CRIMINOLOGY

CRIMINOLOGY
Human Rights, Criminal Law, and Crime

John F. Galliher
University of Missouri-Columbia

Prentice Hall
Englewood Cliffs, New Jersey 07632

LIBRARY OF CONGRESS
Library of Congress Cataloging-in-Publication Data

Galliher, John F.
    Criminology : human rights, criminal law, and crime / John F.
Galliher.
        p.   cm.
    Includes bibliographical references and index.
    ISBN 0-13-193145-8
    1. Crime and criminals--United States. 2. Criminal law--United
States. 3. Criminal justice, Administration of--United States.
I. Title.
HV6789.G35 1989
364'.973--dc19   88-12443
                                                                  CIP

To "Lindy"
Alfred R. Lindesmith

Editorial/production supervision and
  interior design: Joy Moore/Jeanne Genz
Cover design: George Cornell
Manufacturing buyer: Ray Keating/Peter Havens

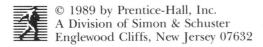 © 1989 by Prentice-Hall, Inc.
A Division of Simon & Schuster
Englewood Cliffs, New Jersey 07632

Printed in the United States of America

10 9 8 7 6 5 4 3 2 1

ISBN 0-13-193145-8

Prentice-Hall International (UK) Limited, *London*
Prentice-Hall of Australia Pty. Limited, *Sydney*
Prentice-Hall Canada Inc., *Toronto*
Prentice-Hall Hispanoamericana, S.A., *Mexico*
Prentice-Hall of India Private Limited, *New Delhi*
Prentice-Hall of Japan, Inc., *Tokyo*
Simon & Schuster Asia Pte. Ltd., *Singapore*
Editora Prentice-Hall do Brasil, Ltda., *Rio de Janeiro*

CONTENTS

PART ONE ■ Causes, Types, and Amount of Crime

PART TWO ■ Origins of Written Law

PART THREE ■ Administration of Criminal Law

PART FOUR ■ Punishment of Crime

PREFACE

It is increasingly apparent that prison rehabilitation programs currently in use hold scant promise of success for the prevention and control of crime. This is also true of the massive prison-building program presently being carried out and of capital punishment, as evidenced by the burgeoning population on death row. In addition, American incarceration and execution systems can be criticized as patently racist in practice. Therefore this text, unlike many other criminology textbooks, adopts an explicit ethical, moral, and political position on crime prevention and control. The human right to meaningful employment must be recognized and observed if crime is ever to be effectively controlled. Without such a commitment we as a nation will all be prisoners, gripped by alienation and fear. Emphasis is placed on why certain behaviors are defined as crime in a given society rather than on the causes of criminal behavior. Since criminal laws are the essential crime-defining mechanisms, considerable attention has been devoted to the origins of the various types of criminal laws, which often serve as instruments of oppression.

     Liberal reforms, such as the public defender system, which was ostensibly designed to provide legal aid to the poor, but which often delivers only the appearance of equality, are addressed. This analysis also recognizes that attacks on women, racial minorities, young people, and the poor are often implemented by the police and the courts, which in turn are usually mislabeled as the "criminal justice system." Such an approach recognizes the police as tools of racial and class oppression yet at the same time recognizes their manipulation and exploitation by societal elites.

Traditionally, criminology has spent considerable time studying the crimes of the poor and powerless rather than the crimes of the rich and powerful. Therefore this text gives special attention to crimes of business leaders and corporations. Attention is also given to the victims of crime, including rape, unnecessary surgery, and corporate crime.

Old friends and colleagues have helped greatly in the development of this book. William J. Chambliss (George Washington University) and Richard Quinney (Northern Illinois University) have lent guidance and support in this task, as they have for over 20 years. Steven Spitzer (Suffolk University), Thomas S. Weinberg (State University College at Buffalo), and Stephen Norland (University of Hartford) read early versions of the manuscript and helped me clarify my thinking on a number of issues, for which I am grateful. Steven Spitzer and Thomas Weinberg also provided the bibliographies concerned with female crime in chapter 3. Mark C. Stafford (Washington State University) had great patience in guiding me through several versions of the manuscript. I also owe a special debt to Jim McCartney, who assisted me in developing many of the ideas in this book. And last, but not least, the professional and personal example set by my teacher and friend, Alfred Lindesmith, has been a continuing source of inspiration.

John F. Galliher

1
INTRODUCTION

In this book the issue of human rights will be drawn on to analyze not only the collective human rights of society to be free from the threat of crime but also the human rights of those persons accused of crime. Human rights should be distinguished from legal rights. Legal rights, unlike human rights, may have nothing to do with justice or fairness, as, for example, the legal rights found in the laws of Nazi Germany or in the laws of South Africa. Interest in the collective human rights of society often appears to expand at the expense of the rights of persons accused of crime. Moreover, an important consideration in determining the human rights of individual actors may be what is seen as their human nature. Only in the context of assumptions about human nature has it been possible to specify the human rights that individuals are capable of enjoying. For example, in South Africa the white-controlled government has long claimed that black Africans are by their very nature incapable of using the same political freedoms as are whites. This book will explore this relationship between human nature and human rights.

Gresham Sykes (1974) suggested that dramatic changes are emerging in academic criminology. These changes run along four lines: (1) a belief that law enforcement agencies such as the police and courts serve the interests of the repression of most citizens by a ruling social class, (2) a belief that the statutes as written are also the work of the ruling class and reflect repressive class interests, (3) a belief that official crime statistics are a product of these repressive interests and, therefore, (4) a total rejection of theories that attempt to explain the causes of criminal behavior as irrelevant once we recognize the arbitrary and imposed nature of what is called crime. This book mirrors many of these changes.

In this book it is claimed that one can best understand crime in a class-structured society such as the United States as the end product of a chain of interactions involving powerful groups that use their power to establish criminal laws and sanctions against less powerful persons and groups that may pose a threat to the groups in power. Most important, the United States is a relatively class-structured society in which such designations as "upper class," "middle class," and "working class" or "lower class" are essential in accounting for how people will be affected by the legal system. Despite a mythology of egalitarianism in the United States, such as that expressed in the phrase "all men are created equal," it seems clear that one's position in the social class structure is associated with great differences in the control of money, property, and political power.

Since the distribution of income and property among the social classes in the United States is extremely unequal, and since defending oneself in the legal system can be expensive, it is not surprising that crime statistics usually seem to establish that crime is most prevalent in the lower class. This inequality suggests that criminal behavior in the lower class may not be markedly different from that in the more affluent classes and that persons in the latter group merely have more resources with which to defend themselves and to elude the consequences of being stigmatized as "criminals."

The title of this book *Criminology: Human Rights, Criminal Law, and Crime,* places human rights, criminal law, and crime in the proper order of importance in understanding criminology. As will be seen in this book, in a study of the causes, consequences, and control of crime, it is essential to begin by considering the human rights of all persons, including both those who commit crimes and those who become crime victims. Next it is necessary to recognize the basis on which *criminal laws* are passed and enforced and the fact that criminal laws are, in turn, the benchmarks for determining what the appropriate data for criminology will be, inasmuch as the criminal law specifies or defines the nature and quality of *crime.*

It undoubtedly seems strange to many people that courses on criminology are routinely taught on college campuses. After all, every American is bombarded with information about the nature, distribution, and extent of crime and the various techniques that are used to prevent crime and punish law violators. Even a casual observer of the mass communications media knows which types of neighborhoods, which types of places in these neighborhoods, and which types of people are most likely to become involved in crimes of various sorts, not to mention knowing the consequences of prison overcrowding and increasingly common stories about executions. The daily newspapers, for example, are filled with such information. In a sense, we are all experts on the nature of crime. Clearly the average citizen is not presented with the same rich diet of information about recent developments in organic chemistry or theoretical physics. In light of the massive amount of public information about crime, if one is to justify teaching a course on criminology, it is important to demonstrate in what ways the course differs from the type of presentation available in the media.

The range of coverage of crime in the American mass media typically extends from conservative to liberal. An example of the former is the famous *Union Leader*, of Manchester, New Hampshire; an illustration of the latter is the *New York Times*. The conservative press would have us believe, first, that the problem of crime is largely a product of judges who mollycoddle criminals and, second, that our country can remain a part of the civilized world only if we as a society show criminals that we "mean business" and have had "enough of this nonsense" by sentencing lawbreakers to longer sentences without benefit of early parole and, ignoring the obvious irony, by starting wider use of the death penalty to demonstrate to convicted murderers that we hold human life to be sacred. An editorial in the *St. Louis Globe-Democrat* (1973:2D) reads:

> The nation should simply go back to administering the death penalty as it once did before the era of sweetness and charity toward criminals was ushered in. It also should demand that judges stop giving non-sentences to serious offenders and crime repeaters, and instead assess penalties as the law intended. Only then will there be a real chance of putting criminals on the defensive and stopping the long flight from the forces of crime.

Conservatives abhor the idea of gun control legislation and often urge citizens to arm themsevles for self-protection when the police and courts do not do their jobs properly (*Manchester* [N.H.] *Union Leader*, 1985).

The liberal press, on the other hand, would have us believe, according to their editorial pages, that crime and its punishment in America are a natural result of both poverty and racial discrimination. The *New York Times* (1985:22), for example, reviewed evidence demonstrating that racial discrimination seems to be an important factor in determining who will be executed for first-degree murder and, in fact, influences the entire process of the administration of criminal law. But the editorial concluded: "That racism may be at work in other parts of the judicial system is no excuse for inflicting the death penalty unfairly." If crime is centered among black males, there is a structural reason, according to liberal editorials. It is well known that ghetto schools are underfunded, in part because of the racism of city officials. It is therefore not suprising that these schools have an astounding dropout rate and that all too few of the graduates of these schools are able to read. According to this liberal reasoning, another predictable result of this racism is an unemployment rate among black male teenagers that often hovers around 50 percent. Given this chronic lack of education, lack of employment, and lack of hope, it is reasonable to expect widespread hatred and violence. Justification for the academic discipline of criminology requires solutions that differ from either of these alternatives.

AN ILLUSTRATION OF ACADEMIC CRIMINOLOGY: ANALYSIS
OF THE PUBLIC DEFENDER SYSTEM

The public defender system features a permanent government office staffed by attorneys whose sole task it is to defend indigent people when they are charged with crimes. Before the development of such agencies, many states made no legal provision for legal counsel for the defendant who was without funds. The early period of the public defender system was during the 1960s. At this time, some jurisdictions already had a public defender system, but 90 percent did not (Paulsen, 1964). When the idea of a public defender system was first seriously discussed, there were wide differences in the reactions of political liberals and conservatives, but as will be seen, the reactions of both groups differed from the analysis of academic criminologists. Conservatives complained that by giving indigent criminals free legal counsel, we would simply be encouraging crime, which was already out of control, because the guilty parties would have one more way to escape prison. They were both angry and worried by this proposal (Kunen, 1983).

Liberals reacted much differently. They saw in the public defender system the promise that at long last the American legal system would, in actual practice, live up to the ideals embodied in our Constitution (Kunen, 1983). Finally, they thought the poor would have the same legal rights as the more affluent, and all people accused of a crime would have an equal opportunity for legal counsel. A new day for American democracy was dawning. The hope and joy of the liberals knew no bounds.

Criminologists found, however, that the actual operation of the public defender system differed considerably from either the hopes of the liberals or the fears of the conservatives. As will be seen in greater detail in chapter 9, because public defender offices are typically underfunded and overloaded with clients, the best that most public defenders can do is to attempt to convince their clients to plead guilty in return for some consideration from the prosecution, in the form of either a reduced charge or a reduced criminal penalty. Therefore, in actual practice, rather than being a zealous defender of lower-class clients, the public defender is typically only one more office of government attempting to manipulate the poor. Clearly, neither the fears of conservatives nor the hopes of liberals were warranted.

Ideally, academic criminolgy should be a nonpartisan discipline, but one cannot truthfully make the claim that it is totally unbiased. Throughout this text I will attempt to demonstrate the ways in which the academic discipline of criminology can concern itself with human rights and equality without resorting to partisan politics. In fact, this text will show again and again how different the analyses of academic criminology can be from the views found in either conservative or liberal politics.

DEFINITIONAL ISSUES: CRIME, MORALITY, AND DANGEROUSNESS

It is typically argued that the reason some acts are outlawed, whereas others are not, is that the former are considered more immoral in a given society. Yet this explanation is called into question when we recognize that much of the behavior that violates criminal law is not considered immoral by many people. For example, widespread marihuana use exists among American citizens and price-fixing by business leaders is routine, but there is abundant evidence (Rossi et al., 1974) that neither of these practices is seen as a truly serious problem by most Americans. The attitude seems to be that we are all aware of these activities but are satisfied when the law enforcement authorities ignore them.

There are further complications with the argument that the most immoral behavior is made criminal. Some behavior that is widely considered very immoral is not a crime. For example, in 1978 a Pittsburgh man was critically ill and for survival required a bone marrow transplant from a cousin (*New York Times*, 1978). Marrow from any other donor would not have provided a suitable match. The cousin refused to cooperate, and people across the nation expressed horror at the cousin's selfishness. Even in the face of this outrage, the courts were unwilling to compel him to provide the transplant, and there was no move in any legislature to legally require such cooperation. The cousin's behavior was considered extremely immoral—but not illegal.

It should also be noted that some acts that are very harmful are not generally defined as either immoral or criminal. There is abundant evidence from company records that the Ford Motor Company intentionally made an unsafe product, in the case of the Ford Pinto, to maximize profits. Some Ford executives knew that the vehicle would explode after even low-speed rear-end collisions, but they reasoned that it would be less expensive to pay off likely insurance claims for death and injury than to modify the car. There is no doubt that much loss of life and injury was caused by this greed, and an Indiana prosecutor therefore brought criminal charges against Ford executives in a case involving the deaths of three young women as a result of a Pinto crash. An Indiana jury failed to hold the corporation leaders criminally responsible (*New York Times*, 1980). The jury simply did not see these deaths as involving moral or criminal responsibility. Thus immoral behavior and criminal behavior can be distinct, and moreover, both can be different from behavior that is harmful to society.

To complicate matters further, we can note that *perceived* dangerousness can also be distinct from law-violating behavior. The late Martin Luther King was considered extremely dangerous by many white Americans, most notably J. Edgar Hoover, the late chief of the Federal Bureau of Investigation (Garrow, 1981), even though Dr. King had committed no more serious crime than parading and praying without a permit during civil rights demonstrations. Hoover considered the Reverend King so dangerous that he had a secret wiretap put on his phone and attempted to use information from it to blackmail King into leaving the civil rights movement. In conclusion, then, we can say that criminal behavior is not necessarily that behavior which is most dangerous to society—or considered most dangerous or immoral. An important issue that will be discussed in chapters 6 and 7 is why certain acts are made illegal when they are not necessarily a result of immorality, dangerousness, or perceived dangerousness.

CRIME AND THE POLITICAL PROCESS

The most obvious fact about crime is that the political entities (for example, nations or states) define crime by creating and then enforcing criminal laws. The critical question is, Which persons or groups in the body politic have the most influence or power in the creation, and eventually in the selective enforcement, of criminal laws? Political sociologists (for example, Goertzel, 1976) have proposed three different models to account for the distribution and exercise of power in society (the passing of criminal laws is just one manifestation of political power): the class model, the elitist model, and the pressure group (or pluralist) model.

The *class model* asserts that economic circumstances determine political life and that persons with wealth dominate the political life of those without wealth. In the Marxist conception, those who own and control the means of production (capitalists) control the political life of the workers (proletarians).

In the *elitist model*, power is also viewed as unequally distributed, and some few persons or groups monopolize political power because of their special qualities of intelligence, expertise, or strength, but not necessarily wealth. This elite group creates laws that affect the masses.

Finally, the *pressure group model* (also called the interest group model) proposes a pluralist conception of the political process. In this view, society is composed of a multiplicity of groups with different interests that try to maintain themselves in a favored position relative to that of other groups. Not infrequently, groups with opposing interests come into conflict. They compete politically by trying to have laws passed that favor their interests or that restrict and limit the interests of other groups. According to this reasoning, most individuals have some interest group than can successfully represent their interests on at least some specific issue.

As a result of the present state of our knowledge about the dynamics and interrelationships of power, law, and crime, it is difficult to accept any one of these three models as totally comprehensive, although it is becoming increasingly clear that the class model seems to explain more cases than the others. Chapters 6 and 7 will examine some specific instances of how criminal laws have originated and will cite examples to support all three models. On the other hand, each model (including the class model) has some weaknesses as a complete explanation of all cases. As will be demonstrated, some laws have their origins in the interests of wealthy corporations, some reflect the views of the middle- and upper-class citizens independent of corporate needs, and some reflect religious interests.

Since none of these models seems comprehensive, some borrowing from their varied assumptions is necessary to understand crime. Yet I am sympathetic with the class model, because as later chapters will show, there is much evidence that persons without wealth and political power are the most likely to be defined as criminals. The upper and middle classes are most often able to control the political process by controlling party nominations through financial support of candidates and officeholders, so that criminal laws preserve wealth and property and punish those who might threaten the existing distribution of wealth and property. If upper- and upper-middle-class persons are apprehended for a crime, they are better able to afford expensive and sophisticated legal counsel, either to avoid conviction or to gain leniency in sentencing. In some instances, as will be seen in the discussion of marihuana laws in chapter 7, persons with wealth and power may be able to change the laws they have violated so that their actions are punished less severely. Chapter 8 will demonstrate how the police serve the interests of the wealthy elites as well.

ETHICAL ORIENTATION

Unlike many social science textbooks dealing with crime, this text openly acknowledges a specific ethical orientation toward social life. Its position is that an ethical social ordering within any society, or among societies, requires that all men, women, and children have an equal chance for personal freedom and physical survival. Such an ethical stance seems required to avoid an unreflective acceptance of the legal system, official crime statistics, and criminal statutes as they are, and it mirrors the Charter of the United Nations, which begins as follows (United Nations Conference, 1945:1):

> WE THE PEOPLE OF THE UNITED NATIONS, DETERMINED
>
> to save succeeding generations from the scourge of war, which twice in our lifetime has brought untold sorrow to mankind, and to reaffirm faith in fundamental human rights, in the dignity and worth of the human person, in the *equal rights* of men and women and of nations large and small . . . (emphasis added)

The statement of purpose of the United Nations reads in part (United Nations Conference, 1945:3): "To develop friendly relations among nations based on respect for the principle of *equal rights and self-determination of peoples*" (emphasis added).

Indeed, the U.S. Declaration of Independence reads: "We hold these Truths to be self-evident, that all Men are created equal, that they are endowed by their Creator with certain unalienable Rights."

Our ethical orientation is also reflected in the first ten amendments to the U.S. Constitution—the Bill of Rights—which guarantee all American citizens protection from self-incrimination, excessive bail, cruel and unusual punishment, and unreasonable search and seizure, as well as the right to a speedy trial and to trial by jury. All of these rights are, of course, directly related to crime and its control (U.S. Constitution, Amendments I to X). This ethical orientation obviously has implications for numerous social and economic issues, such as the distribution of food, petroleum, and other resources, but it will be developed here only in relation to the issue of crime and its control. Ethical orientation has important consequences for the initial assumptions that inform a study of crime and its control.

An excellent test of the morality and justice of an ethical position was proposed by John Rawls (1971). Rawls suggested that to determine what is, indeed, a just society, people must return to what he calls the "original position," a position in which they are without information on their social or economic status in society. Only from this position, behind what Rawls called the "veil of ignorance," can people make just or fair decisions on how society should be organized. Since people in the original position are deprived of knowledge of their position in society, their predictable and rational decision for ordering social life would be true equality. For people in such a position to select a highly stratified society modeled after a nation such as czarist Russia, for example, would be very risky, because the chance of being powerless peasants would be much greater than the chance of being members of the nobility. However, once people occupy a position of privilege in an established society, leveling is not attractive to them. In a society with great inequality in the distribution of resources, only the poor would most readily accept equality for all.

Dworkin (1977:177–183) observed that freedom and equality are two fundamental rights central to Rawls's theory. According to this line of reasoning, people have a right to maximum freedom from coercion by government. But the most fundamental right is that individuals have a right to equal input into the creation and administration of the political institutions that govern them. Individuals possess this right not by their particular merit but simply as human beings.

TRADITIONAL ASSUMPTIONS

The traditional assumptions of social science in general, and of criminlogy in particular, include the position usually referred to as cultural relativism. This position argues that although there are observable differences in cultural practices and beliefs among various societies, including differences in legal codes and their enforcement, it is impossible to assess these different practices and beliefs in terms of moral superiority or inferiority. Cultural relativism suggests that societies are only different from one another, not better or worse. Because it is impossible to develop any scientific measures for use in evaluating values and cultures, cultural relativism views all societies as having equal merit. It is sometimes claimed that such an orientation, which assumes equality of differing value patterns, should generate tolerance and understanding among the various cultures of the world (Bidney, 1968:545). Cultural relativism seeks to avoid the error of ethnocentrism, which is the belief that one's own values and way of life are superior to all others and that it is therefore proper to judge all cultures according to how far they diverge from the observer's culture. To avoid this possibility, cultural relativists make no judgments of others' cultures (Bidney, 1968:546). In much of the traditional academic discipline of criminology, cultural relativism has led scholars to accept the legal codes of a society as given, without fundamental moral examination of those codes.

A second traditional assumption often made in American criminology, which is not explicitly rejected in most of the professional literature, is that written statutes more or less represent the will of most of the people in a society, at least in a democracy such as the United States. Some discussions of crime and criminal law mention how elites and powerful interest groups create the criminal law and then proceed to ignore this issue, implicitly treating crime as having an existence independent of the will of elites or interest groups. Sutherland and Cressey (1970), for example, mention the elitist theory regarding the nature of crime and criminal law as one of many possible orientations and then proceed largely to ignore this perspective in favor of a focus on criminal behavior, devoting chapters to such topics as the relationship between race and crime and between home life and crime. According to Newman (1966), such concern with the causes of individuals' criminal behavior has been the major thrust of the work of sociological criminologists, and this emphasis is clearly reflected in criminology texts. In any event, by not emphasizing the role of power and elites, the impression is maintained that in states with elected governments the majority rules in all major political issues, including the structuring of the criminal code. This majority-rule orientation is seen in the following statement: "The only common characteristic of all crimes is that they consist . . . in acts universally disapproved of by all members of each society" (Durkheim, 1933:73).

Another traditional assumption of criminologists is the discriminatory nature of the criminal justice process, including the systems of both arrest and trial. As will be shown in the following chapters, criminologists have demonstrated that police and the courts often discriminate against racial and economic minorities. In the United States, blacks are more likely than whites to be arrested, convicted, and sentenced for the same offense. Therefore official records of arrests or convictions for crimes reflect not only the law-violating behavior in the community but also the biases of the legal system (Matza, 1969:96–98).

Yet another traditional assumption is that criminal behavior and criminals are objects amenable to scientific study. That is, it is assumed that the unit of analysis is the individual, called a criminal, and that something about the individual can be isolated as the cause of the criminal behavior. In addition, crime and criminals are assumed to be morally inferior to noncrime and noncriminals (Matza, 1969:17ff; Vold, 1958). It is taken for granted that the people and behavior in question should be controlled. Naturally, if it is assumed that crime and criminals are morally inferior, then it follows that crime must be prevented or, failing that, that crime and criminals must at least be controlled within limits.

During the early 1960s there developed a boom in research on the causes of juvenile deliquency that was largely atheoretical and that never explicitly mentioned any moral judgments about delinquency and its control, although the implication was always very clear: deliquency of all types should be controlled. Predictably this research surge was largely a product of support from the federal government (Galliher and McCartney, 1973). A good illustration of this type of research is found in the work of one deliquency researcher, who suggests that envy or relative deprivation is a major cause of crime and delinquency (Toby, 1979). He claimed that this idea helps account for the overrepresentation of ethnic minorities in delinquent gangs. White Americans, it seems, are more immune to such petty concerns than are others. What provides the prophylaxis for whites is not clear, but this researcher admits that envy is not alone in causing crime and delinquency. "Overurbanization" brought on by rapid growth of cities is another cause, as is a low level of occupational commitment. Thus we are left with the understanding that "a little of this and a little of that" cause crime and delinquency, seemingly in a chaotic fashion with no theoretical integration.

During the late 1960s there developed another boom in criminology research. This one attempted to demonstrate the extent to which variations in criminal penalties across jurisdictions are responsible for deterring crime in these areas. This so-called deterrence research was practically unknown before the late 1960s, but by the 1970s it had become the dominant type of research in criminology (DiChiara and Galliher, 1984). This research, like delinquency research before it, is typically atheoretical in that it looks for any criminal penalties that could be correlated with lower crime rates. It also made the claim of being value free—of just presenting the facts without moral or political bias.

The assumptions made in traditional academic criminology, such as in research on juvenile delinquency and deterrence, suffer from several internal inconsistencies. The social scientists working in these traditions are supposedly dispassionately studying commonsense assumptions but, in fact, accept them as their own because traditional criminology accepts the commonsense position that crime is a moral problem. A nondiscriminating cultural relativism which holds that all cultural practices are of equal ethical merit is inconsistent with the proposition that certain behavior within a society, namely crime, is inferior to other behavior and should be controlled. All the nonjudgmental social scientist should logically claim is that criminals and criminal behavior are defined differently from other people and behavior. Moreover, if criminal codes, the police, the courts, and official crime records are recognized as often discriminatory, then it is inconsistent to view those behaviors officially termed crime and those people labeled criminals as necessarily morally different from other behaviors and people. By not assuming any blanket moral reality to crime and criminals, and by recognizing the role of power in society, one avoids the inconsistencies found in the assumptions of traditional criminology.

ALLEGED VALUE NEUTRALITY IN CONTEMPORARY CRIMINOLOGY*

Deterrence Research

A prominent researcher (Gibbs, 1968) seems to have set the moral and intellectual tone for most of the research on crime deterrence that has been published recently. He claims to be personally opposed to the death penalty but was still determined to demonstrate the degree to which it serves as a deterrent. Whereas an earlier generation of criminologists saw punishment as an evil to be overcome, contemporary deterrence researchers typically have followed this more recent example of purporting to develop a value-free endeavor. Contemporary deterrence researchers emphasize criminal punishment in the control of crime while ignoring the role that greater social justice could have in crime control (for a recent example, see Piliavin et al., 1986). These researchers do so while still claiming value neutrality.

Unlike deterrence researchers who hold deterrence of crime to be an empirical issue, some sociologists have claimed that punishment invariably increases criminal self-concepts and criminal behavior (Becker, 1963). It is predictable that researchers who hold this view would, while studying deviants, including convicted criminals, develop a "deep sympathy" for these "subordinates" and see them as "more sinned against than sinning" (Becker, 1967:240). Proponents of this alternative view predict that such an orientation would be quickly discounted by some critics as biased, whereas taking the side of persons in positions of authority is generally not seen as having such an effect. Indeed, deterrence researchers do not admit to any bias, and they have seldom been so criticized. This is true even when deterrence researchers discuss how deterrence can serve political leaders (Gibbs, 1979:81):

> Those who seek power will look to the social sciences for an answer to the question: How can we control human behavior in the aggregate? If sociologists provide no answer, those who operate the purse strings will decide that they can do without us.

*In this section, much of the material was taken from A. DiChiara and J. F. Galliher, "Thirty Years of Deterrence Research: Characteristics, Causes and Consequences," Contemporary Crisis 8(July 1984):243–263.

This writer (Gibbs, 1975:25) recognizes the opposition to such a view:

> The State purportedly serves the interests of some classes or groups more than others. That line of argumentation leads some critics to oppose, openly or tacitly, any research on the deterrence question. They see such research as providing a service or tool for members of the "establishment," that is, the research will enable the oppressors to control the oppressed more effectively.

But as a pioneer of modern deterrence research, this sociologist harbors none of these doubts about the wisdom and morality of conducting such investigations. It is arguable that the potential dangers of deterrence research are apparent in two recent conclusions of another deterrence researcher:

> There is considerable indication that people of lower status do perceive sanction threats differently. Therefore their behavior is likely to be more conformist in response to sanctions than is the behavior of those of other status levels. (Tittle, 1980:301.)

Further:

> Since the data suggest greater deterrence among nonwhites, especially for arrest fear, the net effect should be considerably more prevention by legal threats among nonwhites. (Tittle, 1980:304.)

These conclusions allege that deterrence research provides the state with increased information that can facilitate the manipulation of the lower classes and black citizens. Presumably, affluent whites are not as responsive to official sanctions. Such findings clearly commend a policy of punitive penal sanctions selectively directed against economic and racial minorities. Yet the potential benefit of such research is that it holds the promise of reducing street crime. Since legislators set criminal penalties whether or not this social science research is conducted, it could be argued that it is better that this legislation be informed by accurate social science research than solely by the prejudices of legislators. The other side of the argument is that such research on the deterrent effects of criminal punishment puts academicians in the position of legitimating state controls without considering who controls the state (Beyleveld, 1982) and therefore indeed represents a political decision.

In spite of these possible dangers, many researchers either have been unaware of them or have neutralized them in some way, because their research has not explored the ethical or political priorities implicit in such activity. For example, an article dealing with capital punishment as a deterrent to murder raises the issue of ethics in a cryptic disclaimer:

> In this paper I will be concerned with the deterrent effect of capital punishment. I will not consider the other important dimensions of this topic, for example, the morality or immorality of capital punishment. (Phillips, 1980a:139.)

Elsewhere this author explains this omission:

> I have some technical expertise which enables me to discover whether capital punishment has a deterrent effect in some circumstances. I have no moral expertise and consequently my opinion on the morality of capital punishment is worth no more and no less than any one else's. (Phillips, 1980b.)

Clearly this writer believes it is both possible and essential to isolate empirical research from questions of ethics. Presumably the latter is solely the business of "experts" on morality, such as philosophers and theologians.

Some, however, question whether it is possible to remove deterrence research from ethical concerns:

> The very concept of deterrence has immediate ethical implications. A conventional utilitarian would say that since the reduction of murder rates is taken as an ultimate ethical good, anything that is required to lower the murder rate is also ethical, including capital punishment. (Vaughan, 1981.)

To the extent that anyone reasons in this fashion, presumably any system of punishment, no matter how extreme, could be justified as long as it was considered the minimum necessary to reduce homicide rates. If such a rationale becomes widely accepted, the human rights of persons convicted of murder will likely be in jeopardy. Indeed, others have argued that the results of deterrence research can make punishment more palatable to citizens and lawmakers who are interested in effective criminal controls. Ehrlich found that "an additional execution per year over the period in question may have resulted, on average, in 7 or 8 fewer murders" (1975:414). He described this as a direct "tradeoff," yet later (1982:137) contended that "the efficacy and desirability of capital punishment are separate issues." It is difficult to believe, however, that legislators could recognize the existence of this tradeoff of seven or eight innocent lives for that of one murderer and nonetheless hold in abeyance the question of the desirability of the death penalty. Clearly, deterrence research has obvious ethical and political implications.

Divergent Assumptions of This Approach

The approach to the study of crime and its control found in this book does not challenge traditional criminology's assertions regarding observable differences in cultural practices and beliefs. Unlike traditional criminology, however, this approach does not concede that it is impossible to make moral distinctions among such beliefs and practices. In other words, it is not necessarily true that one culture's legal practices are as just and fair as another's. The mass execution of Jews by the Third Reich in wartime Germany is not merely different from other cultural practices but represents one moral low point in any cross-cultural comparison.

Indeed, we even assume that some crime may be morally superior to some noncrime. For example, obeying the law and carrying out orders to exterminate Jews in Nazi Germany certainly would be judged as morally inferior to disobeying the law and fighting the organized state. Nor is conformity to southern U.S. state statutes that required the segregation of races by definition morally superior to open and consistent violation of those statutes. According to Mouledous (1967:229), "What is critical is that the behaviors which we are encouraging or discouraging should not be determined by existing social norms nor by administrative judgment. Sociologists cannot abdicate the responsibility of judgment and accept the state's criteria of crime. A superior referent must be sought."

One measure of the morality of specific criminal statutes has been proposed by Mouledous (1967), who suggests that exclusive criminal statutes that apply only to specific groups of people (such as laws restricting the voting or residential location of a specific racial group) are morally inferior to statutes that apply to all persons living in a society, irrespective of racial or class characteristics. It is hoped that this proposal will provide a beginning for the development of a general set of principles against which written law can be judged with equality established as the primary moral referent.

The orientation used in this book, unlike that of traditional criminology, assumes that many written statutes are not the will of all the people or even of a majority; rather, they represent the orientation of organized interest groups with the political power to make legislation reflect their will. For example, laws prohibiting embezzlement represent mainly and most directly the interests of employers who desire protection from employees. Yet some sample surveys of Americans' attitudes show something approaching a consensus on various issues relating to crime and its control. Much of this consensus can be explained as follows. Contrary to the myth of an independent and constitutionally mandated free press in the United States, the media are a part of the larger corporate structure and generally represent that structure's definitions of reality, including what is and what is not defined as crime and how crime can be controlled. This media orientation manufactures much of the consensus on crime and crime control (Cohen and Young, 1973). Even though there is seldom any government censorship, wealthy corporations nonetheless largely control the mass media indirectly through advertising and directly through actual ownership of the media. These corporations effectively use the media to set the limits within which public debate on issues is confined (Sallach, 1974).

In some instances, such as the laws governing rape and homicide, it can be convincingly argued that class or corporate interests are not reflected in the written law and that all classes derive the same benefits from the protection provided by the law. However, in laws involving personal assault and some offenses against property, class interests are reflected not in the terms of the law itself but it its differential enforcement. For this reason, one of the chief complaints among economic and racial minorities is that they do not receive adequate police protection (Hahn, 1971). Many blacks believe, for example, that the police consider offenses against their homes or assaults against their persons to be less serious than similar incidents occuring in the white community (Ennis, 1967). In this sense, even laws protecting persons and property do not serve all classes. In other words, even if the written law represents a broad range of class interests, it often becomes discriminatory in its administration.

The approach used in this book does not dispute the assumption of traditional criminology that the legal process is often discriminatory and arbitrary, making official records distorted reflections of crime. A system of law enforcement that gives special privileges to the affluent is a critical moral problem in a society that claims to afford equal rights under law to all people, as does the United States. Finally, this approach, unlike that of traditional criminology, does not assume a reality to crime and criminals independent of the application of culturally specific social definitions (Becker, 1963). It claims that there are no universally valid statutory distinctions separating crime from noncrime or criminals from noncriminals. Specific crimes and criminals may be legally condemned only within a particular society, and this should sensitize the social analyst to make moral judgments independently of any particular social order. Indeed, the social analyst can arrive at some moral conclusions about many of a given culture's practices in the definition and control of crime, rather than assume, as does traditional criminology, that behavior defined as criminal in a society should necessarily be studied, controlled, and implicitly considered immoral.

METHODOLOGY FOR A DEMOCRATIC CRIMINOLOGY*

The long-standing professional morality of most sociologists and criminologists seems to require the cooperation of our subjects; therefore the only secret information obtainable is from individuals and groups who are too ignorant, too powerless, or both, to demand limitations on the researchers. Much more is known about the indiscretions and alleged abnormalities of the ignorant, poor, and powerless than about those of any other groups higher in the social stratification system. Apparently the poor and powerless are the least able to keep their private lives private from the social scientist. As a consequence of our professional ethics, therefore, the image we portray of American society is highly distorted. What the social scientist often describes is a great deal about the personal lives of the poor and powerless and little about the secrets of the more affluent. Even if only the aggregate characteristics of the poor are described, such information may still have adverse effects on the group. For example, a description of the work and sex habits and the modes of family organization of

*Much of the material in this section was taken from J. F. Galliher, "The Protection of Human Subjects: A Reexamination of the Professional Code of Ethics," American Sociologist 8(August 1973):93–100.

poor blacks may influence government social welfare policy, adversely affecting the subject group. The detailed view of the poor, together with the veneered image of the more affluent, can be used to legitimate a highly economically stratified and racist society. And is not the failure of sociology to uncover corrupt, illegitimate, covert practices of government or industry because of the supposed prohibitions of professional ethics tantamount to supporting such practices?

Lofland (1961:366) has therefore defended disguised participant observation as a legitimate research technique. He dismissed the idea of professional rules that would prohibit such techniques:

> A professional rule to this effect would not only make for great past, present and future loss to the discipline, but would be an active violation of many people's moral standards who think that there are some groups, such as professional crime groups, that should be studied whether they are asked and give permission or not. In other words, in accepting this rule, we could not study "bad" groups, which, as it happens, are also especially likely to be groups that do not want to be studied.

In a study of police behavior, Black and Reiss (1970:65) admit to "systematic deception" of officers whose behavior they observed. They indicated to the officers that they were interested only in citizens reaction toward the police, when they were, in fact, studying police treatment of citizens. Black and Reiss apparently believed that this subterfuge was required because it is well documented that there is a widespread concern among police to maintain secrecy from outsiders. And Rainwater and Pittman (1967:365–366) issued a challenge to increase the accountability of elites in business and government. They concluded:

> Sociologists have the right (and perhaps also the obligation) to study publicly accountable behavior. By publicly accountable behavior we do not simply mean the behavior of public officials (though there the case is clearest) but also the behavior of any individual as he goes about performing public or secondary roles for which he is socially accountable–this would include businessmen, college teachers, physicians, etc.; in short all people as they carry out jobs for which they are in some sense publicly accountable. One of the functions of our discipline, along with those of political science, history, economics, journalism, and intellectual pursuits generally, is to further public accountability in a society whose complexity makes it easier for people to avoid their responsibilities.

Presumably, Rainwater and Pittman would applaud the efforts of Black and Reiss, even though they engage in a form of subterfuge required for their investigations and would defend similar research on conduct in accountable roles.

Becker and Horowitz (1972:48) observed that sociological research has generally serviced elites at the expense of the less powerful:

> Prison research has for the most part been oriented to problems of jailers rather than those of prisoners; industrial research, to the problems of managers rather

than those of workers; military research, to the problems of generals rather than those of privates. . . . Wherever someone is oppressed, an "establishment" sociologist seems to lurk in the backround, providing the facts which make oppression more efficient and the theory which makes it legitimate to a larger constituency.

Becker and Horowitz (1972:55) then concluded:

A sociology that is true to the world inevitably clarifies what has been confused, reveals the character of organization secrets, upsets the interests of powerful people and groups.

Similarly, Gans (quoted by Woodward, 1974:78) commented about economic as opposed to political leaders: "Since the rich don't let themselves be studied, and it's pretty hard to get into a fancy club on your own, sociologists go where they have easier access." For example, Domhoff (1975) relied heavily on key informants in his research on private ruling-class vacation retreats. High-ranking people do not want social scientists around, in part merely because the latter are lower in rank. Even with limited resources, a researcher can spend a summer in Harlem, but few, if any, social scientists have the money or prestige to be welcome as observers in prestigious eastern clubs or in a General Motors board meeting.

The point of ignorance of the powerful is forcefully brought home by Green (1971), who cited the lack of any independent academic studies of an organization such as the Standard Oil Company of New Jersey, a mammoth corporation with vast national and international influence. Whatever the reasons, more is known about the private lives of the poor than of most other citizens. The detailed view of the poor, in contrast to the veneered image of the powerful, suggests that the poor are poor because they are the most abnormal. Surely those scholars interested in the study of crime in America recognize, especially after the events of the Watergate burglary, that they must concern themselves more with studying persons who are above them in the stratification system, as urged by Nader (1969:299). Indeed, Chambliss (1978) has demonstrated that to understand organized crime adequately, one must study the link between leaders in business and government and those who are more obviously involved in racketeering.

LAW AND MORALITY

Most sociologists who study the law believe, as do most criminologists, that morality has no place in what they believe should be a scientific pursuit (Schur, 1968: 51–58; Quinney, 1973: 1–16). However, the early criminologist Beccaria (1775) made the moral value judgment that all people should be equal before the law. Certainly not all writers have accepted this premise. Plato (Taylor, 1934) and Aristotle (Barker, 1946) rejected such equality as unjust. For example, both accepted slavery and the inequality of slaves and masters as morally legitimate.

As indicated earlier, social scientists studying crime and the law have been highly relativistic. The crux of the issue seems to hinge on whether or not law can be subjected to moral evaluation independent of the biases of a given culture. One position, called the natural theory of law, is that through the exercise of reason, humans can determine the core qualities of all people at all places and at all times (independent of any given culture) and that this knowledge can provide the basis for a legal system ideally suited for human existence. The natural law is a set of principles against which to assess actual written law, and when written law is not congruent with these principles, it is said to be unjust law. Dr. Martin Luther King (1963) was a proponent of the natural theory of law and proclaimed that because all people are made by their creator with the same moral worth, laws that do not treat them equally are unjust.

In other words, the law contains two components, the *is* and the *ought* (Fuller, 1966:9–10). Both statutes and court decisions involve a set of written words (the is), as well as an objective that it is hoped will be brought about by these words (the ought). Laws prohibiting rape and burglary are not only a collection of words but provide a vision of an ideal state of affairs where one's home and body would not be violated as a matter of a universal human right. Therefore attempts to consider the law as it is without also considering the moral issue of what ought to be are impossible.

Opponents to the natural law position argue that there is no way to determine the core qualities of human beings, and even if these qualities could be determined, there is no way to use this information to arrive at just laws. Yet some legal scholars (Hart, 1961: 189–195) recognize that any system of law must enforce rules such as those protecting people against violence and imposing liability for breach of promise. This is true because of a few core qualities of human life, including the physical vulnerability of human beings and a typical scarcity of resources. Because of these natural qualities of human life, there is a corresponding natural necessity for a legal code to provide for these needs and rights.

Whatever the universal human qualities and universal human needs and human rights, if sociology makes no moral judgments independent of criminal statutes, it becomes sterile and inhumane—the work of moral eunuchs or legal technicians. Recognizing that cultural definitions of crime are a product mainly of powerful interest groups, the analyst of crime should not necessarily be tied to the moral judgments reflected in those statutes. If moral judgments above and beyond criminal law were not made, the laws of Nazi Germany would be indistinguishable from the laws of many other nations. Yet the Nuremberg trials after World War II advanced the position that numerous officials of the Nazi government, although admittedly acting in accord with German law, were behaving in such a grossly immoral fashion as to be criminally responsible. Some obedience to law was held by the Nuremberg tribunal to be morally reprehensible and therefore criminal.

As might be expected, the advocates of a higher morality than that embodied in written law have often been those outside government who were rebelling against governmental authority, as did Martin Luther King (1963; see also Gandhi, 1951). However, in the Nuremberg trials, representatives of the Allied governments—France, England, the Soviet Union, and the United States—explicitly and publicly supported the idea of a moral order and moral judgments independent of written law. No claim was made by the Allied prosecutors that those on trial had violated German statutes; rather, the claim was that, by enforcing those statutes, the defendants had committed atrocities against humanity. At Nuremberg, four major world powers endorsed the idea of a higher moral order than that necessarily found in written laws, which perhaps lends a credibilty to this position that it might otherwise not enjoy. The example of Nuremberg shows that moral judgments by students of crime can be made independently of particular cultural definitions of crime.

On October 7, 1942, President Roosevelt released the following statement:

> It is our intention that just and sure punishment shall be meted out to [those] responsible for the organized murder of thousands of innocent persons and the commission of atrocities which *have violated every tenet of the Christian faith.* (Jackson, 1949:9; emphasis added.)

And on March 24, 1944, President Roosevelt declared:

> In one of the blackest crimes of all history—begun by the Nazis in the day of peace and multiplied by them a hundred times in time of war—the wholesale systematic murder of the Jews of Europe goes on unabated every hour. . . . It is therefore fitting that we should again proclaim our determination that *none who participate in these acts of savagery shall go unpunished.* The United Nations have made it clear that they will pursue the guilty and deliver them up in order that justice be done. *That warning applies not only to the leaders but also to their functionaries and subordinates* in Germany and in the satellite countries. All who knowingly take part in the deportation of Jews to their death in Poland or Norwegians and French to their death in Germany are equally guilty with the executioner. All who share the guilt shall share the punishment. (Jackson, 1949:12–13; emphasis added.)

Bereft of moral judgment, the social analyst can provide only description of the development or administration of the laws and must at least pretend not to make any critical judgments. Yet the social analyst does make moral judgments, even if only in picking topics for study (Black, 1973:48) and even if unaware of making those moral judgments. For example, the selection for study of the effects of social stratification on the administration of the law, which Skolnick (1965:4) says is typical of the sociology of law, often reflects the view that nothing is fundamentally wrong with the basic assumptions of the system of criminal law. The argument continues that the system requires only a few minor modifications, such as the provision of legal counsel for the indigent and the use of better educated, less prejudiced police, to operate with proper equality for all. (This argument is criticized in chapter 8). In any case, to be completely honest, rather than claim an objectivity that is impossible, perhaps it is best to recognize and be explicit about our moral biases so that the observer can take them into account in considering our work.

The alternative assumptions of the orientation in the chapters that follow stress (1) the unjust and class-based nature of what is usually called crime, (2) the law as a defining mechanism of crime, and (3) the failure of law enforcement agencies to produce data suited to the scientific study of people or their behavior. Finally, it seems appropriate to observe that not all persons who place morality above the written law will arrive at the conclusions enbodied in this text. Those who oppose equality for women, blacks, and other minorities, even in opposition to statutory provisions, are able to find moral justifications for their positions. Resolution of the issue of the relationship between law and morality therefore requires the activation of individual conscience, and this may well usher in an increased professional awareness of the role of conflict and lack of consensus, which will in turn be reflected in a new direction for theory and research in criminology. No longer can the thoughtful student of law, crime, and morality claim that "it must be immoral or it would not be illegal." Duly constituted laws can command the segregation of educational facilities along racial lines or the mass murder of religious or racial minorities—and violation of such laws is not necessarily immoral.

The four chapters that immediately follow deal with the causes, types, and amount of crime. Chapter 2 provides a historical discussion of the theories of crime and criminal behavior. Next, chapter 3 introduces a discussion of types of crime, and then organized crime is analyzed in chapter 4. Chapter 5 presents a discussion of the measurement of crime. Chapters 6 and 7 deal with the social basis of law and the origins of marihuana laws, respectively, such laws being the defining mechanisms of crime. Three chapters address the administration of criminal law, including the police (chapter 8), the courts (chapter 9), and the role of psychiatrists in the court system (chapter 10). Chapter 11 deals with the variety of rationales used to prevent and control crime, chapter 12 with the history of incarceration, chapter 13 with prison organization, and chapter 14 with the problems of rehabilitating prisoners. The final chapter (chapter 15) summarizes the human rights position of contemporary criminology.

REFERENCES

Barker, E. (trans.)
  1946 The Politics of Aristotle. Book 1. London: Oxford University Press.
Beccaria, C. B.
  1775 An Essay on Crimes and Punishments. 4th ed. London: E. Newbery.

Becker, H. S.
  1963 Outsiders. New York: The Free Press of Glencoe.

  1967 "Whose side are we on?" Social Problems 14:239–247.

Becker, H. S. and I. L. Horowitz
1972 "Radical politics and sociological research: observations on methodology and ideology." American Journal of Sociology 78:48–66.

Beyleveld, D.
1982 "Ehrlich's analysis of deterrence." British Journal of Criminology 22:101–123.

Bidney, D.
1968 "Cultural relativism." Pp. 543–547 in International Encyclopedia of the Social Sciences, vol. 3. New York: Macmillan and The Free Press.

Black, D. J. and A. J. Reiss, Jr.
1970 "Police and control of juveniles." American Sociological Review 35:63–77.

Black, D.
1973 "The boundaries of legal sociology." Pp. 41–56 in D. Black and M. Mileski (eds.), The Social Organization of Law. New York: Seminar Press.

Chambliss, W. J.
1978 On the Take: From Petty Crooks to Presidents. Bloomington: Indiana University Press.

Cohen, S. and J. Young (eds.)
1973 The Manufacture of News. Beverly Hills, Calif.: Sage Publications.

DiChiara, A. and J. F. Galliher
1984 "Thirty years of deterrence research: characteristics, causes, and consequences." Contemporary Crises 8(July):243–263.

Domhoff, G. W.
1975 The Bohemian Grove and Other Retreats. New York: Harper & Row.

Durkheim, E.
1933 The Division of Labor in Society. (George Simpson, trans.) New York: The Free Press of Glencoe.

Dworkin. R.
1977 Taking Rights Seriously. Cambridge, Mass.: Harvard University Press.

Ehrlich, I.
1975 "The deterrent effect of capital punishment: a question of life and death." American Economic Review 65:397–417.
1982 "On positive methodology, ethics, and polemics in deterrence research." British Journal of Criminology 22:124–139.

Ennis, P. H.
1967 Criminal Victimization in the United States: A Report of a National Survey. National Opinion Research Center, University of Chicago. Washington, D.C.: U.S. Government Printing Office.

Fuller, L.
1966 The Law in Quest of Itself. Boston: Beacon Press.

Galliher, J. F.
1973 "The protection of human subjects: a reexamination of the professional code of ethics." American Sociologist 8(August): 93–100.

Galliher, J. F. and J. L. McCartney
1973 "The influence of funding agencies on juvenile delinquency research." Social Problems 21:77–90.

Gandhi, M. K.
1951 Non-violent Resistance. New York: Schocken Books.

Garrow, D. J.
1981 The FBI and Martin Luther King, Jr.: From "Solo" to Memphis. New York: W. W. Norton.

Gibbs. J. P.
1968 "Crime, punishment, and deterrence." Southwestern Social Science Quarterly 48:515–530.
1975 Crime, Punishment, and Deterrence. New York: Elsevier.
1979 "The elites can do without us." The American Sociologist 14:79–85.

Goertzel, T. G.
1976 Political Society. Chicago: Rand McNally College Publishing.

Green, P.
1971 "The obligations of American social scientists." Annals of the American Academy of Political and Social Sciences 394:13–27.

Hahn, H.
1971 "Ghetto assessments of police protection and authority." Law and Society Review 6(November):183–194.

Hart, H. L. A.
1961 The Concept of Law. London: Oxford University Press.

Jackson, R. H.
1949 International Conference on Military Trials. Department of State Publication No. 3080, International Organization and Conference Series 2. Washington, D.C.: U.S. Government Printing Office.

King, M. L., Jr.
1963 "Letter from Birmingham Jail." The Christian Century 80(June 12): 767–773.

Kunen, J. S.
1983 How Could You Defend those People? New York: Random House.

Lofland, J.
1961 "Comment on 'initial interaction of newcomers in Alcoholics Anonymous.'" Social Problems 8:365–367.

Manchester (N.H.) Union Leader
1985 "Liberal principles tested by collapse of law and order." February 7:34.

Matza, D.
1969 Becoming Deviant. Englewood Cliffs, N.J.: Prentice Hall.

Mouledous, J. C.
1967 "Political crime and the Negro revolution." Pp. 217–231 in M. B. Clinard and R. Quinney (eds.), Criminal Behavior Systems: A Typology. New York: Holt, Rinehart & Winston.

Nader, L.
1969 "Up the anthropologist: perspectives gained from studying up." Pp. 284–311 in D. Hymes (ed.), Reinventing Anthropology. New York: Random House.

New York Times
1978 "Judge upholds transplant denial." July 27:A10.
1980 "Ford auto company cleared in 3 deaths." March 14:A1,D12.
1985 "Does racism prompt executions?" [Editorial]. February 9:22.

Newman, D. J.
1966 "Sociologists and the administration of criminal justice." Pp. 177–187 in A. B. Shostak (ed.), Sociology in Action. Homewood, Ill.: Dorsey Press.

Paulsen, M. G.
1964 Equal Justice for the Poor Man. New York: Public Affairs Committee.

Phillips, D. P.
1980a "The deterrent effect of capital punishment: new evidence on an old controversy." American Journal of Sociology 86:139–148.
1980b Personal Communication (October 23).

Piliavin, I., R. Gartner, C. Thornton, and R. L. Matsueda
1986 "Crime, deterrence and rational choice." American Sociological Review 51(February):101–119.

Quinney, R.
1973 Critique of Legal Order: Crime Control in Capitalist Society. Boston: Little, Brown.

Rainwater, L. and D. J. Pittman
1967 "Ethical problems in studying a politically sensitive and deviant community." Social Problems 14:357–366.

Rawls, J.
1971 A Theory of Justice. Cambridge, Mass.: Belknap Press.

Rossi, P. H., C. E. Bose, and R. E. Burke
1974 "The seriousness of crimes: normative structure and individual differences." American Sociological Review 39:224–237.

Sallach, D. L.
1974 "Class domination and ideological hegemony." Sociological Quarterly 15(Winter): 38–50.

Schur, E. M.
1968 Law and Society: A Sociological View. New York: Random House.

Skolnick, J. H.
1965 "The sociology of law in America: overview and trends." Law and Society (supplement to Social Problems) (Summer):4–39.

St. Louis Globe-Democrat
1973 "Stop the retreat from crime" [Editorial]. January 6–7:2D.

Sutherland, E. H. and D. R. Cressey
1970 Criminology. 8th ed. Philadelphia: J. B. Lippincott.

Sykes, G. M.
1974 "The rise of critical criminology." Journal of Criminal Law and Criminology 65(June): 206–213.

Taylor, A. E. (trans.)
1934 The Laws of Plato. Section 757. London: J. M. Dent and Sons.

Tittle, C. R.
1980 Sanctions and Social Deviance: The Question of Deterrence. New York: Praeger Publishers.

Toby, J.
1979 "Deliquency in cross-cultural perspective." Pp. 105–149 in L. T. Empey (ed.), Juvenile Justice: The Progressive Legacy and Current Reforms. Charlottesville: University of Virginia Press.

United Nations Conference on International Organization
1945 Charter of the United Nations Together with the Statute of the International Court of Justice. U.S. Department of State Publication No. 2353, Conference Series 74. Washington, D.C.: U.S. Government Printing Office.

Vaughan, T.R.
1981 Comments made in session on "Ethics and Social Science: Research on Capital Punishment." Midwest Sociological Society Annual Meeting, Minneapolis (April).

Vold, G. B.
1958 Theoretical Criminology. New York: Oxford University Press.

Woodward, K. L.
1974 "Secrets of the very rich." Newsweek (October 7):78.

2
CRIMINOLOGICAL THEORIES OF THE NATURE OF CRIME AND THE NATURE OF PEOPLE

SOME HISTORICAL ORIGINS OF MODERN CRIMINOLOGY

In this chapter the historical development of contemporary criminology will be traced, and the various theoretical assumptions and research strategies that have emerged will be discussed. It will be demonstrated that certain theoretical assumptions are related both to the choice of specific research strategies and to specific proposals for the control of crime.

Classical and Other Early Criminology

The earliest scholarship that can be called criminology, or the study of crime-related issues, was the work of Cesare Beccaria (1738–1794), who is usually referred to as an advocate of the classical school of criminology (Vold, 1958:18–24; Monachesi, 1973:36–50). Unlike most of the later criminologists, Beccaria was not concerned with explaining the causes of criminal behavior but dealt with what he considered to be injustices in the administration of the law, which gave special privileges to the clergy and the nobility. Beccaria observed that laws typically represented only the interests of a few powerful members of a society. He also complained that the same crimes were often punished in a different manner at different times in the same courts. He recommended a literal enforcement of all laws, irrespective of the mental condition or social status of the accused or the social status of the victim. He deliberately ignored

Much of this chapter was taken from J. F. Galliher, "The Life and Death of Liberal Criminology," Contemporary Crises 2(July 1978):245–263.

questions regarding the individual's motives, and in any event considered them unimportant because he believed that all people have a free will and in this sense are alike (Beccaria, 1775).

The problem with completely ignoring the characteristics of the individuals accused is that in no society has the criminal law been administered without consideration of who is being accused. It is unrealistic to imagine that institutions created by human beings and operated by human beings could function in a totally impersonal and mechanical fashion. Moreover, in strict form, classical criminology would have treated minors and obviously insane persons in the same way as any other accused. In addition, classical criminology would treat first offenders like repeat offenders because it considers the crime committed, not the characteristics of the accused, to be the proper basis for the legal response (Vold, 1958:24). Yet, Beccaria's ideas, however unrealistic, are of lasting importance because they have served as a starting point for a recurrent theme in criminology, namely, demands for legal reforms. When Beccaria's ideas are placed in historical context, we can see that they appeared in the late 1700s during a period in the Western world in which a number of revolutionary movements originated, including those in the United States and, later, in France and Russia. This period saw the emergence of new ideas about the dignity of human beings and their innate rights to freedom and equality. Beccaria's ideas provided the intellectual foundation for modern democratic societies. In such societies a strong myth of equality, if not the actual practice, is necessary to gain the voluntary cooperation of citizens. Past and present police states have not required such ideas of legal justice.

Somewhat later, Jeremy Bentham (1748–1832) also produced a treatise on criminal behavior, criminal law, and legal reform (Bentham, 1823). How Bentham's works can best be categorized is a disputed question (Vold, 1958:14–26; Mannheim, 1973:24). Bentham was concerned with the development of a just legal structure, as was Beccaria, and like Beccaria, Bentham viewed people as possessing a free will. However, unlike Beccaria, Bentham is remembered more for his concern with criminal behavior and its control. He is often remembered for recommending that a set of penalties be developed to control criminal behavior. His idea, which he called the principle of utility, although it is often referred to as the hedonistic calculus, is that the criminal laws should prescribe punishment just severe enough to offset the pleasure that people receive from committing a given criminal act. Any more severe punishment is unnecessarily brutal and therefore unjust.

The central pleasure-pain thesis of the hedonistic calculus is questionable from at least two perspectives. First, there is no evidence that all people derive the same amount of pleasure from the same criminal act. Clearly, some people enjoy stealing. In the famous book by Victor Hugo, *Les Misérables* (1862), the central character, Jean Valjean, dereived no pleasure, but rather considerable guilt, from stealing a loaf of bread, but he felt forced to do so to keep his sister's children from starving. Moreover, there is no evidence that all people suffer the same amount of pain from the imposition of identical criminal sanctions. For example, some prison inmates adjust well to prison life and serve "easy time," whereas for other inmates, each day in prison is a nightmare. Carroll (1974:105) demonstrates that the alienation and poverty of many black Americans is so great that prison is no threat to them. One black prisoner was quoted as saying, "I'm doing time all my life, man. Don't make much difference if I do it here or out there. It's still time." "We be used to time, so we be immune to it," another black inmate remarked, "because we been slaves for 400 years." Prison holds no threat for these men. Despite these considerable shortcomings, Bentham's general orientation is still often used by public officials and others to justify harsh penalities for what they consider serious crimes. For example, it is often said that "we can't lower the penalty for marihuana possession, or everybody will be using it." Clearly, people do not reason in the manner Bentham imagined, since many other factors are known to influence human behavior besides the threat of criminal punishment.

POSITIVISM IN CRIMINOLOGY

Next to develop were the ideas of a heterogeneous group of scholars who are known collectively as positivists. Although differences abound in this group, the positivist writers share several central premises. They all assume that people are controlled in some specifiable manner, by either their biological, psychological, or social characteristics, that these controlling characteristics can be isolated through the use of scientific measurements and of official crime records, and that in this way criminal behavior can be more effectively predicted and controlled. The origins of criminological positivism are often neglected and almost forgotten. One can begin to trace this history in France during the nineteenth century, when there was widespread fear of urban crime and the "dangerous classes." This specific fear was made worse by working-class insurrections. In addition, around 1815 and shortly thereafter, there were great increases in the crime rates—especially in thefts and public disturbances—and the number of convictions nearly doubled during this period.

It is in this context that Adolphe Quetelet

> learned how to apply algebra and geometry to demographic tables. . . . Quetelet reasoned, "We are compelled to believe in the analogue that the influence of [the] laws [of nature] should be extended to the human species." The identification of such laws in the social world was dependent on statistical calculation. . . . The apparent constancy of crime rates in the [official crime records of France] suggested to Quetelet that, whatever the idiosyncrasies of human agency, criminal behavior obeyed laws of the same order as those that regulate the motion of inanimate objects, . . . [with] young males, the poor, the less educated, and those without employment [the most likely both] to commit crimes and to be convicted of them (Beirne, 1987:1150, 1153–1155).

But poverty did not in itself cause crime, because some of the poorest areas, such as Luxembourg, had very low crime rates. Rather, what was more significant was great inequality in wealth and rapid economic change that plunged many into poverty. These factors caused the greatest irritation, he believed. Given the perceived association between crime and the dangerous classes, Quetelet's idea that "crime was an inevitable feature of social organization" was an affront to the law-abiding citizenry. The judiciary also disapproved, because ideas of legal responsibility seemed to fit best with the classical notion of free will, "for if crimes had social rather than individual causes, then perhaps criminals could not be held strictly accountable for their misdeeds" (quoted in Beirne, 1987:1161–1162).

If Quetelet has been frequently neglected, historical accounts of positivism in criminology always mention Cesare Lombroso (1835–1909) as having stressed the role of biological factors in criminal behavior. Lambroso's early research convinced him that convicted crimnals in disproportionately high numbers evidenced physical characteristics of the human's less evolved apelike ancestors. This suggested to Lombroso, in line with the then new notion of evolution, that criminals were throwbacks to earlier stages in the evolutionary process. For this reason he believed that criminals were unable to adjust to civilized society. In short, according to Lombroso's reasoning, many convicted criminals are literally forced by their physical characteristics to commit crimes.

A sampling of the apelike characteristics that Lombroso found among convicted criminals follows:

- Unusually large ears, or occasionally very small, or standing out from the head as in the chimpanzee;
- Fleshy, swollen, and protruding lips;
- Pouches in the cheek like those of lower animals;
- Receding chin, or excessively long, or short, or flat, as in apes;
- Exceedingly long arms. (Lambroso-Ferrero, 1911:14–19.)

Consistent with his other findings, Lombroso found that biological conditions in women led to their criminal activity. In *The Female Offender* (Lombroso and Ferrero, 1895), he found a series of unique biological traits in women convicted of crime. Similar reasoning continues today with the recent discussion of the premenstrual syndrome, which is alleged to trigger many violent crimes by women (*New York Times* 1982a; 1982b; 1982c).

Although Lombroso (1911) later discarded this biological determinism when he found similar biological characteristics among a noncriminal group of Italian soldiers (Vold, 1958:50–52), his early research is of lasting importance because its general assumptions are reflected in contemporary biological positivism. One contemporary variant of biological positivism is found in the considerable amount of popular attention that has been directed to genetic, chromosomal linkages with crime. Some studies have pointed to such a causal link between crime and the presence in some male criminals of an extra Y, or male-producing, chromosome (XY is normal). The evidence from these studies purports to show that XYY males can be characterized as subnormal in intelligence and hyperaggressive and that they appear with greater frequency in institutionalized populations (prisons and mental hospitals) than in the general population (Report on XYY Chromosomal Abnormality, 1970). Even so, a conference of experts convened by the National Institute of Mental Health was reluctant to conclude that the XYY abnormality was definitely or invariably associated with behavioral abnormalities (Report on XYY Chromosomal Abnormality, 1970:33). One major problem in Lombroso's work that continues in the more recent chromosome research is that at best these investigations are conjectural because they ground the relationship between the alleged biological abnormalities and criminal behavior in statistical associations but have established no causal linkages.

Another biologically based approach to criminality is found in psychiatric theories, primarily those emanating from the work of Sigmund Freud. These theories emphasize that the learned aspects of a person's personality can be overcome by biological drives, with criminal behavior as a consequence (Alexander and Staub, 1931; Abrahamsen, 1964). Although these psychiatric theories regard all people as born criminals, they state that most people learn after birth to control their criminal biological impulses. According to this psychiatric orientation, humans are innately aggressive, and although the veneer of civilization has prevented total chaos, it has not changed fundamental human nature. This reasoning holds that people do not choose to commit crime but are literally driven to it by a combination of physical drives and relatively weak learned inhibitions.

Some biological positivists have claimed that one could separate the effects of heredity and environment by studying the behavior of identical twins. According to this reasoning, any differences in the behavior of identical twins must be due to environment because their biological inheritance is the same. Using this technique, some researhers have found remarkable similarities in the criminal biographies of such identical twins and have therefore concluded that heredity is more significant than environment. Although some research continues to find support for the claim of biological sources of the similarities in the behavior of identical twins (Rowe, 1985; Rowe and Osgood, 1984), such a conclusion overlooks the obvious, that because identical twins look alike, they often have identical social environments as well. Often their own parents cannot tell them apart, and they are referred to as a single social unit, "the twins." Yet the studies of identical twins who have been reared apart often find remarkable similarities in their lives. Contrary to some claims, however, these studies do not verify the power of biological inheritance. Many of the identical twins who were reared apart were raised by aunts, sisters, or best friends or neighbors of their parents in the same town, thus the social environment of both twins was very similar (Lewontin, 1982:101).

Mental deficiency or hereditary feeblemindedness has been used as a causal explanation for criminal behavior, the notion being that mentally defective persons have more difficulty than others in adjusting to society. Early works using this approach appeared in the nineteenth century, but not until Henry Goddard (1914, 1921) translated the Binet-Simon intelligence scale for American use did the approach become widespread in this country (Fink, 1962:211ff). Goddard not only found that criminal behavior was caused by feeblemindedness but also claimed that his research indicated that Jews, Hungarians, Italians, and Russians were far below the intelligence of native-born Americans (1917a; 1917b). On the basis of such reasoning, the U.S. Congress, early in this century, passed immigration quotas setting strict limits on the numbers of southern and eastern Europeans who could immigrate to this country in any given year. When World War II broke out and the Nazi holocaust was beginning to become evident, the United States, because of these quotas, could not provide a haven for European Jews. Clearly this demonstrates the pernicious consequences of biological positivism. The racist thinking in the United States, buttressed by biological positivism, made it impossible for the United States to mitigate the consequences of the Nazi genocide. (For other criticisms of Goddard's work, see Gould, 1981.) Even though Goddard's work has had lasting and deadly consequences, the irony is that after an initial surge of popularity in 1910 and shortly thereafter, its use diminished when, after appropriate comparison groups were established, it was shown that prison populations showed approximately the same range of intelligence as the so-called normal population (Vold 1958:75–89).

Sociological Positivism

The latest development in criminological positivism is that of twentieth-century sociology. Emile Durkheim (1858–1917) is often cited as an early sociological positivist with a professional interest in criminal behavior. His position was that social phenomena are just as real as the behavior of individuals or physical objects and that the external characteristics of "social facts" can therefore be studied by objective means (Durkheim, 1938). Durkheim believed that these external characteristics were adequately reflected in official records, which permitted the calculation of such things as suicide and crime rates, and ultimately made possible the analysis and explanation of such rates.

Within contemporary sociological positivism in criminology, several major theoretical traditions have developed. The earliest is found in the works of Shaw (1929) and Shaw and McKay (1942). Rather than focus on characteristics of individuals as causal agents in crime, Shaw and McKay looked to the social disorganization or lack of community control found in specific innercity neighborhood districts as responsible for generating high official rates of law violation. High rates of adult crime are found in these areas, along with similarly high rates of juvenile delinquency, mental illness, and poverty. Shaw and McKay found that the high rates of law violation are remarkably consistent in such neighborhoods, irrespective of the particular ethnic group living in these areas. This suggests that the deteriorating character of neighborhoods characterized by impersonality and transiency gives rise to those rates.

Within sociological positivism, two other theoretical traditions developed in the late 1930's. One orientation was that of anomie theory as developed by Robert K. Merton (1938), and the other was the differential association theory of Edwin Sutherland (1939:1–9). Anomie theory attempts, as did Shaw and McKay, to explain the high rates of crime among the poor, and maintains that crime is a consequence of discrepancies between culturally prescribed goals and the socially approved means available to achieve those goals. In the United States, according to anomie theory, all people are subject to strong social pressures to achieve economic success, and yet some people are in relatively unfavorable competitive positions for attaining that goal legitimately. Consequently, people in such positions experience frustration and strain. Since American society stresses economic success more than the means used to achieve this success, these people are strongly motivated to resort to deviant or illegitimate means. This theory, Merton claims, explains the high rate of officially recorded crime among the poor.

Differential association theory, on the other hand, suggests that people engage in criminal behavior because their predominant intimate contacts have been with criminal behavior patterns. Both criminal techniques and values are learned through such associations. Sutherland claims that a high ratio, or "differential," of criminal to noncriminal associations makes it more likely that a person will commit a crime, because such associations shape and control the person's worldview. In short, "the principles of the process of association by which criminal behavior develops are the same as the principles of the process by which lawful behavior develops" (Sutherland, 1939:5). Sutherland asserted, therefore, that contrary to the claims of psychiatrists, crime does not necessarily represent a pathological condition. Sutherland was very much the champion of sociological criminology and never missed an opportunity to defend sociologists' interests against the competing ideas of psychiatry.

Later, Walter Reckless (1961) developed what is called the containment theory of criminal behavior. The idea is that when conformity occurs, it can be a result of either inner or outer containment. That is, conformity can occur because of external controls on an actor, such as police surveillance, or as a consequence of an individual's ability to control his or her own behavior independently of external forces. Inner control is magnified to the extent that individuals (1) believe in the essential justice and fairness of the rules of society, (2) have the capacity to withstand frustration and adversity, (3) have goals in life that they can easily attain (because if their aspirations are too high, they will be chronically disappointed and frustrated), and (4) have a self-image that is incompatible with law violation—indeed some people would rather starve than steal. Reckless had earlier found that he could successfully predict which of a group of 12-year-old boys in high delinquency areas would get into trouble with the law. The prediction was based on whether or not the boys had self-concepts as "good boys" (Reckless and Dinitz, 1972).

Some individuals are in groups with a high degree of outer containment and at the same time possess a high degree of inner containment. The possibility of crime is then relatively remote. Other individuals possess a high degee of inner containment, but outer containment is weak. There is still only a slight possibility of crime, and such individuals need not be watched because they carry their controls around with them. In still other persons, outer containment is strong and inner containment is weak. Now the possibility of crime is increased because, for example, no matter how many police are on the streets, they cannot be everywhere to watch persons with no commitment to the law. Finally, the possibility of crime is the greatest when there are few inner or outer controls.

A situation in which there are few inner and outer controls is a living hell that almost no one can tolerate. Such a situation seems to have developed in the infamous Pruitt-Igoe federal housing project in St. Louis, Missouri. Built in 1955 and 1956, these high-rise buildings almost immediately began to experience serious crime problems caused by residents of the area (Meehan, 1975). Police were often fired on when responding to calls for help and understandably became less eager to intervene. As a consequence of these continuing crime problems and police inaction, the vacancy rate in this project began to rise steadily. Finally, by 1974, almost all units were vacant, and then all the buildings were closed and then razed. There were simply too few inner and outer controls for people to tolerate living there.

An even better known illustration of a lack of inner and outer controls is found in the massive looting that ocurred in New York City in 1977, when there was a citywide power failure and the city was without lights for approximately 24 hours (Curvin and Porter, 1979). When the lights went out at 9:35 P.M., law enforcement became almost impossible and looting began almost immediately. There developed a frenzy of looting that lasted all night and into the next day. All legal restraints against stealing were removed once the lights went out. The feeling of all looters is reflected in the following quote from one participant: "There's a wallet on the floor and some money sticking out of it, and nobody's going to see you take it. That's what it was like, the same situation. I saw an opportunity and took advantage of it" (Curvin and Porter, 1979:73). Apparently the looters had few existing inner controls, and once outer controls were lifted, looting began immediately.

Containment theory has been discussed in considerable detail in part because it is an ideal means to demonstrate how new ideas develop in criminology or, for that matter, in any science. What passes for a totally new idea is typically only a summarization and recombination of older ideas. Remember that Reckless discussed identification with the rules and laws of society—which comes from Sutherland's differential association theory. Reckless also mentioned frustration—earlier mentioned also by Merton. Reckless' discussion of self-image as an insulator against delinquency comes from his own earlier research.

What all positivists have in common, then, is that they see people as essentially compelled to commit crimes because of their biological, psychological, or social condition. For example, Lombroso claimed that many convicted criminals were compelled to commit misdeeds by their relatively less highly evolved biological capacities; Goddard considered feeblemindedness to be the main controlling agent; and Sutherland focused on group pressures. Moreover, it is such conditions that make criminals essentially different from noncriminals. These twin assumptions of constraint and differentiation, Matza (1964:1–32) observed, leave unexplained the consistent features of the lives of most criminals and delinquents. If crimnals are forced to commit criminal acts, and if they are indeed so different from other people, then how can patterns of occasional law violation, separated by long periods of conformity, be explained? Matza's point is that if persons are forced to commit crime because of their unique characteristics, logically they should be forced to do so continually. Positivism cannot explain intermittent law violation, even though it is typical even of persons called habitual criminals. According to Matza, people can "drift" into and out of criminal and delinquent behavior without the total commitment claimed by positivists.

The heavy emphasis on the study of criminal individuals is expected of biological positivists, but it is somewhat surprising to find sociologists, who should be more attuned to group processes and social forces, also emphasizing individual characteristics. Moreover, these sociologists, like other positivists, rely heavily on the scientific measurement of individual characteristics, such as the self concept or frustration, and on official crime statistics as appropriate sources of information on criminal individuals. This emphasis is reflected in a review of the social science research on juvenile delinquency published over the past 30 years. The review indicates a heavy use of official records, statistical tests, and hypothesis testing, all of which are part of the traditional scientific model, and a heavy use of individual variables, such as respondents' attitudes and values as measured through interviews and questionnaires (Galliher and McCartney, 1973). There are, however, a few excellent qualitative descriptions that analyze crime as it is situated in the community. These provide a convincing picture of crime and of persons called criminals (Liebow, 1967).

As might be expected, positivism was originally dominated by biologists and physicians until approximately the late 1920s, when sociological positivism emerged (Gibbons, 1974). Unlike in Britain, where criminology developed largely in medicine and law, criminology in the United States eventually developed in the social sciences partially because of American optimism concerning remediable social forces as causes of crime (Cohen, 1974). As indicated earlier, this sociological positivism is well known for emphasizing such things as peer pressure and neighborhood disorganization as the social causes of criminal behavior. The Great Depression of the 1930s and the massive social upheaval that it caused sensitized people to social issues and made the idea of social causes for crime an appealing one. Perhaps the sociological positivism of the period is best exemplified by Merton's anomie theory, which stresses blocked legitimate opportunities for success as the cause of the problem of high official rates of crime and delinquency among the poor. Merton's anomie theory is a good illustration of the emphasis on liberal reformism in sociological positivism.

According to Merton's conception of crime, the problem could be solved by opening the American dream of success to the poor. Moreover, liberal formulations such as Merton's accept the government's definition of the crime problem, namely official police records showing that most crime is among the poor.

As part of the positivistic tradition, the subfield of criminology called *corrections* blossomed during the 1950s and 1960s (Matza, 1969). Numerous studies of parole prediction and prison organization are a part of this tradition. Much of this writing asks why and how prisons operate in such a way that many prisoners return to prison after release. Stated in positivistic terms, what is it about the prison or parole experience that forces so many prisoners to violate parole or commit another crime? Among criminologists studying prisons there has been little interest in research on rehabilitation. Perhaps this is true because of criminologists' lack of belief in rehabilitation as a result of their positivist inclinations.

Another important subfield of positivistic criminology is juvenile delinquency research, which, as indicated in chapter 1, experienced a boom in the 1960s (Galliher and McCartney, 1973). We noted that the increase in published articles dealing with this topic appears to have been stimulated by increases in support for this type of research from government funding agencies. Among the most widely cited theorists in this subfield are Richard Cloward and Lloyd Ohlin (1960), who stressed as did Merton, blocked legal or legitimate means for success. But neither Merton nor Cloward and Ohlin adequately distinguished between illegal and illegitimate means for success. The interchangeable use of the terms *illegal means* and *illegitimate means* implies a moral consensus supporting written laws; it suggests that all illegal acts are considered by citizens to be illegitimate or immoral. Moreover, using the terms *illegality* and *illegitimacy* synonymously ignores the illegal behavior of the affluent, which is often not widely condemned—that is not considered illegitimate. As indicated above, both the emphasis on political consensus and the deemphasis of law violation by the affluent has been typical of liberal criminology.

Moynihan (1969) observed that Cloward and Ohlin's position was politically attractive because it claimed that the only thing delinquents want is the opportunity to meet the same success goals as other Americans, not radical social change. For this reason, their theoretical position was adopted in the 1960s' federal war-on-poverty programs as the guiding force behind the federal youth projects. As might be expected of ideas chosen for their political safety rather than their intellectual merit, programs based on these ideas were a total failure. Yet positivism, as discussed here, is attractive to government officials because it is concerned with finding answers to the practical problems of crime control. Positivists have described a simple society composed of normal persons and others—the criminals or delinquents—and in so doing have been able to help legitimate commonsense morality.

Sociological positivism continued to be the dominant force in criminology until the late 1960s and early 1970s, when it began to disappear. Yet it is true that some researchers continue to investigate the causes of criminal behavior. They are somewhat less likely to be sociologists, however, and once again, are more likely to be biologists or physicians, as was true before 1920. One indication of this movement away from sociological positivism and toward biological positivism is reflected in National Institute of Mental Health (1976) expenditures for crime and delinquency research, showing support for numerous XYY chromosomal studies and little support for research into the social causes of crime. But more recently, even social scientists have begun calling for a renewed consideration of the biological roots of criminal behavior (Wilson and Herrnstein, 1985). Biological positivism, past and present, does not have the liberal or reformist implications of sociological positivism, and in this sense liberal positivism is disappearing. Biological positivism reflects a less optimistic orientation toward easy policy changes for crime control.

The Demise of Delinquency

There currently exists a hardening of spirit against children identified as deviants. To the extent that there is growing sentiment to treat juveniles as young criminals, and to the extent that criminal punishment and retribution are replacing the rehabilitative ideal, most of what was the original humanitarian support for the juvenile court movement has vanished. We may be observing the demise of delinquency. Indeed, many American political leaders currently are claiming that youthful law violators should be referred to as young criminals and not as juvenile delinquents. Given the current crisis in American political and economic institutions, one can understand the disappearance, among politicians, citizens, and social scientists, of liberal sympathy for deviants (Platt and Takagi, 1977; Galliher, 1978). The economic crisis in the Western world, long predicted by social scientists, is now becoming obvious to all. Industrial productivity is plummeting and unemployment is reaching new heights, especially among the young. In response, some Western governments are turning to more conservative leadership and are cutting back on social welfare spending, replacing such allocations with political attacks on the working class. The parallel developments in the United States and Great Britain serve as prime examples of this pattern. This loss of faith in liberalism and reform among political leaders and much of the electorate is also found among social scientists. Whereas social scientists studied juvenile delinquency and advocated liberal reforms such as slum clearance and government employment programs in the 1950s and 1960s, now there is a rush of publications reporting the type of penalties that deter crime most effectively. Whereas both juvenile delinquency research and deterrence research hold the promise of lower crime rates, deterrence research, unlike many studies of juvenile delinquency, assumes no concomitant improvements in the material conditions of the poor.

Bayer (1981) traced this decline in liberal ideology through a review of articles published from 1945 to 1975 in major American magazines. As a result of his survey, he concluded: "The mood of self-confidence has been shattered. More than three decades after the end of World War II, liberalism appears to have lost its sense of vision, of mission" (1981:170). Traditionally liberals, unlike conservatives, have not emphasized moral categories when judging crime and criminals and have claimed that the entire society is to blame when crime occurs. Liberal analysts focused on the miserble conditions of lower-class life in urban ghettos, including chronic unemployment. And liberals rejected punishment as a response to crime, not only as unjust, but as counterproductive in that it only produced more, not less, crime (Cullen and Gilbert, 1982). In recent years this sympathetic liberalism has come under increasing pressure with the realization that lower-class people themselves have been the most frequent victims of crime. Finally, there has been the increasing belief that the great hopes for the rehabilitation of prisoners were misplaced. This demise of liberalism, Bayer argued, is more profound and more general than just a loss of faith in liberal crime control policies and reaches to all areas of American life.

SOCIAL CONTROL AND SOCIETAL REACTIONS

As indicated earlier, Durkheim is usually cited as an early sociological positivist. He was also the first social analyst to suggest that, contrary to the traditional view that crime is only a burden to society, it may serve a positive function in social life. His notion was that if a society is so rigid and binding that no crime occurs, then no other creativity will occur either, and no change or progress will be possible.

> To make progress, individual originality must be able to express itself. In order that the originality of the idealist whose dreams transcend his century may find expression, it is necessary that the originality of the criminal, who is below the level of his time, shall also be possible. One does not occur without the other. . . . Crime implies not only that the way remains open to necessary changes but that in certain cases it directly prepares these changes. (Durkheim, 1938:71.)

Moreover, Durkheim suggested that society's very act of punishing crime mobilizes support for the social norm that has been violated. In this sense as well, crime serves a positive function in society, because the violation and consequent punishment symbolize to everyone the importance of the social norm (Durkheim, 1933:70–110). Durkheim's concern with the social reactions of a citizenry toward criminal behavior represented a significant departure in the literature dealing with crime, for before his work attention was focused mainly on the criminal.

Another step toward a thorough analysis of citizen reactions and defini-tions of crime and criminals is seen in Frank Tannenbaum's discussion (1938:19–21) of what he called the "dramatization of evil." The idea is that once a person has been arrested and taken into court, a process of public redefining and labeling begins that emphasizes to the public and to the arrested person that he or she is indeed a criminal. Not only does the public become convinced of the person's new identity, but the arrestee becomes convinced as well and changes his or her behavior to bring it in line with this new self-image. Very often, children who have been sent to a reformatory emerge from the correctional institution with a clear view of themselves as bad, and they behave accordingly. Thus the very behavior that the community complains of is reinforced by the community's reaction.

The distinction between "primary and secondary deviation," first discussed by Edwin Lemert (1951:75–78), also deals with the effect of citizen reaction to crime. Some law violation occurs before an actor is publicly labeled a criminal or delinquent. Lemert referred to this as primary deviation. However, once actors' deviance has been identified, this new public knowledge can alter how they are perceived by themselves and others. The new deviant role thus created for the actor encourages further law violation—called secondary deviation. In other words, secondary deviation is a result of the dramatization of evil. In the works of Tannenbaum and Lemert, at least a slight shift of emphasis has been made away from the exclusive study of the behavior of criminals and toward some analysis of the impact of broader social events on the actor once he or she has been identified as a criminal. Public definitions of crime and criminals become objects worthy of study in their own right.

A somewhat more extreme position is the labeling theory perspective of Howard Becker. Becker (1963) maintained that the *audience reaction* to deviance should be of primary interest to social analysts beause one cannot determine whether acts are criminal or delinquent independently of that reaction. The definition of "what happened" is recognized as not inherent in the behavior itself (cf. Douglas, 1967). Becker (1963) stated:

> From this point of view, deviance is *not* a quality of the act the person commits, but rather a consequence of the application by others of rules and sanctions to an "offender." The deviant is one to whom that label has successfully been applied; deviant behavior is behavior that people so label (page 9). . . . Whether an act is deviant, then, depends on how other people react to it (page 11). . . . Just because one has committed an infraction of a rule does not mean that others will respond as though this had happened. (Conversely, just because one has not violated a rule does not mean that he may not be treated, in some circumstances, as though he had.) (page 12). . . . Some people may be labeled deviant who in fact have not broken a rule (page 9).

Jumping around while shouting and frothing at the mouth can be defined as a glorious religious experience deserving respect and awe, as evidence of mental illness requiring hospitalization, or as an indication that the actor is a witch and merits burning at the stake. The meaning of the act can be determined only by observing the act's significance for the participants. Prostitution, gambling, drunkenness, and begging, which are crimes in our society, are not so defined in all cultures (Vold, 1958:141–146) but may be seen as behaviors that are appropriate and even honorable on special occasions or when committed by special persons, as in ritual drunkenness at athletic events or ritualized prostitution in temples. What killing a person with an ax is called is a matter of variable human definition. It can be seen as murder, self-defense, battlefield valor, or routine performance of one's job as an executioner. The labeling pespective is useful in demonstrating social and legal variability among cultures, but although we make use of some of its observations, we do not try to avoid making moral judgments about certain cultural practices.

If one uses the labeling perspective, then official crime records become suspect as reflections of actual behavior and tend to be seen as a measure of the reactions to various types of behavior by the organizations that compile those records (Kitsuse and Cicourel, 1963). Within this context, crime rates become useful as a reflection of police activity and decision making and irrelevant as indicators of the amount of criminal behavior taking place in a community. For example, a high rate of narcotics arrests may not mean that an area is being flooded with drugs in comparison with neighboring areas but, rather, that the police there are less tolerant of, and more vigilant in dealing with, such offenses. Not only do labeling theorists reject official records as measures of deviance, but also they criticize and abandon scientific methods that use such data. The labeling perspective claims that there is a dynamic or processual aspect to human existence that is not adequately described in official records and is retrievable only through field observation. Yet the labeling theorists, like the positivists, continue to view the actor as essentially controlled or dominated by his or her environment (Schervish, 1973). Their usual argument is that the actor labeled as a lawbreaker is forced into a life of crime.

In the late 1960s and early 1970s, the labeling perspective enjoyed a considerable amount of popularity. The labeling perspective's consideration of the social process involved in defining crime and criminals and its insistence on the arbitrary nature of consequent definitions proved convincing in an era when government was increasingly distrusted. During such an era, official definitions of reality, including official definitions of crime, are less likely to be accepted without question. When the government and its law enforcement agencies are widely suspected of bias and corruption, the official records and official definitions of crime and criminals come to be seen as questionable and come to be regarded as subjects suitable for study in their own right. As Jerome Hall (1945:345–346) observed, the positivist orientation toward the study of crime develops only when governments are trusted and above question.

Various developments have contributed to the credibility of the labeling position. In the southeastern United States during the various civil rights demonstrations and other related racial clashes of the 1960s, the police and courts often failed to enforce the law when whites assaulted or even killed local blacks. Indeed, the southern police often assumed a leadership role in physical brutality toward black demonstrators, including women and children. With the aid of national television networks, all Americans could easily learn about racist segregation statutes and the racist administration of other criminal laws, at least in the South. More recently, the deceitful actions of a former U.S. president, Richard

Nixon, and his attorney general, the chief law enforcement officer of the nation, ensured the continued credibility of the labeling position.

Labeling and Liberalism

Although sociological positivism's study of criminal behavior continued to flourish through the 1960s, Tannenbaum's creation of the "dramatization of evil" in the late 1930s was an important development in the sociological study of crime that went almost unnoticed. Tannenbaum developed the notion of dramatization of evil in 1938 at the beginning of the Nazi holocaust and this was not an opportune time to argue the artificially created or concocted nature of deviance. When Lemert introduced the notion of secondary deviance in 1951, during the height of the cultural paranoia of McCarthyism and the Cold War with the Soviet Union, this again was not the best time to argue for the created nature of deviance to an American audience seemingly convinced of the menace of communists. Although the 1930s, 1940s, and 1950s were not ideal periods for a labelling type of orientation, these years were clearly suitable for criminological positivism and its unquestioning view of crime.

The emphasis on societal reaction in the study of deviation became widely recognized and used only after Becker's book *Outsiders* appeared in 1963. At this point it began to be referred to as the labeling perspective. In this case the actors are viewed as compelled to respond to negative labeling by some type of deviation, crime, or delinquency. This perspective flourished during the halcyon years of liberalism and of the Great Society: the Kennedy-Johnson years of the 1964 Civil Rights Law and of the beginning of various federal social welfare programs.

A parallel development with the popularity of the labeling perspective was a new identifiable subfield of sociology called deviance. The term *deviance* was used only occasionally before Becker's labeling theory was published, but since labeling theory appeared in the 1960s, numerous new college courses and texts on this subject have appeared. The ideas of Tannenbaum, Lemert, and Becker have generated a series of essays criticizing, defending, or explaining and extending this orientation. These essays deal with the adequacy, usefulness, consistency, and application of what has come to be called labeling theory.

What makes this perspective of special significance, however, are the other developments it appears to have stimulated or triggered. Much as social disorganization did earlier in the century, the new term deviance has provided an umbrella under which one can include not only crime and delinquency but also many other types of behavior. Mental illness can be subjected to a labeling perspective analysis as can other noncriminal behavior such as that of jazz musicians, "Jesus freaks" and carnival freaks, skid-row bums, homosexuals, prostitutes, strippers, and transvestites.

This labeling perspective seems to have encouraged a concern with the unique or bizarre and with the exotic and erotic. Such an orientation focuses on powerless deviants but ignores power elites. Yet unlike positivistic criminology, labeling theory, to its credit, does not suggest a societal consensus. The labeling tradition, unlike previous criminology, does not imply that deviants must be changed or controlled and for this reason rarely studies crime involving property relations. Rather, it concentrates on crimes without victims. In addition, unlike previous criminology, this tradition concentrates on the subjective meanings of deviance, but like its predecessors, it ignores the social and historical setting of crime.

Labeling and the Sociology of Law

The labeling perspective, because it emphasizes audience reaction, has set the stage for the beginning of a sociological effort to study both the operation and the origins of criminal law. This sociology of law is concerned with the social and politial origins of the law and with the operation or administration of the law, especially by the police departments but also by the courts. The research concerns of the sociology of law reflect the labeling perspective's emphasis on external forces and a tendency to place the blame for the crime problem on local government authorities. In fact, both Tannenbaum and Becker mention the importance of government agencies in the labeling of crime and delinquency. Before the labeling perspective emerged, police departments and the origins of law had only rarely been studied by sociologists.

After the development of labeling theory, liberal sociologists often studied the police and often criticized them. As will be seen in chapter 8, however, liberal sociologists usually studied the police in isolation from institutionalized power and structural arrangements, in the same way that they have studied deviants. Taylor et al. (1975) observed that even at best, liberal social theory rarely tries to account for the workings of the total society. C. Wright Mills (1962) claimed that liberalism has little interest in theory and is concerned with piecemeal observations rather than broad structual issues. Moreover, Mills showed that, in the name of tolerance, liberalism seldom makes explicit moral judgments. All these characteristics are reflected in the labeling pespective.

Applications of the Societal Reaction Perspective

Once the social processes involved in defining crime and criminals are recognized, new topics that seem especially relevant to contemporary society can be better understood. Objects, behaviors, and events not usually associated with crime and criminals can be presented in a new light outside the protective shield of commonsense opinion.

It has been convincingly argued that what is usually considered a "drug" or "narcotic," and therefore what is considered drug abuse, has no basis in chemical or pharmacological fact but is merely a cultural fabrication. *"A drug is something that has been arbitrarily defined by certain segments of society as a drug"* (Goode, 1972:18; original emphasis). Marihuana is routinely classified as a drug, whereas coffee, cigarettes, and alcohol are not. "What this means is that the effects of different drugs have relatively little to do with the way they are conceptualized, defined, and classified" (Goode, 1972:18).

It has been well known for several decades (Nader, 1965) that automobile manufacturers have collaborated to manufacture cheaply produced autos but have disregarded the safety of the occupants. The manufacturers' knowledge of engineering clearly indicates to them that such autos will kill and maim the occupants in low-speed crashes. Yet no claims have been made by the public, the press, or prosecutors that auto manufacturers are guilty of conspiracy to commit highway genocide. When a family is slaughtered on the highways, the disaster is blamed on driver fatigue, drinking, or poor visibility but never on Henry Ford II or other corporate executives, even though the elements of a conspiracy resulting in unnecessary deaths seem to be present. Our cultural image of the responsibility for auto accidents comes from the National Safety Council (NSC), an agency supported in large part with funds from the auto industry (Gusfield, 1975). The NSC does not call attention to the design characteristics of the specific automobiles associated with auto accidents and deaths. The clear implication is that if anyone is to be blamed for auto accidents, it is the driver. Furthermore, as indicated in chapter 1, there is no evidence that such acts as illegal price-fixing by business executives create public moral indignation, even though such behavior violates criminal statutes and annually costs the American public millions of dollars.

As another case in point, one can observe that much of the American public was not aroused by the endless bombings of civilians in Southeast Asia during the 1960s and 1970s as a result of presidential decrees by Richard Nixon, in a conflict seldom now justified in military or political terms. Yet many citizens were outraged when the same leader was implicated in what seems to be the relatively minor crime of conspiracy to obstruct justice in a burglary (the Watergate case). Curiously, the destruction of human life seems to have been considered less serious than was burglary.

In contrast to dictionary definitions of violence, most American men interviewed in a nationwide survey (Blumenthal et al., 1972) did not see war as violent, nor did a majority see the shooting of looters by police as violent, even though the vast majority of the respondents saw looting itself as violent. The point is that even though a behavior is destructive of life or property, this does not guarantee that the public will define it as violent or as criminal. Public definitions of violence, crime, criminals, and immorality are not based on objective measures of physical destruction and human suffering—or even on gross and open violation of criminal statutes. Violence is typically seen by laymen and social scientists solely as a product of the behavior of persons outside government, even when it is recognized that the representatives of government kill and injure. Only rarely has an attempt been made to provide the tools to see the normative violence of the powerful in the same terms as the violence of others (Ball-Rokeach, 1980).

Most recently there has developed a massive debate about the morality of legalized abortion. In the 1973 Supreme Court decision in *Roe* v. *Wade*, abortions were interpreted to be a constitutional right for American women. Since the early 1980s there has developed a vocal and politically powerful minority that seeks to outlaw this procedure, either through new Supreme Court decisions reversing the 1973 decision or through a Constitutional Convention to amend the Constitution. Persons opposed to legalized abortion argue that abortion is killing, the taking of a human life. On the other hand, the pro-choice advocates argue that abortions are procedures on fetuses—not on babies—and therefore that abortions are not killing. The two sides totally disagree on the definiton of this act, even though they totally agree on the procedures involved in the various types of medical abortion operations. Describing, even in great detail, the physical behavior involved tells us nothing about how it will be defined.

Once consensus is achieved regarding what acts have occurred, then the matter of responsibility for those acts must be addressed. The judgments in answer to such questions also have no basis independent of cultural designations. One issue is whether an individual or a gang is responsible for a criminal act. In fact, only a part of an individual's body is held responsible for certain crimes in some Arabic societies, as reflected in their traditional practice of cutting off the hands of thieves. Although this may seem ridiculous to Americans, it seems logical to others not to blame the entire body for what is seen as the act of a person's hand. In the Western world, on the contary, we routinely hold people responsible for crimes they have commissioned, including killings, even though they did not participate in the criminal act. This example shows how unimportant the objective physical behaviors may be in human definitions. One can be 2,000 miles away from a murder and still be held legally and socially responsible for it. At times, the individual who has been attacked may even be blamed for the assault, as is often true of rape victims. It is frequently alleged that rape victims, by their seductive dress or manner, created the conditons resulting in their own victimization (Brownmiller, 1975).

The problem of assessing responsibility for actions was addressed in trials conducted by the Allied powers in Nuremberg, Germany, after World War II, which established a principle that was unusual in the history of war among modern nations. Historically, after a war the individual operatives of the defeated nation have not been held legally or morally responsible for its acts. The Nuremberg trials, however, abandoned this principle and held various government officials and army officers criminally responsible for the atrocities of the Third Reich. In addition, what many regard as a crime crisis in America is alternatively blamed on a communist conspiracy, the Mafia, the mass media, or liberal judges and permissive parents. Indeed, some juvenile court judges have suggested punishment for the parents of youths found to be delinquent. As in definitions of crime, designations of responsibility are totally dependent on varying cultural judgments. By using this labeling perspective, chapters 3 and 4 will explore the created nature of a variety of criminals and criminal behaviors.

CONFLICT THEORY

In the late 1960s there reemerged in the United States what is usually called the conflict perspective in the study of crime and deviance. More than the labeling perspective this orientation stresses the role of *power* in winning control over government operations, including the law enforcement (crime-defining) machinery (Quinney, 1970; Turk, 1969).

Quinney developed a well-known conflict orientation embodied in a series of theoretical propositions that include the following:

- **Proposition 1 (Definition of crime):** Crime is a definition of human conduct that is created by authorized agents in a politically organized society. (Quinney, 1970:15.)
- **Proposition 2 (Formulation of criminal definitions):** Criminal definitions describe behaviors that conflict with the interests of the segments of the society that have the power to shape public policy. (Quinney, 1970:16.)
- **Proposition 3 (Applications of criminal definitions):** Criminal definitions are applied by the segments of society that have the power to shape the enforcement and administration of criminal law. (Quinney, 1970:18.)

The conflict approach to the study of crime can be summarized as follows:

> [Crime emerges when] individuals or loosely organized small groups with little power are strongly feared by a well-organized, sizable minority or majority who have a large amount of power. (Lofland, 1969:14.) Then, the existence of state rulings and corresponding enforcement mechanisms . . . provide for the possibility of forcibly removing actors from civil society, either by banishment, annihilation or incarceration. Again, it is precisely those actors who have little power and who are not organized toward whom such actions can most successfully be undertaken. (Lofland, 1969:18.)

The conflict position takes as its primary article of faith the view that crime is first and foremost a political topic. Black radicals' claims of being political prisoners and the trials of Vietnam war protesters have undoubtedly contributed to the visibility, if not the credibility, of this position in contemporary America. The evidence in chapters 6 and 7 regarding the role of elites in shaping most criminal statutes also seems to support this theoretical orientation. The conflict perspective is not new, however, having European origins in the work of the Marxist-socialist Willem Bonger (1876–1940), whose book *Criminality and Economic Conditions* was published in this country in 1916. Somewhat later the conflict perspective emerged in the United States (Sellin, 1938; Taft, 1942; Vold, 1958). Most recently, in the 1970s, some proponents of the conflict perspective placed more emphasis on the work of Karl Marx in their explorations of the nature of class conflict and domination, crime, and crime control (Quinney, 1973; Taylor et al., 1975).

According to Marxist analysis, as capitalism develops, a greater and greater proportion of the labor force is unneeded and is thus referred to as the surplus population. According to Quinney (1977:58):

> Crimes of economic gain increase whenever the jobless seek ways to maintain themselves and their familites. Crimes of violence rise when the problems of life are futher exacerbrated by the loss of life-supporting activity. Anger and frustration at a world that punishes rather than supports produce their own forms of destruction. Permanent unemployment—and the acceptance of that condition—can result in a form of life where criminality is an appropriate and consistent response. Hence, crime under capitalism has become a response to the material conditions of life. Nearly all crimes among the working class in capitalist society are actually a means of *survival*, an attempt to exist in a society where survival is not assured by other, collective means. Crime is inevitable under captalist conditions.

Other exponents of the Marxist perspective qualify these claims as follows (Reiman and Headlee, 1981:45):

> This is not to say that every person at the bottom of society will automatically become a criminal. Rather, the point is that if a sufficiently large number of people are kept in conditions of instability and need, some will give in to the temptation to prey on others.

The explanations of Marxists fit nicely with empirical research of other writers, which shows that "high rates of criminal violence are apparently the price of racial and economic inequalities. In a society founded on the principle 'that all men are created equal' economic inequalities rooted in ascribed positions violate the spirit of democracy and are likely to create alienation, despair, and conflict" (Blau and Blau, 1982:126). Thus it is not the amount of poverty per se that is important but, rather, the amount of spread or the range in economic situations that creates the conditions which encourage criminal violence. Indeed, it has also been found in international comparisons that the magnitude of social and economic inequality is strongly associated with the levels of violence found in specific nations (Avison and Loring, 1986).

Like labeling theory, the conflict perspective usually gives some recognition to the notion that definitions of crime and criminals are arbitrary. Yet, as with positivists and to some degree labeling theorists, the conflict perspective's view of humankind is still usually that of actors who are subject to the dictates of social and economic conditions. This view is undoubtedly a result of the pespective's historical roots in Marxism, which has always stressed a class-controlled view of human behavior.

Labeling and Conflict Theory

The appearance of a conflict perspective in the late 1960s and early 1970s seems to be another possible spin-off from the labeling perspective. Since the work of Sellin (1938), emphasizing the role of culture conflict in crime, little attention has been devoted to the role of conflict and power in creating criminal definitions and criminal behavior. The popularity of the labeling perspective, with its emphasis on societal reaction and created deviance, seems to have provided the conditions in the discipline for the swift reemergence of the conflict orientation once it was triggered by the political milieu. The Black Power and civil rights movements of the 1960s seem to have revitalized an interest in conflict and power in the control of government processes, and the conflict perspective seems to have been fed by the ever-increasing distrust of government during the late 1960s and early 1970s. The deception of the United States government in the cases of Vietnam, Cambodia, Kent State University, and, ultimately, the Watergate burglary did not go unnoticed by some studying the American legal system, as Sykes (1974) observed. By putting the "blame" or focusing attention on powerful "others" besides the deviants themselves, labeling helped create the intellectual conditions in which a conflict orientation could emerge, although it was directly spawned by social and political conditions. And labeling theory and conflict theory can be easily joined once it is recognized that the labeling process is always grounded in the existing political and economic environment (Melossi, 1985). The conflict perspective, stressing powerful interest groups' control of the law, police, and courts, in turn created the intellectual basis for the emergence of Marxism in criminology in the 1970s. This perspective has little historical precedent except for the European socialist Bonger (1916), and no precedent in the United States. The development of the career of Richard Quinney, who was initially a conflict theorist (1970) and later became a Marxist (1973), is an excellent example of how this metamorphosis has occurred.

Marxist criminology portrays crime as a natural and inevitable product of modern capitalism. This is seen as true not only because of the economic exploitation of the masses by the propertied class but also because of the latter's control of government, including a domination of the police, legislatures, and courts. Unlike other criminology, radical research is not content with mere description of behavior, or even prescription of alternatives, but strives to change social situations through the research activity. This change can be fostered by feeding back research results, not to the powerful as is usually done, but to those most negatively affected by any inequality being studied. Unlike other social science research, no effort is made to avoid the "Hawthorne effect"—the influence of the research activity on the data base. Schumann saw the following question for a Marxist or critical criminology as central: "Why are some conflicts regulated by criminal law while many others are not?" (1976:288). Further, Shumann (1976) and Taylor et al. (1975) believe that such a criminology must study the processes involved in the origin and change of criminal law. The radical criminologist should develop a model of society and work toward a society in which no group's special interests will ever be guaranteed by criminal law.

Some criticism of this Marxist criminology suggests that the works and ideas of Marx do not extend to a systematic analysis of crime and its control and that attempting this mix of ideas is not an appropriate use of Marxist thought, which, in fact, deals with broader economic and historical issues. The argument continues that Marx saw criminals as part of the lumpenproletariat, a drain on society, and irrelevant to the revolution. Marx and Engels, it is claimed, saw crime and criminals not only as irrelevant but even in opposition to the struggle of the proletariat (Hirst, 1975). Criminals, such as the prostitute, rather than working as do the proletariat, service the corrupt desires of the ruling class and often are recruited as police informers. Moreover, the thief steals from all classes, workers as well as the wealthy. Schumann (1976) also observed that not all social conflicts and their regulation can be explained by a Marxist class analysis of capitalism (e.g., the widespread discrimination against women). Perhaps Marx and Marxism, however, are chosen as much for symbolic reasons—to communicate a total perspective, or world view—as for the particularities of what Marx wrote about crime or law. Few claims so succinctly and cogently communicate a complete contempt and rejection of American society as the adherence to Marxism. And clearly the broad outlines of Marxist thought can be and are used to sensitize social analysts of crime and crime control to the ways in which capitalist societies both cause and control crime.

DETERRENCE: TWENTIETH-CENTURY NEOCLASSICISM

Both the positivistic and the labeling perspectives assume, as do most conflict theorists including Marxists, that people are constrained in some way, and this has been the dominant position in criminology since Lombroso. Recently, however, there has been a return among some sociologists to Beccaria's and Bentham's belief that people may have the potential for voluntary action, and there has been an increase in the associated concern with directing this behavior and deterrence of crime through appropriate passage and administration of laws (DiChiara and Galliher, 1984). This belief in the human capacity for voluntary action distinguishes deterrence research from sociological positivism, as does the fact that deterrence research implies no liberal reforms such as those reflected in Merton's writing (1938). Much of this research has explained how legislation and enforcement practices deter or fail to deter various types of crime.

Although there are differences in method among these studies of deterrence, they usually rely heavily on statistical techniques in their analysis. Disputes among scholars in this area of research have often been technical in nature, such as disputes concerning the most appropriate measure of criminal behavior to use: self-reported behavior, or official statistics, or whether *actual* severity and certainty or *perceived* severity and certainty are the appropriate independent variables. Curiously, deterrence research uses the classical theory of free will in combination with the scientific-technological approach to the prediction and control of human behavior. Simply stated, this is a theory of freedom and a method of control. If people are free, they, not society, can be held responsible for their acts, while at the same time science promises to increase the state's capacity to control human action.

Several studies in the 1950s and 1960s seemed to be statements of principle against capital punishment rather than empirical investigation of whether punishment, in fact, deters crime. These studies sometimes included the claim (in standard liberal positivistic fashion) that murders are crimes of passion that people usually do not choose to commit and for this reason cannot be deterred. Usually these early studies compared states in the same region with and without capital punsihment, or the researchers studied states before, during, and after abolition of capital punishment. They seldom found significant differences in homicide rates.

SUMMARY AND DISCUSSION OF RECENT DEVELOPMENTS

The two recent developments in criminology are the deterrence and the Marxist orientations, and both reflect concerns of the 1970s and 1980s. These contemporary concerns are different from the dominant liberal idealism of the 1960s, when Lyndon Johnson won the presidency by a landslide over a conservative opponent by promising Americans both "guns and butter," which meant both guns for the military and butter for Americans on welfare. Johnson's program, which he called the "Great Society," is now gone, and in its place we have had the Nixon-Ford-Reagan years. Liberalism has been discredited, as have social scientists who continually seek the environmental causes of crime (Moynihan, 1969). Neither the programs of liberal politicians nor the research of liberal social scientists has made progress in solving America's social problems. The cities are increasingly seen as dangerous in spite of considerable spending on social science research and on social welfare programs.

There is an increasingly hard line on crime, as reflected in the number of states that have recently passed and used death penalty laws and enacted mandatory minimum sentences for conviction of certain offenses (Cullen and Gilbert, 1982). Consideration of deterrence is becoming more popular because it is increasingly clear that rehabilitation programs, no matter how well financed and planned, do not reduce recidivism. The attitude of both politicians and academicians seems to be that the only alternative left is to consider punishment as a deterrent.

Earlier it was observed that positivism has flourished only when government is trusted. This is true because positivism requires the acceptance of government definitions of crime. Government seems to have generated the required trust in the l940s, 1950s, and the early 1960s. It seems likely that the various changes noted in sociological criminology in the 1960s and 1970s were influenced by the political milieu of the times, the years of optimistic liberalism, which shifted into the distrust and pessimism of the late 1960s and the 1970s. Labeling theory and its criticism of local officials provided the academic language and initial professional justification for this shift of concerns. As Shover (1975:98) observes, "the context of criminological theories, and the variation in the degree to which they are uncritically accepted, are to some extent determined by politial economic variables. . . . In this respect, they are not unlike political ideologies.

Deterrence and Marxism (to say nothing of biological positivism) represent a distrust of liberalism and are two new and divergent intellectual reactions to two distinct themes found in contemporary America. Concern with deterrence represents the widespread opinion of the time that streets can be made safe if law violators are punished. The Marxists, of course, reflect a profound distrust of American government. At just the time when government is most distrusted, citizens appear most dependent on government to control crime.

In sum, the development, growth, and eventual decline of liberal criminology, in both its positivistic and labeling variants as here described, seem to have resulted at least in part from concurrent political and social changes in the United States. In place of the hegemony of the 30 to 40 years of liberal criminology, there is now the wide hiatus between Marxist research and deterrence research. The great differences in the theoretical, methodological, and political assumptions of Marxists and deterrence researchers strain the tolerance of both. Whatever the future of American criminology, it is clear that it has experienced a major shift and split in theoretical concerns.

Assumptions Regarding the Nature of People

Assumptions about the nature of people and the nature of crime may be found in all theoretical orientations. People may be seen either as free or as totally or partially constrained, and crime may be seen as real or contrived.

Most of the study of crime has uncritically accepted the official government definitions of the nature of crime and criminals and in this sense has not differed much from the commonsense explanations of the general public (Phillipson, 1974:2–3). "Moreover, most of this work has been done within a positivistic frame of reference which typically dehumanizes man by reducing him to an object of study; in doing this the work covers its own value commitments by laying spurious claims to scientific status" (Phillipson, 1974:3).

My orientation supports the view expounded by labeling and conflict theorists regarding the constructed, arbitrary nature of crime, and therefore challenges the positivists' implicit assumption that crime has some reality independent of human interpretaton. However, I disagree with the positivists, as well as the labeling and conflict theorists, when they picture people as necessarily constrained beings. As the classical criminologist Beccaria would have claimed, we suggest that even relatively powerless individuals can and do make decisions—that is, they choose among alternatives, at least some of the time. Therefore even such people help create, to some degree, the environment to which they in turn react. This orientation is true to the dynamic nature of human existence as seen by the actors themselves. It views people not as puppets to be manipulated at government whim but as creatures with inner direction that is, to some degree, independent of immediate controls. It is important to affirm what people everywhere believe: that they are capable of self-direction even if a given society does not encourage this freedom. Perhaps the wide consensus that criminals are controlled and without reason has developed because the individuals who commit most traditional crimes are recruited from the poorest strata of society and, indeed, have fewer choices than do other, more affluent citizens. In addition, as Matza (1964:7) observed, it is relatively easy to accept the notion that those called criminals do not possess free will or the capacity for reason. In other words, it is easy to define criminals as "crazy".

This historical discussion of criminological theories is of significance in understanding the development of contemporary conceptions of crime causation. Equally important, however, is the recognition that only when one understands what theories people hold regarding the causes of crime, will one be able to understand and even predict what social policy measures such people will advocate in the contol of crime. Those who accept Bentham's ideas of a hedonistic calculus will undoubtedly argue for more severe penalties to deal with rising crime rates. Legislators at both the state and federal levels frequently argue for crime control along these lines. Biological positivists have predictably been proponents of both execution and the sterilization of convicted offenders, because of what they see as the impossibility of reforming what they consider to be inferior biological types. On the other hand, social scientists who support Merton's anomie theory have argued for vocational training programs in both high-crime areas and prisons to open up new legitimate opportunities for economic achievement (see chapter 14). And those who locate the source of crime in the individual's mind often suggest some type of psychological treatment or therapy as a soluton to the problem of crime.

CRIMINOLOGICAL RESEARCH METHODS

Historically, positivism in criminology has relied heavily on science. The heart of this scientific method has usually been used to contrast exact measurements of biological, psychological, or social traits of criminals with comparable measurements of noncriminals. The assumptions of this method have been challenged— for example, in the works of Herbert Marcuse (1964). Marcuse contends that people are increasingly dictated to by science and technology. In the name of rationality, the demands of "scientific progress" have become a form of political domination that is all the more effective because it is not recognized as such (Habermas, 1969:81–122).

Social scientists, and especially criminologists, have not typically recognized that the development of science is responsive to the governmental and private agencies that pay the research bills. Because of what is now known about funding agencies, the policies of these agencies can usually be expected to represent the interests and biases of the elites that have the greatest political and economic power. Although there has recently been a growing criticism of science, it is still sacrosanct to many, and its very hallowed nature allows it to create and maintain, unchallenged, a rich folklore about the nature of reality, including the reality of crime. As a case in point, observations of the types of research on juvenile delinquency supported by funding agencies indicate that these agencies have furthered the notion that juvenile delinquency and crime are problems of individuals, since individuals, and not institutions or organizations, are usually the unit of analysis in such funded research. Moreover, funding agencies support research that defines juvenile delinquency as a problem adequately reflected by official statistics, and this in turn makes it seem that delinquency is a proclivity of urban black youths (Galliher and McCartney, 1973). Persons who study crime have given most attention to the illegal behavior of the powerless and poor and have largely ignored the "illegal, and destructive actions of powerful individuals, groups, and institutions in our society" (Liazos, 1972:111; see also Thio, 1973).

Marcuse's observations about the enslaving quality of science are accurate, except that it should be emphasized that where there are slaves, there are also masters. The interests of government leaders are furthered by the picture of crime created by the criminologist that describes crime as an individual, as opposed to a structural, problem and one in which official arrest statistics and therefore arrest practices go essentially unchallenged. Most governments and their funding agencies can be expected to find favor in this positivism, relying as it does on science and official records. Positivists who claim that humankind is controlled strive, through science, to isolate the specific mechanisms for controlling behavior, including criminal behavior. Marcuse's challenge to scientific technology is in contrast to the approach of most students of crime and deviance. Even the conflict theorist Bonger, who was a Marxist socialist, used official statistics and the scientific method. Awareness of the implicit assumptions of the scientific method seems largely absent in the study of crime. An alternative to this concern with science, and its emphasis on exacting measurements of individual characteristics, is an attempt to be conscious of a society's historical traditions and of the influence that a society's changing patterns of power has on the passage of criminal law and the administration of the law by the police and the courts.

Data Sources

A final question regarding the means of studying crime, which criminologists seldom ask and yet always, at least implicitly, answer, concerns what the data of criminology are taken to be. As indicated, most criminologists implicitly assume that their appropriate data center on the criminal behavior of individuals. This is, of course, true of positivists, but perhaps more surprising, it is also often true of labeling and conflict theorists (Schervish, 1973; Bonger, 1916). In contrast, C. Ray Jeffery (1956) contends that criminal law alone can provide the data for criminology. He argues that one must begin with the study of criminal law, because only the law and its administration can create the environment in which behavior can take on the meaning of crime.

It is also possible, of course, to study criminal behavior within the guidelines presented by Jeffery by considering how the law and the criminal justice system affect people labeled as criminals. It must be recognized, however, that studying behavior as opposed to legal institutions is as much a political as an academic decision. If the problem for criminology is defined as dealing with the individual's behavior to the exclusion of a study of the development and administration of the law, one's research indirectly lends credibility to persons with the power to control the legislatures, the police, and the courts, and it opposes the interests of persons against whom the law is usually enforced. If one studies only the individuals and groups officially defined as the problem, rather than the groups that do the defining, such as the police, the courts, and the legislatures, one is actively, even if unwittingly, taking a position in support of the status quo. It is important for criminologists to be self-conscious about criminology's historical development and the forces involved in that development, including the influence of funding agencies, as well as to be aware of the historical development and administration of the criminal law, which provide the definitional boundaries for what is called crime.

Looking at the whole of the legal process, one sees clearly that not all people are as completely constrained as criminologists so often picture them. I will attempt to demonstrate (1) that lawmakers, and those whose interests they represent, are least constrained and most supported by the entire legal system and (2) that persons who are called criminals are by definition of the label the most constrained by the law, although far from being totally controlled, as police and prison guards will testify. The revival of the issue of equality before the law, raised by Beccaria two centuries ago, seems appropriate in an economically stratified and racist society such as our own, where—as this book will demonstrate—despite the prevailing myth of democracy and equality before the law, lawmakers and their coteries are largely affluent whites, and those against whom the law is enforced are disproportionately poor and black. As Matza (1969:94–100) observed, despite frequent criticism of official records of crime by criminologists, because those records are usually seen as the only information available, they are used anyway in conducting empirical research and generating theories. Science and official records must be recognized as serving the interests of some people while compromising the interests of others, and the substantive and theoretical boundaries of criminology must be provided by a thorough knowledge of the social bases of criminal law and its administration.

Research Assumptions

Hughes (1971) developed a set of ideas for analyzing research of any type that seems especially applicable to research on crime and delinquency. He claimed that research can be seen as consisting of three components: the minor premise, the major premise, and the conclusion. The minor premise is the statement of alleged fact, such as the finding that a high percentage of men who are serving sentences for violent crime evidence the XYY syndrome. The logical conclusion of such a finding is that the community needs and deserves some special protection from those with the XYY pattern to prevent violent crime before its occurs. The major premise of research is the underlying or basic reason for conducting such research. These underlying reasons are typically implicit or unspoken. The underlying, or basic, reason for conducting studies of the XYY syndrome and its relationship to crime is the assumption that any biological condition that can be statistically associated with high rates of violent crime can legitimately be used to deprive persons who have these characteristics of their basic civil rights, even before they have committed any crime.

Such XYY findings could be used to deny parole to XYY prisoners, to encourage more severe sentencing of such offenders because of their limited rehabilitation potential, and to develop special predelinquency programs for children with the characteristic. But whatever the results of such research, the researh itself is fundamentally an undemocratic activity. Merely conducting such research suggests that it is a credible idea in a society such as our own, which is accustomed to thinking in biological categories, even if most of the results are inconclusive, as indeed they are (Report on the XYY Chromosomal Abnormality, 1970). All research on crime and delinquency is presumably undertaken to shed light on some policy alternatives, and the question becomes, What social policy is suggested by biological positivism, including XYY research? If crime problems are determined to have biological origins, then crime control solutions must take these biological conditions into consideration. Whereas the far right wing in American politics often supports biological positivism, political liberals often support sociological positivism. The implication of sociological positivism, such as Merton's anomie theory, is that slum environments, underfunded schools, and unemployment lead to high crime rates through blocked legitimate opportunities. Therefore if crime is to be controlled, all the problems of poverty and racism must be addressed. Liberal opposition to biological positivism typically consists of challenging the findings, or the minor premise, of the research (Fox, 1971). But a more fundamental criticism of such research is that even if there is, indeed, empirical merit to the idea of an XYY offender, the political implications of such findings have no place in a democracy.

CONCLUSION

This chapter has briefly traced the historical development of modern criminology, beginning with the "radical" ideas of the classical criminologist Beccaria, who demanded equal justice for all. Next, Bentham's notion of using the hedonistic calculus to control criminal penalties and behavior was discussed. Both Beccaria and Bentham believed that people possess reason and a free will. Several varieties of criminological positivism, including biological positivism, psychological and psychiatric positivism, and the most recent development—sociological positivism—were then discussed. All criminological positivism involves a concentration on the study of criminal individuals through the scientific measurement of their individual characteristics and the use of official records. These records reveal what appears to be a great amount of crime among the poor. The positivist perspective also assumes that criminals are forced to commit crimes because of some unique biological, psychological, or social condition. More recently there has emerged in criminology some recognition of the arbitrary nature of the definitions of crime and criminals, and therefore some recognition of the importance of audience reactions. A critical look at criminological research methods and at the types of data that these methods produce was also taken. The demise of liberal criminology was described, as was the rapid growth of deterrence research and modern Marxism. Finally, it was argued that the boundaries of criminology, that is, what is and what is not an appropriate subject of study for researchers interested in crime and criminals, can be provided only by a thorough knowledge of the social and historical origins of criminal law. Whatever the origins of specific criminal laws, the social analyst should feel free to make moral judgments of those laws on the basis of their consequences. Moreover, since both traditional criminology and this alternative stress the importance of the administration of the criminal law as an arbitrary and discriminatory defining agent, an analysis of the police and the courts is essential. First, however, chapter 3 will present a survey of the types and amount of crime found in modern America.

REFERENCES

Abrahamsen, D.
  1964 The Psychology of Crime. New York: John Wiley & Sons.
Alexander, F. and H. Staub
  1931 The Criminal, the Judge, and the Public: A Psychological Analysis. New York: Macmillan.

Avison, W. R. and P. L. Loring
  1986 "Population diversity and cross-national homicide: the effects of inequality and heterogeneity." Criminology 24(November): 733–749.
Ball-Rokeach, S. J.
  1980 "Normative and deviant violence from a

conflict perspective." Social Problems 28(October):45–62.

Bayer, R.
1981 "Crime, punishment, and the decline of liberal optimism." Crime and Delinquency 27(April):169–190.

Beccaria, C. B.
1775 An Essay on Crimes and Punishments. 4th ed. London: E. Newbery.

Becker, H. S.
1963 Outsiders. New York: The Free Press of Glencoe.

Beirne, P.
1987 "Adolphe Quetelet and the origins of positive criminology." American Journal of Sociology 92(March):1140–1169.

Bentham, J.
1823 An Introduction to the Principles of Morals and Legislation. Reprinted 1948. New York: Hafner Press.

Blau, J. R. and P. M. Blau
1982 "The cost of inequality: metropolitan structure and violent crime." American Sociological Review 47(February):114–129.

Blumenthal, M. D., R. L. Kahn, F. M. Andrews, and K. B. Head
1972 Justifying Violence: Attitudes of American Men. Ann Arbor: Institute for Social Research, University of Michigan.

Bonger, W.
1916 Criminality and Economic Conditions. (H. P. Horton, trans.) Boston: Little, Brown.

Brownmiller, S.
1975 Against Our Will: Men, Women, and Rape. New York: Simon & Schuster.

Carroll, L.
1974 Hacks, Blacks, and Cons: Race Relations in a Maximum Security Prison. Lexington, Mass.: D. C. Heath.

Cloward, R. A. and L. E. Ohlin
1960 Delinquency and Opportunity: A Theory of Delinquent Gangs. Glencoe, Ill.: The Free Press.

Cohen, S.
1974 "Criminology and the sociology of deviance in Britain." In P. Rock and M. McIntosh (eds.), Deviance and Social Control. London: Tavistock Publications.

Cullen, F. T. and K. E. Gilbert
1982 Reaffirming Rehabilitation. Cincinnati: Anderson Publishing.

Curvin, R. and B. Porter
1979 "Blackout looting!" Society(May–June): 68–76.

DiChiara, A. and J. F. Galliher
1984 "Thirty years of deterrence research: characteristics, causes and consequences." Contemporary Crises 8(June):243–263.

Douglas, J. D.
1967 The Social Meanings of Suicide. Princeton, N. J.: Princeton University Press.

Durkheim, E.
1933 The Division of Labor in Society. (G. Simpson, trans.) Glencoe, Ill.:The Free Press.
1938 The Rules of Sociological Method. (S. A. Solovay and J. H. Mueller, trans.; G. E. G. Catlin, ed.) Glencoe, Ill.: The Free Press.

Fink, A. E.
1962 Causes of Crime: Biological Theories in the United States 1800–1915. San Diego, Calif.: A. S. Barnes.

Fox, R. G.
1971 "The XYY offender: a modern myth?" Journal of Criminal Law, Criminology and Police Science 62(March):59–73.

Galliher, J. F.
1978 "The life and death of liberal criminology." Contemporary Crises 2(July):245–263.

Galliher, J. F. and J. L. McCartney
1973 "The influence of funding agencies on juvenile delinquency research." Social Problems 21(Summer):77–90.

Gibbons, D. C.
1974 "Say, whatever became of Maurice Parmlee, anyway?" The Sociological Quarterly 15:405–416.

Goddard, H. H.
1914 Feeble-Mindedness: Its Causes and Consequences. New York: Macmillan.
1917a "Mental tests and the immigrant." The Journal of Deliquency 2(September): 243–277.
1917b "The criminal instincts of the feeble-minded." The Journal of Delinquency 2(November):352–355.
1921 Juvenile Delinquency. New York: Dodd, Mead.

Gould, S. J.
1981 The Mismeasure of Man. New York: W. W. Norton.

Goode, E.
1972 Drugs in American Society. New York: Alfred A. Knopf.

Gusfield, J. R.
1975 "Categories of ownership and responsibility in social issues: alcohol abuse and automobile use." Journal of Drug Issues 5(Fall):285–303.

Habermas, J.
1969 Toward a Rational Society: Student Protest, Science, and Politics. (J. J. Shapiro, trans.) Boston: Beacon Press.

Hall, Jerome
1945 "Criminology." Pp. 342–365 in G. Gurvitch and W. E. Moore (eds.), Twentieth Century Sociology. New York: Philosophical Library.

Hirst, P. Q.
1975 "Marx and Engles on law, crime and morality." In I. Taylor, P. Walton, and J. Young (eds.), Critical Criminology. London: Routledge and Kegan Paul.

Hughes, E. C.
1971 "Principle and rationalization in race relations." Pp. 212–219 in The Sociological Eye: Selected Papers. Chicago: Aldine-Atherton.

Hugo, V.
1862 Les Misérables, vol. 1.

Jeffery, C. R.
1956 "Crime, law, and social structure" Journal of Criminal Law, Criminology, and Police Science 47(November–December):423–435.

Kitsuse, J. I. and A. V. Cicourel
1963 "A note on the uses of official statistics." Social Problems 11(Fall):131–139.

Lemert, E. M.
1951 Social Pathology. New York: McGraw-Hill.

Lewontin, R. C.
1982 Human Diversity. New York: Scientific American Books.

Liazos, A.
1972 "The poverty of the sociology of deviance: nuts, sluts, and perverts." Social Problems 20(Summer):103–120.

Liebow, E.
1967 Tally's Corner: A Study of Negro Street-corner Men. Boston: Little, Brown.

Lofland, J.
1969 Deviance and Identity. Englewood Cliffs, N.J.: Prentice Hall.

Lombroso, C.
1911 Crime: Its Causes and Remedies. (H. P. Horton, trans.) Boston: Little, Brown.

Lambroso, C. and W. Ferrero
1895 The Female Offender. New York: D. Appleton.

Lombroso-Ferrero, G.
1911 Criminal Man, According to the Classification of Caesare Lombroso. New York: G. P. Putnam's Sons.

Mannheim, H. (ed.)
1973 Pioneers in Criminology. 2nd ed., enlarged. Montclair, N.J.: Patterson Smith.

Marcuse, H.
1964 One-Dimensional Man. Boston: Beacon Press.

Matza, D.
1964 Delinquency and Drift. New York: John Wiley & Sons.
1969 Becoming Deviant. Englewood Cliffs, N.J.: Prentice Hall.

Meehan, E. J.
1975 Public Housing Policy: Convention Versus Reality. New Brunswick, N.J.: Center for Urban Policy Research, Rutgers–The State University.

Melossi, D.
1985 "Overcoming the crisis in critical criminology: toward a grounded labeling theory." Criminology 23(May):193–208.

Merton, R. K.
1938 "Social structure and anomie." American Sociological Review 3(October):672–682.

Mills, C.
1962 The Marxists. New York: Dell.

Monachesi, E.
1973 "Caesare Beccaria." In H. Mannheim (ed.), Pioneers in Criminology. 2nd ed., enlarged. Montclair, N.J.: Patterson Smith.

Moynihan, D. P.
1969 Maximum Feasible Misunderstanding: Community Action in the War on Poverty. New York: The Free Press.

Nader, R.
1965 Unsafe at Any Speed. New York: Grossman Publishers.

National Institute of Mental Health
1976 Active Research Grants. Center for Studies in Crime and Delinquency. Washington, D.C.: U.S. Government Printing Office.

New York Times
1982a "Premenstrual syndrome: a complex issue." July 12:C16.
1982b "Defense linked to menstruation dropped in case." November 4:B4.
1982c "Premenstrual tensions and criminal behavior." November 15:C18.

Phillipson, M.
1974 Understanding Crime and Delinquency. Chicago: Aldine.

Platt, T. and P. Takagi
1977 "Intellectuals for law and order: a critique of the new realists." Crime and Social Justice 8(Fall–Winter):1–16.

Quinney, R.
1970 The Social Reality of Crime. Boston: Little, Brown.
1973 Critique of Legal Order: Crime Control in Capitalist Society. Boston: Little, Brown.
1977 Class, State, and Crime: On the Theory and Practice of Criminal Justice. New York: David McKay.

Reckless, W. C.
1961 "A new theory of delinquency and crime." Federal Probation 25(December):42–46.

Reckless, W. C. and S. Dinitz
1972 The Prevention of Juvenile Delinquency: An Experiment. Columbus: Ohio State University.

Reiman, J. H. and S. Headlee
1981 "Marxism and criminal justice policy." Crime and Delinquency 27(January):24–47.

Report on the XYY Chromosomal Abnormality
  1970   National Institute of Mental Health, Center for Studies on Crime and Delinquency. Public Health Service Publication No. 2103. Washington, D.C.: U.S. Government Printing Office.
Rowe, D. C.
  1985   "Sibling interaction and self-reported delinquent behavior: a study of 265 twin pairs." Criminolgy 23(May):223–240.
Rowe, D. C. and D. W. Osgood
  1984   "Heredity and sociological theories of delinquency: a reconsideration." American Sociological Review 49(August):526–540.
Schervish, P. G.
  1973   "The labeling perspective: its bias and potential in the study of political deviance." American Sociologist 8(May):47–57.
Schumann, K. F.
  1976   "Theoretical presuppositions for criminology as a critical enterprise." International Journal of Criminology and Penology 4: 285–294.
Sellin, T.
  1938   Culture Conflict and Crime. New York: Social Science Research Council.
Shaw, C. R.
  1929   Delinquency Areas. Chicago: University of Chicago Press.
Shaw, C. R. and H. D. McKay
  1942   Juvenile Delinquency and Urban Areas. Chicago: University of Chicago Press.

Shover, N.
  1975   "Criminal behavior as theoretical praxis." Issues in Criminology 10:95–108.
Sutherland, E. H.
  1939   Principles of Criminology. 3rd ed. Philadelphia: J. B. Lippincott.
Sykes, G. M.
  1974   "The rise of critical criminology." Journal of Criminal Law and Criminology 65(June):206–213.
Taft, D. R.
  1942   Criminology. New York: Macmillan.
Tannenbaum, F.
  1938   Crime and the Community. Boston: Ginn.
Taylor, I., P. Walton, and J. Young (eds.)
  1975   Critical Criminology. London: Routledge and Kegan Paul.
Thio, A.
  1973   "Class bias in the sociology of deviance." American Sociologist 8(February):1–12.
Turk, A. T.
  1969   Criminality and Legal Order. Chicago: Rand McNally.
Vold, G. B.
  1958   Theoretical Criminology. New York: Oxford University Press.
Wilson, J. Q. and R. J. Herrnstein
  1985   Crime and Human Nature. New York: Simon & Schuster.

3
CRIME AND CRIME VICTIMS

VIOLENT CRIME

Although it may be conceded that some crime is a result of arbitrary definitions, for example, victimless offenses such as gambling and prostitution, some crime strikes us as a real threat because we can empathize with the injured victim. The victim of an armed robber has actually been robbed and may be injured or dead. Nevertheless, death at the hands of another person is not necessarily defined as murder. Former President Richard Nixon ordered the bombing of thousands of Asians during the war in Vietnam and was subsequently reelected to a second term as president. The number of civilians killed by American police is six times as great as the number of police killed in the line of duty (Robin, 1963). Yet police are still largely defined as defenders of law and social order. Violence is typically seen as a product of persons outside government, even when it is recognized that representatives of government kill and injure.

Wolfgang and Ferracuti (1967) developed the notion that a subculture of violence exists among lower-class people and used that concept to explain assaultive behavior among poor whites and ghetto blacks. This emphasis on lower-class violence ignores the evidence of personal aggression committed by more affluent persons and by the government. A survey conducted by Stark and McEvoy (1970) found, for example, that a higher percentage of middle-class than of lower-class persons admitted that they had physically assaulted another person. This finding is contrary to police statistics showing more violence among the poor. Stark and McEvoy suggest that the affluent are underrepresented in arrest data because they can rely on private resources, such as marriage counselors, to settle disputes, whereas the poor must often rely on the police. In addition, the middle classes typically have greater privacy in their disputes, whereas the quarrels of the poor often take place in bars, on sidewalks, or in crowded apartments and are therefore more likely to become known to the police.

The lack of predictability in the definitions of killing and assault has been systematically investigated by Blumenthal et al. (1972). As noted in chapter 2, they surveyed American men and found no relationship between gross destruction of property or injury to people and the percentage of men who called such acts violence. A higher percentage of their respondents defined looting as violence than the percentage who defined the beating of students or the shooting of looters by police as violence. Thus, even on a supposedly concrete issue such as the definition of violence, there is no necessary relationship between the dictionary definition—the exertion of physical force to injure or abuse (Webster's New World Dictionary 1956)—and human perceptions. In a survey of Baltimore citizens, Rossi et al. (1974) found that selling marihuana was generally considered as serious as beating up a police officer and much more serious than knowingly selling defective used cars as completely safe. Although defective used cars, unlike marihuana, have a proven potential for human destruction, selling such cars was defined as less serious than selling marihuana. Other researchers have struggled to achieve greater precision in the use of a term such as violence so that the normative violence of government and business corporations can be discussed in the same way that the violence of individuals is discussed (Ball-Rokeach, 1980).

Moreover, public and official definitions of crime can shift drastically. "To mention a more modern example, the abrupt and rapid changes in the lawmaking power structure at the time of the Hungarian revolution in 1956 resulted in criminals becoming heroes and then again criminals, and law-abiding citizens turning into criminals and then again into conformists—all within eight days" (Schafer, 1974:33). It may well be that if the Axis powers, rather than the Allies, had won World War II, instead of the Nuremberg trials, there might have been Washington trials to sentence Generals MacArthur and Eisenhower for war crimes, and President Truman for genocide in ordering atomic bombings of Japan. Had this happened, it is also likely that American-born children would be learning different definitions of these men and their acts.

Murder in America

Whatever definition of violence is used, it is generally recognized that the United States has one of the highest levels of domestic violence in the world. This nation leads all industrialized nations in per capita murder rates. For example, in 1978 there were 20,432 homicides in the United States, for a rate of 9.4 per 100,000, compared with 5.7 for Northern Ireland, which is generally considered to be violent beyond belief (Statistical Abstract of the United States, 1983:181). For the remainder of Western Europe the rates range from 3.0 to 0.7 per 100,000. Thus the United States has almost twice the murder rate of Northern Ireland and at least three times the murder rate of many other nations. The United Nations (1985) reported that in 1983 the United States had a rate of 9.9 murders per 100,000, behind only three other nations (Puerto Rico, Guatemala, and El Salvador).

A disproportionate amount of this violence is committed by black Americans. And there is a reason. Racial and economic inequalities appear to be positively related to the extent of violence in a community, undoubtedly because of alienation and despair (Blau and Blau, 1982; Blau and Golden, 1986). Silberman (1978) explains this violence as a consequence of black hopelessness and anger due to the obvious inability of black Americans to find the type of success experienced by other minorities. Since the earliest phase of the history of our nation, blacks have lived in America. Over the years, blacks would begin to make some small movement upward in social and economic mobility. Just when they would begin to experience some success, a wave of European immigrants would come to this country and quickly displace the black workers, leapfrogging over them. When one such group would continue its course of upward mobility and blacks were again beginning to experience some upward mobility, another influx of immigrants would begin and the blacks would be displaced again. First it was the Germans, next the Irish and Italians, and finally the Mexicans and Puerto Ricans. All of these other groups found mobility much easier because they did not suffer from the stigma associated with slavery.

And violent black Americans have excellent white role models. The United States seems unique among modern nations in that it was founded on a policy of systematic genocide that resulted in the elimination of numerous Native American cultures. The Native Americans that were not killed were forced from their homes and onto reservations. This history of savagery toward Native Americans may be related to the fact that in the United States, unlike most other industrial nations of the world, there is widespread private ownership of handguns. From the beginning of this nation, there has been a constitutional provision for this, and in many quarters there is something that amounts to worship of weapons, especially guns. It will come as no surprise to learn that over the past 10 years an average of over 60 percent of American murder victims died from guns (Statistical Abstracts, 1982–1983:179). But the bulk of material in this chapter on violent crime will be devoted to topics other than traditional street crimes such as murder or armed robbery. Most Americans already have a considerable amount of information from the mass media on street crime, but they have much less understanding of the other violent crimes considered in this chapter.

Violence in American Industry

The 1972 President's Report on Occupational Safety and Health noted that "at least 390,000 new cases of disabling occupational disease" (Berman 1978:44) can be counted yearly, and "there may be as many as 100,000 deaths per year from occupation-caused diseases" (Berman, 1978:46), or five times the number of deaths officially labeled as homicide. A federal study estimated that somewhere between 20 and 40 percent of cancer deaths were caused by exposure on the job. To mention just one industry, among the 560,000 American textile workers exposed to cotton dust, 100,000 suffer from byssinosis, which causes wheezing and shortness of breath, and at least 35,000 workers are permanently disabled from this disease, commonly known as brown lung disease (Claybrook et al., 1984). In 1970 the National Safety Council reported 2.2 million disabling injuries due to industrial accidents. These figures on injury exclude many seriously injured workers who are reassigned to "soft" jobs so that their company can avoid counting them as disabled (Page and O'Brien, 1973: 161–162). The traditional method of estimating the amount of employee injury has been to rely on employer self-reporting. Clearly it is not in the industry's interest to keep complete accident records that will reflect badly on themselves (Berman, 1978). Thus, as frightening as the figures on occupational death and injury are, they undoubtedly underreport the full extent of the tragedy.

In 1976 the federal Resource Conservation and Recovery Act was passed. These new regulations greatly increased the restrictions on hazardous waste hauling and disposal (Szasz, 1986) and were designed to prevent the disease and death known to be caused by these substances. The Environmental Protection Agency (EPA) estimated that, in 1974, ten million metric tons of hazardous waste was generated: by 1980 the estimate was 40 million, and by 1983 the federal estimate was 250 metric tons. The EPA also estimated in a study published in 1985 that two out of seven corporate hazardous waste generators illegally disposed of such wastes in the 2 years preceding the study. Such wastes have been mixed with garbage and dumped in city landfills, contrary to the provisions of federal law. Some liquid hazardous wastes have been sprayed on roadways for dust control or dumped into rivers and oceans. Flammable liquid wastes have been mixed with fuel oil (Szasz, 1986).

These results are an obvious consequence of lax, incompetent, and corrupt law enforcement (Szasz, 1986). Moreover, the existing law is not strongly worded. Under pressure from corporations the final version of the federal law did not require specific hazardous waste practices during the production process, but only at final disposal. In other words, the corporations remained free to produce as much—and as dangerous—waste as they pleased. Nor did the law require that generators remain responsible for their wastes after assigning them to a hauler. Thus generators had no responsibility to turn in haulers whom they suspected of not disposing of chemicals properly. Moreover, these corporations would not likely want to turn in the low bidders for their hauling and disposal needs (Szasz, 1986). The costs of such practices in human suffering, including death and disease, are now well known.

Assaults on Females

Brownmiller (1975) presented convincing evidence that rape is often not perceived as genuinely violent by male social scientists, historians, journalists, or police. Since these groups, for the most part, do not take this crime seriously, rape has seldom been reported or, until recently, studied. This is true even though the number of rape cases is staggering. For example, a study of "930 women in San Francisco provides a basis for estimating that there is at least a 26 percent probability that a woman in that city will become the victim of completed rape at some point in her life, and a 46 percent probability that she will become a victim of rape *or* attempted rape" (Russell and Howell, 1983:694–695). Even so, a common assumption is that "good" women do not get raped: "A woman with her dress up can run faster than a man with his pants down" seems to be the common assumption. The conventional wisdom, supported by Freudian psychiatric theory, is that if the truth were known, women who are raped actually enjoy it and secretly desire to be raped. Therefore, Brownmiller contended, when a woman is raped, the crime is often held to be at least partly the victim's fault, for wearing sexy clothing, or staying out late at night, or going to dangerous places alone. In other words, taking adequate precautions against rape involves living like a cloistered nun. Unlike victims of robbery and other assaults, victims of rape are sometimes legally required to prove that they resisted. Indeed, rape is often referred to as victim-precipitated crime. Juries have often acquitted male defendants on rape charges if the female victim either dated them or drank with them before the rape. The feeling among juries seems to be that the victim was at least partially responsible for the crime by putting herself at risk (Wood, 1973).

One might assume that such thinking exists only among the most conventional and politically conservative elements of society, and yet Brownmiller (1975) showed that even persons who consider themselves to be political liberals do not usually consider rape to be a serious problem and have usually become concerned with this crime only when white women's accusations of rape have led to the execution or lynching of black men. Here again, mistrust of the raped woman is revealed. In fact, Brownmiller indicated that black radicals, such as Eldridge Cleaver, have viewed the rape of white women as an appropriate revolutionary act against the white man's property—women. The punishment of rapists has been most severe where such punishment has reflected a need to protect the white man's property—in this case, white women against black men—and in such instances the person seen as most wronged by rape has usually been a man, the father or the husband, rather than the female victim.

Until very recently the law gave women no protection from rape by their husbands. Thus it appears that rape and other assaults on women such as wife beating are condoned. Indeed, there are an estimated 1.8 million cases of wife beating in the United States per year, amounting to approximately one fourth of all assaults on married women (Bowker, 1981). Unfortunately, most battered women do not leave their husbands, both because of their economic dependence, with the prospect of rearing their children in poverty, and their own shame and self-blame for what has happened (Bowker, 1981).

Rape often goes unreported because of victims' realistic fears of police and prosecution indifference and the equally realistic prospect of humiliation during the process of a public trial. Approximately 56,000 rapes were reported to the police in 1975, whereas surveys of victims provide estimates of four times this number (Robin, 1977). Reporting is discouraged by questions from police such as "How many orgasms did you have?" or "Don't you ever wear a bra?" (Robin, 1977:140). Yet wife battering undoubtedly goes unreported even more frequently than rape (Martin, 1978). Even so, research by the Kansas City, Missouri, police department from 1971 to 1972 reported that over 46,000 domestic disturbance calls, which typically involve such battering, were received in 1 year. A full 40% of the city's homicides were found to involve cases of such spouse abuse (Martin, 1978). Sometimes it is wrongly assumed by psychiatrists and others that because of masochistic needs, women enjoy being raped or beaten. Thus police officers are usually instructed to have couples who are involved in such disturbances "work out their differences" and to avoid making an arrest. In this manner, police refuse to take most of these cases seriously.

FEMALE CRIME

If the rape of women has not always been taken seriously, with only a few exceptions, the misbehavior of women has not been taken seriously either and has only rarely been a subject of writing and research by students of crime. Most major positivist orientations are explicitly or implicitly limited to the study of the criminal behavior of male offenders, and female criminality is usually ignored. This inattention seems to reflect the idea that female misbehavior is not crime in the same sense as are offenses committed by male offenders. Scholarly inattention to the study of female offenders and female offenses mirrors a societal lack of concern for female criminality (Adler, 1975). Unlike male crime, female crime does not seem to demand attention by striking fear into the hearts of observers. Except in unusual cases, even women convicted of assault or homicide are not feared. Because they are not feared, less attention is given to their imprisonment, as will be discussed in chapter 12.

The typical view that women commit mainly sex-linked crime is not supported by self-reported behavior. Such self-reports give a picture of female crimes that reflect the same variety found among men (Chesney-Lind, 1973;1974). Yet females charged with nonsexual offenses have been subjected to gynecological examinations to determine whether they have venereal disease, and younger, single females have been examined to determine whether they have ever had sexual relations. If the latter have been discovered to have a ruptured hymen, they have often been charged with promiscuity (Chesney-Lind, 1973;1974). The sexualization of nonsexual offenses reflects the assumption that females accused of any type of crime are also promiscuous and supports the view that criminal definitions are imposed and artificial.

According to stereotype, women are thought to present a genuine crime problem only with regard to sex-linked offenses. If criminologists do discuss female criminality, they usually focus on prostitution. Since prostitution takes two participants—most often a man and a woman—it is noteworthy that men are absent both from scholarly discussion of prostitution and from arrest records for this offense. As indicated in chapter 6, Roby (1969) discussed an unsuccessful attempt in New York to hold the patrons of prostitutes to be as criminally responsible as the prostitutes themselves. Such a law passed the state legislature but was not enforced, in part because of concerns about the possible arrest and embarrassment of the prostitutes' businessmen-customers. This example clearly shows the operation of powerful class interests.

In recent years a debate has emerged regarding whether the women's liberation movement has been responsible for increases in female crime rates. One argument is that as women gain more equal opportunity in legal activities, they will also, of necessity, achieve this same equality with men in illegal endeavors and thus become involved in more serious crime, including violent crime (Adler, 1975). Another, related argument is that women's occupational gains have made possible equal gains in the opportunity to commit white collar crimes such as embezzlement (Simon, 1975). Such analyses are misinformed on two counts. First, only approximately 10 percent of the persons arrested in 1980 for serious crimes were female, and only approximately 15 percent of all arrests were of females, including many arrests for very trivial offenses (Chesney-Lind, 1986). Women are not catching up with men in the commission of violent crime or white collar crime; the increases are mainly in traditional female crimes such as shoplifting, prostitution, and check forgery (Steffinsmeier, 1980). Most important, "since women have not experienced major gains in the economic world, it seems implausible that any wave of female crime could be laid at this door" (Chesney-Lind, 1986).

CRIME WITH UNAWARE VICTIMS

Crimes of Physicians

In 1965 the federal government enacted the Medicaid program to provide medical care for poor persons and Medicare to provide care for elderly persons. At the time, lawmakers were little concerned with the possibility of fraud and abuse of these programs by physicians (Pepinsky and Jesilow, 1984), perhaps because of the traditional hero worship of the medical profession. Law-makers were much more fearful that the medical profession would simply refuse to participate in the programs and refuse to treat patients covered by these programs, because at the time the American Medical Association opposed this legislation. With these problems in mind, the government imposed few rules and regulations on physicians. One enforcement agent recalled years later: "We built this giant edifice and failed to put any control into it. We sort of said, 'Come in and take what you want' " (Pepinsky and Jesilow, 1984:49).

By the late 1970s it had become very clear that some legal controls on physicians were required, especially after the U.S. House of Representatives held hearings on the resulting abuse. Examples of abuses described at these hearings included a physicians's charging nursing-home patients while he was on a vacation in the Bahamas. "Some doctors would simply walk through a nursing home, saying 'Hi' to the patients in their path, count the salutation as a visit to each of them, and bill the government accordingly" (Pepinsky and Jesilow, 1984:49). And in New York City, clinics that serve welfare recipients developed the practices referred to as "ganging" and "ping-ponging." The first is the prac-tice of billing the government for treatment of all family members present in the clinic when only one is ill, and the latter involves unnecessary referral of patients to other physicians in the clinic. There is also evidence that unnecessary surgery has been encouraged by this seemingly bottomless pit of federal funding to physicians. This needless surgery clearly represents an assault on the individual patient and qualifies as a violent crime, just as surely as any other assault. It is sometimes argued, therefore, that justice would be served if physicians who can be proven to have performed unnecessary surgery would be charged with assault; in addition, if the patient died as a consequence of the surgery, the physician would be charged with manslaughter (Pepinsy and Jesilow, 1984).

Crimes of Business People

There appears to be little public understanding of the myriad crimes committed by the business community. The economic crimes committed by busi-ness people in the course of their work are usually referred to as white-collar crimes (Sutherland, 1949). White-collar crimes are generally committed by per-sons of high status and respectability who commit the crimes in the course of their occupational endeavors. When caught, such offenders are almost never prosecuted in criminal courts; if they are punished at all, punishment is through civil damages. Sutherland documented the myriad crimes committed by Amer-ica's largest corporations, including such offenses as price-fixing, tax evasion, misrepresentation in advertising, and such unfair labor practices as the coercion and intimidation of union organizers. Many types of crime are routinely explained as a direct consequence of poverty, but such an explanation clearly fails in this instance.

There is no evidence that the public is outraged by the crimes of business people, even when there is proof of the nature and extent of such crimes. One reason that the public is not angered by many of these crimes is that the general public is not always the victim of such offenses. In the case of the embezzlement of corporation funds, stockholders are likely to be the primary victims. Other corporations are the most direct victims in cases of infringement of patents or copyrights. Employees are the victims of unfair and illegal labor practices. In the case of price-fixing, the general public is the victim, but even here there is no evidence of great moral outrage of a sort that would demand full prosecution of such offenders.

There are several interrelated reasons for this lack of outrage. The first and most obvious explanation is that many corporations own the mass media and therefore are able to control the formation of public opinion (Sutherland, 1949). And the high social status of these corporate leaders makes many persons believe that the mere humiliation caused by the public disclosure of their misdeeds is enough punishment in itself. For example, there appears to have been the widespread opinion that former President Nixon had suffered enough by being forced to resign from office, so that futher prosecution or incarceration was not appropriate. Finally, as will be demonstrated later in this chapter, business leaders can use their vast financial resources to control political campaigns and thereby control judges, prosecutors, and presidents.

When Sutherland originally published his classic book *White Collar Crime* in 1949, he was threatened with lawsuits if he included the names of the corporations involved in these activities. Therefore his publisher convinced him to drop the names. But by 1983 such fears had subsided (perhaps in part because the information was by that time extremely dated and no longer reflected on the current operation of these corporations), and an "uncut version" of the book was published. Now at long last we at least can know the historical record of various corporations. Among the 70 largest manufacturing, mining, and mercantile corporations surveyed by Sutherland, the leading offenders—those with 25 or more decisions against them—included the following (Sutherland, 1983:16–18):

- American Tobacco: 25
- Armour and Company: 50
- Ford: 28
- General Electric: 25
- General Motors: 40
- Lowe's: 31
- Montgomery Ward: 39
- Paramount: 25
- Sears, Roebuck: 39
- Swift and Company: 50
- U.S. Steel: 26
- Warner Bros.: 25

Apparently something is involved in the economic circumstances of making automobiles and movies and of processing meat that lends itself to criminal behavior. Only 16 percent of these decisions were made by criminal courts (although criminal prosecution was a possibility in all of these cases), and for this reason Sutherland's publisher was concerned about liability if the term *white collar crime* was used to describe specific cases.

Limited enforcement staffs make control of corporate crime impossible. Less than 200 assistant U.S. attorneys are responsible for the prosecution of white-collar or corporate crime, even though corporate crime costs billions of dollars a year (Clinard, 1979). The U.S. Senate estimated in the 1970s that manufacture of faulty goods and monopolistic practices costs consumers $174 to $231 billion a year, compared to the typical burglary of $350. The largest robbery in U.S. history took place in 1978 and involved a theft of $5.4 million from a New York City warehouse. By contrast, in 1979 nine oil companies were charged by the Justice Department with overcharging consumers more than $1 billion (Clinard, 1979).

As noted in chapter 1, Rossi et al. (1974) found that traditional crimes, such as robbery and assault, are seen as more serious than white-collar crimes. In a survey of citizens in Baltimore, where respondents ranked a list of offenses according to their seriousness, selling marihuana was seen as more serious than such white collar crimes as "manufacturing and selling autos known to be dangerously defective," "knowingly selling defective used cars as completely safe," "a public official accepting bribes in return for favors," and "fixing prices" (Rossi et al., 1974:228–229). In fact, price-fixing was considered to be among the least serious of the behaviors ranked, approximately equivalent in seriousness to "shoplifting a book in a bookstore" or "repeated refusal to obey parents."

In a survey of public reaction to violations of pure food laws by business people, such as selling contaminated foods, Newman (1957) also found little public outrage. He found that "respondents viewed food adulteration [by large corporations] as more comparable to serious traffic violations than to burglary" (Newman, 1957:231). Reasons (1974:230) suggested one possible explanation for public indifference to the crimes of business people:

> Our interest and concern with the "organized underworld" has directed our attention away from the "organized upperworld." While the terms "organized crime," "Mafia," and "Cosa Nostra" conjure up images of insidious, ruthless, sly, machine-gun-toting gangsters who are a major threat to our national viability, we fail to recognize that "they" merely represent the tip of the iceberg [with so-called legitimate corporations reaping the biggest benefits from crime].

Geis (1973) suggested that the low level of public awareness of and concern about white-collar crime is a result of the fact that the injuries and costs of most corporate crimes, such as price-fixing, are highly diffused and widely scattered, making the effects almost imperceptible, in comparison with the effects of the larger sums often stolen from each victim by burglars. Air and water pollution assaults victims in a slow and subtle fashion, although it is no less damaging than street muggings. There is some indication that the public is beginning to see corporate crimes as somewhat more serious offenses, but still less so than most other crimes (Cullen et al., 1982).

To increase public awareness of white-collar crime, Geis (1973) suggests some alternative means of collecting and distributing information on such offenses. One idea is for the Federal Bureau of Investigation to include white-collar offenses in its reports as, he notes, was done originally. Geis also recommends the infiltration of corporations suspected of crimes by police agents trained in undercover work, much as other criminal operations are infiltrated. The cost would be minimal, since agents would, of course, be paid a salary by the corporations and because corporation fines would help pay informer fees.

Black Marketing   During World War II there emerged a new type of business crime that involved dealing in black market goods. At this point the possibility of committing this type of crime existed for the first time because laws had been passed making it a criminal violation to charge more than a specified price for nearly all commodities. For the first time in American history there was compulsory rationing of goods by the government (Clinard, 1952).

Persons involved in black-marketing operations had generally not been involved in previous criminal practices. They were simply the business people who were in the line of supply. Before the passage of the price-fixing law, they were usually not considered to be violating any statutes. When these statutes were changed, they continued to charge what the market would bear, but when they continued their old practices after the passage of the law, they were in violation of a statute. Only one in ten of the business people known to have been involved in the black market had a previous record. The infrequency of a previous record, along with the high social class standing of many black marketers, may help explain why there were only a small number of prosecutions for such violations. The absence of a previous record made conviction or imprisonment more difficult, and this may have discouraged prosecutors from taking official action.

Some of the behavior engaged in by black marketers, such as representing a product as being of higher quality than it actually was, was illegal before the establishment of wartime price controls. But a great deal of the black-marketers' behavior was legal before controls were imposed, or if not strictly legal, such as paying bribes to secure contracts, it was at least overlooked in peacetime. Finally, even if new laws had not been enacted, the war gave business people greater opportunities to engage in law violation because there was a greater scarcity and a greater competition for the goods the business people controlled, and it was therefore easier for them to exploit their customers.

Clinard (1952) claims that an effort was made by the government to convince the American public that the black marketers were dangerous criminals who were jeopardizing the national interest. However, this government effort was not completely successful, perhaps for at least two reasons. First, abstract reasoning is required to understand the harm done by the crimes of black marketers. For example, the result of diverting gasoline and tires from the war effort and selling them at high cost is inflation, which weakens the economy. Armed robberies and assaults are easier to understand. Second, as indicated above, much black marketing was simply traditional business behavior that was abruptly made illegal, and public sentiment toward such behavior did not change as quickly as did the law. Even though the American public never reacted strongly against merchants who dealt in the black market, it is clear that at least some of these activities diverted materials from the war effort and therefore cost the lives of civilians and soldiers by prolonging the war.

Bribery and American Business A recent survey of the largest American corporations found three major categories of illegal behavior (Browning and Gerassi, 1980:411–412). Fourteen percent had been charged with creating consumer safety hazards or deceptive advertising, 24 percent had been charged with antitrust violations, including price-fixing, and 38 percent had admitted making "illegal or improper political payments" (Browning and Gerassi, 1980:412). "In the pecking order of big-time crime, bribery is king" (Browning and Gerassi, 1980:415). Since bribery is so common, a company sought to deduct from their corporate taxes the bribes paid to gas company employees who had harassed the company to prevent it from performing its contract (Reisman, 1979:53–55). The tax court disallowed these deductions because the company had not demonstrated that it was usual to have such expenses. But later a tax court allowed income tax deductions for bribes paid by opticians to prescribing physicians who referred patients to these specific opticians. Lockheed Aircraft Corporation has admitted paying large bribes to the leaders of a number of foreign nations in return for orders, and the Department of Defense accepts this practice among weapons producers (Reisman, 1979:67–68). The true attitude of government officials toward bribery was demonstrated in the comments of a member of the Interstate Commerce Commission in a private meeting with his colleagues that were leaked to the press (*Washington Post,* 1982). This commissioner told the others that he believed there was nothing wrong with a trucker's paying bribes to a shipping manager in return for business. This practice makes it possible for truckers to drive out all of their competition and ultimately set monopolistic prices. Yet the commissioner said that such bribes "are probably one of the clearest instances of the free market at work" (*Washington Post,* 1982).

In these particular cases the government seems to have accepted the existence of bribes, but that is not always true. It is possible to distinguish three different types of bribes, only some of which are tolerated (Reisman, 1979). *Transaction bribes* are payments routinely made to a public official to hasten the performance of the prescribed task. Examples include payments made to customs officials to go to the head of the line and move quickly through customs. *Variance bribes* involve, not a speedy performance of a task, but payment for nonperformance of a task. In this case a briber pays, not to go to the head of the inspection line, but to ensure that his or her bags will not be checked at all. The transaction bribe is usually very difficult to trace because it involves no illegal behavior, whereas variance bribes are easier to discover and therefore more expensive. The most extreme form of bribery is the *outright purchase.* In such a case a public official is actually an employee of a briber while still appearing to act as a public servant. For example, a customs official may be bribed, not to allow one person to pass through customs with illegal drugs, but to be ready to help any agents of a criminal conspiracy through customs no matter what they possess.

Bribery, in fact, is so common that government investigators often feel forced to accept the existence of some bribery, and they attempt to stop only the most flagrant cases (Reisman, 1979). For example, the Knapp Commission, investigating corruption among the New York City police in the 1970s, distinguished between "honest" and "dishonest" graft and attacked only the latter. Possible examples of "honest" graft include taking small bribes to allow double parking of construction company trucks on city streets near construction sites. The trucks must park somewhere, but when there are no parking spaces, a small bribe solves the problem and no one seems to be any worse off because of the practice. Here again, the government ignores and indirectly endorses some bribery.

Chambliss (1971) tells about a city health code for controlling restaurants. There were so many technical provisions that one could not serve meals without violating some section of the code. Therefore corrupt city health inspectors could shut down any restaurant that refused to pay continual bribes. Perhaps without realizing it, most of us have seen a hint that something of the sort exists in most cities. Local laws typically require that elevators be inspected at regular intervals by city inspectors, and on an interior wall of elevators there is typically a small glass case containing the record of inspections, with their dates. What is usually noteworthy about this record is that few or no inspections are recorded. As in the case of health inspectors, it is probable that the elevator inspectors have not forgotten about all these elevators but, rather, are paid a bribe not to inspect them. Thus there is a real possibility that a major disaster could be brought on by such corruption.

Unfortunately, such threats to life and limb rest on more than such speculation. In Kansas City, Missouri, on July 17, 1981, several elevated walkways in the new Hyatt Regeny Hotel collapsed, killing 114 people congregated there for a dance. A later investigation demonstrated that city building inspectors, rather than actually inspecting the hotel while it was under construction, spent their days loafing in bars and cafes, apparently with the knowledge and cooperation of the inspectors' supervisors and the owners of the hotel (*Columbia Missourian*, 1982; 1983a; 1983b). The inspectors were being paid a salary but were encouraged not to perform this or any other inspection. This arrangement suggests a type of *variance bribe*. Although civil suits have been filed and cash settlements made to the victims of this tragedy, to date no criminal charges have been filed.

From the late 1950s to the mid-1970s the Lockheed Aircraft Corporation, in exchange for aircraft orders, paid millions of dollars in bribes to government officials in Japan, Germany, Italy, the Netherlands, Indonesia, and Saudi Arabia. At the time these bribes were paid, the paying of such bribes was not a violation of American law, even if accepting them was a clear violation of the laws in these other nations. (In 1977 the U.S. government did outlaw such practices.)

But even if such bribes were not a violation of American law at the time they were paid, they were clearly immoral, because these foreign governments, often as a consequence of having accepted these bribes, bought inferior products or products they could not use. Italy, for example, purchased Lockheed C-130 aircraft, which can fly to Brazil and back nonstop but which the Italian military did not need (Pierce, 1986). Obviously, both Lockheed and the officials who received the bribes profited from these transactions. The victims of these bribes were the citizens of these foreign nations.

In spite of the massive amount of bribery in this country, the myth that all bribery is morally wrong is supported in public pronouncements by political leaders, especially those who are extorting bribes from others (Reisman, 1979). Corrupt politicians know better than anyone that the myth of an honestly operated government builds stability into the system and protects their corrupt practices. As a result, the most common response to bribery is an attempt to create the public impression that corruption has been rooted out and stopped, when in fact it continues unabated. This insincere attempt to control bribery is called a "crusade." A genuine effort to stop these corrupt practices is called a "reform." A sure sign that a mere crusade, rather than a reform, is under way is a grossly inadequate law enforcement budget or the presence of manifest incompetents on the law enforcement staff.

DEMOCRATS, REPUBLICANS, AND THE LATE HOWARD HUGHES   Perhaps the most dramatic illustration of bribery was described recently through the publication of a best-selling exposé based on the life of the late billionaire Howard Hughes (Drosnin, 1985). The details of Hughes's use of bribery were uncovered in thousands of pages of his handwritten confidential memos, which were stolen from his headquarters in 1974. This burglary has never been solved. Somehow these notes came into the possession of Michael Drosnin, and he has been sued for releasing their contents in his book on Hughes (*Los Angeles Times*, 1985). In 1968, preparing for the presidential election, Hughes wrote in a note to a top aide, "I am determined to elect a President of our choosing this year, and one who will be deeply indebted, and who will recognize his indebtedness. . . . Since I am willing to go beyond all limitations on this, I think we should be able to select a candidate and a party who knows the facts of political life" (Drosnin, 1985:44). Hughes ordered many payoffs to politicians in both political parties, both liberals and conservatives, with only one guiding principle, "Find the right place, and the right people, and buy what we want" (Drosnin, 1985:44).

Hughes's reasons for bribery were many and diverse. He was extremely worried about the damage from nuclear testing to the environment of the state of Nevada, where he lived during the last years of his life and where he owned a considerable share of the casino industry. When his attempts to bribe the Atomic Energy Commssion to postpone any further nuclear testing in the state failed, he hit on the idea of moving all the testing to Alaska at his expense. So keen were his arguments and so large his fortune that he convinced both the governor of Nevada and a U.S. senator from Alaska to support his cause. He also attempted to bribe President Johnson in 1968 to delay a scheduled nuclear test. And Hughes knew that Johnson could be bribed, "'I think you should try to determine who is the real, honest-to-God, bagman at the White House,' he urged [a top aide]. 'And please don't be frightened away by the enormity of the thought. I have known for a number of years that the White House under this particular Democratic administration is just as crooked as it can be'" (Drosnin, 1985:222). Johnson wanted a large library built in Texas in his honor, and it seemed that if Hughes would help with this endeavor, Johnson promised, according to a memorandum from a Hughes aide, that he would "do everything in his power to stop future big blasts in Nevada" (Drosnin, 1985:232). Hughes was also troubled that the Justice Department was attempting to contol his plans for the acquisition of casinos under federal antitrust law provisions.

When Hubert Humphrey announced his candidacy for president, Hughes delivered $100,000 to him, half in secret cash that he could use in any way he saw fit. And Hughes had other reasons for controlling the presidency. He planned to attempt for a second time to acquire the American Broadcasting Company television network, and this required Federal Communications Commission approval. The Hughes Aircraft Company depended almost entirely on defense contracts, and his legal battle to retain control of Trans World Airlines would come before a U.S. Supreme Court shaped by any new president. For all these reasons, and more, Hughes wanted to control the presidency. To hedge his bets, Hughes also delivered $100,000 to Richard M. Nixon, the Republican candidate. After becoming president in 1968, Nixon used much of the money for improvements at his home in Key Biscayne, Florida. Larry O'Brien, while serving as chair of the Democratic National Committee in 1972, was also on the Hughes payroll, getting $15,000 a month. This connection of O'Brien to Hughes worried Nixon because he feared that O'Brien knew of Nixon's acceptance of the Hughes money. The president must have believed that it was important to obtain proof of O'Brien's acceptance of bribes before O'Brien could blow the whistle on him. Ultimately the Watergate burglars were dispatched to the Democratic Party headquarters in 1972 to find proof of the Hughes-O'Brien connection (Drosnin, 1985:412).

Duplicity and Automobile Dealers Both new-car and used-car dealers have a well-deserved reputation for dishonesty, and bribery has a role in this business. Rather than blaming only the automobile dealers for these practices, it has been suggested that the manufacturers create an economic situation that forces dealers to adopt dishonest practices to survive. For their part, the manufacturers recognize that they must operate on an economy of scale to survive. It has been demonstrated (Farberman, 1975:438–439) "how one elite, namely, automobile manufacturers, creates a 'criminogenic market structure' by imposing upon their new car dealers a pricing policy which requires high volume and low per unit profit." The more cars the manufacturers produce, the less the cost of each car will be and the more profitable their corporation will become. Therefore the manufacturers force their dealers to purchase, with cash on delivery, a very high volume of new cars. The new-car dealer must therefore borrow large sums of money to pay for these cars. Because of the high interest the dealers must pay on these loans, they are willing to sell new cars for very little profit. They then have a considerable amount of capital invested in a massive number of used cars taken in as trade-ins. The new-car dealer therefore has a substantial interest in selling most of these trade-ins en masse to wholesalers as soon as possible.

These conditions then provide the economic environment for a practice referred to as the "short sale" (Farberman, 1975). This is the way the practice works: Used-car wholesalers who deal directly with retail customers often reduce the recorded sale price to be paid by check and take the rest of the total price in cash. The advantage to retail customers is that they save some of the state sales tax. The advantage to the wholesalers is that they now have some unrecorded income that they can use to bribe the used-car managers of new-car dealerships to keep their line of supply of used cars open. These used-car managers must sell a large number of used cars at very low prices very quickly, and every wholesale dealer would like to be the beneficiary of the new-car dealers' need to sell these cars quickly. The owners of new-car dealerships must know that their used-car managers are taking bribes, but they may not care so long as their used cars are sold quickly. All these illegal practices seem forced on these participants by the market pressures.

Punishment of Crimes with Unaware Victims

By the end of the nineteenth century, many Americans recognized that they were very much exploited by the nation's giant corporations. Thus, in 1890, federal antitrust legislation was passed—but it was seldom enforced (McCormick, 1977). Because no special funds to enforce this legislation were originally provided by Congress, it was clearly a symbolic type of legislation designed to falsely convince the citizens that their interests were being protected. It was not until the electric companies' conspiracy case in 1961 that any business people were actually imprisoned for price-fixing under this legislation. The problem is that the critical period for changing the public's definition of behavior is immediately after the law has been passed. If the law is not enforced, it will be impossible to change public attitudes at a later time (McCormick, 1977). It is in this context that great public tolerance of price-fixing is predictably found.

Embezzlement and Price-Fixing Because of the early and well-known work by Cressey (1953), most of the information that criminologists have relied on in discussing white-collar crimes and white-collar criminals came from his study of embezzlers. However, the generalizations arrived at by studying embezzlers do not hold for other types of white-collar crime. Violations of antitrust laws, for example, present a different set of circumstances from embezzlement. Not only are the offenders from a different socioeconomic class, but the techniques and justifications for carrying out the crimes differ. Cressey indicated that the white-collar crime of embezzlement arises from a situation in which previously honest white-collar workers find that they have a problem involving money, such as gambling debts, that they are ashamed to share with others. Such individuals also realize that they can solve the problem by taking their employer's money "temporarily," as a "loan." They justify the act to themselves by telling themselves that they are not actually stealing, because they intend to pay back the money. Perhaps because of their high status, embezzlers find it difficult to perceive themselves as criminals.

The information available about price fixers leads to the belief that the description of embezzlement does not supply an adequate picture of price-fixing (Geis, 1967). Price-fixing does not appear to be an individual solution to an individual money problem. Rather, it is a group solution to a group money problem. The individuals involved do not commit the crime because of personal need or gain; they claim that it is merely part of their job. Corporations would like to know in advance, for example, what share of government contracts they will receive in a given year. This makes future budgeting, hiring, and plant expansion less risky. If they know which, and how many, contracts they will be awarded, then their probability of spending money on plant expansion or on training of new employees, when neither is needed, is small. Price-fixing, then, may serve to maximize corporate profits.

Price-fixing, like embezzlement, is usually done with secrecy, but unlike embezzlement, several people necessarily know about it. Also unlike embezzlement, no guilt feelings attach to this activity. Embezzlers are humiliated and mortified when their defalcations are made public, because they have violated their own code of behavior—not so for price fixers.

The scandal of the electric companies' price fixing in 1961 was the focus of a considerable amount of attention. The defendants, executives of several large American corporations, did not contest the charges of the government, thus avoiding a public trial. This case was unusual in that seven of the defendants were given short jail sentences. In cases of this kind, fines are usually levied against the company and its employees, with the company usually paying the employees' fines.

Originally, General Electric's position was that the behavior of its employees was not harmful, because even with price-fixing, its products were a bargain (Geis, 1967). The defendants justified what they had done on the ground that it was just part of their job. They recognized that their behavior was technically illegal but argued that it served the worthwhile purpose of stabilizing prices. They distingushed between illegal and immoral acts. There was general admission that their behavior had been illegal, but they still believed that is could not be characterized as immoral.

Being publicly labeled a price fixer was not grounds for dismissal from Westinghouse, and the imprisoned price fixers whose corporations did fire them were quickly hired by other companies after their release from jail (Geis, 1967).

This indicates that no stigma or public outrage was attached to the price fixers' behavior. An embezzling bank teller will not be hired in any position of trust again. But for some high-level executives, the ability to be flexible with the law, not honesty, seems to be a prime occupational requirement. This comparison clearly indicates how elite class interests operate; yet the character of those operations would not usually be disclosed by the commonly used example of embezzlement.

The Revco Drug Company Caper   Revco Drug Stores, Inc., is one of the largest retail drugstore chains in this country, with 825 stores in 21 states. On July 28, 1977, Revco was found guilty of a double-billing scheme that resulted in the theft of over a half million dollars from the Ohio Department of Public Welfare (Vaughan, 1983). The story begins in May 1976, when a pharmacist at an Ohio Revco drugstore observed that a local podiatrist was prescribing large quantities of tranquilizers, apparently outside the usual scope of podiatry. The pharmacist notified the Ohio Board of Pharmacy, which then began an investigation by examining the drugstore's prescription records.

Just by chance, the investigators noticed something in these records that they had not been looking for originally. They noticed the following pattern: A request for compensation for a prescription to a Medicaid recipient was forwarded to the Ohio Department of Public Welfare for reimbursement. Then, 3 days later, the same prescription was claimed again, but with the last three digits of the prescription number transposed. These officials then broadened their investigation to include the records of 12 other Revco stores, where they found the same pattern. Further investigations found no actual prescriptions to back up any of these second claims for reimbursement. This investigation found over 60,000 bogus claims, with a total loss to the Ohio Department of Public Welfare of over $600,000.

Because this practice of double billing existed in several stores, it seemed unlikely that a store manager was behind the theft. Any scheme involving so many store managers would have been sure to unravel. Indeed, when confronted with evidence of their involvement, two high-level executives accepted full responsibility. They had hatched a scheme to recover money from Revco Medicaid claims rejected by the Ohio welfare department computer. Rather than taking the time to correct faulty claims, which would be time-consuming and expensive, these executives reasoned that it would be quicker to report bogus claims which they knew were in a form that would clear the computers, because they waited a few days until the first claim had been paid. Although the executives admitted these falsifications, Revco placed the blame for the entire problem on the Ohio welfare department for refusing to pay the original claims. Revco claimed that it was the victim, and not the offender. One wonders how much of this type of theft goes on among other companies, because it would never have been discovered except for the chance request for an investigation by the Revco pharmacist.

The two executives were fined $2,000 each for this offense. One was transferred laterally to another executive position at Revco, and the other resigned and accepted a position as an executive with a firm providing computer services to pharmacies. (The latter's conviction apparently demonstrated his professional expertise to others in the industry.) No action was taken against the top executives of Revco, although it is difficult to believe that such practices to recover over a half million dollars could exist without the top management's knowing of the operation. The welfare department could have terminated Revco's participation in the Medicaid program, which would have cost Revco $2 million annually, or 2 percent of total sales. But it was reasoned that to terminate Revco's participation in Medicaid would have worked a hardship on Medicaid recipients who depended on nearby Revco stores and would have punished a large group of Revco stockholders, who were blameless. The question is, Should a government agency representing citizens in a democracy punish so many of these citizens for something that they did not approve? Instead of terminating Revco's Medicaid participation, the company was forced to make restitution of over $500,000 and pay a $50,000 fine. Out of $650 million annual sales, these sums were only a tiny percent of gross sales. As in the electric company conspiracy case, no one was punished severely by the courts, and no one's career suffered as a result of this criminal conviction.

Bad Checks at E. F. Hutton and Bad Charges at General Dynamics The large investment firm E. F. Hutton recently pleaded guilty to an elaborate fraud that essentially allowed the company to use millions of dollars of bank funds interest free (*New York Times*, 1985b). The company had so many accounts in so many banks that a check could be written on an account that contained no funds, and by the time the check cleared, the funds to cover the check would be in place. Often this meant that E. F. Hutton had the use of a bank's money for 2 or 3 days without paying any interest. It is estimated by the U. S. Department of Justice that by these means the company had defrauded various banks out of $8 million from 1980 to 1982. As a part of plea bargaining, the company agreed to pay the $8 million back to the banks and to pay a $2 million fine, but no one in the company went to prison. The message from the Justice Department is clear: persons who write bad checks will ordinarily go to prison unless the theft involves millions of dollars stolen by the executives of a large corporation. Or as cynics said in a parody of a company slogan: "When E. F. Hutton talks, the Justice Department listens."

A very small story went almost unnoticed in the business news of the *New York Times* (1985a:2). Its full text reads: "General Dynamics has agreed to withdraw a bill of $491,840 charged to the federal government for 76 corporate flights its chairman, David Lewis, made to his farm in Georgia." Apparently if government defense contractors are caught redhanded in billing the government for grossly improper items, it is enough for the contractors to tell the Pentagon that the bill no longer has to be paid. It is similar to writing a bad check and, if detected, telling the bank that the check doesn't have to be cashed. Part of the motivation of David Lewis is suggested in a taped telephone conversation that was leaked to the press indicating that he had boasted about his agreement to drop the requests for disputed funds in 1981 "in hopes that his company might get higher profits on nuclear submarine contracts in the future" (*St. Louis Post-Dispatch*, 1985).

Corporate Greed and the Dalkon Shield In 1971, the A. H. Robins Company, a major pharmaceutical manufacturer, began to market the Dalkon Shield, selling 4.5 million of the intrauterine devices (IUDs) for birth control in the United States and 80 foreign countries before halting sales in the mid-1970s in the United States (Mintz, 1985). It was advertised as the "modern," "superior," and "safe" method of birth control, even though Robins had made no studies of any potential harm that might be caused by the IUDs. Over 2 million women in the United States had this device inserted, and nearly 1 million women in other nations had done so.

The problem was that this device seriously injured tens of thousands of its users. It caused pelvic inflammatory disease (PID), killing at least 18 women in the United States, and most of the infections impaired or destroyed the women's ability to bear children. Moreover, the device was less effective than other such devices, with approximately 110,000 users becoming pregnant, nearly five times the advertised claims. Estimates are that 60 percent of American women who conceived while using this device suffered miscarriage, or about 10,000 more than if they had used other IUDs. Many of the babies who did survive had birth defects such as blindness, mental retardation, and cerebral palsy (Mintz, 1985). In 1974 the U.S. government became aware of these problems and asked the company to suspend sales, which it did but only in the United States. Even after 1974 it continued to sell the device abroad.

In 1977 the company was twice warned in writing by a concerned attorney of the potential danger to women who were still using these devices, but the company did not respond. In 1981, after 4 more years of ignoring the evidence of continuing deaths, the chief district judge for Minnesota pleaded for an immediate recall of all these devices by the company and publicly reprimanded the three senior company officers (Mintz, 1985:24):

> The only conceivable reasons you have not recalled this product are that it would hurt your balance sheet and alert women who already have been harmed that you may be liable for their injuries. . . . You are the corporate conscience. Please, in the name of humanity, lift your eyes above the bottom line. . . .Please, gentlemen, give consideration to tracing down the victims and sparing them the agony that will surely be theirs.

But Robins contended that its IUDs were no more dangerous than others and that no campaign was needed. Only in 1984 did Robins begin a recall campaign, while still maintaining that its IUD was safe and effective when "properly used" (Mintz, 1985:24). It is now abundantly clear that this company attempted to conceal information on effectiveness and hazards from consumers, from the medical profession, and from the government. Unfortunately, this same tactic is found in the case of cigarette companies, whose executives deny that there is any scientific evidence linking smoking to lung cancer, and in the case of auto manufacturers such as Ford, whose representatives failed to inform consumers of the risk of fatality if certain Ford cars sustained a rear-end collision. Thus government regulation is only an illusion, rather than a truly adequate protection. In August 1985, Robins filed for bankruptcy, which may make it impossible for victims ever to collect damages from the company. Thus corporations and their officers are simply not accountable for the death and injury that they cause.

Who's to Blame for Business Crime?

Ghetto Merchants   To help assess the responsibility for crimes committed in the business community, this discussion will begin with what is generally considered by liberals to be a loathsome character, the ghetto merchant. Such business people are generally believed to feed on the misery and poverty of those Americans who have the greatest problems of survival. If the government and the general public are victimized by much white-collar crime, one might predict even greater victimization in the black ghettos, where the victims are among the least powerful citizens.

Consumption may be even more important for low-income people than for those in higher classes, because the former have no prospect of upward occupational mobility and can thus share in the success that is the American dream only through consumption (Caplovitz, 1967). This emphasis on consumption makes such people easy victims for scheming business people. It is exceedingly easy to sell goods to them. Yet low-income people often cannot buy with cash and usually have unstable jobs, making them poor credit risks. States limit the amount that can be legally charged for credit, but ghetto merchants often cover their risks by not letting the customer even know the interest being charged and giving the customer only a payment card. This practice, of course, violates the law. Although interest is regulated by law, the price of merchants' goods is not. In addition to charging predictably high prices, ghetto merchants carry low-quality goods. Both their pricing practices and the low quality of their goods give ghetto merchants some protection, which they feel is necessary because of their risky credit business.

In fact, at times the actual price of a product is misrepresented (Caplovitz, 1967). Caplovitz described a case in which a salesman told a customer that the price of a television set was $250. The customer signed a contract to buy the set on time payments and later received a contract in the mail specifying a $300 purchase price. In another case, a woman bought a lamp for $29 from a door-to-door salesman and made an initial deposit. A week later the salesman came back to her home and told her that the price had gone up. She could not pay the extra amount, so he took the lamp back and did not return the deposit.

According to Caplovitz (1967), ghetto merchants sometimes use false advertising of a special sale when no such goods exist at the advertised price and then try to sell something more expensive to the people they have lured into their stores in this way. In addition, the goods these merchants sell are sometimes misrepresented. A man bought what he believed was a new television set, but it lasted only a short time. A television repairperson informed him that it was a reconditioned set in a new cabinet.

The bill collection practices of ghetto merchants are also often illegal. Yet there is no evidence that law enforcement officials view the ghetto merchant as a lawless predator. In one instance, two police officers came to a man's apartment to collect the money he owed on lamps, and then physically assaulted him and took all the money in his wallet. When the low-income consumer fails to make payments, merchants can use the law to protect their rights and sometimes even use the police to achieve what are not their legal rights, as in such strong-arm collections. When a merchant fails to back up a promise or guarantee, however, low-inome consumers are powerless because of ignorance of their legal rights and because of laws that favor merchants, such as a lack of government controls on the price and quality of goods (Caplovitz, 1967). Like many other crimes of business people, this behavior is usually not discussed as crime either by the press or by professional criminologists.

Assigning Blame   As we noted earlier in the case of automobile dealers and short sales, it is a mistake to blame only corporation vice presidents or retail merchants for their illegal practices, because at times they feel forced into these practices by more powerful elites that control an entire market. The high-volume, low-profit pattern forced on auto dealers by manufacturers forces the dealers into fraudulent service operations for financial survival. Such practices include "billing for repairs not actually done, replacing parts unnecessarily, and using rebuilt parts but charging for new parts" (Farberman, 1975:455; see also Leonard and Weber, 1970).

In the interest of locating the moral responsibility for crime and establishing reasonable policies to control such crime, it is essential to understand the economic environment that produces such problems. In the case of the ghetto merchant, we must ask whether it would be possible for a merchant to operate honestly in the ghetto, servicing the needs of the local community, offering credit at legal rates, selling high-quality goods at reasonable prices. The only hope for such a development would be some type of government subsidy for ghetto merchants similar to that offered to most farmers, including tobacco growers, to maximize the possibility of their making a profit. If the government can use tax dollars to ensure that farmers who grow tobacco for cigarettes do not go out of business, surely we can do as much for merchants who are operating in a terribly unstable but nonetheless critical part of America's domestic economy.

THE OFFENDER AS VICTIM: JUVENILE DELINQUENCY

It is sometimes argued that certain behaviors are prohibited and designated as crime to protect the offenders from themselves. The vices such as drug use, homosexual relations between consenting adults, and prostitutes' activities are usually included on this list. In reality, some argue that there is no such thing as a crime without a victim. But the clearest and least ambiguous illustration of the offender as the victim is found in the case of juvenile delinquency.

Definitions of Delinquency: Old and New, at Home and Abroad

Juvenile delinquency is also easy to recognize as a cultural creation, given the great variation in this designation at different times and in different places. Not all nations have the same concept of juvenile delinquency (Lejins, 1961). The concept of juvenile delinquency assumes the concept of adolescence, a transitional stage between childhood and adult status, and not all societies have this stage (Cavan and Cavan, 1968). In cultures where individuals pass directly from childhood to adult status, the notion of juvenile delinquency cannot develop. Moreover, in many countries that recognize the existence of juvenile delinquency, it includes only criminal code offenses committed by persons below a certain age (Lejins, 1961).

In traditional English common law the concept of juvenile delinquency did not exist:

> Children under the age of seven were presumed incapable of committing a crime, whereas "on the attainment of fourteen years of age, the criminal actions of infants are subject to the same modes of construction as those of the rest of society." Children between the ages of seven and fourteen were also presumed to be "destitute of criminal design," a presumption which could be rebutted by the prosecution if "guilty knowledge was clearly and unambiguously demonstrated. The burden of proof was on the prosecution and any doubt had to operate in favor of the defendant. (Platt, 1969:188.)

Youths were either considered capable of having criminal intent and subject to the criminal law or were exempt. However, no special law was applicable to them.

In the contemporary United States, however, we have a greatly altered and much broader conception of juvenile misdeeds that are alleged to require government intervention. Although there is considerable variation from state to state, the following list of violations, published soon after World War II, reflects the broad range of prohibited behaviors found in laws applying to the behavior of American juveniles (Rubin, 1949:2):

- Violates any law or ordinance
- Immoral or indecent conduct

- Immoral conduct around school
- Engages in illegal occupation
- (Knowingly) associates with vicious or immoral persons
- Grows up in idleness or crime
- (Knowingly) enters, visits house of ill repute
- Patronizes, visits policy shop or gaming place
- Patronizes saloon or dram house where intoxicating liquor is sold
- Patronizes public poolroom or bucket shops
- Wanders in streets at night, not on lawful business (curfew)
- (Habitually) wanders about railroad yards or tracks
- Jumps train or enters car or engine without authority
- Habitually truant from school
- Incorrigible
- (Habitually) uses vile, obscene, or vulgar language (in public place)
- Absents self from home without consent
- Loiters, sleeps in alleys
- Refuses to obey parent, guardian
- Uses intoxicating liquors
- Is found in place for which adult may be punished
- Deports self so as to injure self or others
- Smokes cigarettes (around public place)
- In occupation or situation dangerous to self or others
- Begs or receives alms (or in street for purpose of)

The outlandish breadth of these prohibitions found in the various juvenile codes is readily apparent. They cover behaviors ranging from violation of the law to public smoking and swearing. Moreover, many of the prohibitions seem too vague to be fairly implemented. It is not clear how incorrigibility is to be defined or what qualifies as vulgar language, growing up in idleness, or indecent conduct. Finally, the language of some of these prohibitions, and many of the regulations themselves, reflect an archaic and dated quality. The definitions of "dram house" and "bucket shops" are undoubtedly unknown to most Americans today, and public smoking by juveniles hardly generates public outrage in contemporary America.

The juvenile codes of all 50 states cover what are often referred to as "status offenses," or conduct that is illegal only because of the culprit's age. As can be seen in the list presented above, such illegal misconduct includes incorrigibility, immorality, idling, and being beyond reasonable parental control or otherwise in need of supervision. Moreover, cases involving dependent children without homes are also usually processed by juvenile courts.

Minimum age limitations are infrequent in juvenile codes, and the maximum age of persons covered by a state's juvenile code varies from 15 to 18 years (Levin and Sarri, 1974:13). The age qualification sometimes refers to age at the time of the offense, but under some statutes only the age at the date of apprehension and detention is relevant (Levin and Sarri, 1974:14). In most states the authority of the juvenile court can be waived so that juveniles above a stated age can be tried as adults for serious crimes when there is a public outcry for retribution. Some states require the juvenile court to make this judgment, and some empower the prosecutor to do so (Levin and Sarri, 1974:17).

Thus the picture we have of contemporary juvenile codes in the United States is one of broad and exceedingly vague statutes that vary from state to state. Included in this variation are differences in juvenile age limits. Moreover, the authorities are often free to waive the use of the juvenile court and to try juveniles as adults. This means that juveniles often get the worst of both worlds—vague laws describing wide liability for minor misdeeds combined with the prospect of losing their juvenile status if more serious charges are involved and law enforcement authorities believe that punishment will be more severe than is possible under juvenile law.

It is apparent that not only is the definition of juvenile delinquency broad and unclear, but also, as might be expected, the operation of the juvenile court is also ambiguous, with the juvenile deprived of some of the constitutional rights of due process afforded other citizens. The question is, How did this unhappy state of affairs come about?

The Invention of Delinquency

A century ago the notion of juvenile delinquency was unknown. Young people accused of serious crime typically were either considered old enough to be held responsible or were released outright (Platt, 1969). Truancy and swearing were either ignored or handled informally, usually with a sound thrashing. The first American juvenile court provided for by law was established in Illinois in 1899. That court became a model for similar courts in other states. By 1917 all but three states had juvenile courts.

These courts were established largely through the efforts of a cadre of middle-class women who Platt (1969) called the child savers. These women were uniformly disenchanted with the city and believed that wayward youth should be institutionalized in rural areas, away from saloons and gangs. The child savers advocated not only reform in the treatment of young people but also the parental discipline of the nuclear family, agricultural life, and the assimilation of immigrants. Although these women viewed themselves as humanitarians, and although others involved in founding the juvenile courts and juvenile institutions are increasingly thought to have had genuine concern and sympathy for these children (Hagan and Leon, 1977; Schlossman, 1977), these reformers brought attention to and, in fact, invented a newly recognized category of youthful misbehavior (Platt, 1969).

Platt (1969) observed:

> Although the child savers were responsible for minor reforms in jails and reformatories, they were most active and successful in extending governmental control over a whole range of youthful activities that had been previously ignored or

dealt with informally. . . . The child savers were prohibitionists in a general sense who believed that social progress depended on efficient law enforcement, strict supervision of children's leisure and recreation, and the regulation of illicit pleasures. Their efforts were directed at rescuing children from institutions and situations [such as] (theaters, dance halls, saloons, etc.) [page 99]. . . . Ideally, the child savers wanted to intervene in the lives of "predelinquent" children and maintain control over them until they were immunized against "delinquency" (page 107). . . . It was not by accident that the behavior selected for penalizing by the child savers—drinking, begging, roaming the streets, frequenting dance-halls and movies, fighting, sexuality, staying out late at night, and incorrigibility—was primarily attributable to the children of lower-class migrant and immigrant families (page 139).

True to the child savers' goals, the original juvenile court statutes enabled the courts to investigate a wide variety of youthful needs and misbehavior—no legal distinctions differentiated the delinquent from the dependent.

Statutory definitions of "delinquency" included (1) acts that would be criminal if committed by adults, (2) acts that violated county, town or municipal ordinances, and (3) violations of vaguely defined catchalls—such as "vicious or immoral behavior," "incorrigibility," "truancy," "profane or indecent language," "growing up in idleness," "living with any vicious or disreputable person." (Platt, 1969:138.)

The juvenile court's initial control mission is reflected in the fact that its staff consisted primarily of police and truant officers. In the early years of the juvenile court, most delinquency cases involved charges of "crimes without victims," such as disorderly behavior, immorality, vagrancy, truancy, and incorrigibility (Platt, 1969:140). Yet the juvenile court was also prepared to process crimes against people and property. Moreover, contrary to the spirit of the act that created the juvenile court, its establishment did little to improve the lot of incarcerated children, who continued to be imprisoned with adults in county and city jails (Platt, 1969:146). Juvenile delinquency is a concept that is so all-inclusive as to be almost without boundaries or definition. Moreover, it includes behavior that is punishable only when committed by persons below a given age. Both of these qualities emphasize the association of age and power in determining what behavior is included under the heading of juvenile delinquency.

IMAGINARY VICTIMS

Many argue that drug use, gambling, prostitution, and homosexual relations between consenting adults are not instances in which the offender is the victim; rather, they are victimless crimes. Perhaps it is easier to demonstrate this concept and the arbitrary and capricious nature of human judgment by looking at another time and place: Europe during the fifteenth century.

Witchcraft

Today we can easily see the crime of witchcraft as a historical curiosity, reflecting the superstitions of an earlier and more naive period. Witchcraft (Currie, 1968) could be proved in fifteenth-century Europe without proving any actual or observable behavior. It came to be defined as a thought crime—making a pact with the devil or putting a hex on someone. Earlier, in the thirteenth century, the Catholic church took the position that the belief in witchcraft was an illusion. But by the fifteenth century, attitudes had changed. No lesser figures than John Calvin and Martin Luther, for example, believed in the existence of witchcraft.

Since no one had ever been seen making a pact with the devil, ordinary sources of evidence were worthless. Indeed, ordinary people were thought to be unable to see the devil. In most cases of witchcraft, direct proof was impossible to come by, so a premium was placed on securing confessions through torture. Since such confessions included the revealing of other witches, a steady flow of witches was ensured. Confessions were publicly read at executions and distributed to the populace at large. This practice justified the trials to the public and helped reinforce the reality of witchcraft itself. The increasing numbers of witches mentioned in confessions frightened the populace and legitimated even more stringent suppression.

If the accused witch had a good reputation in the community, he or she was clearly a witch, for according to sterotype, witches sought to be well thought of, as a disguise. If the accused was not well thought of, this was also understandable, because no rational person would approve of witches. Stubbornness in refusing to confess was considered a sure sign of alliance with the devil, who was known to demand silence from witches. Thus no negative evidence was possible.

In England the response to witchcraft took place within a framework of effective limitations on the power of the state. English citizens, unlike their counterparts on the Continent, had explicit rights of due process. In addition, because the property of suspected witches was not confiscated in England, as on the Continent, English officials did not have the same vested interest in the discovery and conviction of witches. There was less torture in England, and confessions were rare. On the Continent, by contrast, court officials, including executioners, torturers, and judges of witches, were paid high wages supported by confiscated property. It is not accidental, therefore, that on the Continent most witches were people of wealth and property, whereas in England they were usually poorer and much fewer in number (Currie, 1968).

Thus in continental Europe, a form of deviance was nurtured by the confiscation of property and maintained largely through the efforts of a self-sustaining bureaucratic organization dedicated to its discovery and punishment. When confiscation was outlawed, this form of deviance ceased to be recognized. Witchcraft is an extreme case, in the sense that it is an invented form of deviance whose definition lacks roots in concrete behavior. By their nature, systems of repressive control tend to foster the growth of officially created deviance and an organizational structure that is oriented toward self-perpetuation.

As noted in the next chapter, the parallels between the "real" Mafia and fictitious witchcraft are not difficult to discover. As witchcraft is a pact with the devil that only the devil can know of, so the pact of the Mafia is with other insiders and known only to them. In both cases no direct empirical evidence of the crime is possible. Therefore, as with witchcraft, confessions are the only evidence of the Mafia. In addition, as with witchcraft, no negative evidence is possible to disprove the existence of the Mafia, because denials only reflect the code of secrecy (Hawkins, 1969). As witches were blamed for assorted problems, so today the Mafia is blamed for a wide assortment of crimes. As with witchcraft, reports of massive organized crime have alarmed the public and elected officials, and consequently the law has been altered to allow police to use more extreme measures in fighting organized crime, including liberalized use of secret wiretaps (Harris, 1969). The inputs to the witch courts were property; the material inputs to the modern police agencies are larger public appropriations.

The Crime of Communism

Just as the artificial nature of witchcraft is apparent today, most contemporary Americans probably also recognize the outrageousness of the accusations associated with the communism panic of the early 1950s. Senator Joseph R. McCarthy, a Wisconsin Republican, accused numerous Americans of criminal conspiracy with Communists. His special skill at propaganda triggered a nationwide panic. McCarthy's accusations of treason were directed especially at government officials in the State Department and the army, and numerous careers were destroyed by his groundless charges (Cook, 1971; Watkins, 1969). Just as the Kefauver Senate hearings captured the public's interest in organized crime during the 1950s, the McCarthy Senate hearings on Communists in government generated a national paranoia about Communists. Neither Kefauver nor McCarthy, of course, was concerned with evenhanded, objective fact gathering and analysis. Ultimately the outrageous accusations of McCarthy so antagonized the Senate that it formally moved to condemn him, and thereafter he was ignored. Yet this episode offers a contemporary example of the way in which powerful government figures, with access to the mass media, can create public designations of crime to suit their personal and political interests.

Drugs and Drug Abuse

If we were to question a sample of American adults, most of them would probably agree that drugs include such things as barbiturates, penicillin, morphine, heroin, LSD, and marihuana. They would probably place coffee, alcohol, and tobacco in a distinctly different category. These respondents might also indicate that all ingested drugs have a physiological impact on the body. On that basis, however, coffee, alcohol, and tobacco would have to be included among drugs. The wary respondent might then reply that these are not drugs because they are not as harmful as "real" drugs. One might point to the thousands of deaths from automobile accidents caused by drinking and to the deaths caused by lung cancer and heart disease that have been linked to cigarette smoking—but probably to no avail. The respondent might then reply that "real" drugs are more addictive than the others, even though in this regard marihuana seems no different from coffee or cigarettes, and marihuana is less addictive than alcohol. The commonsense perception of drugs includes marihuana but not martinis, even if this perception cannot be empirically defended. Goode (1972:18) has correctly observed that "the concept 'drug' is a cultural artifact, a social fabrication. *A drug is something that has been arbitrarily defined by certain segments of society as a drug.*"

Substances called drugs do not share pharmacological traits setting them apart from nondrugs. If the category "drugs" is an artificial construct, then the category "drug abuse" is also artificial. Clearly, what is considered "abuse" is also a cultural artifact with no basis in chemical fact. Alcoholism or the three-pack-a-day cigarette habit is not usually considered drug abuse, of course, because alcohol and cigarettes are not usually considered drugs. Even within the category of real drugs, some use is considered abuse, but some use, even though massive, is not. Many Americans probably consider any consumption of marihuana and—especially—heroin as drug abuse. However, the use of morphine administered by a physician before an operation is considered appropriate, whereas the sale of the same amount of morphine by a street pusher is regarded as drug abuse. The common addiction of affluent adults to barbiturates is not typically seen as drug abuse either, again perhaps because it is a legal addiction, whereas addiction to heroin is not. And there is no evidence that heroin is, in itself, a more dangerous drug than are the barbiturates (Reiman, 1979:31–34). The violent crime (armed robbery to support a 200-dollar-a-day habit) and the disease or death (from dirty needles) associated with heroin is a consequence of its being illegal and is not inherent in the drug itself. Thus the addiction itself is not the central problem. Rather, legality becomes the important commonplace referent for the definition of drug abuse. The logic seems to be that specific drug use would not be illegal if there were not something terribly wrong with it, and if not illegal, then the use cannot be very bad.

CONCLUSION

In this chapter, crime such as personal assault was distinguished from other, more subtle forms of crime that have not evoked such widespread public outrage. Examples of the latter include price-fixing and occupation-caused deaths. Contrary to popular opinion, these are classifications imposed by societal elites on specific human behaviors. Even intentional killing is not necessarily defined as murder. The discriminatory nature of cultural definitions of human behavior is well illustrated in what has been defined as juvenile delinquency. Social scientists who study crime often believe that they are at their liberal muckraking best when they describe the illegal policies of electric company vice presidents or of automobile dealers. Yet it has been demonstrated that even such criminal behavior of affluent business people is often necessitated by elites who control the economic situation in which persons who are guilty of that behavior must survive. Most important for this analysis is the conclusion that the distinctions between crime and noncrime, and between serious and other crime, work to the advantage of powerful segments of American society, such as business leaders, and to the disadvantage of the poor and racial minorities. Designating certain behavior as juvenile delinquency seriously erodes the freedom of another American minority, the young. The primary reason for largely ignoring traditional street crimes such as armed robbery, burglary, and auto theft is that Americans already know a good deal about such crimes from the mass media. This is in sharp contrast to the lack of information and misinformation about the crimes of business leaders. Such misinformation is especially pronounced in the case of American organized crime, and therefore an entire chapter will be devoted to its analysis.

REFERENCES

Adler, F.
 1975   Sisters in Crime: The Rise of the New Female Criminal. New York: McGraw-Hill.
Ball-Rokeach, S. J.
 1980   "Normative and deviant violence from a conflict perspective." Social Problems 28(October):45–62.
Berman, D. M.
 1978   Death on the Job: Occupational Health and Safety Struggles in the United States. New York: Monthly Review Press.
Blau, J. R., and P. M. Blau
 1982   "The cost of inequality: metropolitan structure and violent crime." American Sociological Review 47(February):114–129.
Blau, P. M., and R. M. Golden
 1986   "Metropolitan structure and violence." Sociological Quarterly 27:15–26.
Blumenthal, M. D., R. L. Kahn, F. M. Andrews, and K. B. Head
 1972   Justifying Violence: Attitudes of American Men. Ann Arbor: Institute for Social Research, University of Michigan.
Bowker, L. H.
 1981   "Wife beating." Pp. 234–239 in L. H. Bowker (ed.), Women and Crime in America. New York: Macmillan.
Browning, F. and J. Gerassi
 1980   The American Way of Crime. New York: G. P. Putnam's Sons.

Brownmiller, S.
 1975   Against Our Will: Men, Women, and Rape. New York: Simon & Schuster.
Caplovitz, D.
 1967   The Poor Pay More. New York: The Free Press.
Cavan, R. S. and J. T. Cavan
 1968   Delinquency and Crime: Cross-Cultural Perspectives. Philadelphia: J. B. Lippincott.
Chambliss, W. J.
 1971   "Vice, corruption, bureaucracy, and power." Wisconsin Law Review 1971: 1150–1173.
Chesney-Lind, M.
 1973   "Judicial enforcement of the female sex role: the family court and the female delinquent." Issues on Criminology 8(Fall): 51–69.
 1974   "Juvenile delinquency: the sexualization of female crime." Psychology Today 8(July): 43, 45–46.
 1986   "Women and crime: the female offender." Signs 12(Autumn):78–96.
Claybrook, J. and the staff of Public Citizen
 1984   Retreat From Safety: Reagan's Attack on America's Health. New York: Pantheon Books.
Clinard, M. B.
 1952   The Black Market: A Study of White Collar Crime. New York: Rinehart.

Clinard, M. B. (with the assistance of P. C. Yeager, J. Brissette, D. Petrashek, and E. Harries)
1979 Illegal Corporate Behavior. National Institute of Law Enforcement and Criminal Justice, U.S. Justice Department. Washington, D.C.: U.S. Government Printing Office.

Columbia Missourian
1982 "Contractor: Hyatt owners knew of faults." December 19:7C.
1983a "Kansas City inspectors say bosses tied to deceit." February 6:4A.
1983b "Kansas City loafers revealed." February 17:4A.

Cook, F. J.
1971 The Nightmare Decade. New York: Random House.

Cressey, D. R.
1953 Other People's Money: A Study in the Social Psychology of Embezzlement. Glencoe, Ill.: The Free Press.

Cullen, F. T., B. G. Link, and C. W. Polanzi
1982 "The seriousness of crime revisited: have attitudes toward white-collar crime changed?" Criminology 20(May):83–102.

Currie, E. P.
1968 "Crimes without criminals: witchcraft and its control in Renaissance Europe." Law and Society Review 3(August):7–32.

Drosnin, M.
1985 Citizen Hughes. New York: Holt, Rinehart & Winston.

Farberman, H. A.
1975 "A criminogenic market structure: the automobile industry." Sociological Quarterly 16(Autumn):438–457.

Geis, G.
1967 "White collar crime: the heavy electrical equipment antitrust cases of 1961." Pp. 139–151 in M. B. Clinard and R. Quinney (eds.), Criminal Behavior Systems: A Typology. New York: Holt, Rinehart & Winston.
1973 "Deterring corporate crime." Pp. 182–197 in R. Nader and M. J. Green (eds.), Corporate Power in America. New York: Grossman Publishers.

Goode, E.
1972 Drugs in American Society. New York: Alfred A. Knopf.

Hagan, J. and J. Leon
1977 "Rediscovering delinquency: social history, political ideology and the sociology of law." American Sociological Review 42(August): 587–598.

Harris, R.
1969 The Fear of Crime. New York: Praeger.

Hawkins, G.
1969 "God and the Mafia." Public Interest 14(Winter):24–51.

Lejins, P. P.
1961 "American data on juvenile delinquency in an international forum." Federal Probation 25(June):18–21.

Leonard, W. N. and M. G. Weber
1970 "Automakers and dealers: a study of criminogenic market forces." Law and Society Review 4(February):407–424.

Levin M. M. and R. C. Sarri
1974 Juvenile Delinquency: A Comparative Analysis of Legal Codes in the United States. National Assessment of Juvenile Corrections. Ann Arbor: University of Michigan.

Los Angeles Times
1985 "Hughes aide sues best-seller's author." Reprinted from the Columbia Daily Tribune, May 2:7.

Martin D.
1978 "Battered women: society's problem." Pp. 111–141 in J. R. Chapman and M. Gates (eds.), The Victimization of Women. Beverly Hills, Calif.: Sage Publications.

McCormick, A. E., Jr.
1977 "Rule enforcement and moral indignation: some observations on the effects of criminal antitrust convictions upon societal reaction processes." Social Problems 25(October): 30–39.

Mintz, M.
1985 "At any cost: corporate greed, women, and the Dalkon Shield." The Progressive (November):20–25.

Newman, D. J.
1957 "Public attitudes toward a form of white-collar crime." Social Problems 4(January): 228-232.

New York Times
1985a "Expense claim withdrawn." February 11:D2.
1985b "E. F. Hutton guilty in bank fraud, penalties could top $10 million." May 3:1, 33.

Page, J. A. and M. W. O'Brien
1973 Bitter Wages. New York: Grossman

Pepinsky, H. E. and P. Jesilow
1984 Myths That Cause Crime. Washington, D.C.: Seven Locks Press.

Pierce, C.
1986 How to Solve the Lockheed Case. New Brunswick, N.J.: Transaction Books.

Platt, A. M.
1969 The Child Savers: The Invention of Delinquency. Chicago: University of Chicago Press.

Reasons, C. E.
1974 The Criminologist: Crime and the Criminal. Pacific Palisades, Calif.: Goodyear.

Reiman, J. H.
1979 The Rich Get Richer and the Poor Get Prison: Ideology, Class, and Justice. New York: John Wiley & Sons.

Reisman, W.
1979 Folded Lies: Bribery, Crusades, and Reforms. New York: The Free Press.
Robin, G. D.
1963 "Justifiable homicide by police officers." Journal of Criminal Law, Criminology, and Police Science 54(June):222–231.
1977 "Forcible rape: institutionalized sexism in the criminal justice system." Crime and Delinquency 23(April):136–153.
Roby, P. A.
1969 "Politics and criminal law: revision of the New York State penal law on prostitution." Social Problems 17(Summer):83–109.
Rossi, P. H., C. E. Bose, and R. E. Berk
1974 "The seriousness of crimes: normative structure and individual differences." American Sociological Review 39(April):224–237.
Rubin, S.
1949 "The legal character of juvenile delinquency." Annals of the American Academy of Politial and Social Science 261(January):1–8.
Russell, D. E. H. and N. Howell
1983 "The prevalence of rape in the United States revisited." Signs 8(Summer):688–695.
Schafer, S.
1974 The Political Criminal: The Problem of Morality and Crime. New York: The Free Press.
Schlossman, S. L.
1977 Love and the American Delinquent: The Theory and Practice of "Progressive" Juvenile Justice, 1825–1920. Chicago: University of Chicago Press.
Silberman, C. E.
1978 Criminal Violence, Criminal Justice. New York: Random House.
Simon, R. J.
1975 Women and Crime. Lexington, Mass.: Lexington Books.
St. Louis Post-Dispatch
1985 "Lewis boast on tape, paper says." February 11:1.

Stark, R. and J. McEvoy III
1970 "Middle-class violence." Psychology Today 4(November):52–54, 110–112.
Statistical Abstract of the United States
1982–1983 103rd ed.:179.
Steffinsmeier, D. J.
1980 "Sex differences in patterns of adult crime, 1965–77." Social Forces 58(June):1080–1108.
Sutherland, E. H.
1949 White Collar Crime. New York: Holt, Rinehart & Winston.
1983 White Collar Crime: The Uncut Version. New Haven: Yale University Press.
Szasz, A.
1986 "Corporations, organized crime, and the disposal of hazardous waste: an examination of the making of a criminogenic regulatory structure." Criminology 24(February):1–27.
United Nations
1985 Demographic Yearbook, 1983. 35th ed. New York.
Vaughan, D.
1983 Controlling Unlawful Organizational Behavior: Social Structure and Corporate Misconduct. Chicago: University of Chicago Press.
Washington Post
1982 "Transcript suggests widespread kickbacks in trucking industry." Reprinted in the Columbia Daily Tribune, December 18:1.
Watkins, A. V.
1969 Enough Rope. Englewood Cliffs, N.J.: Prentice Hall.
Webster's New World Dictionary of the American Language
1956 Cleveland: World Publishing.
Wolfgang, M. E. and F. Ferracuti
1967 The Subculture of Violence: Towards an Integrated Theory in Criminology. London: Social Science Paperbacks.
Wood, P. L.
1973 "The victim in a forcible rape case: a feminist view." American Criminal Law Review 11(Winter):335–354.

4
ORGANIZED CRIME

Organized crime is selected for extensive analysis because it is arguably the least understood of all types of crime in America today. It is a type of crime that is seen as real and threatening by Americans whether it is called the Mafia, La Cosa Nostra, or the syndicate. If the flood of government reports, newspaper articles, books, and movies involving American organized crime is any indication of citizen awareness, then surely Americans are currently very conscious of this phenomenon. Numerous popular books on the subject, both fiction and nonfiction, have been published in recent years. Several have been made into movies, and one, *The Godfather*, broke all box-office records. Although there is some variation from source to source, the central image is that of a multibillion-dollar-a-year conspiracy of Sicilian origin, in which a code of secrecy (in Italian called *omertà*) is enforced—by violence if necessary. This conspiracy is purportedly international in scope and yet is organized around 24 families in America's largest urban areas. It is thought to be involved in a large share of the illegal gambling and narcotics trafficking in this country and to have infiltrated and corrupted legitimate business. Currently, in the absence of direct personal experience with this thing called organized crime, public views are based largely on fiction (Smith, 1975:91). The book *The Godfather* seemed credible to journalists and to the public and demonstrated the truth of the government's claims of organized crime as an Italian Mafia (Smith, 1975:276–277).

Much of this chapter originally appeared in J. F. Galliher and J. A. Cain, "Citation Support for the Mafia Myth in Criminology Textbooks," American Sociologist 9(May 1974):68–74.

Social scientists have been much less active than journalists in collecting information about organized crime. Perhaps the reason, as Polsky (1967: 117–149) suggested, is that scientists mistakenly believe that such research is impossible. Polsky does admit that criminologists who collect information about organized crime may face some problems, such as being subjected to criminal charges for withholding information on criminal activity from the police, but he indicates that criminology textbook writers invariably give the false impression that to conduct such research, one must pass as a criminal or even engage in a crime as the only means of gaining cooperation. However, in the 1920s John Landesco (1968:xiv–xv) conducted a pioneering study of organized crime in Chicago that involved "not only the collection of newspaper and other printed sources but, in the tradition of Chicago sociology, the development of extensive contacts with criminal groups in the city." More recently, Ianni (1972) conducted a study of organized crime, relying mainly on participant observation supplemented by interviews with key informants. Another contemporary study, by Chambliss (1971), used interviews with persons involved in organized vice or its control. Albini (1971) also used such interviews, along with a variety of existing records, in his study of organized crime. None of these studies mentions the problems often alleged to exist by criminology textbook writers, and significantly, none of these studies have uncovered any evidence of a national conspiracy. But such social science research on organized crime is not common. Albini (1971:8) observed:

> There is no question that much of the material written in the area of organized crime thus far is not scholarly in nature, all too frequently falling into the medium of the journalistic and sensation-oriented style of writing where documentation of sources is either at a minimum or completely absent. Too often these writings are value-laden, resulting in outright distortion of fact and, in many cases, the creation of utter nonsense.

The lack of "scholarly" material and the dominance of "journalistic and sensation-oriented" writing present a dilemma to the social scientist writing a criminology text. The choice apparently is either to ignore the topic of organized crime or to use the available sources with all their obvious limitations. Unfortunately, in answer to this dilemma, there is a heavy reliance among criminologists on journalistic and especially official government documents. This dependence on journalistic and official documents to understand the nature of organized crime is at least partially a consequence of the limitations of traditional social science research techniques. Assuming the code of secrecy, the usual sociological techniques of data collection through interviews, questionnaires, or participant observation seem irrelevant or even dangerous. Moreover, the morality or ethics guiding most social science would hamper the study of any such secret society. The American Sociological Association Code of Ethics, for example, appears to compel the researcher to secure voluntary subject cooperation and prohibits the release of information about subjects against their will (American Sociologist, 1968:316–318).

The reliance of researchers on official documents is not unlike the well-known dependence of criminologists on official arrest records in their other areas of study (Matza, 1969:94–100). Matza illustrates how criminologists typically acknowledge the limitations of arrest records and yet still use them in their research, bemoaning the fact that no alternatives are available. Undoubtedly, this same reasoning helps explain the widespread use of government records, such as U.S. Senate investigative hearings, as a basic source of data on organized crime.

Yet the image of organized crime reflected in the streets and in the businesses of all American communities, as some researchers have found, involves more widespread and more diverse types of corruption and dishonesty than alleged in Senate and Justice Department press releases (Chambliss, 1971; 1978). This more accurate image of organized crime knows no ethnic bounds and involves corrupt police, politicians, and business people. But even if distorted, the Justice Department's publications are useful for detailed study because they reflect what law enforcement functionaries apparently believe and thus show why these agencies adopt certain policies in attempting to combat organized crime. As will be seen in this chapter, the international Mafia, so much a part of our common discourse, may in fact be no more than an image created largely by government propaganda.

DEFINITION OF ORGANIZED CRIME

It is now becoming more widely recognized that there is no clear definition of organized crime. Sometimes the term is used to refer to the crimes committed by organized criminal groups, including gambling, narcotics, loan-sharking, theft, and fencing of stolen goods. At other times the term is used to refer, not to crimes committed, but to *any* activities of groups identified as involved in organized crime (Blakey et al., 1978). Thus even the same writer can slip back and forth between definitions, much like Humpty-Dumpty in Lewis Carroll's *Alice's Adventures in Wonderland.* "'When I use a word,' Humpty-Dumpty said, in rather a scornful tone, 'it means just what I choose it to mean—neither more or less. . . . The question is,' said Humpty-Dumpty, 'which is to be master—that's all.'"

The U.S. comptroller general (1977:8–9) released a report listing the myriad definitions used by federal law enforcement authorities in fighting organized crime. Following are some of the definitions that various agency officials provided:

- Any organized group involved in the commission of a crime
- Activities normally associated with La Cosa Nostra figures or with corrupt public officials
- Any criminal activity performed on a large and sophisticated scale, such as gambling
- A continuous pattern of criminal activity by the same group or individual which has a monopolistic impact on an industry or area

Thus the definitions ranged from the narrow (only persons proved to be members of La Cosa Nostra) to the inclusive (any group of two or more persons formed to commit any criminal act). Given these disparate definitions, the number of organized crime gangs is either a handful or tens of thousands, or somewhere in between.

Part of the confusion in the definition of organized crime is that there are, in truth, different ways in which crime can be considered organized crime. Many types of legal businesses are subject to the pressures of the economy of scale—that is, to survive, they must become larger and larger. In twentieth-century America, this is true of automobile production and banking, but it is not true of all businesses. The practice of law and the making of machine tools are not subject to these same pressures (Schelling, 1967). These same differences of economies of scale seem to be true of illegal businesses. Prostitution may not be subject to the same economy of scale as are heroin production and distribution.

Thinking of crime, one should distinguish between a highly organized criminal enterprise and the organized economy within which crime operates. Not all crime is organized in the first sense of the word. International heroin distribution possibly fits the first definition of the word, but bulglary is organized only in the second sense. Burglary typically does not involve large-scale gangs but does at times involve organized marketing, or fencing. Still other crimes, such as those typically committed by amateurs, occur completely outside the organized illegal economy. This is true of most shoplifting and embezzlement. The problem is that in discussions of organized crime, it is not always clear precisely what type of organization is being referred to: the organization of the gang, of an economy, or both.

The confusion about the definition of organized crime is dramatically reflected in the words chosen for press reports. There are reports of a Black Mafia (NBC News, 1977; Ianni, 1974), an Israeli Mafia ("NBC News Magazine," 1981), and a Japanese Mafia (*Columbia* (Mo.) *Daily Tribune*, 1984). The term "Mafia" implies Italian control, but the other words used as modifiers contradict this image. The new ethnic label, when attached to the term "Mafia," performs two functions (Smith, 1975:7): "It supplies an easily identified criminal label for one group, while perpetuating the criminal identity of another." This contradictory imagery has tended to "overwhelm fact and blur our vision of the real world" (Smith, 1975:8). The U.S. Senate's first investigation of organized crime during the 1950s, in fact, made no reference to the Mafia but spoke, instead, of the "Mob" and the "Syndicate" (King, 1977:69).

Block and Chambliss (1981:195) show that the definition of organized crime is terribly distorted because it "is not applied to crimes that are really organized, such as anti-trust violations of large corporations." Because of the distorted definitions of organized crime, which are evident in the mass media and in government agencies, effective law enforcement is impossible. The federal government has recently recognized that this distortion may be at the heart of its law enforcement problem. The federal General Accounting Office reported (Block and Chambliss, 1981:197): "The lack of specific definition of organized crime, . . . also makes it difficult to define the problem the [organized crime] strike forces were created to reduce."

These problems in defining organized crime ultimately rest on the shoulders of law enforcement: the police, prosecutors, and judges. And because of the great freedom allowed to persons engaged in business activities, it is difficult for the authorities to know whether a particular individual who is violating the law should be considered essentially a business person or a racketeer (Tyler, 1962). If the individual is essentially a respectable business leader, the tendency is for law enforcement to ignore most law violation, but if the person is defined as a racketeer, then law enforcement agencies feel justified in attempting to disrupt all of the individual's activities, including entry into legal businesses. With such individuals, even legal business enterprises are considered likely fronts for criminal activity. Indeed, in recent years law enforcement leaders have often bemoaned the fact that persons in organized crime are increasingly moving into legitimate businesses, where they are more difficult to prosecute. But Smith (1975:323) found that "illicit enterprise is a game that anyone can play. It does not require a total commitment." Thus the distinction between legal and illegal businesses is not always clear. There is little or no difference between credit companies that frequently violate the law and the loan shark (Smith, 1975:337). It appears to some that the activities of a loan shark, who is defined as a racketeer, are less like those of a narcotics dealer and more like those of a banker who happens to loan money at interest beyond the legal rates (Smith, 1975:17).

Block and Chambliss (1981) concluded that rather than defining organized crime on the basis of the types of people allegedly involved, it is better to rest the definition directly on the type of activities considered. Block and Chambliss (1981:12) claimed that organized crime can then be seen as involving

> those illegal activities connected with the management and coordination of racketeering (organized extortion) and the vices, particularly illegal drugs, illegal gambling, usury, and prostitution. This definition does not suggest *who* is involved, thereby leaving that question open for research

Indeed, the title of their book, *Organizing Crime*, intentionally emphasizes activities rather than actors.

Much of our current definition of, and fascination with, organized crime comes from television. The U.S. Senate hearings on organized crime in the 1950s had extensive television coverage. Smith (1975:134) observed that the Senate committee hearings were a great public relations success. The reason for this coverage is that the Mafia story is tailor made for television news. Television requires good pictures—and colorful Mafia figures with gaudy clothing and flashy nicknames fit this need very nicely. The clever nicknames, such as Tony "Big Tuna" Accardo and Jimmy "The Weasel" Fratianno, not only make a colorful story even better but give these reports an air of authenticity. Obviously the persons who are close enough to the situation to know the participants' nicknames must know what is going on. Because Americans are increasingly reliant on television for the news, all the other mass media have changed somewhat in an attempt to compete with television, and they appear to follow television's lead in reporting practices.

The Appalachian meeting of alleged Mafia bosses during the U.S. Senate McClellan hearings in 1957 and 1958 was widely reported and helped boost the Mafia myth (Smith, 1975:154–78). A New York State trooper set up a roadblock to keep people from escaping from the meeting, but he had no right to do so because there were no outstanding warrants for the arrest of these men and no evidence that they were committing any crime. Even so, the guests appeared to panic after the roadblock was set up. Many of these Italian-American men had long criminal records, and many were related to one another by marriage. But it is still not known why they were meeting, and contrary to government claims, it is not known whether there was a Mafia meeting.

THE NATURE OF THE PROOF OF ORGANIZED CRIME

If there are serious problems in the definition of organized crime, then it stands to reason that there will also be problems in the types of demonstrations of the proof of this phenomenon. Much of the current belief in the nature of organized crime comes from the numerous congressional investigations. But Moore (1974:75) lamented:

> What has rarely been appreciated is that congressional committees were better dramatists than investigators, that the limited staff and training available, the political atmosphere in which committees worked, and the necessity of arriving at solutions rather than in-depth understanding of problems severely curtailed the amount of serious research a committee could pursue. . . . Investigating committees do little real investigating, but rather, they dramatize a particular perspective on a problem and place the prestige of a Senate body behind the chosen point of view.

The Kefauver Committee of the 1950s asked for testimony only from police officers and politicians and requested no information from academic experts (Moore, 1974:79). During the late 1960s the federal Task Force on Organized Crime used expert consultants only sparingly (King, 1977:69). The other task forces appointed at the time to deal with other aspects of crime and crime control made much greater use of academic resources. In the Task Force Report on Organized Crime, Robert Blakey (1967) argued that the U.S. Constitution had to be changed to fight organized crime by allowing greater freedom in the collection of evidence from secret electronic surveillance through wiretapping.

Cressey (1967:25–60; 1969) collected information on organized crime in his role as a consultant to the task force, and he observed (1969:x):

> Upon being invited to work for the Commission, I was not at all sure that a nationwide organization of criminals exists. . . . I changed my mind. I am certain that no rational man could read the evidence that I have read and still come to the conclusion that an organization variously called "the Mafia," "Cosa Nostra," and "the syndicate" does not exist. . . . [The] Deputy Director of the President's Commission invited law-enforcement and investigative agencies to submit reports on organized crime to the Commission. A summer spent reading these materials, exploring other confidential materials, and interviewing knowledge-able policemen and investigators convinced me.

This conversion of Cressey was to be expected. As a parallel example, if one were going to do research on the truth of the story of the virgin birth of Jesus Christ, and if research was limited to the Vatican library in Rome, presumably even the most skeptical person could be convinced. As one of the few academic consul-tants to the federal Task Force on Organized Crime, Cressey's essay in the 1967 federal Task Force Report, endorsing the government's claims, gave these ideas academic legitimacy. Later, in his book *Theft of the Nation*, he was ready to claim that organized crime was synonymous with the Mafia (Smith, 1975:306–308).

Much of what has been written in government reports and in the mass media about organized crime does not seem to be dealing with an empirical or scientific matter. Rather, the logic used in these writings seems more like that used in theology than science (Hawkins, 1969). Sometimes it is reasoned that there must be such a thing as organized crime, or a Mafia, because the pattern in crimes cannot be a mere coincidence. Several Italian-Americans are simul-taneously murdered in different parts of the same city. That proves a wide-spread conspiracy, as does the sale of the same illegal drugs from coast to coast. This is called the argument of design, and has been used to prove the existence of God. It is reasoned that there must be a God who created the earth, or how could there be something as perfect as a tulip or a spring sunrise?

In the case of both God and the Mafia, it is not clear what could be used as significant evidence against their existence (Hawkins, 1969). When witnesses have testified to their membership in the Mafia at U.S. Senate investigating committee hearings, and when they have explained how organized crime oper-ates, their testimony has been accepted at face value by the government and much of the media and has been used to prove that a Mafia truly exists. However, if subpoenaed witnesses deny the existence of a Mafia, as they usually do, this also proves that there is a Mafia because everyone knows that it is a secret conspiracy. Everything proves the existence of a Mafia, just as everything proves to the Christian faithful the existence of God. If someone is stricken at an early age with cancer and dies, the Christian believes that this is God's will. But if the person recovers, that is also God's will. Although this is acceptable, and even necessary, reasoning for religious faith, it surely is inadequate as a basis for setting government policy.

The routine denials of witnesses, combined with their professed ignorance of organized crime, suggest "either a sinister organization or a romantic myth" (Smith, 1975:143–144). It seems unlikely that, if there indeed exists a large-scale Italian conspiracy, it could remain so well hidden (Morris and Hawkins, 1969:204). And if there are many instances of internal violence, they should demonstrate that organized crime is not so well organized (Morris and Hawkins, 1969:230). But the story is still convincing, perhaps because Americans are always looking for conspiracies, as in the deaths of John F. Kennedy and Martin Luther King.

The belief in a Mafia myth serves the same function as do other myths (Hawkins, 1969). Myths are necessary in all societies because they help explain and give meaning to an otherwise meaningless existance. If Americans are alarmed about crime, as they usually are, they can always blame the Mafia. Irrational scapegoating is common in all societies and serves as a means of venting collective hostility.

There is no doubt that large-scale, highly coordinated criminal activities do exist. Gangs of people steal cars, quickly strip them, and sell the parts to local fences. Other large groups are involved in heroin production and international distribution of this drug. The only question in real dispute is whether there is, in fact, an Italian-dominated syndicate that controls racketeering in this country, as is usually claimed.

Much of the current belief in the Mafia is a result of the testimony of an alleged Mafia member, Joe Valachi, who decided during the 1960s to become a government informer in return for government protection from other Mafia members. But his testimony is suspect on several grounds. Most of his testimony was not confirmed by other sources. He called organized crime La Cosa Nostra, rather than the Mafia. No federal law enforcement officials had ever heard this term before. This suggests that either federal agents are incompetent or that Valachi was not telling the truth. Valachi described the internal structure of the typical Mafia family, and again there was no independent confirmation. There was a surface appearance of confirmation from others, but these other witnesses, in fact, used Valachi's testimony as their source of information (Smith, 1975:232).

Aside from these problems, there were internal inconsistencies in Valachi's testimony. He claimed that the internal discipline in the Mafia was very strict and that the organization leaders had decreed in 1957 that there would be no further trafficking in drugs because of pressure from federal law enforcement, but later he admitted that this ruling was disregarded. Finally, Valachi was a low-level operative in the rackets and was never in a position to learn the details of any national or international organization; instead, he could be counted on only to provide details on operations of the rackets on the streets.

More recently, at least a minor media event was created by the publication of *The Last Mafioso* (1981), by David Demaris, which deals with the life of Jimmy "the Weasel" Fratianno. The January 5, 1981, issue of *Newsweek* contained a long essay based on this book, with Fratianno's picture appearing on the cover. On January 7, ABC News devoted most of its "Nightline" program to the book, as did CBS News in its January 4 edition of "60 Minutes." Among the numerous publications reporting on this engaging story was the *Kansas City* (Mo.) *Times*, which on January 5 began a five-part series based on the book.

Who is this Jimmy Fratianno, and why were so many people talking about him? ABC News described him as "the highest-level Mafia figure ever to turn informant." As was just indicated, the answer to this crucial question indicates the number of organizational details that the informant was in a position to know. Yet there is some doubt about Fratianno's actual stature in the Mafia. One of his former colleagues in organized crime was quoted by the *Kansas City Times* (Vitello and Royce, 1981): "He's nowhere near a Valachi. Jimmy was somebody they used when they had to. He was the guy who would go and get the sandwiches and the cream sodas. . . . The last time he got arrested, he couldn't even afford his own lawyer." In *The Last Mafioso*, it is learned that Fratianno was personally involved in at least four murders and was sentenced to prison three times and served about 20 years. During his second prison sentence, he learned that only one other Mafia member was in the entire California prison system.

At this point, he clearly recognized that he was being used. Indeed, by his own admission he felt like an outsider among Mafia members, telling a friend (Demaris, 1981:100): "Except for you, I've got no real friends in this thing. I thought how could I have been so dumb. All they ever used me for was to kill people, set up people, and I never got nothing for none of it." Because of these details of Fratianno's life, it is impossible to believe the claim that his testimony is of great value because of his high Mafia position.

Without more satisfactory evidence, journalists and government agencies appear to be confused.

ITEM: *Time* magazine (1977b) described Mafia control of prostitution on the streets with imprecise wording. The Mafia was *"alleged* to control many topless and bottomless bars, where youthful dancers are enticed into prostitution. The racketeers are also *believed* to own quick-turnover hotels where prostitutes work" (emphasis added). Notice how vague the verbs in these sentences are: It is "alleged" and it is "believed."

ITEM: *Time* magazine (1978) stated: "Hotel and restaurant employees are being recruited by teamsters locals from Philadelphia and northern New Jersey with the *blessing* of Mafia muscleman Anthony 'Tony Pro' Provenzano" (emphasis added). It is not at all clear what the "blessing" of Provenzano actually means.

ITEM: NBC News (1977) stated: "In Florida, Sam 'the plumber' DeCalvacante is a don among dons, a boss among bosses." No proof or even source for this assertion was given.

ITEM: The U.S. Justice Department (1972), as an aid to local police departments, produced a manual entitled *Police Guide on Organized Crime*, which includes the following advice (p. 35): "During a routine check of a restaurant, a patrolman recognizes several organized crime figures at a table, or many double-parked cars are spotted in front of a bar that is either known or suspected as a meeting place for racketeers." The Federal Bureau of Investigation provides the very helpful tip that the Mafia always double-parks.

ITEM: The 1967 Task Force Report has been criticized for attempting to prove that organized crime "has an impact on American life" by noting that Frank Costello (an alleged Mafia boss) formerly "lived in an expensive apartment, . . . was often seen dining in well-known restaurants, . . . [and] was shaved in the barbershop of the Waldorf" (King, 1977:69).

HISTORICAL ORIGINS

By studying the historical record, one can discover problems in the notion that the Mafia was imported directly from Sicily or Italy (Nelli, 1969). In the early 1900s, problems with Italian organized crime were centered mainly in Chicago. In other American cities, including Boston, where there were large Italian-American groups, there was no crime problem. In South America there was no crime problem associated with Italian immigrants; the problem was one of political radicalism. Thus it was not always the case that large groups of Italians necessarily imported traditions of organized crime. It also appears that in Sicily and southern Italy the dominant cultural trait was an intense loyalty only to the immediate nuclear family. Therefore loyalty to a larger group such as a large criminal organization must have originated elsewhere than Sicily or Italy. Although it is probably true that some Italians who came to America were involved in organized crime in the Old Country, probably the most powerful organized crime bosses never came to America because they did not want to leave their power base (Moore, 1974:6). And before the 1920s the image of Italian crime involved mainly acts of passion, the family vendetta, and extortion, not racketeering involving prostitution, gambling, or drugs.

It is typically contended that until the national prohibition of alcohol, there was no large-scale organized crime in the United States. When national prohibition was repealed in 1933, the underworld faced a crisis in losing its largest business because the demand for bootleg liquor almost vanished. Their task was to find an alternative service or product to support their large organization. Criminal organizationas have special problems of survival and therefore have employees with special skills unlike those in legal enterprises. Since law enforcement agencies are in business to put criminal organizations out of business, the criminal organization will usually have emloyees who have special skills in bribery or other techniques to neutralize law enforcement. The organzations that had employees who were especially skilled in producing and distributing illegal goods and illegal service were often not prepared to enter the legitimate liquor business after prohibition but, instead, selected another illegal commodity or service such as drugs or prostitution. Other illegal services and goods require the same general type of organization and the same general type of employee skills.

Block and Chambliss (1981) illustrated that a constant commodity in organized crime in the United States over the years had been a crucial involvement and control by corporate leaders. These authors show that as long ago as the eighteenth century, the opium industry was controlled by an illegal alliance of business and government officials from various nations. And during the period from 1930 to 1960, leaders of major corporations controlled the American heroin industry. These leaders have also corrupted and controlled many labor unions, thereby ensuring greater profits for themselves. Leaders of the business community involved in racketeering are in an ideal position to secure large loans for either their legal or illegal business ventures. They also have such power that they dominate the mass media, which ensures that the public is seldom told of their machinations. This control explains why we have such distorted ideas about who, in fact, is involved in organized crime. Aside from outright ownership of the mass media, Block and Chambliss described the techniques that business leaders use to dominate the media. There is the example of a magazine that published an article suggesting that several local political leaders were corrupt. In response, business leaders in the area canceled advertising in the publication and refused to allow the publication to be sold on their property.

At the highest levels of American government, Block and Chambliss found support of, and involvement in, organized crime. The Central Intelligence Agency was shown to have been involved in narcotics trafficking to reward the anticommunist opium growers of Indochina. And the Nixon administration pursued only the organized crime syndicates that were unfriendly to the Republican Party. The rest were intentionally left unscathed.

ETHNICITY

According to the federal government, La Cosa Nostra consists of 24 exclusively Italian families in the United States, of which the most powerful and wealthy are in New York City (Task Force Report, 1967). Each family has a membership of anywhere from 20 to 700. Most cities have only one family, but New York City has five. The organization of each family is similar to that of the Mafia in Sicily, in that each family is headed by one man, the boss. His job is to maintain order in the family and maximize profits. The authority of the boss is subject to review only by a national executive group called the Commission. The Commission settles all disputes between families that individual leaders cannot settle. Although the Commission has authority over all 24 families, it is composed of only 9 to 12 members from the most powerful families.

There are some glaring inconsistencies in this story, however. As indicated earlier, there is frequent discussion of a Black Mafia, an Israeli Mafia, and a Japanese Mafia, with no real indication of how these disparate ethnic groups fit together into one criminal conspiracy. And there is reference to Meyer Lansky as a leader of organized crime in America (NBC News, 1977), even though he was hardly an Italian-American.

Although Italians are typically blamed for organized crime, Block and Chambliss (1981) convincingly argued that the federal government should have known from their own records that only about 16 percent of those convicted of organized criminal activity from 1953 to 1959 had Italian surnames. These authors further demonstrated that organized crime is central to American economic life and therefore involves all American ethnic groups. Indeed, Block and Chambliss (1981) noted that early in this century, Jews were alleged to control organized crime in New York City, although the Irish were also visibly involved. A correlate of this ethnic diversity is that organized crime is less centralized then is typically alleged. There is no evidence of a scale of organization comparable to General Motors or Standard Oil, for example.

The Task Force Report on Organized Crime (1967) conceded that at the very bottom level of the Mafia family organization are those people who are not actual members of the family. These are the functionaries on the streets that conduct the business of the family such as taking bets and selling drugs. Many non-Italians are involved in this activity, and they are usually from the same ethnic groups as the local customers. In an indirect way, this concession protects the myth of ethnic purity, because otherwise it would be obvious that the Mafia is composed of many ethnic types. This diversity is explained away by claiming that these non-Italians are not actually in the family. The report also concedes that in America, unlike the initial situation in Sicily, Mafia families are not necessarily real families, because they now admit members that are not relatives (Cressey, 1967).

The Mafia originally took root in a rural peasant country, but now it has changed in response to changing environmental pressures (Anderson, 1965). In the modern Mafia the social relations are no longer necessarily close or affectionate. Of course, this revelation comes as no surprise when one considers that some Mafia families allegedly number in the hundreds. No one could have hundreds of close friends. And for greater flexibility, members of the modern Mafia family can now be recruited through marriage and through the ritual kinship of godparenthood. As the Mafia organization has continued to grow, it appears that individual members have occupied more and more specialized jobs. They may specialize as drivers, accountants, or gunmen, or they may specialize in particular goods or services such as drugs or prostitution. And although the family still has a single head, the chain of command is becoming more and more complex. Everyone in a very small social group can report directly to the same leader, but as the group grows, a more complex hierarchy must develop. In all these ways, modern organized crime is becoming more and more like any other commercial bureaucracy. As in any other commercial organization, these changes are forced on organized crime by the changing economic situation.

Before the 1960s the public image of organized crime was not confined to Italians (Smith and Alba, 1979). At this earlier time, organized crime leaders included such famous names as Dion O'Banion, Louis Buchalter, Dutch Schultz, and Louis Lepke, along with the Italians. But in recent years the history of organized crime has been rewritten. Because of the pattern of Italian-American settlement, it is not suprising that, according to the Justice Department, most major cities outside the Northeast do not have a Mafia family. Yet this admission makes the other Justice Department claims of the nationwide Italian domination of organized crime seem doubtful. Rather than seeing organized crime as a foreign parasitic force, it is clear that it contains all ethnic groups because it is an integral part of the United States. Smith and Alba (1979) also noted that individuals who commit crimes together are vulnerable because they need to have complete trust in each other. Yet their agreements cannot be put in writing. Such complete trust, without the support of written contractual agreements, does not easily extend beyond a small circle of friends—and certainly not to a large organization.

In the Jimmy Fratianno book (Demaris, 1981), as in other Mafia stories, there is only infrequent discussion of mob links to the activites of people involved in what is called legitimate business. It is as though these Mafia characters live in an isolated world all their own. Even the few contacts they do have with the outside world are, in turn, tainted with suspect family, ethnic, or religious ties, as in the case of Fratianno's alleged ties with Frank Sinatra or a former San Fransisco mayor, Joseph Alioto.

Time reported (1977a): "As reckoned by the FBI, the Mafia numbers about 5,000 'made men,' or members. All are of Italian ancestry, most with roots in Sicily. Of course, the nationwide number of mobsters involved in organized crime is far higher and knows no ethnic limits." But then this article goes on to describe the behavior of only those with Italian surnames, and thus the image of ethnic purity is maintained. Even when explicit disclaimers are made that organized crime is not an exclusively Italian-American enterprise, as Ted Koppel did on "Nightline" (ABC News, 1981), the impression still persists because, again, only Italian names were mentioned. And if organized crime is dominated by Italians, it is by definition also dominated by Roman Catholics, as Mike Wallace reasoned on "60 Minutes" (CBS News, 1981). *Newsweek* (1981:35) followed the journalistic tradition of dealing in ethnic stereotypes by allowing that the Italian monopoly of organized crime had been broken by "Jewish and Irish hoodlums"; yet it devoted a section of its Mafia article to mob control of the pizza industry, again emphasizing Italian imagery.

We are left with the impression that it is either the Irish, the Italians, or the Jews who control organized crime. It is curious that Protestants and Anglo-Saxons are seldom involved in the same type of illegal money-making schemes. These stereotypes, in fact, are transparently vacuous, for how can one refer to Irish or Italian control of American rackets in the 1980s, some 60 to 70 years after European immigration nearly ceased? The usual Mafia myth of Italian domination of organized crime suffers from a type of dated ghetto mentality. Americans with Italian names are not really Italian after all. After nearly a century of intermarriage with other groups in the United States, as well as nearly complete social integration in our nation's countless suburbs, who is an Italian-American or an Irish-American anyway? The typical answer found in the mass media is that anyone with an Italian or Irish surname qualifies even if he or she is a fourth-generation, suburban-reared American and about as biologically pure as Hitler's Aryans.

The easiest journalism is that which relies on stereotypes of some kind. Even mediocre research and writing can be an instant success with an audience if the message fits with existing stereotypes and biases. Yet such writing does not so much inform an audience as pacify it. The enormous success of *The Godfather* book (Puzo, 1969) and *The Godfather* movies surely reflects the power of the mythology of the Mafia. These stereotypes allow us to focus blame and anger on identifiable "foreigners" for America's considerable crime problem. It will later be shown how the false distinction between organized crime and legitimate business protects the depredations of many American business leaders from citizen reaction.

ORGANIZED CRIME: SECRET OR PUBLIC?

The testimony of Joe Valachi was spawned when he realized that someone associated with organized crime was attempting to have him killed (Mass, 1968). Fratianno's morale was finally destroyed, and he decided to become a government witness, when he learned that he was on an organized crime hit list. Fratianno claimed that such threats in the rackets had convinced many other members that only the government could protect them, and thus informers were everywhere. There have been others over the years to defect from organized crime and tell all of the organization's secrets (see for example, Teresa, 1973). Nevertheless, Ted Koppel insisted:

> *Omertà*, the Mafia's code of silence, is a good deal more than a romantic myth. Because of that code and what happens to people who violate it, only rarely does anyone emerge from the underworld of organized crime to tell us what goes on there. Right now there is such a man, Fratianno.

In point of fact, the Nixon White House had better success at keeping secrets than does the Mafia.

The federal Task Force Report (Cressey, 1967) indicates that there are at least two types of authority and that this becomes relevant to questions of secrecy. A person may have authority over others by virtue of rank in an organization—for example, a military general. Authority may also be a consequence of the possession of certain expert knowledge, such as the authority of an engineer who instructs workers in a factory on precisely how a machine must be assembled. Authority in dictatorships is usually based on rank, whereas in business enterprises it is more typically based on expertise.

In organized crime there appears to be a clear trend away from authority based on rank toward authority resting on the use of expert knowledge. Organized crime increasingly requires the services of lawyers, accountants, and investment experts. The leaders of organized crime cannot dictate to these professionals exactly how to perform their jobs. Moreover, as organized crime becomes more and more like any other business, there is less need for conformity and total silence. All this has happened as organized crime has moved out of the rackets and into legitimate businesses. In all ways the differences between organized crime and legitimate business seem to be disappearing.

Even so, it is generally argued that little is known about organized crime because there are few failures in their activities, and it is mainly through failure that we learn about crime. Therefore, what little can be known about organized crime can be uncovered only through the massive resources of the Justice Department—in other words we must rely on the federal government for the truth about organized crime. The average researcher, whether a journalist or a criminologist, who gets too close to the truth about organized crime, according to traditional reasoning, will be killed. But an increasing number of criminologists have studied the traditional operations of the rackets, such as drug sales and illegal gambling, and have found little of this secrecy (Chambliss, 1971; Albini, 1971). Racketeering must be fairly open if the potential customers are to locate these operations. The way the rackets have always operated is not to emphasize secrecy but, rather, to have relatively well-known locations for illegal operations and to routinely make payoffs to politicians and to the police in return for allowing these illegal businesses to continue.

ORGANIZED CRIME: STRONG OR WEAK?

The Task Force Report (1967) claimed that organized crime is so powerful that it has accumulated sufficient funds to manipulate the stock market prices and control the prices of retail goods and therefore destroy legitimate businesses. One criminal synidicate alone was estimated to own $300 million in real estate. With all of these financial resources, organized crime can manipulate government officials and thereby avoid income taxes and even prosecution for serious crimes, including murder. *Time* magazine has also commented on this massive wealth (1977a): "Justice Department officials believe that the Mafia may own as many as 10,000 legitimate firms, which generate annual profits estimated at $12 billion." In spite of all this muscle, the Task Force Report complained that few resources are allocated to fight organized crime, and even cities with well-known problems with organized crime commit only a token force.

The persons who write on the subject of organized crime have deeply divided opinions on its power. The late Robert Kennedy, the former attorney general and U.S. senator from New York, wrote a book (1960) about the Mafia and warned of its massive power and destructive potential. The sociologist Donald Cressey came to similar conclusions and therefore as will be shown later in this chapter, argued for treating organized crime much as we do powerful foreign enemy nations (1969). This image of a rich and powerful cartel can also be found in fictionalized accounts such as *The Godfather*.

Other commentators are more sanguine. There are a few journalists and other writers who have questioned the dominant image of organized crime. For example, a novel by Jimmy Breslin (1969) characterized a Mafia family in New York City as being totally incompetent, in disarray and poverty, and engaged in continual conflict with other Mafia families. A similar picture of internal decay and internecine conflict emerges from Gay Talese's study (1971) of the Bonannos, one of the better known New York City families. Talese described organized crime as crumbling because of squabbles triggered by FBI pressure and better opportunities outside the rackets. Using government wiretap evidence that was presented in court, Murray Kempton (1969) demonstrated that the members of a New Jersey Mafia family were involved, not in multimillion-dollar drug shipments or nationwide gambling syndicates, but in crimes netting no more than a few hundred dollars. This family had difficulty in paying the rent and sometimes found legitimate occupations more lucrative than crime. Kempton's revelations are especially convincing if one accepts the government's traditional argument that one of the few methods of learning the truth about organized crime is through such wiretap information. Former CIA director William Colby recalled the agency's attempt to use organized crime to assassinate Cuban leader Fidel Castro and was quoted as saying (*Time*, 1980), "You couldn't find a more inept crowd than the Mafia."

Moore (1974:113) concluded that the evidence strongly indicates a more decentralized pattern of organization than the government investigators wanted to admit. The essential requirement for successful illegal gambling and other vice operations appears to involve influence with local law enforcement officials (Moore, 1974:113; Chambliss, 1978). Block and Chambliss (1981) also describe an organized crime that is less centralized, more diverse, and more pervasive than reflected in government reports. Much of the power of organized crime allegedly comes from their use of violence, and it appears that it isn't all that violent. It was reported that as a result of a protracted internal Mafia war, there were 21 victims in 3½ years (*Time* 1977a). "These feared Sicilians are not even all that deadly. . . . To credit La Cosa Nostra with a few dozen, or even a few hundred, hits per year would not say much for it: the number of felony murders (murders commited in connection with some other crime) tallied by the FBI in the United States in 1957 was 6,645" (King, 1977:75).

LEGITIMATE BUSINESS AND ORGANIZED CRIME

One of the reasons that organized crime may seem so powerful is that it is not clear where organized crime ends and legitimate business begins. Chambliss (1978) studied the relationship between the business community and organized crime. Not only did he find the close linkages that worry the Justice Department;

he also found no distinction between the two. One quality that makes organized crime possible is the investment of large sums of money by corporation leaders. These leaders provide the cash and arrange the loans that can make possible the purchase of massive amounts of drugs, for example. These people are the financiers behind criminal operations, and they consequently reap huge profits.

Even the boundary between legitimate business people and lower-level organized crime operatives is difficult to see. Chambliss (1971) found that in Seattle a new restaurant owner was asked to continue to allow illegal card playing and bookmaking on the premises, as had the previous owner, as well as to continue illegal payoffs to the police. He did not agree to allow bookmaking, but for a while he agreed to continue to make the payments to the police, as had the previous owner. But later, when he decided to reduce and ultimately terminate these payments, the police harassed his customers. The city health inspectors used other ammunition. The local health code was written in such a way that no one could actually serve meals and not be in technical violation of some ordinance. Therefore, once he stopped paying bribes, these inspectors found him in technical violation of many minor provisions of the city health code. Ultimately he found that he could not run the business and sold it back to the previous owner at a great loss. This story shows that it was impossible to operate a restaurant in that city without becoming involved in illegal gambling and illegal payments to the police. This story also suggests that the ethnic Mafia image does not emphasize corruption of local officials sufficiently and that the image of gamblers' corruption of political officials is misplaced; if anything, politicians are a corrupting influence on persons we call racketeers. Moore (1974:99) found that the evidence suggests that "politicians used the gamblers, their funds, and their organization more frequently than gamblers used the politicians."

Moore (1974:4) demonstrated that both criminologists and government prosecuters have adopted an artificial distinction between organized crime and the crimes of persons in legitimate business, usually referred to as white-collar crimes. Toward the latter morally acceptable enterprises, prosecuters applied antitrust laws and sought minor civil penalties in the form of fines, but for the former they sought outright suppression and prison sentences. Because most observers see organized crime in conspiratorial rather than economic terms, often when persons who were once involved with gambling and prostitution attempt to diversify their investments into other, more lucrative and stable businesses, this attempt is seen as the infiltration of legitimate business by organized crime (Moore, 1974:ix).

For example, the complaint is often made that organized crime has begun to invest heavily in legitimate businesses, and it is always assumed that this investment is to be used as a front for other activites (Woetzel, 1963). It is claimed that in some cases such investors have embezzled funds from the corporation where they have gained control. They have also used bribery to corrupt labor leaders, keeping their wage costs very low and giving them an unfair advantage over their business competitors. Assuming that every one of these charges is true, it is also the case that all of these activities have been proved to have been committed by persons who were never linked to organized crime. At times it is also alleged that those in organized crime gain a foothold in businesses by force and extortion, but it is acknowledged that entry is often gained by investments (Woetzel, 1963).

Time magazine also complained (1977a):

> The criminals plow lots of their profits back into their rackets or, even more ominously, into a wide range of legitimate business. . . . Justice Department officials believe that the Mafia may own as many as 10,000 legitimate firms, which generate annual profits estimated at $12 billion. . . . Chicago authorities estimate that because of Mob operations, the average citizen pays an additional 2 cents on the dollar for almost everything.

No evidence was provided of precisely how this 2-cent figure was determined. But still NBC News (1977) moaned that "the mob is baking bagels and is using profits from street rackets to move into a number of businesses: banking, cigarettes, trucking, shopping centers, clothing, construction, cable TV, even cheese. Federal organized crime prosecuters say mobsters of today are seeking legitimacy in unions and businesses. So far in Florida and the other places where the mob has moved seeking new identity, police have been able to do little more than watch." It is also alleged that they have a virtual monopoly on Italian cheese and now can force pizzeria owners to pay any price they demand (NBC News, 1977). In conclusion, the U.S. assistant attorney general said that the government is moving against these people and expects results soon: "We expect progress in two years and in 5, 6, 7 years in efforts to drive organized crime out of legitimate business" (NBC News, 1977). Presumably the idea was to drive these former racketeers out of the cheese business and back into heroin. There is clearly no rejoicing for a prodigal son coming home.

ATTEMPTS TO CONTROL ORGANIZED CRIME

The largely unchecked folklore regarding organized crime provides an important rationale for the provision in the Omnibus Crime Control and Safe Streets Act (1968:14) for court use of wiretap information. The bill reads:

> Organized criminals make extensive use of wire and oral communications in their criminal activities. The interception of such communications to obtain evidence of the commission of crimes or to prevent their commission is an indispensable aid to law enforcement and the administration of justice.

Regarding the legislative provision for the use of secretly collected wiretap information, one wonders just how well organized an "organized criminal" would have to be before qualifying for secret surveillance under this law. Would a conspiracy of any size qualify, or how about any crimes committed by persons with Italian surnames? Since the law does not define organized criminals, there is no way of knowing who is and who is not to be covered by this law. The danger in the absence of a clear definition of organized crime is that almost anyone could be subject to the provisions of this law because there are no specific limitations. Such an alteration in constitutional guarantees would not be sensible and could not be justified in combating local criminal gangs—about whose existence there is, of course, no dispute—but it can be defended, if at all, only on the assumption that organized crime is operated by a massive, well-integrated, interstate conspiracy. Cressey's research (1969:x) as a consultant to an official crime commission, using reports from law enforcements agencies, predictably convinced him of the government's claims of organized crime's massive proportions and certain threat. Because of organized crime's allegedly gigantic scale, he concluded (1969:323–324) that it cannot be effectively controlled by means of traditional law enforcement techniques. As a possible solution, he suggested that government agencies might attempt to control organized crime by means of a treaty much like those entered into with foreign enemy states. Such a document, Cressey said, might stipulate that [The] "Cosa Nostra would agree to give up its political involvements and its illegal operation of legitimate businesses . . . if it could be assured that it will be permitted to keep the profits, after taxes, on bet-taking" (1969:324). Obviously such an extreme proposal could seem credible only to persons who accept the image of a large-scale conspiracy that is especially ominous because of its movement out of the rackets and into legal businesses.

One need only to go back to the McCarthy era in the early 1950s, or to the relocation and internment of Japanese-Americans after the bombing of Pearl Harbor, to recognize that extreme measures are easily justified when people believe they are facing widespread conspiratorial threat. Unfortunately, criminlogists have purveyed the common belief in the conspiratorial threat posed by organized crime, usually without indicating the limitations of their sources.

Rufus King (1977), an attorney who served as legal counsel for the U.S. Senate committee that investigated organized crime during the 1950s, told of how the Washington, D.C., police force set up a sting operation by pretending to be a fencing business called PFF, Inc. (or Police FBI Fencing Incognito). This operation purchased stolen goods for five months and then threw a large party for all of the persons who had been selling the stolen goods to the undercover police. A mass arrest of the guests followed. The undercover police officials had pretended to be Mafia members, since "everybody knows" that the Mafia controls all such operations. "Most interesting of all, however, was the absence of any genuine Italian connection in any quarter. These career officers, with access to the intelligence resources of the nation's greatest law-enforcement agencies, had to improvise their Mafia roles from Hollywood" (King, 1977:71). And King concluded that no one from the "real Mafia" showed up to punish them for their deception in imitating the real thing, perhaps because such an organization never existed in the first place.

King also noted that despite all of the U.S. government's apparent concern with organized crime, there has been no serious reassessment of the realities of the Mafia since the 1950s. "One explanation may be that so long as the money keeps flowing, neither mercenary scholars nor affluent crimefighters want to jeopardize a good thing" (1977:74). King concluded that billions of dollars are being squandered and that both incompetence and gross corruption, as well, are excused on the ground that organized crime is an adversary that is beyond reach.

Some (Ruth, 1967) complain that the public does not react strongly to the threat of organized crime, and even some legal experts do not take the problem as seriously as they should, a prime example being Ramsey Clark, the former U.S. attorney general who claimed that organized crime is only a small part of the total crime problem. And not only is public apathy a problem, but it is sometimes claimed that the language of the average criminal statute is also an obstacle to effective enforcement. The language of the typical criminal statute is directed toward the operation of racketeering, not its organization. Statutes dealing with gambling, for example, control the bookmaker but not the organizers of these illegal activities if they are not involved on the functionary level (Reckless, 1967:339). Therefore one of the few means of prosecuting the leaders of organized crime is for tax evasion, and not for the actual racketeering. The recommendation is often made that criminal laws should be changed for easier prosecution of the rackets. But even if the written laws were more adequate to their task, there is still the problem of the corruption of political and law enforcement officials through bribery, making control of organized crime impossible.

There is not only the problem of the impossiblity of effective law enforcement but also the issue of what can be called the ethics of the legal control of vice in a democratic society (Tyler, 1962). What should the state do in a democracy if a sizable proportion of its citizens desire a specific service or commodity? This issue is well illustrated in a study by Gardiner (1970) of a community in which, at two different times during two different decades, local officials were voted out of office after outside investigators demonstrated that racketeers had corrupted these local politicians. For each scandal, the revelations caused a temporary crisis in which voters elected politicians of a different political party from the usual one in power. The local people were very indignant when corruption was made apparent to them, but otherwise they seemed little concerned about local gambling.

In fact, most local residents believed that there was nothing wrong with gambling itself (88 percent thought that bingo should be permitted and, in any event, believed that gambling could not be stopped by the law). These same people were hostile to corruption, but they did not infer corruption from the simple presence of gambling or prostitution in their community. The recurrent public disclosures of official corruption forced these residents to see that there was a contradiction between their tolerant attitudes toward gambling and their intolerance of corruption, and that gambling and corruption are necessarily related. But soon after the reform government would take office, the voters apparently would forget about this connection and vote for their usual political party. Gambling would then begin again until another outside investigation renewed public outrage.

It should be noted that, in the community under discussion, gambling permitted many otherwise outmoded businesses to survive, such as small grocery stores and other small shops. By selling "numbers," these stores could make enough profit to stay in business. When gambling was stopped by reform politicians, they were forced out of business. In addition, when the city had plenty of illegal gambling, many other retail businesses in the city thrived, including the bars and cafés that serviced the gamblers visiting the city. Even though these latter types of businesses did not violate the law, they benefited from illegal gambling nonetheless. Much of the business of racketeers involves prostitution, illegal drugs, and gambling, all of which involve supplying services or products that are illegal. It has been suggested that if these goods and services were legalized, this avenue for corruption would be greatly altered and possibly completely closed.

SUMMARY AND CONCLUSION

This chapter reviewed the imprecise definition of what is called organized crime, the Mafia, or La Cosa Nostra. Given this lack of clarity, it is not suprising that the logic used in proving the nature of organized crime has more in common with mythology than with science. There are considerable differences of opinion concerning the ethnicity of persons involved in organized crime, but the history of racketeering clearly demonstrates that it has existed since our nation's origins and has not been dependent on Italian immigration. There is accumulating evidence that organized crime is not nearly so strong nor so secret an enterprise as is often claimed. The relationship between organized crime and legitimate business is also the subject of considerable dispute, some researchers demonstrating not only close linkages but no essential difference. All these points of contention become of special importance because the answers to these questions determine what will ultimately become law enforcement policy.

In conclusion, there appears to be a difference between the social definition of actors and their acts. If white-collar crime is compared with organized crime, it becomes clear that the social definition or stigma attached to the actors is much more important in determining how others respond to them than the actors' behavior per se. For example, compare two persons—one an alleged Mafia chieftain and the other a top executive of an American corporation. Even if a business leader is involved in price-fixing or other corporate crime, the public may not be outraged, because a business leader is generally accorded great respect in our society. Sutherland (1949:46–51) observed that this respect for business leaders exists among the legislators responsible for drafting criminal laws and among the general public, in part because the mass media are controlled by business interests and usually describe these interests in the most favorable light. Sutherland also recognized, however, that legislators' respect for business leaders is supplemented by a measure of fear that corporate moneys will be used to unseat them should they pass legislation contrary to business interests. On the other hand, even if alleged Mafia figures are in a legitimate business, many law enforcement officials believe that they should be harassed and pursued. The widespread definitions of violence and organized crime can be demonstrated to serve the ends of specific elite, class, and powerful interest groups. These definitions include the notions that violence does not include deaths associated with structural defects of automobiles and that organized crime does not include large U.S. corporations but, rather, involves 24 Mafia families. As Reasons (1974:230) observed: "Our interest and concern with the 'organized underworld' has directed our attention away from the 'organized upperworld.' "

REFERENCES

ABC News
1981 "Nightline," January 7.
Albini, J. L.
1971 The American Mafia: Genesis of a Legend. New York: Appleton-Century-Crofts.
American Sociologist
1968 "Toward a code of ethics for sociologists." 3(November):316–318.
Anderson, R. T.
1965 "From Mafia to Cosa Nostra." American Journal of Sociology 71(November): 302–310.
Blakey, G. R.
1967 "Aspects of the evidence gathering process in organized crime cases: a preliminary analysis." Appendix C. In Task Force Report: Organized Crime, The President's Commission on Law Enforcement and Administration of Justice. Washington, D.C.: U.S. Government Printing Office.
Blakey, G. R., R. Goldstock, and C. H. Rogovin
1978 Rackets Bureaus: Investigation and Prosecution of Organized Crime. Washington, D.C.: National Institute of Law Enforcement and Criminal Justice, Law Enforcement Assistance Administration, U.S. Department of Justice.
Block, A. A. and W. J. Chambliss
1981 Organizing Crime. New York: Elsevier.
Breslin, J.
1969 The Gang That Couldn't Shoot Straight. New York: Viking.

CBS News
1981 "60 Minutes," January 4.
Chambliss, W. J.
1971 "Vice, corruption, bureaucracy, and power." Wisconsin Law Review 1971:1150–1173.
1978 On the Take: From Petty Crooks to Presidents. Bloomington: Indiana University Press.
Columbia (Mo.) Daily Tribune
1984 "Asian Mafia serious crime threat in U.S." October 23:3.
Cressey, D. R.
1967 "The functions and structure of criminal syndicates." Appendix A. In Task Force Report: Organized Crime. The President's Commission on Law Enforcement and Administration of Justice. Washington, D.C.: U.S. Government Printing Office.
1969 Theft of the Nation. New York: Harper & Row.
Demaris, O.
1981 The Last Mafioso: The Treacherous World of Jimmy Fratianno. New York: Times Books.
Gardiner, J. A.
1970 The Politics of Corruption: Organized Crime in an American City. New York: Russell Sage Foundation.
Hawkins, G.
1969 "God and the Mafia." The Public Interest 14(Winter):24–51.

Ianni, F. A. J.
  1972 A Family Business: Kinship and Social Control in Organized Crime. New York: Russell Sage Foundation.
  1974 Black Mafia: Ethnic Succession in Organized Crime. New York: Simon & Schuster.
Kempton, M.
  1969 "Crime does not pay." New York Review of Books 13(September 11):5, 6, 8, 10.
Kennedy, R. F.
  1960 The Enemy Within. New York: Harper & Row.
King, R.
  1977 "Looking for the Lost: Mafia." Harpers (January):68–75.
Landesco, J.
  1968 Organized Crime in Chicago. Chicago: University of Chicago Press.
Mass, P.
  1968 The Valachi Papers. New York: Bantam Books.
Matza, D.
  1969 Becoming Deviant. Englewood Cliffs, N.J.: Prentice Hall.
Moore, W. H.
  1974 The Kefauver Committee and the Politics of Crime, 1950–1952. Columbia: University of Missouri Press.
Morris, N. and G. Hawkins
  1969 The Honest Politician's Guide to Crime Control. Chicago: University of Chicago Press.
Nelli, H. S.
  1969 "Italians and crime in Chicago: the formative years, 1980–1920." American Journal of Sociology 74(January):373–391.
Newsweek
  1981 "How the Mob really works." January 5:34–43.
NBC News
  1977 "Five-part series on the new Mob," December 12, 1977, to December 16, 1977.
NBC News Magazine
  1981 "The Israeli Mafia," September 11.
Omnibus Crime Control and Safe Streets Act
  1968 Public Law 90–351, 90th Congress, H.R. 5037 (June 19).
Polsky, N.
  1967 Hustlers, Beats and Others. Chicago: Aldine.
Puzo, M.
  1969 The Godfather. New York: Fawcett World Library.
Reasons, C. E.
  1974 The Criminologist: Crime and the Criminal. Pacific Palisades, Calif.: Goodyear.
Reckless, W. C.
  1967 The Crime Problem. 4th ed. East Norwalk, Conn.: Appleton-Century-Crofts.

Ruth, H. S., Jr.
  1967 "Why organized crime thrives." Annals of the American Academy of Political and Social Science 374(November):113–122.
Schelling, T. C.
  1967 "Economic analysis and organized crime." Appendix D. Task Force Report: Organized Crime. U.S. President's Commission on Law Enforcement and Administration of Justice. Washington, D.C.: U.S. Government Printing Office.
Smith, D. C.
  1975 The Mafia Mystique. New York: Basic Books.
Smith, D. C. and R. D. Alba
  1979 "Organized crime and american life." Society 16(March/April):32–38.
Sutherland, E. H.
  1949 White Collar Crime. New York: Holt, Rinehart & Winston.
Talese, G.
  1971 Honor Thy Father. New York: World.
Task Force Report: Organized Crime
  1967 The President's Commission on Law Enforcement and Administration of Justice. Washington, D.C.: U.S. Government Printing Office.
Teresa, V.
  1973 My Life in the Mafia. Garden City, N.Y.: Doubleday.
Time
  1977a "The Mafia: big, bad and booming." May 16:32–42.
  1977b "Youth for sale on the streets." November 28:23.
  1978 "Trouble in Las Vegas East." January 16:14.
  1980 "On the record." December 29:45.
Tyler, G.
  1962 Organized Crime in America: A Book of Readings. Ann Arbor: University of Michigan Press.
United States Comptroller General
  1977 Report to the Congress: War on Organized Crime Faltering: Federal Strike Forces Not Getting Job Done. Washington, D.C.: Department of Justice (March 17).
United States Justice Department
  1972 Police Guide on Organized Crime. Washington, D.C.: Law Enforcement Assistance Administration.
Vitello, P. and K. Royce
  1981 "'Small-time hood' makes it big as government witness." Kansas City (Mo.) Times, January 5:A1, A4.
Woetzel, R. K.
  1963 "An overview of organized crime: mores versus morality." Annals of the American Academy of Political and Social Science 347(May):1–11.

5
THE MEASUREMENT
OF CRIME

THE CREATION OF CRIME WAVES

Americans are constantly told by political leaders, police, and the press that our society is facing crime rates that, with few exceptions, increase from year to year. These same general claims about soaring crime rates are nothing new. As early as 1895, Emile Durkheim wrote that crime statistics demonstrated that in France, criminality had increased approximately 300 percent since the beginning of the nineteenth century (Weis and Milakovich, 1974). Moreover, Weis and Milakovich observed (1974:29) that even as early as 600 B.C. in the Promised Land, it was reported in Ezekiel 7:23 that "the land is full of bloody crimes, and the city is full of violence." Obviously there is a logical impossibility in these claims of an ever-increasing rate of crime.

The Federal Bureau of Investigation (FBI) has used the picture of a clock, called the Crime Clock, in its annual reports. In 1980, for example, it indicated that someone was murdered every half hour in this country. The Crime Clock is misleading, however, because although there are twice as many murders today as in 1933, the population has also approximately doubled; the likelihood of being a murder victim has not increased (Wright, 1985). And we are no longer a nation of farms and small towns. Most of us live in or near massive cities with many reported crimes, and therefore our perception is that we are exposed to more crime. Thus the first problem in the measurement of crime is that it is a socially defined event (Wright, 1985).

On the heels of President Ronald Reagan's first inauguration, the new U.S. attorney general called a press conference and declared crime to be officially "out of control" (*Los Angeles Times,* 1981). In that same week, and in fact on the same day, both *Time* and *Newsweek* (March 23, 1981) published cover stories supporting the attorney general's claim. *Time* used the headline "The Curse of Violent Crime," and *Newsweek* used "The Epidemic of Violent Crime." Both magazines had pictures of pistols pointed at the reader to help make their point. To add more zip to an already frightening story, the *Time* essay quoted a former director of the Bureau of Justice Statistics, who made the ridiculous prediction that "within four or five years every household in the country will be hit by crime" (1981:17). A little later that year (October 12), *U.S. News & World Report* again had a pistol pointing at the reader on its cover with the headline "Our Losing Battle Against Crime." Early the following year (April 1982), *Life* magazine used a picture of this same type of pistol but now used the headline "Guns Are Out of Control." Clearly there seems to be something artificial about these sudden claims of crime's being out of control, coinciding as they did so closely with the assertion of the attorney general.

Indeed, recent research (Fishman, 1978) demonstrated that crime waves do have something of an artificial quality. For crime waves to occur, journalists must first be sensitized, or ready to observe a specific type of crime wave, and this readiness may or may not be related to evidence of actual increases of crime in the community. In 1976 and 1977, journalists in New York City were expecting, and indeed were predicting, a war among the area's various organized crime families. Even so, these writers never got enough reports on this topic to develop such a theme into a media-created crime wave. On the other hand, recently there has apparently developed a crime wave against elderly persons—that is, there has been a great increase in articles reporting such crime. But no such increase in actual crimes against elderly persons can be found in police records. Apparently the press was ready for a surge in such stories, and enough elderly victims were available to be used in such increased reporting.

Fishman (1978) explained how reporting of a crime wave can happen. In large cities there are simply too many crimes occurring and too many crimes known to the local police for the police beat reporters to know them all. Therefore journalists depend on a police summary of these events, known as the "police wire." For example, all the major media in the city receive teletype reports from the New York City Police Department's Office of Public Information; the number of reports ranges from 12 to 25 a day. If the local police of a city believe that the press is interested in writing about specific types of crime, such as crimes against elderly persons or among leaders of organized crime, such cases will be included in the crime summary whenever they arise.

Of course, if the police have the power to emphasize certain types of crimes, they also have the power to refuse to report certain types of crime themes. In the crime summary, police seldom include information on victim-offender relationships, and the specific location is mentioned only if the crime occurred in a public place such as the street, a schoolyard, an apartment hallway, or a subway (Fishman, 1978). Since victim-offender relationships are rarely mentioned, and since only public places are mentioned, this leaves the impression that most crime occurs between strangers in public places. In point of fact, nothing could be further from the truth. Some evidence shows that people have a greater chance of being victimized in their own home and by someone whom they know well, such as a lover, spouse, or other family member (Wolfgang, 1958).

There are some other artificial qualities to these crime waves. Certain types of offenses never become a part of this police wire (Fishman, 1978:539); the police do not report to the press on such offenses as "price-fixing, consumer fraud, sub-standard housing, unhealthy food, environmental pollution, political bribery and corruption." Police do not report on these offenses because they do not enforce these laws. Police are responsible only for controlling street crime and therefore can report only on such offenses. Certain crimes, such as bicycle theft, and rape or wife beating that does not result in death or hospitalization, are considered too common by the police to be reported. And not all street crime that appears on the police wire will end up in the press. Political leaders and other government authorities can use their power to stop certain themes from becoming crime waves. These leaders can deny the existence of a crime wave and demand that coverage be directed elsewhere. For example, when several articles on subway crime appeared in the *New York Daily News*, the head of the city transit authority told the news reporter that there was no subway crime wave; articles on this topic stopped.

Recently, there has been mounting evidence that the widespread paranoia about missing children may be in large part a consequence of exaggeration (*Denver Post*, 1985). The problem of missing children became a visible national issue after 28 children disappeared in Atlanta between 1979 and 1981, and after a 6-year-old Florida boy, Adam Walsh, was abducted and murdered in 1981. Adam's father, John Walsh, launched a national campaign to locate missing children, and his story was made into a made-for-television movie, which has been broadcast several times. His efforts also helped create a national agency that tracks missing children. In testimony before Congress that was portrayed in the movie, Walsh maintained that 1.5 million children disappear each year. As a consequence of such claims, the faces of missing children are now found on milk cartons and flashed on television screens. Indeed, the fear is so great that one company advertized an electronic transmitter that can be attached to a child's clothing to keep track of his or her exact location (Best, 1987). But the FBI reported that it had only 67 cases of child kidnapping in 1984, and the National Safety Council places the number at 80. Law enforcement authorities indicate that about 95 percent of missing children reports are on runaways, and most of these children return within 3 days. In March 1985, for example, 27,489 missing children reports were entered into the FBI's computer, but by the month's end, 27,520 cases had been removed. One additional problem associated with this hysteria is that many communities across the nation have initiated programs on

"Stranger Danger" to instill warnings in the children and have begun to fingerprint and photograph all local youngsters, scaring them greatly in the process *(St. Louis Post-Dispatch,* 1985).

Conklin (1975) observed that the feeling that a crime crisis exists is more likely to be generated by crime reporting in the mass media than by official crime rates. Crime reports in the mass media are more accessible and more easily understood than official crime rates, and therefore people's ideas about the gravity of the crime problem are more closely tied to mass media reports than to official reports. This, Conklin noted, is especially true in the United States, where newspapers have typically given more attention to sensationalist crime reporting than have the newspapers of other nations. The seemingly capricious nature of crime reporting in American newspapers was reflected in a Colorado study (Davis, 1952), which found great variation in the amount of space devoted to crime stories in various Colorado newspapers but no relationship between local crime rates and the amount of crime news in the local newspapers. At times there was a negative relationship between official rates of crime and the amount of crime news. Conklin (1975:24) suggested that the distorted nature of crime reporting is also reflected in the great variation in the space devoted to crime problems in competing daily newspapers in the same cities. Some newspapers devote relatively little space to crime, whereas others give the subject considerably more coverage.

The motivation for artificially created crime waves may appear to be a mystery to most Americans, especially those who believe in a truly independent watchdog press, such as that guaranteed by the First Amendment to the U.S. Constitution. However, as Sallach (1974) observed, most of the nation's mass media not only are owned by large corporations but require advertising from large corporations. Journalists' claims of an independent news media that serves the public interest is largely a myth, because journalists give relatively little attention to the misdeeds of giant corporations. A public with an unquestioning conception of crime serves the interests of the giant corporations in their efforts to protect themselves from a potentially rebellious and demanding citizenry. It is in the interest of these corporations to control the public image of the amount, and especially the nature, of crime. The typical media message is that the nation faces a crime crisis involving purse snatching, burglary, and the Mafia, but usually nothing is said about the criminal activities of large corporations. (See also Molotch and Lester, 1974:104–105, for a discussion of media control by elites.)

VARIOUS OFFICIAL CRIME RECORDS

The various methods of measuring crime include the use of police records, records of court proceedings, and records of correctional institutions. Insurance company records of claims made for property losses through theft and destruction provide an alternative avenue of gauging the frequency of some property crime. Anonymous questionnaires can be used to estimate the magnitude of criminal behavior in a given population, and interviews with samples of citizens can be used to determine whether, during a given year, they have been victims of any of a variety of crimes. The most widely used and most commonly accepted measures of the magnitude of crimes are the frequencies found in police records, which are usually expressed in rates per 100,000 population in a given political jurisdiction. In this chapter the various measures of crime will be evaluated in terms of how accurately they report criminal behavior.

There is some debate as to whether court or police statistics are the best measures of crime (Sellin and Wolfgang, 1964). Among persons who opt for one or the other of these choices, there are other differences. Among those who argued for the use of court statistics, many conclude that counting convictions is the most adequate measure of crime, whereas others hold that all cases coming before the courts should be counted. Among advocates of the use of police records, some adhere to the use of arrests or other crimes that the police know to have occurred, whereas others argue that all crimes reported to the police should be counted, including those whose existence the police have been unable to verify. As will be seen below, the amount of crime reported will vary considerably, depending on which of these crime measures is ultimately selected.

Although at present there is considerable acceptance of the FBI's Uniform Crime Reports (which are based on police records) as a reflection of actual crime, some believe that court records may have advantages over these police records (Sellin and Wolfgang, 1964). For those who think of the Uniform Crime Reports as the only reasonable way of reporting crime, it is instructive to learn that before World War I, most countries used only judicial statistics and that the switch to police records has been made only recently in the twentieth century. One argument against the use of judicial records is that people are frequently accused of a number of crimes but are tried only for the most serious one. Thus the judicial records would exaggerate most serious crimes and minimize lesser crimes. It is also argued that the number of violators disclosed by judicial records does not reflect the number of law violations; one person may commit many crimes, or several persons may conspire to commit the same crime, and these differences do not necessarily balance each other out. On the other hand, some crime cannot be accurately counted until the personal responsibility of the suspect has been assessed by the court and all the facts of the case have been presented and weighed as evidence. This, of course, argues for the use of judicial records (Sellin and Wolfgang, 1964). But one problem with court records is that a trial cannot be held until a suspect has been captured; if the accused person is never found, the crimes will never be placed into the court records. It should also be noted that the existence of many types of crimes can be determined before any person has been prosecuted for them. Most homicides clearly illustrate crime that is proved before any hearing is held.

Pepinsky (1976a) traced the development of official crime records and observed that, in 1827, France became the first jurisdiction to collect nationwide conviction statistics. In the United States the earliest figures recorded on a state-wide basis involved judicial statistics in New York State in 1829. Massachusetts began collecting prison statistics in 1834. By 1905, a total of 25 states were compiling statistics on persons who had been tried and convicted. By the early 1900s, it was argued that judicial statistics were superior to prison statistics because the former were "far more complete" (Pepinsky, 1976a:25). Therefore, if one follows this logic, it was recognized by the 1930s that arrest statistics were even more complete than judicial records. Even more inclusive than arrest records are those crimes "known to the police." Thus it is not surprising that by 1930 the FBI began to compile this last type of information.

Police reports are not without their problems, however (Sellin and Wolfgang, 1964). Many types of crime, such as prostitution, gambling, and narcotics offenses, are seldom reported to the police, and therefore the police must collect all information on these offenses on their own, with little or no help from the community. This being true, if there is any change in the amount of emphasis placed on these offenses by a police department, the rates of such crimes will fluctuate accordingly. Indeed, some sociologists have argued that official records of crime indicate almost nothing about the amount of crime in a community but a lot about the operation of the agency that compiles these reports (Kitsuse and Cicourel, 1963). Further, because the police cannot be everywhere in the community at once, much of what finds its way into police records is reported to the police by private citizens, and what is reported will depend on whether the behavior is considered a serious infraction by the local community. Such community standards vary substantially from one community to another, even within the same nation. Perhaps the best illustration in the United States is the special tolerance of the public expression of homosexual attraction in San Francisco, California, which is unmatched in much of the rest of the nation. And toleration of drug use is undoubtedly greater in Greenwich Village, in New York City, than in Tulsa, Oklahoma, or Jackson, Mississippi.

In an assessment of conviction rates as a type of crime statistic, it should be noted that the relationship between the police and the courts must be considered (Tappan, 1960:364–365). Some judges may be willing and eager to convict defendants, even in cases where the evidence has been illegally seized. Other judges may insist on a careful hearing of the evidence and thus may discharge a greater percentage of defendants. Thus a high rate of dismissal at the trial court does not necessarily mean that the court is poorly run. To make an informed assessment of the meaning of these rates of conviction, one must also know what is happening at earlier stages in the legal process. One cannot assess the operation of the trial court without knowing something of the operation of the police. If the police are ineffective, severe limits will be placed on what a trial court can accomplish.

Clearly there are some crimes that have direct and obvious victims, such as assault or theft, in which either the victim or the victim's relatives or friends will be likely to report the offense to the police (Sellin and Wolfgang, 1964). But there are other crimes in which there are no personal victims or in which there are no victims who recognize that they have been victimized. The illegal and artificial inflation of consumer prices by business leaders through price-fixing is one such illustration. There are some types of crimes that do not directly affect any person, such as crimes of public drunkenness, prostitution, and vagrancy. Police only rarely receive complaints about any offenses without direct and personal victims. Only in cases with direct and personal victims can there be even a minimal certainty in police or court records.

POLITICAL AND TECHNICAL PROBLEMS IN CRIME RECORDING

Police Records

When crime rates are discussed, the source of information is usually the FBI Uniform Crime Reports. The Uniform Crime Reports is an annual FBI publication that gives a detailed description of crime patterns in the United States for the year. For each state and every city over 10,000, it itemizes the frequency of all major types of crimes reported to, or discovered by, the police. A separate report of all arrests is also included. The FBI also records information about juvenile misbehavior, including crimes committed by juveniles and two juvenile-status offenses, running away and curfew violations. The FBI Uniform Crime Reports distinguishes two types of offense categories—Part I and Part II crimes. Part I crimes, which are used to make up the highly publicized Crime Index, originally included only seven offenses: criminal homicide, forcible rape, robbery, aggravated assault, burglary, automobile theft, and larceny-theft. By an act of Congress in 1978, arson was added to this list of Part I crimes. Indeed, it is hard to understand how it ever happened that the destructive, costly, and life-threatening crime of arson was ever categorized as anything other than a major crime. Crimes are included in this count of Part I crimes if they are reported to, or in any other way known by, the police. Part II crimes include all other offenses, including such allegedly minor crimes as driving while intoxicated, fraud, embezzlement, and child abuse. Here the count is limited to cases in which suspects are apprehended and arrests made.

What is most curious about these "minor crimes" is that many, if not most, of them seem as serious as the Part I crimes. Any larceny, including the theft of a bicycle, is considered major crime, whereas child abuse is considered minor crime. Apparently, abusing a child is not considered as grave a malfeasance as similarly mistreating an adult (an assault) or stealing a bicycle. And the embezzlement of millions of dollars is apparently not considered as serious as bicycle theft. Finally, once again it appears that everybody loves a funny drunk, even one behind the wheel of a car—apparently forgetting that drunk drivers kill and maim thousands every year on America's streets and highways. American humor is built on drunk drivers, as in the following old and tired joke: "A very intoxicated patron of a bar is preparing to leave and is asked by the bartender: 'Are you going to drive home in your condition?' To which the drunk replies, 'Of course I'm going to drive home. I'm certainly too drunk to walk.' " In the case of drunk driving, at least, the placement of this offense in the category of minor crime does appear to reflect American ambivalence toward this behavior. And if only comparisons within the Part I category are considered, it seems curious that minor theft should be included in the same category of crime as rape and murder. It seems as though this categorization denigrates the importance of both rape and murder.

The crime rates published in the Uniform Crime Reports are based on the results of a questionnaire that all police departments are asked to complete annually. The FBI has no legal power to force departments to report, and some departments, especially the smaller ones in rural areas, do not report. Moreover, there is no provision for auditing department reports. Police recognize that the crime rates reported to the FBI may be used to rate their department's effectiveness. If they accurately report all crime, the high rates in their areas may convince some people that they are not doing a good job.

Police often attempt to persuade the public that they are doing a good job in controlling crime, but they also want to convey the message that crime is still a great threat. This apparently contradictory message of both decreases and increases in crime seems logically impossible, but it was achieved by the recent Justice Department claims that crime was increasing at a decreasing rate (Weis and Milakovich, 1974:27). Government officials can argue, for example, that an 8 percent increase in crime in a given year actually represents a reduction in comparison with a previous yearly increase of 10 percent, but this, of course, ignores the fact that smaller percentage increments are predictable as the base from which the increments are calculated increases. One problem with official police records is that the temptation to alter the figures may be very strong. If a police force has received public funds to show a crime decrease, the pressure is very great to do just that. And politicians running for reelection may feel the need to credit their leadership with similar reductions. The FBI does not have the legal responsibility of auditing local police figures that are reported to them. Even if such audits were possible, one could conclude that because arrest data reflect on police activities, a police organization such as the FBI should not be collecting the data (Weis and Milakovich, 1974:30). Clearly some trusted and disinterested agency should be charged with the collection, analysis, and publication of this information.

In 1950, New York City reported crime figures to the FBI that seemed very low. The FBI typically accepts police department reports at face value, but in this instance the FBI did some checking and found that the number of property crimes reported by the police was approximately half the number reported to insurance companies (Bell, 1960:152). In this case, it appears that the police department was not telling the whole story to the FBI to avoid the embarrassment that a high crime rate might cause to city officials. A more recent distortion of police records occurred in Washington, D.C. The political scientist David Seidman (*Time*, 1972:55) found that "the police tend not even to record crime they believe they have little or no chance of solving." Moreover, the accounting firm of Ernst and Ernst audited the Washington, D.C., police records and found that more than 1,000 thefts of over $50 had been purposely downgraded to below $50. That made these thefts misdemeanors and dropped them from the roster of major crimes, which the department was committed to reducing. The chief of police in the District of Columbia, Jerry Wilson, firmly, if unconvincingly, denied any wrongdoing: "Where did 202 crimes a day go? I mean, I didn't eat them!" In fairness to Chief Wilson, it should be noted that Washington was President Nixon's primary demonstration area for his "war on crime" policies (Pepinsky, 1976a). With the Nixon administration, history records that anything was possible and that it became administration policy that crime rates would come down. Chief Wilson had two choices: report a lower crime rate in accordance with President Nixon's predictions or lose his job.

However, it should be mentioned that an effect of inflation is to increase the number of thefts of over $50, independent of any real increases in thefts. A $25 item stolen 10 years ago may now be valued at over $50. A consequence of prosperity has been an increase in burglary and theft insurance, which requires the reporting of losses to the police as a condition for making an insurance claim (Biderman, 1966:119–120). Thus a greater proportion of reported losses might also make it falsely appear that property crime is increasing. Perhaps as a result of these problems of political abuse and inflation, since 1973 the FBI has included all larcenies in its major crime index, not just those over $50, as was previously the case.

As indicated above, among persons urging the use of police data in the study of crime, some support the procedure of counting as crimes only those events that the police have seen or discovered to have been crimes, whereas others support the idea of using as data all events known to, or reported to, the police as crimes to avoid ignoring important information on crime (Sellin and Wolfgang, 1964). The problem of missing information is especially common for Part II crimes, because many of these offenses never result in clearance by arrest and are therefore not recorded.

Although most Americans seem to have become accustomed to crime statistics reported from police records, the accuracy of police statistics varies with the type of crime. Crimes such as vice, including gambling and prostitution, almost never become known to the police through reporting, either because there are no victims in the traditional sense or because the victimized do not know that they are victims. Such crimes must be discovered by the police through routine patrol, undercover work, or informants. This means that changes in the intensity of law enforcement activity, and not changes in the amount of such crime, may account for changes in the number of such offenses detected. The police are more often notified if the victims are harmed directly, as in assaults and theft. In such cases there is often someone—the victim or a friend or relative of the victim—who will call the police. Even when there is a victim in the traditional sense, however, a crime may not be reported to the police because of a belief that the police either cannot or will not do anything about it (Gould, 1971:89). Crime victims may correctly recognize that the chance that the police will locate their television set is very remote, and some minority people may believe that the chance that the police will actually make a thorough investigation of their assault is very remote.

Cicourel (1968) suggested that a very different picture of the extent and distribution of juvenile delinquency is obtained (1) by looking at official police records and (2) by looking at all cases known to the police. For one thing, the attitude of the youth is important in determining how his or her behavior will initially be interpreted by the police officer and how it will ultimately be reported in the official record. Moreover, the middle- or upper-class child typically has the advantage of a conventional family unit that can show its concern, which, in an officer's judgment, bodes well for the youth's future behavior. Both of these elements are important in determining whether an officer will see a particular behavior as serious. Such characteristics as a "bad attitude" or a "poor home environment" transform the juvenile into a person in need of formal disposition irrespective of the seriousness of the behavior in question. Even the repeated relatively violent acts of middle- and upper-class youths may be defined away as evidence of a natural phase of growing up in a troubled world or, at worst, as evidence that the youths need professional and medical help. On the other hand, crimes committed by children from racial and economic minority groups, especially if the children are defiant, supply evidence to the police of the beginnings of a criminal career that must be nipped in the bud by some official action, such as incarceration. This shows how formal arrest records reflect both American racism and an interest in the protection of the affluent.

Other Official Crime Statistics

Whether court or police statistics are used, changes in the number of arrests, trials, or sentences may not represent actual changes in the amount of crime but, rather, changes in the capacity of various elements of the legal system. Increases or decreases in the number of police, judges, courtrooms, or bed space in correctional institutions will undoubtedly influence these statistics (Lejins, 1961). There is no doubt about it; more police, more judges, and more prisons appear to have a nearly infinite capacity to increase the amount of officially recorded crime.

Van Vechten (1942) demonstrated that a loss of cases occurs at each stage in the criminal justice process, beginning with the crimes known to the police and continuing through arrests, prosecutions, convictions, and sentences. Sellin (1931:335–336) also argued that the adequacy of a crime index decreases as the distance increases between the criminal act and the statistical base used in record keeping in terms of the steps in the criminal justice process. Sellin (1931:346), stated that *"the value of a crime rate for index purposes decreases as the distance from the crime itself in terms of procedure increases.* In other words, police statistics, particularly those of 'crimes known to the police,' are most likely to furnish a good basis for a crime index." The records of a crime—from the time it becomes known to the police to its disposition by arrest, prosecution, conviction, and commitment to a penal institution—represent successive steps in procedure. Crime rates based on these steps are all end results of a selective process into which enter the willingness to report a crime, the desire to record it, the ability on the part of the police to detect and arrest the criminal, the policy that guides the prosecutor in deciding whether to bring the offender to trial at all, or to trial on the crime charged, the desire on the part of the jury or the judge to convict, and, finally, the sentencing policy of the judge (Sellin, 1931:34).

Sellin's argument holds that for a variety of reasons, including bargained-for guilty pleas for lesser charges, police records are of more value in reflecting the actual crime situation than are either court or institutional records. But it is also true that some innocent people are ultimately found not guilty in court, and in such cases the court records are more adequate. With Sellin's argument, however, the most *representative* measure of the crimes that actually occur consists of the crimes known to the police, including those not recorded by them, followed, in order, by measures of crimes recorded by the police, suspects charged, suspects tried, suspects convicted, and finally, convicted persons sentenced to a correctional institution.

Unfortunately, the most representative measure—crimes known to the police—is least likely to provide an *accurate count* of the cases known to law enforcement officials at this level. Going into a police department and securing information about the total number of crimes known to the police, including those which for various reasons do not result in arrests, would be difficult, if not impossible, because of the concern of the police for secrecy about their activities. Asking police officials about how they use their discretion is sure to cause them great concern. The inference they are sure to make is that the questioner is attempting to find out about the special deals they make, sometimes for financial considerations, sometimes because of political pressure on the department, and sometimes for other reasons. On the other hand, officials willingly provide the most accurate counts on the least representative data of all, those obtainable from institutional records (Taft and England, 1964:53). Any prison staff can quickly and accurately supply data on the number of persons it has in custody and the crimes for which they have been sentenced. In fact, most prison staff members are accustomed to counting, and a prison population is typically counted several times each day; even a discrepancy of one is cause for great alarm because of a possible escape.

Interpretation of Official Crime Records: An Illustration

Even when agreement is reached on the use of a given crime index, its interpretation may be problematic. Common opinion holds that modern American cities are becoming more and more violent and dangerous. However, one study of a major American city shows that this assumption may be false and that it may be a result of considering only very recent trends in crime rates. Ferdinand (1967) indicated that in Boston the rate of both minor crime and major violent crime has decreased over the preceding 100 years. Per capita arrests for minor crimes have dropped steadily during this period because in modern Boston the police appear to be less vigilant in making arrests for such minor offenses. However, there probably has been little change in how murder, forcible rape, robbery, or burglary has been handled by the police and courts over this same period. In any case, the official overall crime rate for Boston is only one third of that in 1878.

The question is, How can crime be increasing in the United States if the crime rate is decreasing in major cities such as Boston? Ferdinand suggests that the increase is occurring because an increasing percentage of our nation's population lives in cities, where, even though the crime rate is going down, it is still higher than the rural rate. The following table, based on an example from Ferdinand (1967:99), demonstrates his point:

Population, 1870	Urban and rural crime rates, 1870	Overall crime rate, 1870
80% rural	40/1000	52/1000
20% urban	100/1000	

Population, 1970	Urban and rural crime rates, 1970	Overall crime rate, 1970
10% rural	40/1000	58/1000
90% urban	60/1000	

The argument is outlined below:

- Crime rates in major cities have been decreasing.
- Crime rates remain higher in major cities than in rural areas.
- The proportion of the population living in cities has been rapidly increasing.
- The overall nationwide crime rate has been going up.
- The overall increase in the crime rate is due to massive population shifts to the cities, where the crime rate, though decreasing, is still higher than the rural crime rate.

Such research contradicts our current crisis orientation toward crime, especially in larger American cities. Puttkammer (1953:52–53) recognized that crime waves, or crime crises, are largely artificially created situations and that they often result from increased press activity and concern. Such intense press coverage may, in turn, generate more police activity, and this activity sends the arrest rates up. The rise in arrest rates has the circular effect of giving the media even more material regarding crime with which to further alarm the public.

THE MEANING AND CONSTRUCTION OF CRIME RATES

Earlier we discussed the arbitrary nature of what is termed crime. The definition of crime varies not only among countries but among states as well. Persons who study the patterns of crime are often interested in comparing nations and states. The problem with this effort is that in many cases the same type of behavior may not be defined as the same type of crime among various states and various nations (Taft and England, 1964:47). An act may be a major crime in one state and a minor crime or not a crime at all in another, as with marihuana possession or homosexual relations between consenting adults. Thus, for example, in some states in the United States possession of even one ounce of marihuana is classified as a major crime, whereas in others it may require possession of several ounces; in other areas, including Alaska, possession of marihuana for personal use is defined as a constitutional right. Obviously such differences in statutory definitions must be considered in interstate and international comparisons.

Moreover, the evidence required to obtain proof of the same crime may require different factual material in different states or nations. This makes the task of comparing crime rates among jurisdictions very difficult (Taft and England, 1964:47). In addition, especially in youth-generated crime, there is wide agreement that at least part of the recent increase can be accounted for by changing definitions of crime and delinquency. Acts that a century ago might have been called orneriness and handled informally with a good thrashing are now subject to official control mechanisms and called crime (Tetters and Matza, 1959).

As the youth in a country increase both in raw numbers and in their proportion to the total population, one would, of course, expect more youth crime. However, if crime rates are calculated on the basis of the number of crimes per 100,000 people committed in a given area during a specific period, as is usually the case, no controls can be made for changes in the proportion of youths in the society. Thus it may falsely appear that the *rates* of youth crime are increasing, when in fact the society is experiencing rapid growth in the relative size of the cohort of young males, who are responsible for most street crime.

A murder rate of 5.0 would indicate that five murders were recorded for every 100,000 people in an area. This method of indicating the amount of crime in a given area has been accepted unquestioningly. The method assumes that all people in the area should be included in the calculations. However, it is by no means clear that this is the most accurate way of showing the propensity toward crime in a given area. We know, for example, that most crime is committed by males between the ages of 15 and 40 years, and therefore perhaps only this group should be used as a base in calculating crime rates. Clearly, if a group of people cannot potentially be included in the numerator of the crime rates as either perpetrators or victims, then they should not be included in the denominator. Two-year-old children should not be included in the denominator in calculating rates of armed robberies, because they can neither commit nor be victimized by such offenses. Moreover, it is not clear that the traditional method of calculating crime rates is meaningful to most citizens. Mayors in many large American metropolitan areas claim that their cities have lower crime rates than do many small towns, but there is no evidence that people find this reassuring: people seem more concerned with the total number of crimes than with crime rates. Obviously, if American cities continue to grow, even if crime rates go down in these cities, as was found by Ferdinand (1967) to be true of Boston, there may be a larger number of crimes for newspapers and other media to report if crime rates remain higher in the cities than in rural areas. According to Wolfgang (1967:253), people are less interested in the rate of crime than in their perceived probability of being victims of crime. This perceived probability may increase, not in accordance with actual crime rates, but as a result of changes in the total number of crimes reported.

Lemert (1951:57–58) suggested that it is useful to think of crime waves in terms of what he called the public's *tolerance quotient.* This is the ratio of actual criminal behavior to the public's tolerance of criminal behavior. If the public's tolerance is initially very low, then even slight changes in the amount of criminal behavior can generate a perceived crime wave. Two communities may have very different tolerance quotients, even though the actual crime is the same in both areas. The public's tolerance may simply be greater in one community than in the other. The public's tolerance of crime in general, or of specific types of crime, can be measured by asking citizens to suggest appropriate criminal sanctions for various crimes and by asking them to rate the relative seriousness of a series of criminal offenses.

It has also been suggested that instead of comparing the occurrence of a specific crime to a total or specific population, the occurrence of a specific crime should be compared to the amount of opportunity for that type of crime in a given area (Boggs, 1965). For example, environmental opportunities for crime vary from one neighborhood to another, depending on the activities that prevail in different sections of the city. The availability of such targets as safes, cash registers, dispensing machines, and people and their possessions is distributed differently across any city. Thus in calculations of rape rates, for example, the number of females might serve as a revised total population figure, or in calculations of automobile theft rates, the amount of space for parking automobiles could be used as the base. Some areas in the center of large cities, such as midtown Manhattan in New York City, may well have little auto theft because there is simply no place to park cars, which would then be available to be stolen.

It is clear that the way crime rates are constructed represents an implicit theory about crime causation. If environmental measures are used as a crime rate denominator, the argument is that the amount of crime is somehow importantly related to opportunity to commit crime. This is in contrast to the usual assumption that crime is somehow importantly related to the size of the total population—including infants. Another issue is that a city proper usually contains only a small proportion of all persons in a total urban area. Therefore the crime rate in the city will be high because the denominator of the rate underestimates the total number of potential victims and offenders. Where a total urban area contains only one central city, this central city attracts many nonresidents and accordingly inflates the crime rate there. Thus, for a more accurate picture of crime rates, the denominator should include all residents of the total urban sprawl (Gibbs and Erickson, 1976).

Moreover, the fact that most crime rate reports, including the FBI's, include rates for various racial groups can easily be interpreted as a form of racism. Gilbert Geis's (1965) question is, If crime rates are reported for black Americans, why not for Baptists and Republicans? His point is that using racial distinctions in crime reporting, and not religious or political distinctions, reflects a form of racial prejudice and discrimination. Race, not religion, is implicitly assumed to be important in crime causation. Students of criminology have become accustomed to reporting on racial differences in crime rates of various kinds, but it is possible to imagine the cries of covert prejudice if one attempted to study Jewish rates of shoplifting or Roman Catholic rates of rape.

In calculating the magnitude of the crime problem, one could consider, along with opportunity to commit crime, the amount of loss to victims, or, alternatively, the damage crime causes to public confidence in, and respect for, law and order (Gould, 1971:92–97). Although denominators based on such alternatives are not easy to construct, an example is possible. When the number of registered motor vehicles, rather than population, is used as the denominator (opportunity to commit crime), auto theft shows a great decrease in recent years rather than an increase, as when population figures are used.

The problem with these alternative denominators is that they do not fit most Americans' concept of "crime," which is inseparable from the concept of the "criminal" as a class set apart from the rest of society. What is important to Americans is not how many crimes are committed per unit of property but how many criminals are loose in the society and whether the citizen's personal risk of being victimized has increased. Therefore, Americans understand per capita crime rates better than they understand crime rates using property loss information.

OTHER CRIME MEASUREMENT TECHNIQUES

Victimization Surveys

In light of all problems with the crime measurements provided by the mass media, as well as by police records and other official data, it might be asked what alternatives are available. Two possibilities exist: victimization surveys and anonymous questionnaires. Victimization surveys involve interviewing a sample population and asking interviewees whether they or any other persons in their home have been victims of any of a series of crimes during the preceding year

(Penick and Owens, 1976; Biderman, 1967; Ennis, 1967). On the basis of responses to these surveys, an attempt is made to arrive at an estimate of the total number of crimes in a given area during a specific period. In one survey (U.S. Department of Justice, 1974a), owners of businesses were also checked. Such surveys always turn up many unreported crimes and imply significant under-counting of crime of all types in police records. Victims often do not report crimes to the police because they believe that the police either cannot or will not do anything about their complaints; victimization surveys are a means of filling in the consequent gaps in police records.

But victimization surveys are not without difficulties in interpretation. Although some research shows that official statistics are at least moderately correlated with survey reports of victimization (Skogan, 1974), difficulties abound. One difficulty involves respondents' failures to recall victimization, especially in the case of minor crimes and of incidents more remote in time (Biderman et al., 1967). These problems of recall seem especially likely in high-crime areas, where victimization is a relatively frequent experience. Other limita-tions of such victimization data include underreporting of crimes without vic-tims, such as drug offenses, prostitution, and gambling, or of crimes in which the respondent-victim may have something to hide, as in the case of blackmail (U.S. Department of Justice, 1974b).

Yet the most persistent concerns regarding these victimization studies do not involve the possibility of underreporting but the possibility of overreporting, that is, reporting more crime than actually exists. Such overreporting can involve the biases of both respondents and interviewers (Levine, 1976). Very often peo-ple make honest mistakes in the definition of what has occurred to them. A smashed window may be reported in a survey as an attempted burglary, when in fact it was nothing more than vandalism. Or a person may believe that his or her wallet has been stolen, when the truth is that it was accidently left on a store counter. Shoving on the subway may be defined as an assault. And a little panhandling on the subway may be defined as an attempted robbery, as may have been true in the case involving the famous "subway vigilante," Bernard Goetz (*Time,* 1984). Even the removal by neighborhood children of loose change from a coffee table, although merely a small irritation when it occured, may be listed in a victim survey as larceny.

To the extent that people are generally afraid of crime, they may be prone to overly dramatic definitions. Moreover, people untrained in criminal law often make incorrect judgments about whether a law has been violated, whether they have been victimized, or to what extent they have been victimized. Police officers are often called into situations where no law has been violated. Even so, the most common reasons respondents give in victimization surveys for not reporting crimes to the police is that the offenses caused very little damage and were not very important. And if such trifling cases are reported to the police, no arrest is made, which keeps the arrest rate down. It is estimated that approximately a third of all complaints made to the police are unfounded; that is, they do not constitute a crime. There is no easy way to correct for this problem in victimization surveys.

As indicated above, attempts to determine the amount of crime victimization during the preceding year are designed to make the estimates comparable to annual arrest rates. But there are some additional features of victimization surveys that make such comparisons of little value. Often people say that it seems to be "just yesterday" that they experienced some horrible event, such as being the victim of a crime (Levine, 1976). This distortion of time is often referred to by psychologists as telescoping, that is, moving something in the distance much nearer. To the extent that telescoping occurs, it will tend to inflate the number of serious crimes reported to have occurred during a preceding year. Levine also reasons that some individuals may believe that they are performing a service to our society in being less than completely truthful and dramatizing the crime problem—that somehow or other their fabrications may help the forces of law and order by demonstrating that the police need more money or that the state requires tougher penalties.

Along with these biases of respondents, interviewer biases may also confound the results of these surveys (Levine, 1976). The paid interviewers may recognize that these surveys are designed for one reason: to find crimes that were not recorded in the official record. They may well fear that if the surveys do not find great numbers of these unreported crimes, the surveys will be stopped and they will lose their jobs. Interviewers also know that previous surveys have found great amounts of unrecorded crime and therefore may strive to find results consistent with the earlier findings.

In addition to all the other problems of attempting to compare victimization surveys to official police records, perhaps the most profound problem is that these two methods of figuring the amount of crime are in fact counting different things (Block and Block, 1980). Police reports record criminal *incidents,* whereas surveys estimate *victimizations.* A criminal incident such as armed robbery may have more than one victim, and in such a case the estimated amount of crime in a victim survey would surely be inflated. Moreover, the geographical areas from which the data are drawn are different for arrest rates and victim surveys. Surveys of victims attempt to estimate the number of victimizations among persons in the sampled region, regardless of where the crime occurred. But victim surveys never account for crimes against nonresidents while they were visiting the area. Police reports, on the other hand, include all types of criminal incidents in the area whether the victims were residents or nonresidents. This distinction can make a big difference in large urban, high-mobility areas. In high-crime, high-mobility urban areas, much of the crime against nonresidents could be masked by local victim surveys. In addition, although official records tend to show a concentration of most types of street crime and street criminals in the center of large cities, victim data often show crime to be widely dispersed, with victims in all social classes and in all areas of the nation. For this reason, as well as the generally inflated crime figures, vicitm surveys are especially disquieting. These surveys not only find more crime than is reported in police records, but also show that it is more widely dispersed as well—and therefore harder to avoid.

Victimization surveys also tend to ignore the thorny problem of victim-precipitated crime. The person who reports to an interviewer that he or she has been the victim of an assault may, in fact, have been the aggressor and responsible for the violence. A police investigation may have uncovered this fact, but there is no way to do so in a victim survey. The fact that crime, like other behavior, is a part of a social process is impossible to recognize within the confines of victim surveys.

In spite of the myriad difficulties with victim surveys, after the first such survey, commissioned by the federal government in 1967 through the President's Commission on Law Enforcement and Administration of Justice, was successful in locating a substantial amount of previously unrecorded crime, by 1973 federal monies had been made available for national surveys on an annual basis.

Anonymous Questionnaires

Through the years a number of studies have been conducted to determine how admitted criminal acts compare with those which are officially recorded. These studies have used anonymous questionnaires that were often given to student groups. Historically, the results of such self-report studies indicated that the image of criminal behavior as typically only a lower-class problem is incorrect. In one classic study, all the college students questioned admitted that they had committed at least one crime (Porterfield, 1943). These admissions seemed to reflect the same types and seriousness of crimes as were found among youths brought before juvenile courts. Bloch and Flynn (1956:11–14) found that 91 percent of middle-class college students admitted a wide variety of felony or misdemeanor offenses, or both. Another such study in New York City found that 89 percent of the men and 83 percent of the women in the study sample admitted having committed some theft, and that 64 percent of the men and 29 percent of the women admitted to a serious crime, showing both the commonness of crime and its prevalence among the various social classes (Wallerstein and Wyle, 1947). More recently, several studies that drew on anonymous questionnaires also questioned the existence of an inverse relationship between social class and delinquency. (See, for example, Tittle et al., 1978; Schwendinger and Schwendinger, 1982.)

A high correlation has been found between anonymous questionnaire results regarding admitted smoking and subsequent measures of smoking behavior through the collection of saliva specimens, which suggests that such questionnaires are valid measures of behavior (Akers et al., 1983). Generally, high correlations have been found between such self-reports and official police and court records (Hindelang et al., 1981), and these various measures indicate the same general demographic characteristics for offenders (Hindelang et al., 1979). Similarly, a review of existing studies found that no consistent relationship exists between social class and criminality when either studies of self-reports or official records are used (Tittle et al., 1978).

A serious problem with such questionnaire information is that usually no tests for truthfulness exist. Some respondents could well underreport their offenses or claim law violations that they had not committed. It has also been noted that such self-reports typically measure trivial offenses (Hindelang et al., 1979). Another limitation of such studies is that they rely heavily on student groups, and it is unlikely that a researcher could gain access, for example, to a group of business executives for such research. Yet, whatever the limitations of such data, they do tend to show that females are more like males than the arrest and conviction data seem to indicate. Arrest records may well overemphasize the sexual nature of female crime because of the stereotypes held by the police (Smart, 1977:22–23). Silberman (1978:322) reports that white female adolescents are especially likely to be incarcerated for "premature" sexual activity. However, these questionnaire studies, along with victimization surveys, indicate significant underreporting of crime in official records. Whatever the methodological problems with the use of anonymous questionnaires, their persistent findings of a considerable amount of middle-class crime and delinquency and surprisingly high levels of female crime help to dispel the myth of a "subculture of violence" that some analysts allege to be unique to lower-class, minority-group males (Wolfgang and Ferracuti, 1967). Schwendinger and Schwendinger (1985) reviewed the recent intense debate about the use of anonymous questionnaires that centers on this issue of the social class concentration of delinquency. The Schwendingers note that it was hard for many American criminologists to accept the idea that delinquency is not mainly a product of the lower class.

As Pepinsky (1976b) observed of both self-reported offenses and victim surveys, they have "been used to expand the scope of the crime problem." Remember that during the nineteenth century prison and conviction data were generally considered to be the most appropriate in reflecting the amount of crime in a society. During this period, some critics of prison records believed that conviction records were the superior of the two because they were more complete, since obviously some cases are lost between conviction and imprisonment. Some convicted persons are never sent to prison but, rather, are given a suspended sentence and probation or perhaps are sent to a mental hospital instead of prison. Later, during the early twentieth century, the same reasoning that led to the original preference for conviction data was used to decide that arrest records are superior even to conviction data. Somewhat later, crimes known to the police were trumpeted as an even better measure than arrests. After World War II there was increasing interest in anonymous questionnaires as the latest entry for candidacy as the most complete measure of crime. Finally, beginning in the late 1960s, victimization surveys, funded by the U.S. Justice Department, became the rage among government officials and traditional criminologists as the ultimate in comprehensive crime measurement.

The attempt to determine the best and most comprehensive measure of crime, which has continued over a period of approximately 100 years, has resulted in an increasingly broad definition of what should be included in a "true" measure of crime. The problem is that as the definition of crime expands, the perceived crime rate will go up even if there is no increase in the amount of crime actually occurring in the community. The consequent steady increase in the crime rate is predictably a source of concern for citizens and seems to justify increased government expenditures to ferret out even more hidden or unrecorded crime. Such new measures include not only annual national surveys to determine the amount of crime victimization but also the appropriation of money for more undercover police agents to spot criminal activity and for new high-powered weapons to aid in the fight against "this ever-growing menace."

Yet the most serious consequences of this escalating figure of the true amount of crime is undoubtedly the hazard it poses to American constitutional freedoms. During the 1980s a more conservative U.S. Supreme Court began to chip away at the constitutional rights of persons accused of crimes, and as an aftermath of the urban riots of the 1960s, the U.S. Congress passed the Omnibus Crime Control and Safe Streets Act (1968), which modified the U.S. Constitution to allow, as evidence in trials, the use of information collected by the police from secret wiretaps on suspects' telephones.

Finally, if it is assumed for the moment that there is some truth to the idea that crime is increasing in America, why is this the case? There is accumulating evidence that prisons and the police do not seem to make a dent in the amount of crime. In fact, there is some indication that prisons actually serve as "colleges" of crime and that prisoners who were not committed to a life of crime on entry into a prison soon become so committed after a few years of incarceration. With all of our American money and scientific knowledge, surely as a nation we could be more successful in combating this menace. The fact that the crime rates continue to increase, Reiman (1979) noted, must therefore be a consequence of the fact that elite American policymakers have no strong interest in using American resources and technology to fight crime. If the average American citizen is consumed with fear of street crime, he or she cannot pay much attention to the depridations of American corporations. Reiman indicated that there is no evidence of a conscious conspiracy among these elites to block efforts to decrease crime; instead, they simply have no strong motivation to improve the operation of the police, the courts, and the prisons. Chapter 3 presented a discussion of some of the behaviors of corporations, including price-fixing and environmental pollution, as well as the massive amount of unnecessary surgery by American surgeons more interested in profits than patients' welfare. Most Americans, Reiman (1979) argued, cannot be adequately concerned about these behaviors because they are overwhelmed with a fear of street crime.

CONCLUSION

Of the various official records on crime, the most widely accepted and used are the police records in the FBI Uniform Crime Reports. Such records, however, have been shown to be beset with technical problems and with many potential distortions due to political pressures. Indeed, other sources of information on crime, such as victimization surveys and anonymous questionnaires, give a picture of the amount and distribution of crime that differs greatly from that contained in official records. Because there is no uniform set of criminal codes among the American states or among nations, interstate or international comparisons of crime rates can be misleading. Moreover, the official crime rates show little or nothing about the actual behavior from which they are constructed. Alternative methods of constructing crime rates are conceivable, and such methods might produce more representative reflections of the magnitude of criminal offenses.

The various measures of criminal behavior, however, can be evaluated not only in terms of their representatives of criminal behavior but also in terms of their use in forming public policy decisions, their intrinsic human interest, their use as a basis for law-and-order rhetoric, and their use as a vehicle for judging the efficiency of the various elements of the legal system. Official crime rates have been routinely used to determine such matters of public policy as the allocation of federal and local funds for police departments and changes in criminal statutes. Increases in crime shown by official data are often followed by arguments for increasing police budgets, penalties in the criminal code, or both. Such increases in crime rates, when paired with mass media hysteria, have impelled many Americans to abandon the cities and flee to what they see as the relative safety of the suburbs, even though they have never personally experienced the direct threat of crime. Official crime rates are also useful as support for a get-tough, law-and-order rhetoric that many politicians find appeals to the frightened voter. These same crime rates are also sometimes used by politicians to assess the effectiveness of various elements of the legal system. In fact, increases or decreases in the official crime rates cannot always be used as a sure measure of police effectiveness, for the very reason that the police sometimes recognize the political use made of these crime rates. Nonetheless, these police records are probably a better measure of police activity than of the amount and type of crime occurring in the community.

Most criminologists are well aware of the shortcomings of crime rates based on official data. Even so, after listing all of these shortcomings, scholars typically proceed to use such data anyway, perhaps because they are the only available data (Matza, 1969). A survey of juvenile delinquency research indicated a heavy reliance on official sources of information (Galliher and McCartney, 1973); yet only in rare cases do criminologists actually attempt a true intellectual defense of such data. However, if official crime records are recognized as arbitrary and as reflective of economic and racial discrimination, then their use as measures of criminal behavior is inexcusable.

REFERENCES

Akers, R. L., J. Massey, W. Clarke, and R. M. Lauer
1983 "Are self-reports of adolescent deviance valid? Biochemical measures, randomized response, and the bogus pipeline in smoking behavior." Social Forces 62 (September): 234–251.

Bell, D.
1960 The End of Ideology. Rev. ed. New York: The Free Press.

Best, J.
1987 "Rhetoric in claims-making: constructing the missing children problem." Social Problems 34 (April):101–121.

Biderman, A. D.
1966 "Social indicators and goals." Pp. 68–153 in Raymond A. Bauer, ed., Social Indicators. Cambridge, Mass.: MIT Press.
1967 "Surveys of population samples for estimating crime incidence." Annals of the American Academy of Political and Social Science 374(November):16–33.

Biderman, A. D., L. A. Johnson, J. McIntyre, and A. W. Weir
1967 Report on a Pilot Study in the District of Columbia on Victimization and Attitudes Toward Law Enforcement. President's Commission on Law Enforcement and Adminstration of Justice, Field Surveys No. 1, Office of Law Enforcement Assistance, U.S. Department of Justice. Bureau of Social Science Research, Inc. Washington, D.C.: U.S. Government Printing Office.

Bloch, H. and F. T. Flynn
1956 Delinquency: The Juvenile Offender in America Today. New York: Random House.

Block, R. and C.R. Block
1980 "Decisions and data: the transformation of robbery incidents into official robbery statistics." Journal of Criminal Law and Criminology 71:622–636.

Boggs, S.L .
1965 "Urban crime patterns." American Sociological Review 30(December): 899–908.

Cicourel, A. V.
1968 The Social Organization of Juvenile Justice. New York: John Wiley & Sons.

Conklin, J. E.
1975 The Impact of Crime. New York: Macmillan.

Davis, F. J.
1952 "Crime news in Colorado newspapers." American Journal of Sociology 57(January):325–330.

Denver Post
1985 "Phony numbers inflate missing child hysteria." Reprinted from Columbia (Mo.) Daily Tribune, May 12:8.

Ennis, P. H.
1967 Criminal Victimization in the United States: A Report of a National Survey. National Opinion Research Center, University of Chicago. Washington, D.C.: U.S. Government Printing Office.

Ferdinand, T. N.
1967 "The criminal patterns of Boston since 1849." American Journal of Sociology 73(July):84–99.

Fishman, M.
1978 "Crime waves as ideology." Social Problems 25:531–543.

Galliher, J. F. and J. L. McCartney
1973 "The influence of funding agencies on juvenile delinquency research." Social Problems 21(Summer):77–90.

Geis, G.
1965 "Statistics concerning race and crime." Crime and Delinquency 11(April):142–150.

Gibbs, J. P. and M. L. Erickson
1976 "Crime rates of American cities in an ecological context." American Journal of Sociology 82(November):605–620.

Gould, Leroy
1971 "Crime and its impact in an affluent society." Pp.81–118 in J. D. Douglas, ed., Crime and Justice in American Society. Indianapolis: Bobbs-Merrill.

Hindelang, M. J., T. Hirschi, and J. G. Weis
1979 "Correlates of delinquency: the illusion of discrepancy between self-reports and official measures." American Sociological Review 44(December):995–1014.
1981 Measuring Delinquency. Beverly Hills, Calif.: Sage Publications.

Kitsuse, J. I. and A. V. Cicourel
1963 "A note on the uses of official statistics." Social Problems 11:131–139.

Lejins, P. P.
1961 "American data on juvenile delinquency in an international forum." Federal Probation 25(June):18–21.

Lemert, E. M.
1951 Social Pathology. New York: McGraw-Hill.

Levine, J. P.
1976 "The potential for crime overreporting in criminal victimization surveys." Criminology 14:307–330.

Life
1982 "Guns are out of control." April:30–36.

Los Angeles Times
1981 "Public puts crime control ahead of defense, poll finds." March 28:Part 1, p. 3.

Matza, D.
1969 Becoming Deviant. Englewood Cliffs, N.J.: Prentice Hall.

Molotch, H. and M. Lester
1974 "News as purposive behavior: on the strategic use of routine events, accidents and scandals." American Sociological Review 39(February):101–112.

Newsweek
1981 "The epidemic of violent crime." March 23:46–50, 52–54.

Omnibus Crime Control and Safe Streets Act of 1968
1968 Public Law 90–351, 90th Congress, H.R. 5037 (June 19).

Penick, B., K. Eidson and M. E. B. Owens III (eds.)
1976 Surveying Crime: Panel for the Evaluation of Crime Surveys. Committee on National Statistics, National Research Council. Washington, D.C.: National Academy of Science.

Pepinsky, H. E.
1976a "The growth of crime in the United States." Annals of the American Academy of Political and Social Science 423:23–30.
1976b "The room for despotism in the quest for valid crime statistics: American crime measurement in historical and comparative perspective." American Society of Criminology meeting, Tucson, November 4–7.

Porterfield, A. L.
1943 "Delinquency and its outcome in court and college." American Journal of Sociology 49(November):199–208.

Puttkammer, E. W.
1953 Adminstration of Crimenle Law. Chicago: University of Chicago Press.

Reiman, J. H.
1979 The Rich Get Richer and the Poor Get Prison: Ideology, Class and Criminal Justice. New York: John Wiley & Sons.

St. Louis Post-Dispatch
1985 "Critics assail efforts to fingerprint children." November 4:1B.

Sallach, D. L.
1974 "Class domination and ideological hegemony." Sociological Quarterly 15(Winter): 38–50.

Schwendinger, H. and J. R. Siegel Scwendinger
1982 "The paradigmatic crisis in delinquency theory." Crime and Social Justice 18(Winter):70–78.
1985 Adolescent Subcultures and Delinquency. New York: Praeger.

Sellin, T.
1931 "The basis of a crime index." Journal of Criminal Law and Criminology 22(September):335–356.

Sellin, T. and M. E. Wolfgang
1964 The Measurement of Delinquency. New York: John Wiley & Sons.

Silberman, C. E.
1978 Criminal Violence, Criminal Justice. New York: Random House.

Skogan, W. G.
1974 "The validity of official crime statistics: an empirical investigation." Social Science Quarterly 55(June):25–38.

Smart, C.
1977 Women, Crime and Criminology: A Feminist Critique. London: Routledge & Kegan Paul.

Taft, D. R. and R. W. England
1964 Criminology. 4th ed. New York: Macmillian.

Tappan, P. W.
1960 Crime, Justice and Correction. New York: McGraw-Hill.

Tetters, N. K. and D. Matza
1959 "The extent of delinquency in the United States." Journal of Negro Education 28(Summer):200–213.

Time
1972 "Street crime: who's winning?" October 23:55–56, 58.
1981 "The curse of violent crime." March 23:17–24, 29–30, 33.
1984 "A troubled and troubling life." April 8:35,38.

Tittle, C. R., W. J. Villemez, and D. Smith
1978 "The myth of social class and criminality: an empirical assessment of the empirical evidence." American Sociological Review 43(October):643–656.

United States Department of Justice
1974a Crime in the Nation's Five Largest Cities: National Crime Panel Surveys of Chicago,

Detroit, Los Angeles, New York, and Phila-
delphia. Law Enforcement Assistance
Administration, National Criminal Justice
Information and Statistics Service. Wash-
ington, D.C.: U.S. Government Printing
Office.

1974b Crimes and Victims: A Report on the
Dayton–San Jose Pilot Survey of Victimiza-
tion. Law Enforcement Assistance
Adminstration, National Criminal Justice
Information and Statistics Service. Wash-
ington, D.C.: U.S. Government Printing
Office.

U.S. News & World Report
1981 "Our losing battle against crime." October
12:39–43.

Van Vechten, C. C.
1942 "Differetial criminal case mortality in
selected jurisdictions." American Sociological Review 7(December):833–839.

Wallerstein, J. S. and C. J. Wyle
1947 "Our law-abiding law-breakers." Probation
25(April):107–112, 118.

Weis, K. and M. E. Milakovich
1974 "Political misuses of crime rates." Society
11(July–August):27–33.

Wolfgang, M. E.
1958 Patterns in Criminal Homicide. Philadelphia: University of Pennsylvania.
1967 "Urban crime." Pp. 237–274 in J. Q. Wilson,
ed., The Metropolitan Enigma. Washington, D.C.: Chamber of Commerce of the
United States.

Wolfgang M. E. and F. Ferracuti
1967 The Subculture of Violence: Towards an
Integrated Theory in Criminology.
London: Social Science Paperbacks.

Wright, K. N.
1985 The Great American Crime Myth. Westport, Conn.: Greenwood Press.

6
THE SOCIAL BASIS OF LAW

IS LAW NECESSARY?

To understand the nature of the crime problem in any society, we must first understand the origins of written crime laws, because these laws provide the defining mechanisims for determining what will be called criminal behavior. A discussion of the social and political basis of criminal law should initially address the question of whether society really needs written laws to exist. The evidence suggests that written laws are not always necessary, because not all societies have had a codified body of rules comparable to a modern criminal code. In smaller, less complex societies than our own, traditions serve a function similar to that of modern laws, but these are often not codified, written statutes (Mair, 1962; MacIver and Page, 1964:166–188). Such traditions cover all aspects of communal life, for sharing goods, protecting property, and settling disputes. However, as societies grow, at some point a written criminal code seems to be required. As Murdock (1950:715) observed, smaller groups of any type can rely solely on unwritten or informal understandings; however, in larger groups, such understandings must be reduced to writing to ensure the necessary coordination of activities:

> [When] human beings found themselves for the first time living in local aggregations of appreciably more than a thousand people, they discovered that informal mechanisms of control no longer sufficed to maintain social order. Face-to-face relationships could not now be maintained with everyone, and tended to be

limited to smaller groups of relatives or close neighbors. Individual deviants were presented for the first time with an alternative to conformity. They could sever old relationships and cultivate new ones among persons ignorant or tolerant of their lapses. Thus was born the possibility of escape from the "tyranny" of social control which is exemplified at its maximum today in the anonymity of the individual in a large city.

Suggesting, as this book does, that criminal laws in a given society often reflect the interests of elites and powerful interest groups is quite another thing than claiming that criminal laws of some type are not necessary for organized social life. In a heterogeneous mass society such as our own, where a variety of people are thrown together in often anonymous relationships, laws are useful and necessary for the organization and coordination of activities. However, because ours is a society with very powerful interest groups and wealthy elites, the particular laws that come into existence will not usually conflict with the interests of those groups.

Nevertheless, anarchists and some Marxist theorists contend that law is not necessary for society. One Marxist argument is that the state, including its laws and its police, is not required by mass society but, rather, is required by the bourgeoisie to control the mass of workers in a capitalist economy; it would not be required in a true communist society, regardless of size. According to this reasoning, after the revolution of the proletariat, citizens will voluntarily cooperate with one another, and coercion by the state will no longer be required. Therefore the state, including the laws and the police, will "wither away" (Schlesinger, 1945; Berman, 1963). Unfortunately, with both China and the Soviet Union used as examples of societies that have had such revolutions, no evidence can be seen that the state is withering away. Both the Soviet Union and China have a large and powerful central government. It does not appear that the revolutions in these two countries have produced such a degree of commitment to the social norms that the force of law is no longer necessary.

Indeed, it appears that a formal, written criminal law comes into existence only when commitment to the social norms of a society becomes too weak to restrain widespread violations of those norms. Before such violations occur on any large scale, it is obviously unnecessary to write laws prescribing penalties to cover such behavior. Joseph Eaton (1952:334) observed:

> New rules . . . are usually proposed . . . to combat a specific innovation in personal behavior of some members, which some . . . regard as a violation of the unwritten mores. The new practice must be more than an isolated deviation of the sort which is controlled effectively through the normal processes of community discipline—punishment of the offender by admonition. . . . Only when a deviation becomes widespread . . . are the leaders likely to appeal for a formal statement of the unwritten community code.

Thus a written criminal code is necessary in a mass society, and especially in a highly stratified society such as our own, in which there is a marked lack of consensus about the social norms. Even in our society, however, there is some evidence that the general degree to which people agree on the social norms increases as their formal educational attainment increases (Rossi et al., 1974).

Originally, no written law existed in what is today the nation of Great Britain. A set of principles emerged that derived "their authority solely from usages and customs of immemorial antiquity, or from judgments and decrees of the courts recognizing, affirming, and enforcing such usages and customs" (Black, 1951:345–346). It is from these principles, called common law, that a good deal of American criminal law has been borrowed.

LAW IN SMALL, NONLITERATE SOCIETIES

In small, nonliterate societies that do not have a complex division of labor, it is exceedingly difficult to distinguish law from other norms or customs. Perhaps it is for this reason that some anthropologists say that primitive society has no law and therefore, of course, no crime. Some observers of primitive life have claimed that "custom is king." They argue that the rule of custom is so strong and pervasive in primitive social groups that no law is required and none emerges. Hoebel (1954) asserted that, on the contrary, custom can and should be distinguished from law. He used as an example of law the case of an Indian warrior whose horse was taken by another warrior of his tribe. The aggrieved warrior submitted his complaint to the tribal chiefs. They had the other warrior brought in from a distant camp. The accused warrior offered both restitution and a suitable explanation for his conduct. After settling the dispute as a court, the chiefs went on to act as a legislature and made a new rule against "borrowing" horses without permission. The chiefs also assumed the responsibility for retrieving goods borrowed without permission and established the rule that henceforth the punishment for borrowers who resisted would be a whipping.

On an even less complex level of social organization, such as that of the Eskimo, the opinion of all male adults may be polled before a given punishment is meted out by a citizen whom the others agree can act as an agent of the tribe in this one case. All the men help make what is both a legislative and a judicial decision—namely that a given act must be punished in a specific way and that a certain person may administer the punishment on behalf of the group. No citizen has a permanent specialized legislative, judicial, or police role. Thus it seems that the fundamental, or most basic, quality of law in any society is not a permanent set of law enforcement officials but the legitimate application of physical coercion by some socially authorized agent.

The development of a formal legal system with specialized occupational roles, however, is not an all-or-nothing matter, as this discussion might suggest. In a study of 51 societies, Schwartz and Miller found that some societies have only partially developed legal systems in this sense. These authors (1964:161) identified the following as the elements of a formal legal system:

> Counsel: regular use of specialized non-kin advocates in the settlement of disputes.

Mediation: regular use of non-kin third party intervention in dispute settlement.
Police: specialized armed force used partially or wholly for norm enforcement.

The least complex societies had none of these elements. Typically, if societies have any elements of a legal system, it is mediation, or the use of nonkin in dispute settlements. In somewhat more complex societies, police are typically found as well. In the most complex societies, legal counsel is also present. As seen in chapter 2, it is not until the development of permanent and specialized law enforcement agencies, such as legislatures, police, and courts, that people begin to reflect on the nature of crime and criminal law. These distinctions between the police, courts, and legislative agencies require parallel distinctions between substantive and procedural law. Substantive law refers to the forbidden acts and their punishments. Procedural law, on the other hand, describes how violators are to be dealt with, including any rights of due process such as the right to a speedy trial by a jury of one's peers. It appears that during times when the power of government is very secure, the substantive law has expanded to its greatest extent (Korn and McCorkle, 1959:90–92). For example, during the height of the British Empire, there were over 200 capital crimes. But during periods when a government is weak and on the defensive, procedural safeguards have been enhanced, since procedural law is generally created by the demands of persons outside of the government who oppose its authority and power. The Magna Charta, which was signed by the English King John in 1215, was forced on a weakened monarchy by the English aristocracy, who demanded more civil liberties. Chapters 6 and 7 will be devoted to discussion of substantive law, and chapters 8, 9, and 10 will cover the police and courts, or procedural law.

LEGAL CHANGE AND HUMAN VALUES

When contemporary laws are compared with those of less complex societies, a massive change in legal structure is evident. It is apparent that written laws change, as do the values of people in society. In modern America, this does not imply a democratic leveling of power, however, because there is some indication, as discussed in chapter 1, that business-owned and -controlled mass media manipulate the attitudes of the mass of citizens (Sallach, 1974: Cohen and Young, 1973). In any event, however, attitudes do change, and one need only consider assorted laws that cover a variety of behaviors ranging from blasphemy and abortion to the use of alcohol and marihuana to recognize that as attitudes change, laws also change, although sometimes only very haltingly and slowly and often lagging behind the changes in attitudes. There is less agreement, however, on the issue of whether a change in the law can bring about a later change in people's attitudes and behaviors. Some supporters of the civil rights legislation of the 1960s argued that laws requiring equal treatment for blacks—covering voting rights, open public accomodations, and equal employment opportunities— would create a social environment that would facilitate later positive attitude change (Civil Rights Act of 1964). Persons opposed to such laws argued that "you can't legislate morality" or even force people to obey laws with which they do not agree, citing the failure of national prohibition of alcohol to support their point. But Wirt (1970:7–8) observed that there are examples where laws did change peoples' attitudes and behavior: "Its *success* could be symbolized equally well . . . by the Thirteenth Amendment which prohibited slavery. A century ago there were many Americans who believed that slavery was right. . . . Today, however, it is a rare American whose mores include this belief." Duster (1970) contended, however, that among persons who argue that morality in race relations cannot be legislated, many oppose the legalization of prostitution on the ground that state approval of sexual immorality would corrupt and weaken the moral foundations of society. In other words, the typical position is that the state cannot legislate morality but that it can legitimate immorality. As might be expected, citizens often argue that the law is effective only in supporting what, in fact, is their preexisting moral persuasion. Thus the claim that morality in race relations cannot be legislated often suggests that the person who advances it does not want a new morality to be enforced under law.

Duster (1970) cited other instances where legal change has been followed by changes in behavior and by changes in values and attitudes. The Harrison Tax Act of 1914, designed to control narcotics, is given major credit for transforming the typically tolerant view of drug addiction that existed before 1900 into our current intolerance. Although we have in this century become more tolerant of physical and mental illness, we have become less tolerant of addiction because, along with the legal change, the social characteristics of addicts have also changed. Unlike the typically middle-class addicts around the turn of the century, today's addicts are typically poor. In light of the Harrison Tax Act, it seems that new morality can be legislated only when the poor are the targets and not the beneficiaries of legal change, and when the legal change does not conflict with the moral concerns of more affluent citizens. This may help explain why alcohol prohibition did not work—too many powerful citizens enjoyed drinking. And, on the whole, research has found little or no influence of the law on human attitudes when research subjects have been told of legal penalties for being drunk in public (Berkowitz and Walker, 1967), for prostitution (Walker and Argyle, 1967), or for mandatory seat belt laws (Walker and Marsh, 1984).

Currently there is a considerable amount of debate over whether more restrictive gun control laws could cut down on the great amount of violence in this country. The position of most political liberals includes a comparison of the massive murder rate in the United States with the few murders found in most European nations. Liberals argue that if we would restrict private ownership of firearms, as do most European nations, our murder rate would greatly decline. Liberals' bumper stickers urge that we "ban handguns." The opposition has generally made the counterclaim that the U.S. Constitution guarantees the right to bear arms and that if this freedom were ever restricted, all of our civil liberties would be in grave danger. A few years ago a bumper sticker supporting this position read, Register Communists, Not Handguns. And another reads, I'll Give Up My Gun When You Pry My Cold Dead Fingers From Around It. National Rifle Association members often parrot the claim that with more restrictive gun control laws, "only the criminals will have guns." Indeed, the situation is even more dismal than this phrase claims. Not only will the "criminals" have guns, but a number of otherwise law-abiding people probably will ignore the law as well. Given the intensity of feeling among those who oppose gun control, more restrictive gun control measures may simply create a large new class of law violators, a possibility that few legislators will ignore.

The point is that a simple legal change cannot fundamentally alter the history and social structure of America, contrary to the liberals' claims. The very beginning of our nation involved the annihilation of numerous American Indian cultures and amounted to continental genocide. The traditions of lynching, rape, and other brutalities directed against black Americans are other portions of this legacy. Our nation's bellicose foreign policy and our increasing reliance on the death penalty—which is unique among Western democracies—are both consistent with this reliance on violence to solve problems. The general point is this: Liberals often seem overly optimistic about the possibility of using the law as an instrument of social change, and they are forever disappointed when history does not turn out as they had hoped.

LEGAL CHANGE AND DISOBEDIENCE

Whether legal change alters society or only reflects other social change, it is apparent that laws do change over time. Therefore some argue that in a democracy, which is also a mass society, complete obedience to the law should not be encouraged. Disobedience to the law may be a good thing because it tests and pushes the limits of the law. Resistance to written laws runs the gamut from covert individual violations, such as the frequent use of marihuana in the United States, to massive violent rebellion, such as the Bolshevik revolution in Russia. Nonviolent civil disobedience falls somewhere between these extremes and will be explored more fully, because it dramatizes ideally the relationship between law and morality. Mohandas Gandhi (1869–1948), the political and moral leader of India during its struggle for independence from Britain, advocated such techniques of nonviolent civil disobedience as nonpayment of fines and taxes, boycott of courts, fasting, picketing, and strikes (Gandhi, 1951). One of the few ways in which citizens in a democratic mass society such as our own can have an impact on the law is through direct nonviolent civil disobedience. In his "Letter From Birmingham Jail," Martin Luther King, Jr. (1963:769), wrote:

> One may well ask, "How can you advocate breaking some laws and obeying others?" The answer lies in the fact that there are two types of laws: just and unjust. I agree with St. Augustine that "an unjust law is no law at all."

Now what is the difference between the two? How does one determine whether a law is just or unjust? A just law is a man-made code that squares with the moral law or the law of God. An unjust law is a code that is out of harmony with the moral law. To put it in the terms of St. Thomas Aquinas, an unjust law is a human law that is not rooted in eternal law and natural law. Any law that uplifts human personality is just. Any law that degrades human personality is unjust. All segregation statutes are unjust because segregation distorts the soul and damages the personality.

I hope you are able to see the distinction I am trying to point out. In no sense do I advocate evading the law, as would the rabid segregationist. That would lead to anarchy. One who breaks an unjust law must do so *openly, lovingly,* and with a willingness to accept the penalty. I submit that an individual who breaks a law that conscience tells him is unjust and who willingly accepts the penalty of imprisonment in order to arouse the conscience of the community over its injustice is in reality expressing the highest respect for law.*

In our mass society of more than 200 million people, town meetings where everyone can have a direct and personal voice in government are not feasible. Since laws do change over time, part of this change can be brought about by nonviolent civil disobedience. Regardless of how one feels about civil disobedience, it is clear that the civil disobedience of Dr. King and his followers in the South was responsible for some legal change, including the ending of legal racial segregation of public accommodations. (For a discussion of the specific process of legal change see Barkan, 1984.) But skeptics ask, Can people violate laws simply because they do not like them? It is further often argued that people cannot take the law into their own hands and must obey all laws, not just those they consider to be acceptable (LeGrande, 1967). It is sometimes argued that civil disobedience encroaches on the rights of others. For example, during the 1960s a favorite practice of black civil rights demonstrators was to go en masse to a racially segregated restaurant and wait for service that never came. In some cases this forced the restaurant owner out of business. The owner would not serve blacks, and yet the blacks occupied all available seats during all opening hours. Legal remedies, thus it is sometimes claimed, provide adequate alternatives to civil disobedience. But Dr. King and his followers believed that civil disobedience is an indispensable vehicle for legal change.

Willing acceptance of punishment is a key component of nonviolent civil disobedience. A person who engages in law violation but rejects the right of the state to punish is more akin to a revolutionary, and a person who attempts to evade legal penalties is exhibiting behavior more like that of burglars or rapists. In any case, suffering punishment from the state is a part of the plan of persons who commit civil disobedience to win sympathy for their position. Without suffering the punishment, civil disobedience would lose much, if not all, of its impact.

*Excerpt from "Letter from Birmingham Jail" from *Why We Can't Wait* by Martin Luther King, Jr. New York: Harper & Row, Publishers, Inc. Copyright 1963, 1964 by Martin Luther King, Jr. Reprinted by permission of Joan Daves.

Moreover, the philosophy of Martin Luther King and the results he achieved are not as unique as they appear to be at first glance. The remaining sections of this chapter will present several examples of how specific powerful interest groups had a similarly direct impact on written laws. The argument that society, government, and the law are structured to benefit most the persons who are in positions of power is reflected in these illustrations. If powerful groups have a direct impact on the law, this fact argues for the legitimacy of the direct influence that others may also have on the law. Although sociologists have typically described how inequality has influenced the administration of the law, a prior question, which will be addressed later in this chapter, involves the effect of inequality on the creation of the written law.

ASSUMPTIONS REGARDING THE RELATIONSHIP OF LAW AND ORDER

The rhetoric of political leaders may lead one to believe that law and order are always associated with each other. The idea is that the rule of law or obedience to law and social orderliness, are necessarily bound together (Skolnick, 1966:1–22). Former President Richard Nixon always stressed this point in his political campaigns. Yet his administration provides a dramatic demonstration that law and order are not, in fact, complementary. During his administration the United States appeared to become increasingly orderly after the tumult of the 1960s, which included urban ghetto riots and campus antiwar demonstrations. This orderliness, however, was not a result of the rule of law, because the evidence presented during the various Watergate burglary investigations shows that the Nixon Administration was systematically and routinely violating criminal laws. This example suggests that social order can be maintained in a number of ways and that use of the law is just one such mechanism. Police states, such as those in South Africa and Chile, have been ruled not so much by laws as by guns, and "a concentration camp is more orderly than a town meeting" (Gaylin and Rothman, 1976:xxviii). Although ruling military juntas have no constitutional authority, they are able to maintain order by the threat of personal injury. In fact, the threat of violence seems to be the most efficient means of maintaining order; for example, before a military coup in the 1970s, Chile had much more political disorder. The rule of law implies some restriction on governmental efforts at social control, such as allowing citizens' constitutional rights of due process against government prosecution. However, the commonsense association of law and order, as well as law violation and disorder, is hard to destroy. Most citizens, and perhaps police especially, are suspicious of anything that seeems out of order and out of place (Skolnick, 1966).

Perhaps part of the confusion over the relationship between law and order can be cleared up when it is recognized that what is defined as order is heavily dependent on human perceptions of the symbolic properties of events, rather than on the events themselves. For example, college students who disrupt traffic and damage some property to celebrate a football victory are often tolerated by local citizens and police. Similar student actions to protest the war in Vietnam were occasionally met with massive arrests, beatings, tear gas, and sometimes even shootings. In both types of activity, students conducted themselves similarly, but their actions symbolized vastly different things, which explains the differential response. The point is that the relationship between the rule of law and the maintenance of order is confusing because of changing definitions of social order.

THEORIES OF THE ORIGINS OF LAW

Social scientists interested in the study of crime have from time to time emphasized that a knowledge of the social origins of criminal law is central to a complete understanding of crime. The assumption is that before one can fully understand the patterns of crime in a society, one must first understand the origins of criminal laws, which are the guideposts indicating what behavior is to be defined as crime. As early as the 1920s the eminent criminologist Edwin Sutherland (1924:11) offered this analysis: "An understanding of the nature of law is necessary in order to secure an understanding of the nature of crime. A complete explanation of the origin and enforcement of laws would be, also, an explanation of the violation of laws." And Jeffery (1956:670–671) contended: "The question of what is crime? is prior logically and historically to the study of the criminal. It is prior historically for a norm has to exist before it can be violated; it is prior logically for before an individual can be studied as a criminal he must first be classified as one." According to Hall (1945:355–356), the general boundaries of criminology require that it "be concerned, firstly, with the meanings of the rules of criminal law—and this requires investigation of their origins, the legislative history, the relevant preceding and accompanying social problems with emphasis on the opinions and attitudes of various groups, marked out from the more or less passive 'majority,' and, of course, the authoritative interpretations of the courts." Therefore, noted Hall, (1945:354): "Hence Criminology, in this view, is synonymous with Sociology of Criminal Law." More recently, Akers (1968:460–461) argued: "We will have to scrutinize more carefully the process by which the criminal law is formed and enforced in a search for those variables which determine what of the total range of behavior becomes prohibited and which of the total range of norms become a part of the law."

Five recognizable intellectual traditions may be found in the criminological literature dealing with the origins of criminal law: (1) Law is a product of widespread consensus in society, (2) criminal law can serve mainly a symbolic or public relations function, as opposed to its actual utility in controlling behavior, (3) law is a product of democratic compromise among competing interest groups, (4) law is a product of political domination by some type of elite interest group, and (5) law is a product of a dominant economic class or a consequence of the economic conditions or institutions prevailing in a society.

The Consensus Orientation

The consensus tradition holds that criminal law is a reflection of widespread public opinion. The idea is that criminal laws proscribe those acts that generally are considered morally wrong. Durkheim (1933) called this consensus on which laws are based the "collective conscience" of a society. Assuming such a consensus, Durkheim (1933:73) defined crime as follows: "The only common characteristic of all crimes is that they consist . . . in acts universally disapproved of by members of each society. . . . Crime shocks sentiments which, for a given social system, are found in all healthy consciences."

Illustrations using this perspective are not easy to locate in a heterogeneous and secular society such as our own, but if we consider the Massachusetts Bay Colony, we find that the theory applies. The founders of the colony turned to the Scriptures for guidance in developing their laws (Haskins, 1960). For example, the penalties for sodomy and adultery were both punished in precisely the way described in the the Old Testament. These colonists especially used the Bible as a justification for inflicting the death penalty.

Erikson's research (1966) dealing with the origins of the prohibition of witchcraft is another illustration from the Massachusetts Bay Colony. Erikson argued that punishment of witches began in the colony when it did because of rapid social changes in the colony, such as internal power shifts and external threats. Witches were punished in an effort to emphasize the moral boundaries of the group through punishment of certain behaviors and people. By punishing certain behavior, the colony publicly affirmed its moral boundaries by asserting that such behavior would not be tolerated. One major problem with this perspective, as indicated in chapter 1, is that even when consensus does exist in modern societies, this consensus may reflect the influence of largely corporate-owned and -controlled mass media. Yet in spite of corporate controls on the flow of ideas in the mass media, currently many Americans probably recognize the role of power, interest groups, and elites in government, including the lawmaking process.

Symbolic Legislation

The consensus orientation assumes that people typically make rational decisions to maximize their actual individual gains. However, Edelman (1964) suggested that this assumption may be incorrect and that citizens often base their political behavior, not on their real or material interests, but on whether or not a given piece of legislation symbolically reassures them. Edelman suggested that the masses are often reassured by the mere passage of legislation that conflicts with the interests of organized pressure groups. Yet such legislation is typically not enforced, which in turn satisfies the needs of organized groups. The history of antitrust laws and national prohibition can be interpreted in this way. Antitrust laws were passed at a time when great public hostility was directed against large trusts. The laws satisfied the public that "something was being done," and yet the corporations continued largely as before. Similarly, national prohibition of alcholic beverages was forced through by largely rural Protestant interests; yet because the interests of many powerful consumers' and producers' groups conflicted with the new law, it was enforced only episodically and was widely disregarded or evaded.

Thus laws have both symbolic and instrumental properties. The instrumental role of law involves its actual enforcement effects: the degree to which the laws are enforced with vigor and the extent of citizen compliance. The symbolic properties of law do not require actual enforcement to have an impact. The symbolic impact of law requires only their promulgation or public announcement, irrespective of actual enforcement. The symbolic role of law can be served merely by affirming the superiority of one set of norms over others. Gusfield (1967:177) described this role of law as "utilizing law to proclaim one set of norms as public morality and to use another set of norms in actually controlling that behavior." Gusfield found this symbolic role of law in the national prohibition of alcohol, since prohibition was widely violated but seldom enforced. The mere existence of the law greatly encouraged rural, middle-class Protestants. In conclusion, one can see that the mere use of the idea of symbolic legislation assumes that there is some conflict or difference in the interests of various groups of citizens and that there is something short of complete consensus or unity of interest in society.

Legal Pluralism

Another view is that through law, people in social groups engage in a democratic give-and-take, compromise on their interests, and ultimately achieve some consensus on what is best for society. This is sometimes referred to as legal pluralism.

> Looked at functionally, the law is an attempt to satisfy, to reconcile, to harmonize, to adjust these overlapping and often conflicting claims and demands, either through securing them directly and immediately, or through securing certain individual interests, or through delimitations or compromises of individual interests, so as to give effect to the greatest total of interests that weigh most in our civilization, with the least sacrifice of the scheme of interests as a whole (Pound, 1943:39).

Dahrendorf (1959) observed that pluralism as a type of conflict exists when workers and property owners contain a wide demographic mix of various religions, races, and ethnic groups. When this is the case, no matter how issues are resolved, this minimizes the possibility that winning and losing will eventually evolve into an economic and racial caste system such as that found in the United

States. Winners and losers will have approximately the same racial and ethnic proportions.

An illustration of the pluralistic perspective is found in Roby's study (1969) of the origins of New York State's prostitution law. The legislation, influenced first by one organization and then another, had a long history. A diverse collection of groups had an influence on the law, including local police officials, the New York Hotel Association, the New York Civil Liberties Union, and even the United Nations. The police believed, for example, that including both patrons and prostitutes under the law would make enforcement more difficult. Officials from the United Nations also complained that including patrons under the state law on prostitution would be unfair to visitors from other nations not familiar with such a law. The hotel association also opposed the law as a deterrent to tourism. Civil liberties groups and legal aid attorneys, however, seemed more concerned with the violations of the rights of the *women* charged under this law. Roby (1969:108) summarized the political give-and-take involved:

> During the five stages in the formulation and enforcement of the Penal Law concerning prostitution, power shifted from first one interested group to another. One group frequently exercised power with respect to one section of the law while another did so with respect to another section. In the final stage of the law's history, civil liberties and welfare groups dominated over businessmen and the police with respect to the clause making prostitution a violation subject to a maximum fifteen day sentence while the police and businessmen dominated over the civil liberties and welfare groups with respect to the nonenforcement of the "patron" clause.

It may indeed be that prostitution laws are of a type that do not activate the greatest concern and power of elite interest groups or powerful classes, and that this is the reason that pluralism is so evident in this case.

Berk et al. (1977), in a statistical analysis of hundreds of penal code bills in California enacted from 1955 to 1971, determined that "at one time or another, virtually everyone gained through the making of laws" (1977:282). Such quantitative analysis treats all bills as being of equal significance and therefore arrives at the happy conclusion that everyone gains something from American democracy. The most telling criticism of this type of research is, however, that very few researchers find this pluralistic model to be useful.

Elite Theory

An alternative view is usually referred to as elite theory and maintains that law is the result of the consistent dominance of some type of interest group over others. Through law, the interests of more powerful groups are enforced by the state, and opposing groups are controlled (Vold, 1958; Quinney, 1970). Vold (1958:208) observed: "As political groups line up against one another, they seek the assistance of the organized state to help them defend their 'rights' and protect their interests. . . . Whichever group interest can marshal the greatest number of votes will determine whether or not there is to be a new law to hamper and curb the interests of some opposition group."

Becker (1963) explained how the power of such interest groups can be exercised. Such groups often have an aggressive moral entrepreneur who

> is interested in the content of rules. The existing rules do not satisfy him because there is some evil which profoundly disturbs him. He feels that nothing can be right in the world until rules are made to correct it. He operates with an absolute ethic; what he sees is truly and totally evil with no qualification. Any means is justified to do away with it. The crusader is fervent and righteous, often self-righteous. . . . The crusader is not only interested in seeing to it that other people do what he thinks is right. He believes that if they do what is right it will be good for them. Or he may feel that his reform will prevent certain kinds of exploitation of one person by another. (Becker, 1963:147–148.)

Becker uses as an example of such a moral entrepreneur the long-time head of the Federal Bureau of Narcotics (FBN), Harry Anslinger. Becker claims that Anslinger was responsible for directing an FBN propaganda campaign against marihuana that was in large part responsible for the passage of the federal Marihuana Tax Act of 1937. Unfortunately, there is insufficient evidence to conclude the Mr. Anslinger did, in fact, conduct such a publicity campaign. And the concept of a moral entrepreneur encourages the observer to ignore social structural issues and focus instead on the behavior of individuals. Thus the power of an interest group seemingly has a great deal to do with whether or not it has, as a chance occurrence, recruited a moral entrepreneur among its ranks.

The idea of the moral entrepreneur and special interest groups has also been applied to American abortion laws (Mohr, 1978). Around 1800, women in England and the United States were free to have what were, in fact, abortions before pregnancy was verified by fetal movement (quickening). But by the late 1800s, all states had passed antiabortion legislation at the prompting of American physicians. Earlier, physicians had discovered that they were losing patients to others who were entering medical practice, such as the homeopaths, who used only chemicals. Unlike physicians, these other medical practitioners would perform abortions, and physicians believed themselves to have lost patients as a consequence. Thus the physicians decided to try to force through legislation—and thereby impose their moral values—to control these other medical practitioners. By the mid-1800s the women having abortions were largely married, Protestant, native-born, white, middle- and upper-class women who wished to limit the number of children or delay childbearing. Because abortions were very expensive, they were largely unavailable to poor women. At this time a number of writers described the women who were having abortions as domestic subversives who threatened the future of the white race and weakened the family, and physicians warned of a reverse Darwinism as the nation became less and less Protestant and native-born.

Thus Protestant fears of being outreproduced by Roman Catholics were more important in this antiabortion crusade than was Catholic opposition to abortion. Catholics were not attracted in large numbers to this campaign, undoubtedly because of its anti-Catholic slant. As a consequence of lobbying from the America Medical Association, the state legislatures outlawed abortion. Making abortions illegal had the ironic consequence of forcing them to be performed in underground clinics and thus making abortion more dangerous at just the time when medical advances could have made it much safer. This apparently increased danger of abortion further hardened the attitudes of legislators.

Another lobbying effort of a group of American physicians is described in Sutherland's study (1950) of the origins of sexual-psychopath laws. During the 1930s and 1940s, twelve American states and the District of Columbia passed laws that gave psychiatrists great power in defining individuals as psychopaths and ordering their confinement, in some cases, even though they had not been convicted of a crime. These laws gave no consistent and verifiable definition of sexual psychopathy, leaving it totally to the discretion of psychiatrists. Sutherland observed that psychiatrists predictably played a major role in the passage of these laws, because they had an economic interest as the experts to be used in giving advice to the courts in enforcing these laws.

If physicians have had an active lobby over the years, women have also been involved as moral entrepreneurs. Platt (1977) found that the development of the juvenile courts and a juvenile code in the United States was in large part a result of the efforts, early in the 1900s, of a group of well-educated and affluent women whom Platt refers to as "the child savers." Their concerns for children were sincere, and they worried about the unwholesome conditions these children experienced, especially in the cities. Although women in the early twentieth century were largely excluded from business and politics, women's advice on children was respected. But most important, as Platt observed, the child-saving movement did not emerge in a political and economic vacuum. "The child-saving movement, in its efforts to augment the family with compulsory education and other measures of state intervention, played an important role in helping to reproduce a specialized and disciplined labor force" (Platt, 1977:xxii). According to Platt's account, as capitalism continued to develop, it was necessary that the economic system exert increasing control over the socialization of these future workers. Although others have argued that the motivations of the legislation's sponsors were humane and not coercive (Hagan and Leon, 1977; Schlossman, 1977), nevertheless the role of this legislation in labor exploitation remains. As will be seen in the following paragraphs, many studies have given primary importance to the economic or class interests involved in the legislative process.

Economic and Class Origins of the Law

The fifth and final theoretical orientation used to interpret the origins of law emphasizes the class, or economic, basis of law. For example, one service provided by the legal system is the prosecution of charges involving checks written on insufficient funds. Citizens are prosecuted, convicted, and incarcerated for writing bad checks, not so much because this behavior threatens the whole community but, rather, because "bad check" writers are an annoyance mainly to merchants, and the legal system gives merchants help in collecting on such checks.

In reflecting on contemporary political domination, Reich (1970) suggested that during this century a situation has developed in the United States that has

> produced law that fell into line with the requirements of organization and technology, and that supported the demands of administration rather than protecting the individual. Once law had assumed this role, there began a vast proliferation of laws, statutes, regulations, and decisions. For the law began to be employed to aid all of the work of the Corporate State by compelling obedience to the State's constantly increasing demands (page 110). . . . The greater the quantity of legal rules, the greater the amount of discretionary power is generated. If a licensed pharmacist is subject to fifty separate regulations, he can be harassed by one after another, as soon as he proves himself to have complied with the first (page 115).

In addition, the state dominates some citizens more than others (Reich, 1970:114):

> It can be seen that for each status, class, and position in society, there is a different set of laws. There is one set of laws for the welfare recipient, one for the businessman . . . for example, the constitutional right of privacy is treated differently for a businessman or farmer than for a welfare recipient. A person receiving Medicare is required to take a loyalty oath; others are not. If "law" means a general rule to govern a community of people, then in the most literal and precise sense we have no law; we are a lawless society.

Moreover, Reich (1970:110) observed that despite the proliferation of corporate power over citizens, corporations have largely not been held subject to the Bill of Rights by the courts and can, for example, fire employees who exercise their "freedom" of speech. Reich (1970:116) concluded: "The point is this: there can be no rule of law in an administrative state. The ideal of the rule of law can be realized only in a political-conflict state which places limits upon official power and permits diversity to exist."

This final perspective, which stresses domination as a consequence of an economic or class system, undoubtedly gives a more convincing picture of the role of criminal law, at least in modern industrial states. Yet, as discussed in chapter l, it might be argued that although some criminal laws, such as those involving embezzlement or bad checks, serve mainly and most directly the interests of the powerful, many laws appear to protect the poor and powerless as well as the more influential members of society. It might seem, for example, that murder and rape laws offer the same protection to all groups. In such cases, however, class interests are usually reflected in the administration or application of laws, a topic that will be covered in chapters 8, 9, and 10, which deal with the police and the courts. Indeed, a continuing complaint of the black community is that offenses against black people are taken less seriously by the police and are responded to with less vigorous official action than are identical offenses committed in the white community (for example, see Ennis, 1967:55; and Hahn, 1971).

This section of the chapter will examine several case studies to determine how various powerful groups in England and the United States have exercised their power to forge new legislation suited to their unique interests.

Chambliss (1964) convincingly demonstrated that the historical origins of vagrancy laws in England can be traced to the needs of the changing power structure. He suggested that the earliest forerunners of modern vagrancy laws originated in the thirteenth century. In a strict sense, these were not vagrancy laws because they did not seek to prevent idleness or the aimless wandering of citizens from one place to another. Rather, their aim was to relieve churches of their traditional responsibility for providing free food and shelter to travelers. These laws merely prohibited people from sleeping and eating at any place other than their own homes, including churches, unless they were invited to do so.

The first real vagrancy statutes that prohibited idleness were enacted in the fourteenth century. At that time it became a crime to give alms to anyone who was able to work and yet was unemployed, and it also became a crime to refuse work or leave a job without permission. These new laws were a product of the Black Death, which decimated the labor force in fourteenth-century England. Because few workers were available, the landowners required such legislation to force laborers to accept employment at low wages.

However, even with this help, the landowners were losing power, and by the fifteenth century there was yet another shift in the vagrancy laws. They were no longer designed to force laborers to work, but to control individuals who looked "suspicious," the type of people who might be robbers or thieves. Now the punishments for vagrancy convictions became very severe. The new vagrancy laws served the interests of the merchant groups. These groups were gaining in power and influence in England at the time and desired to have their goods in transit protected under law. Thus three powerful interest groups—the church, the landowners, and the merchants—were served at different periods by the changing vagrancy legislation.

Hall's study (1952:3–40) of embezzlement also vividly demonstrated the role of economic power in the development of written criminal laws in England. Under early English common law it was not considered criminal for people to convert to their own use property that an employer had given them to use in working for the employer. In other words, there was no known crime of embezzlement. Apparently, it was thought that owners had the obligation of protecting themselves by selecting a more trustworthy person to use their property while working for them. Such common-law practices seem to have been satisfactory during the Middle Ages, when the economy was dominated by employers who owned feudal estates and when their employees were serfs and thus legally tied to the land. At that time the essential method of commercial exchange was barter, trading one commodity for another. In such a situation an embezzlement law was not required.

At the end of the Middle Ages, however, several changes occurred that forced the emergence of some government control of what we today call embezzlement. Merchant trading companies were growing rapidly, and the feudal estates were breaking up. Therefore employees were no longer bound to the land. Moreover, barter was being replaced by the widespread use of paper money. The new mobility of employees, plus the increased use of paper money, make embezzlement much easier, and eventually court decisions began to recognize this new form of criminality; ultimately the growing power of commercial groups forced the required legislation through Parliament. The first of these laws protected only the Bank of England and the South Sea Company, clearly demonstrating the special interests served by this legislation. Of such court decisions, Hall (1952:33) declared: "A new set of major institutions required a new rule. The law, lagging behind the needs of the times, was brought into more harmonious relationship with the other institutions by the decision[s]." This illustrates that new legislation is not generated merely because a group has a specific need for such legislation; it is also necessary that the group be powerful enough to have its needs protected by law.

The rise to power of the merchant class had another interesting effect on the law. Nineteenth-century merchants objected to the capital penalty that was prescribed for many nonviolent crimes involving property, such as theft. The merchants argued that the severity of the prescribed punishment discouraged the prosecution of property crimes. Because of their reluctance to inflict the prescribed punishments, judges and juries used any pretext to render a verdict of not guilty even in the face of convincing contrary evidence. Thus theft and other property crimes went unpunished, and the severity of the laws actually encouraged criminality. Ironically, the merchants' support for less severe legal penalties was motivated by a desire for more, not less, punishment (Hall, 1952:110–152).

Indeed, Jeffery (1957) showed how the modern state and modern law emerged in England out of an earlier tribal system as a consequence of the changing economic system. Under tribal law, individuals were tied together by virtue of their bloodlines. When wrongdoing occurred, the whole family was held responsible and any member of the family could be punished. Thus order was maintained through the family. Punishments that were imposed included compensation to another family for injuries to one of its members; failing that, a feud between the families could begin. In the modern state, individuals are bound together through their ties to a common territory. There is individual rather than group responsibility, the state is the unit of justice and order, and punishment, rather than feuding, is the response to wrongs. As England was transformed from a tribal to a feudal and finally to a modern capitalist economy, all these legal changes were required.

The history of American colonies also provides support for the contention that the interests of powerful groups are protected by the laws. Originally there was a close association between sin and crime in the colonies because the Puritan leaders looked to the Bible in drafting criminal statutes (Nelson, 1967:450–482). Therefore court records up until the Revolution indicate that most prosecutions were for sin-crimes, such as fornication, violation of the Sabbath, and adultery. Since crime, like sin, could strike anywhere, offenders were found in all social classes. However, by the early 1800s the basic use of the criminal law had shifted from the preservation of morality to the protection of property. By the early 1800s, probably as a consequence of an economic depression and widespread unemployment, most convictions were for property offenses. Predictably, the records show that the typical offenders were now the urban poor, as is currently true. This example clearly shows that the function of the law had shifted to protect the interests of the more affluent, the property owners, against the less affluent. Economic distress and consequent increases in property violations seem to have caused concern with sin-crimes to be forgotten.

According to Becker (1963:135–146), the influence of the Protestant ethic was also responsible for the repressive governmental policy toward the use of some types of drugs. Yet Musto (1973) pointed out that the narcotics laws in the United States are also a product of the fear that certain drugs make specific minorities more difficult to control. White Southerners alleged that cocaine enabled blacks to withstand bullets that would kill normal persons and stimulated sexual assault among blacks. Such fears are reflected in the 1914 Harrison Tax Act, which legally controlled opium and coca products, including cocaine. Fear among whites in California that smoking opium encouraged sexual contacts between Chinese and white Americans was a factor in its prohibition.

According to Musto (1973), there was little fear of marihuana until the 1930s, and for this reason it was not prohibited under federal law until 1937. Mexican nationals came into the United States in great numbers during the 1920s and brought with them the tradition of marihuana use. Although Anglos in the Southwest may have disliked the habit, it was usually tolerated because the Mexicans provided an inexpensive source of labor during this period of economic boom. However, during the depression of the 1930s, Mexicans were seen as competitors for scarce jobs and their habits began to seem more threatening. This was especially true in the Southwest, where the Mexican immigrants were concentrated.

Physicians recognize that barbiturates, like heroin, are addictive (Smith and Wesson, 1973) and that barbiturates are undoubtedly more widely used than heroin (Brecher, 1972). Yet barbiturates, unlike heroin, are easily available from physicians by prescription. One explanation for the different handling of heroin and barbiturates is the different social status and power of the users of these drugs. The users of heroin are predominantly poor, whereas barbiturate addicts are generally more affluent (Smith and Wesson, 1973). The addiction of the poor is legally proscribed and is subject to police harassment, whereas the addiction of the more affluent is not. Similarly, the prohibition of alcohol was ultimately defeated not because it is safe to use alcohol but because of the power of its users.

The influence of elites has also been reflected in other drug legislation. Graham (1972) observed that 8 to 10 billion amphetamine pills are produced and consumed in the United States each year. According to expert medical testimony presented to Congress, only a samll percentage of these drugs are actually needed for legitimate medical purposes. The remainder of this massive overproduction, Graham indicated, is improperly used by students, housewives, and truckers as pep or diet pills, causing widespread physical addiction as well as traffic accidents that result from the drug's hallucinatory effects. Although Congress was also told of a widespread diversion of these pills to illegal channels, it failed to control the production of amphetamines in the misnamed "Comprehensive Drug Abuse Prevention and Control Act of 1970." This failure to control amphetamines, Graham demonstrates, was due to the powerful lobbying efforts of drug manufacturers who were reaping a bonanza of profits from the sale of these drugs. So intense were the manufacturers' efforts that the staff of the president of the American Pharmaceutical Association actually helped the Justice Department draft the bill to ensure its safety to the drug industry.

This is not to say that the mass of citizens never react successfully against societal elites or powerful economic interest groups. Martin Luther King's nonviolent civil disobedience is usually credited with having had some impact on the passage of the new civil rights legislation of the 1960s, and the campus war protests are believed to have helped deter the United States from waging further war in Southeast Asia and to have helped end the military draft. More recently, during the 1980s, widespread protests involving nonviolent law violation have been directed against both South Africa's system of apartheid and organizations with investments in that nation. These protests are widely believed to have exerted great pressure on the South African government, as well as on corporations with South African investments. Even if one ignores the fact that these influences have not been thoroughly documented, these alleged changes become insignificant in comparison with the changes in the law that have been documented as the work of elites and powerful economic interest groups.

CONCLUSION

This chapter demonstrated that a written criminal code has understandably developed in a mass society such as the United States and that this code helps coordinate activities among a heterogeneous people who often lack consensus on the societal norms. In a highly stratified society such as the United States, the law predictably reflects the interests of powerful interest groups, and even when it appears to protect the interests of less powerful groups, as in antitrust legislation, it is only an effort to pacify and contain those groups. The operation of various elites and powerful interest groups is reflected in the laws discussed in this chapter. At first, vagrancy laws reflected the interests of the church, then the interests of landowners, and finally the interests of merchants. In all instances, the transient poor were the objects of control. Severe penalties for property offenses were altered on behalf of business interests to ensure more likely punishment of the "dangerous classes." Owners of businesses obtained embezzlement legislation to protect their property against their clerks. In the United States at the beginning of the nineteenth century, the criminal code began to reflect less concern with sin and more concern with the protection of property owners' interests. Many drug laws show the influence of another influential group: there is some evidence that fundamentalist Protestant interests were behind the national prohibition of alcohol, as well as other narcotics legislation. Yet even here some section of the nation's poor is the object of control—blacks, Mexicans, or Chinese. It will be shown in the following chapter that the power of economic elites is sometimes reflected not only in the drug-related legislative activities they sponsor but in the drug-related legislation they oppose or help repeal.

REFERENCES

Akers, R. L.
  1968 "Problems in the sociology of deviance: social definitions and behavior." Social Forces 46:455–465.
Barkan, S. E.
  1984 "Legal control of the southern civil rights movement." American Sociological Review 49(August):522–565.
Becker, H. S.
  1963 Outsiders. New York: The Free Press of Glencoe.
Berk, R. A., H. Brackman, and S. Lesser
  1977 A Measure of Justice: An Empirical Study of Changes in the California Penal Code, 1955–1971. New York: Academic Press.
Berkowitz, L. and N. Walker
  1967 "Laws and moral judgment." Sociometry 30(December):410–422.
Berman, H. J.
  1963 Justice in the U.S.S.R. Rev. ed. New York: Vintage Books.
Black, H. C.
  1951 Black's Law Dictionary. 4th ed. St. Paul, Minn.: West.
Brecher, E. M. and Consumer Reports editors
  1972 Licit and Illicit Drugs. Mount Vernon, N.Y.: Consumers Union.
Chambliss, W. J.
  1964 "A sociological analysis of the law of vagrancy." Social Problems 12(Summer):67–77.

Civil Rights Act of 1964
  1964 Public Law 88–352, 88th Congress, 2d Session (July 2, 1964):241–268.
Cohen, S. and J. Young, eds.
  1973 The Manufacture of News. Beverly Hills, Calif.: Sage Publications.
Dahrendorf, R.
  1959 Class and Class Conflict in Industrial Society. Stanford, Calif.: Stanford University Press.
Durkheim, E.
  1933 The Division of Labor in Society. (George Simpson, trans.) Glencoe, Ill.: The Free Press.
Duster, T.
  1970 The Legislation of Morality. Law, Drugs, and Moral Judgment. New York: The Free Press.
Eaton, J. W.
  1952 "Controlled acculturation: a survival technique of the Hutterites." American Sociological Review 17(June):331–340.
Edelman, M.
  1964 The Symbolic Uses of Politics. Urbana: University of Illinois Press.
Ennis, P. H.
  1967 Criminal Victimization in the United States: A Report of a National Survey. National Opinion Research Center, University of Chicago. Washington, D.C.: U.S. Government Printing Office.

Erikson, K. T.
1966 Wayward Puritans: A Study in the Sociology of Deviance. New York: John Wiley & Sons.

Gandhi, M. K.
1951 Non-violent Resistance. New York: Schocken Books.

Gaylin, W. and D. J. Rothman
1976 "Introduction." Pp. xxi-xLi in A. von Hirsch, Doing Justice: The Choice of Punishments. New York: Hill & Wang.

Graham, J. M.
1972 "Amphetamine politics on Capitol Hill." Transaction 9(January):14–22, 53.

Gusfield, J. R.
1967 "Moral passage: the symbolic process in public designations of deviance." Social Problems 15:175–188.

Hagan, J. and J. Leon
1977 "Rediscovering delinquency: social history, political ideology and the sociology of law." American Sociological Review 42(August): 587–598.

Hahn, H.
1971 "Ghetto assessments of police protection and authority." Law and Society Review 6(November):183–194.

Hall, J.
1945 "Criminology." Pp. 342-365 in Georges Gurvitch and Wilbert Moore (eds.), Twentieth Century Sociology. New York: Philosophical Library.
1952 Theft, Law, and Society. 2nd ed. Indianapolis: Bobbs-Merrill.

Haskins, G. L.
1960 Law and Authority in Early Massachusetts: A Study in Tradition and Design. New York: Macmillan.

Hoebel, E. A.
1954 The Law of Primitive Man. Cambridge, Mass.: Harvard University Press.

Jeffery, C. R.
1956 "The structure of American criminological thinking." Journal of Criminal Law, Criminology and Police Science 46:658–672.
1957 "The development of crime in early English society." Journal of Criminal Law, Criminology and Police Science 47:647–666.

King, M. L., Jr.
1963 "Letter from Birmingham jail." The Christian Century 80(June12):767–773.

Korn, R. R. and L. W. McCorkle
1959 Criminology and Penology. New York: Holt, Rinehart & Winston.

LeGrande, J. L.
1967 "Nonviolent civil disobedience and police enforcement policy." The Journal of Criminal Law, Criminology and Police Science 58:393–404.

MacIver, R. M. and C. H. Page
1964 Society: An Introductory Analysis. London: Macmillan.

Mair, L.
1962 Primitive Government. Baltimore: Penguin Books.

Mohr, J. C.
1978 Abortion in America: The Origins and Evolution of National Policy. New York: Oxford University Press.

Murdock, G. P.
1950 "Feasibility and implementation of comparative community research." American Sociological Review 15(December):713–720.

Musto, D. F.
1973 The American Disease: Origins of Narcotic Control. New Haven: Yale University Press.

Nelson, W. E.
1967 "Emerging notions of modern criminal law in the revolutionary era: an historical perspective." New York University Law Review 42(May):450–482.

Platt, A. M.
1977 The Child Savers: The Invention of Delinquency. 2nd ed. (enlarged). Chicago: University of Chicago Press.

Pound, R.
1943 "A survey of social interests." Harvard Law Review 57(October):1–39.

Quinney, R.
1970 The Social Reality of Crime. Boston: Little, Brown.

Reich, C. A.
1970 The Greening of America. New York: Random House.

Roby, P. A.
1969 "Politics and criminal law: revision of the New York State penal law on prostitution." Social Problems 17:83–109.

Rossi, P. H., E. Waite, C. E. Bose, and R. E. Berk
1974 "The seriousness of crimes: normative structure and individual differences." American Sociological Review 39(April): 224–237.

Sallach, D. L.
1974 "Class domination and ideological hegemony. Sociological Quarterly 15(Winter): 38–50.

Schlesinger, R.
1945 Soviet Legal Theory. London: Kegan Paul, Trench, Trubner.

Schlossman, S. L.
1977 Love and the American Delinquent: The Theory and Practice of "Progressive" Juvenile Justice, 1825–1920. Chicago: University of Chicago Press.

Schwartz, R. D. and J. C. Miller
   1964   "Legal evolution and societal complexity."
          American Journal of Sociology 70(Sep-
          tember):159–169.
Skolnick, J. H.
   1966   Justice Without Trial: Law Enforcement in
          Democratic Society. New York: John Wiley
          & Sons.
Smith, D. E. and D. R. Wesson, eds.
   1973   Uppers and Downers. Englewood Cliffs,
          N.J.: Prentice Hall.
Sutherland, E. H.
   1924   Criminology. Philadelphia: J. B. Lippincott.
   1950   "The diffusion of sexual psychopath laws."
          American Journal of Sociology 56:142–148.

Vold, G. B.
   1958   Theoretical Criminology. New York:
          Oxford University Press.
Walker, N. and M. Argyle
   1967   "Does the law affect moral judgments?"
          British Journal of Criminology
          4(October):570–581.
Walker, N. and C. Marsh
   1984   "Do sentences affect public disapproval?"
          British Journal of Criminology 24(January):
          27–48.
Wirt, F. M.
   1970   Politics of Southern Equality: Law and
          Social Change in a Mississippi County. Chi-
          cago: Aldine.

7

THE ORIGINS OF AMERICAN MARIHUANA LAWS

One reason that marihuana laws are especially instructive is that there has been wholesale alteration of these laws within the past decade. Records of the dynamics of these changes are therefore easy to locate. In great part the changes have been a result of the recent widespread use of marihuana. In 1979 a national survey (Fishburne, el al., 1979) found that 68 percent of 18- to 25-year-olds reported that they had used marihuana. In 1984, fifty-five percent of high school seniors had used marihuana at least once (Johnston et al., 1985). Thus the marihauna prohibition laws have the capacity to create many millions of "marihuana criminals" and, in the process, seriously affect their families. This suggests the awesome potential of these laws and helps justify devoting a chapter to this one type of prohibition.

In the 1920s few states prohibited marihuana, but by the late 1930s all states prohibited its possession and sale (Becker, 1963). Federal legal controls were also created in 1937, and federal penalties increased during the 1950s (Musto, 1973). In 1956 the federal penalty for first-offense possession of marihuana was raised to 2 to 10 years in prison. But during the 1960s some states began to lower marihuana possession penalties. Since late 1968, of the 50 states in the United States, 49 have reduced first-offense possession of a limited amount of marihuana from a felony, usually punishable by more than a year in

Much of this chapter was taken from *Morals Legislation Without Morality: The Case of Nevada* by John F. Galliher and John R. Cross. Copyright 1983 by Rutgers, the State University.

prison, to at most a misdemeanor, usually punishable by a fine, less than one year of confinement in a local jail, or both. The growing awareness that marihuana use is no more hazardous than the use of other drugs, such as tobacco and alcohol, and that it should not be treated with severity, is undoubtedly tied to the recent widespread use of marihuana among affluent citizens (Clausen, 1961; Goode, 1970:35–40, 1972:36–37). In the 1970s eleven states totally removed jail sentences for most cases of possession of small amounts of marihuana. Since 1978 no further reforms of marihuana laws have occurred. As with other types of laws, the pressure from powerful groups also helps to explain the recent change in attempts to control marihuana use in the United States.

Another reason for studying marihuana laws is the symbolic punch they carry. Kaplan (1970) demonstrated that marihuana offenses are unique, even among other drug offenses, because the meanings that have been associated with marihuana have been particularly intense. During the 1960s the use of this drug was associated, in the minds of many, with young people who were hedonistic, self-indulgent, and lacking in patriotism and respect for authority. And because marihuana is such a chemically mild drug in comparison with heroin and LSD, observers have a maximum amount of freedom to define it in any way they see fit. A corollary of blaming marihuana use on Mexicans is that the word *marihuana* is often spelled with a Spanish silent *j*, which implies that this drug is a foreign substance imposed on Americans from a foreign culture. Writers who use such a spelling predictably often see the drug as a menace associated with some threatening minority group in the United States, with some foreign nation, or both. The minority group or foreign nation is seen as responsible for growing the drug and selling it here—as imposing it on Americans. Persons who use the hard Anglo *h* in spelling *marihuana* are both more likely to be tolerant and less likely to see the drug's use as associated with local minorities or foreign nations. This difference in usage and understanding amounts to a politics of spelling. The subliminal message carried with the Spanish *j* is that marihuana is a foreign drug that is being imposed on Americans from without.

There is a long tradition in the United States of blaming outsiders for our drug problem (Musto, 1973). It is either Turkey or Thailand—or even more likely Cuba, Mexico, or Colombia—that is defined as responsible for our drug problems, including our marihuana problems. There is a continuing massive effort to interdict the flow of all illegal drugs, including marihuana, into the United States. Obviously the reason drugs are smuggled into this country is that there is what economists call a massive and an inelastic demand for these drugs here. Therefore, if the government officials were ever to be effective in shutting off the supply of marihuana into this country, it seems reasonable to assume that American marihuana consumers would rely on domestic varieties, which grow wild in many states and can be, and are, cultivated in every state in the Union. Yet blaming foreign countries for our drug problem coincides with the effort to blame ethnic minorities in the United States for our illicit drug use. As noted in the previous chapter, Musto (1973) observed that the greatest support for punitive drug penalties is in the case of drugs associated with some dreaded minority group. And whenever our nation has been in a serious international conflict, such as during the Cold War of the 1950s, legal control of drugs and drug users have become much more punitive. The recurrent pattern is that drug abuse is associated with fear of, and conflict with, outsiders.

Himmelstein (1983) showed, through a review of the *Readers' Guide to Periodical Literature* from 1890 to 1976, that the dangers associated with marihuana use have changed over the past century. Before the 1930s, the drug was at times associated with Arabs and called hashish, was sometimes associated with American Indians and called Indian hemp, and also was associated in some cases with Mexicans and called marihuana. By the 1930s the first two images of marihuana had receded and only the third meaning of the substance remained. And during the 1930s marihuana was defined in the press as a "killer weed" that leads its users into homicidal rampages. In part, this image developed because the perceived users were Mexicans who were stereotyped as violent. By the late 1960s the imagery had changed to what Himmelstein (1983) called the "dropout drug," which allegedly caused something called the amotivational syndrome. It was claimed that all interest in achievement vanished in persons who used the drug. Himmelstein reasoned that these altered fears associated with the drug were a consequence of the changing characteristics of its users. Although during the 1930s the greatest fear of Mexicans was their violence, once it was recognized in the late 1960s that the primary users were middle-class youths, the main fears associated with this group was not their violence but, rather, their ultimate possible failure because of a loss of motivation.

THEORIES AND EMPIRICAL RESULTS

Despite repeated calls for research on the social origins of laws, studies of this kind have been produced only on selected types of laws. Alix (1978:xxv) claimed that few have studied laws that deal with what are considered the most serious crimes. Carson (1974:71) contended that the concentration on controversial criminal laws has caused researchers to ignore the widespread consensus that exists on most legal sanctions. Yet research on drug laws in general, and marihuana laws in particular, is significant precisely because of their controversial character. During public debate and political maneuvering on such legislation, one can discover some of the nature of the political process not evident in laws involving crimes such as burglary or armed robbery, where there is something approaching complete consensus and little public debate.

In comparison with the massive amount of research on the deterrence of crime, very little research has been done on the origins of criminal law. And no systematic, integrated research tradition has developed. Perhaps this is a consequence of a lack of researcher commitment to this type of investigation, together with the fact that existing studies span several academic fields, including law, history, and sociology. The lack of integration seems to be a major factor in limiting theoretical and methodological advances in this body of literature. Indeed, at present there does not seem to be an even rudimentary consensus on the meaning and use of methodological techniques or theoretical constructs (Galliher and Walker, 1978), which results in collective confusion in the interpretation of data from such studies (Galliher and Walker, 1977).

Alix (1978:xxvi) observed that "some writers have been concerned with championing, on ideological grounds, various models of law creation as characterizing criminal law in general." Indeed, it is evident in the work of some researchers that they zealously defend a specific theoretical assumption that law either is a result of a pluralistic political process, with no one group or type of group always in control (Hagan and Leon, 1977), or is a consequence of domination of all spheres of the political process by elites (Platt, 1969). Coexisting with these differing theoretical assumptions are variations in the findings, or empirical results, regarding the types of interests served by the laws studied. As noted in the preceding chapter, some studies allegedly demonstrate that laws serve moral interests such as those of specific religious groups; other research emphasizes that laws serve economic interests such as those of certain groups of workers and social classes.

As might be expected, the relationship between the initial theoretical assumptions and the ultimate results is far from random. Those studies of law which assume a pluralistic interest-group theory usually find that moral interests are served by legislation. Unlike material resources, morality is not easily subject to accumulation and hoarding in the hands of a few. As indicated earlier, Becker's study (1963) of the moral entrepreneur's role in the creation of new public morals legislation implies that a wide variety of groups could have such an entrepreneur working on their behalf. Becker claimed that, even with the exercise of such leadership, drug laws have their essential foundations in a considerable degree of moral consensus in society. He noted that traditional Protestant values require self-control, encourage humanitarianism, and proscribe ecstasy states—"three values that provided legitimacy for attempts to prevent the use of intoxicants and narcotics" (Becker, 1963:135–136). Conversely, those studies of the origins of law which are informed by some variety of elite theory, or Marxism, stressing total domination by unified and powerful interests, typically find that economic interests are served by laws. Musto (1973), for example, demonstrated that federal marihuana prohibitions were essentially a result of pressure from southwestern, Anglo political leaders concerned about the inroads Mexican-Americans were making in the job market.

CONCEPTUAL PRECISION

There is a lack of conceptual precision in the study of the social origins of laws, and it creates disagreement over what sort of data can be used to address such questions. Such disagreements are inevitable without agreement on what type of research problem such questions about the social origins of law involve. Gibbs and Erickson (1975:38) claimed that such research "must end with potentially falsifiable assertions about (a) the distinguishing characteristics of individuals who control the enactments of criminal law, [and] (b) the process by which laws are enacted." Category "a" includes information on individual legislative sponsors' motivations, and category "b" contains data on legislative sponsors' tactics. Gibbs and Erickson clearly were calling for information on microscopic details of legislative sponsors' or opponents' tactics or motivations. Such details are referred to as the triggering events of legislation.

Yet Jeffery (1956:426) claimed that such a mechanical "A causes B" orientation toward research is essentially ahistorical and ultimately will shed little light on the world in which criminal laws are passed. As Hall (1952:14) observed, information about structural features, such as "existing legal, social, political and economic institutions," is often reflected in the "common and recurring" events found over a relatively broad historical period, whereas "changes *within a short period of time* suggest the operation of individual, unique influences" (original emphasis). The historical, demographic, and economic features of society provide the milieu within which these individual influences develop and are referred to here as the structural foundations of the law. Both Jeffery and Hall seem to have been calling for information on the structural foundations of laws.

Each type of data has its own strenghts and limitations. Data on triggering events give convincing and often detailed information on exactly *how* a law was passed, that is, on the legislative process. Because of the narrow focus of such data, however, little is revealed about *why* a law was passed. To understand why a law was passed requires a broader range of information on the structural foundations of the law. These data usually provide information on historical epochs and how they, in turn, are associated in time with specific legislation. This distinction between structural foundations and triggering events draws attention to differences in methodology and type of data that, unlike theoretical differences, are often glossed over by researchers. Writers often argue past one another without recognizing that they are dealing with different research questions and different types of data. Thus both recognized theoretical differences and unrecognized methodological divergences contribute to the polemics that appear in the literature.

Often the same legislation has been studied by researchers emphasizing moral interests and political pluralism and also by researchers stressing economic interests and elite theory. Predictably, these researchers come to vastly different conclusions. Applying the methodological distinction between triggering events and structural foundations reveals that many researchers dealing with the origins of criminal law are not, contrary to what they say, arguing about the same issue. They find different origins because they are analyzing different types of data, some studying triggering events, some studying structural foundations, and some studying both. For example, Erikson (1966) argued that the punishment of witchcraft and other religious deviation in the Bay Colony in

Massachusetts had its origins in a collective search for meaning in an increasingly heterogeneous society. By punishing this behavior—by demonstrating that such bahavior would not be tolerated—the society established moral boundaries and new meaning for the group. Chambliss (1974) argued, however, that the punishment was triggered by colony leaders who feared the loss of their high position during periods when their authority was being challenged. Persons who challenged their position usually were singled out for punishment. Erikson seemed to deal more with the structural foundations of the punishment by focusing on the religious heterogeneity of the society, whereas Chambliss dealt with the motivations of the sponsors of the punishment, that is, with the triggering events.

Platt (1969) argued that American juvenile codes and juvenile courts, which are a part of civil law, have their origins in the changing ethnic and religious composition of American society around the beginning of the twentieth century. Native-born Protestants looked with fear on the increasing numbers of immigrants from southern and eastern Europe who shared neither their religious nor their ethnic heritage. The Protestants thought that some legislation was required to control the deviant behavior of children in the immigrant groups. Platt rested his argument essentially on the changing religious and ethnic composition of America early in the 1900s—that is, he emphasized structural characteristics. Yet Hagan and Leon (1977) convincingly demonstrated that the motivation of sponsors of Canadian delinquency legislation was humane and not coercive or punitive. Focusing on triggering events, Hagan and Leon found a much different origin of delinquency laws, which, they maintained, destroys the credibility of Platt's claims, but they failed to recognize that they are dealing with a different order of events.

Similarly, Becker (1963) argued that the federal Marihuana Tax Act of 1937 was triggered by the lobbying of the Director of the Federal Bureau of Narcotics, Harry Anslinger. Yet Musto (1973) ignored this claim in a later study of the same law and asserted that the legislation was directed at the repression of Mexicans and was a result of racial and economic conflicts between Anglos and Mexicans in the southwestern states. He focused, instead, on the law's structural foundations.

Even within a single study, such conflicts in interpretation of the origin of a law are apparent (Galliher et al., 1974). Nebraska was one of the first states to reduce the penalty for marihuana possession during the 1960s. The motivation of legislative supporters varied. Some supporters wanted more certain punishment of college student drug users, inasmuch as few were being prosecuted under the felony marihuana law. Others, more sympathetic to college student marihauna smokers, wanted reduced penalties that would not ruin students' lives. Although the motivations of this law's two kinds of supporters were diametrically opposed, the two groups agreed on penalty reductions. This case of deep divisions of opinion among this legislation's sponsors demonstrates that the structural foundations of a law are not necessarily obvious from the motivations of any given legislative supporter. Discovering the nature of structural foundations requires consideration of a broader range of historical detail.

Without more conceptual precision, it is difficult to anticipate and interpret changes in American drug laws. The morally conservative states of Nebraska and Utah were among the leaders in 1969 in reducing penalties for first-offense marihuana possession. The comparatively liberal state of New York increased its penalty for sale and possession of most types of drugs in the early 1970s. Drawing on the distinction between structural foundations and triggering events, one can show that in Nebraska the early marihuana penalty reduction, and in Utah the reduction of the penalty for marihuana possession and for a variety of other drugs, were passed into law because no threatening minority that could be associated with drug use existed in either state. In contrast, many large and often threatening minorities associated with drug use live in New York State. Remember that the notion of structural foundations draws attention to relevant racial, political, and economic disputes in a given historical epoch; the idea of triggering events draws attention to the moral sentiments people use to justify support of particular legislation. As an introduction to the use of these concepts, it is helpful to review their use in analyzing the origins of marihuana laws in Nebraska, Utah, and Nevada and of federal marihuana legislation.

STRUCTURAL FOUNDATIONS AND TRIGGERING EVENTS

Since by the late 1960s, marihuana use was becoming widespread among middle- and upper-class youth (Goode, 1970), it was not surprising that late in 1968 and early in 1969, several states changed their narcotics-control laws, reducing the maximum penalty for possession to a misdemeanor punishable by less than 1 year of confinement. The purpose of this chapter is twofold: (1) to illustrate the utility of structural foundations and triggering events in analyzing the origins of law and (2) in this manner to provide the basis for comparing the development of marihuana laws in three states—Nebraska, Utah, and Nevada—and in the federal government.

NEBRASKA'S MARIHUANA LAW

Structural Foundations

The demand for leniency in marihuana offenses can be clearly shown to result in part from class interests in the case of Nebraska, which in April 1969 became the second state to make the possession of marihuana a misdemeanor punishable by less than a year of confinement. Nebraska was an unexpected leader among the states in reducing the penalty for possession of marihuana. It has a small population (approximately 1.5 million in 1970) and according to the

1970 census figures was relatively homogeneous, with almost 97 percent of the population white and less than 3 percent black. The state has only two cities with a population of over 50,000, and it seems to be culturally dominated by a farming and small-town way of life. In April 1969 the penalty for possession of up to 1 pound of marihuana was reduced from 2 to 5 years' imprisonment to a maximum jail term of 7 days. The question is, Why would such a conservative state pass legislation that many persons would see as extremely liberal?

Drug abuse was a relatively minor problem in Nebraska before the late 1960s. News reports in the *Lincoln Star* in the state capital, a city with a population of more than 100,000, list an average of one case a year between 1950 and 1967. The Nebraska State Highway Patrol kept records of drug offenses during this period; the averge was 15 cases a year for the entire state between 1960 and 1967. In 1968 drug arrests in Nebraska increased sevenfold over the number in 1967. Many of the arrests involved students. It is in this context that a very conservative state senator introduced legislation (LB2, April 11, 1969) that reduced the penalty for possession of marihuana.

Triggering Events

Newspapers in two urban areas of the state, Lincoln and Omaha, were reviewed to determine public response to the proposed legislation. The interval reviewed was from January to June 1969, which included the periods immediately preceding the introduction of the bill, during its consideration, and after its passage. It seemed likely that most of the interest in drugs and related legislation would be concentrated in these two cities because both had experienced greater increases in drug arrests than other Nebraska communities and because colleges and universities are in both communities. There was no published debate in these papers on the bill by politicians or citizens. The newspaper in the hometown of the bill's senate sponsor was reviewed to gauge the response of his constituents; again, there was no citizen or editorial response. The introduction and passage of the bill were merely noted and then apparently forgotten.

The public hearings on the bill also show a lack of interest. Only one witness testified. A county prosecutor argued in support of the new law as more reasonable and humane than the old law, which treated "experimenting" with drugs by young people as a felony. The motivations of the senate sponsor of the bill, however, seemed more punitive and directed toward more certain punishment of drug-law violators: "The penalty of a felony was so great, it was the belief of the County Attorneys (prosecutors) that they wasted their time trying to enforce it, because the judges would not apply the felony penalty."

In August 1968, six months before the new marihuana-control bill was passed, the son of an outstate county prosecutor was arrested in Lincoln, the state capital, where he was a student at the state university. He was charged with marihuana possession. The boy's father resigned his office, vowing to fight to change what he now had decided was an unjust law. Another student, arrested with the prosecutor's boy, was the son of a local university professor. At first the prosecutor represented his son, but he soon hired a prominent Democratic lawyer who later would become president of the Nebraska Bar Association. The university professor's son was represented by a popular Republican ex-governor who had declined to run for reelection. According to the outstate prosecutor, both attorneys were picked because of their political influence. Explaining the use to which this influence was applied, the ex-governor said, "We recognized the case on our clients was airtight so [we] figured it was best to attack the law." He wrote a draft of a first-offense marihuana-possession misdemeanor law and, after discussing the issue with the county attorney who was prosecuting the boys, sent the proposal to him. The prosecutor, in turn, forwarded it to the senator, who ultimately sponsored the bill.

The county prosecutor handling the case indicated that the state County Attorneys Association unofficially endorsed the idea because of the difficulties in getting convictions in drug cases. Moreover, the members of the association were concerned about a felony conviction for "college kids just experimenting with marihuana," a concern reflected by another county prosecutor who testified at the public hearings. Only one journalist characterized the senate sponsor of the marihuana misdemeanor law as too permissive on drug offenses. Characterizing this man as soft on drugs apparently exceeded credibility for most observers, because of his conservative politics and his argument that the reduction would make convictions easier. Yet the senator recognized the wisdom of leniency for at least some persons in the middle and upper classes, because during the public hearings he volunteered to make the misdemeanor bill retroactive to the day before the boys' arrests, which he later did.

The triggering events clearly centered around the arrest of the sons of the two prominent Nebraskans. The events must be understood, however, in the context of the structural foundations of the legislation. Because Nebraska is such a homogeneous state, it is unlikely that severe drug penalties would be supported as a means of harassment and domination of local minorities. In such a setting, one can understand why prosecutors and lawmakers would dislike the idea of sending local youths to prison. As will be seen later in this chapter, a much different set of circumstances must be involved in the maintenance of severe marihuana penalties.

UTAH'S DRUG LAWS

Structural Foundations

If a leadership role in reducing drug penalties was unexpected for Nebraska, it surely was for Utah. Yet at approximately the same time that Nebraska reduced its penalty for first-offense marihuana possession to a misdemeanor, Utah also did so (Galliher and Basilick, 1979).

Utah is a contemporary Mormon equivalent of historical theocracies.

Most residents are Mormons, and there are few minorities of any kind. The 1970 census shows few blacks (6,617, or 0.06%), and Jonas (1961) cited evidence of only 46,766 Roman Catholics (approximately 4%). Part of the collective identity of Mormons comes from church prohibitions against the use not only of tobacco and alcohol but also of coffee and tea. The last two prohibitions obviously separate Mormons, or Latter-day Saints (LDS), from most other Christians. Joseph Smith, the LDS church's founder, advocated these prohibitions to protect the human body, and the church expends considerable effort demonstrating the harmful effects of these substances. Surely, in Utah, tolerance of marihuana would not be expected.

The church's opposition to drugs has been emphasized by its president and by numerous other church leaders. As might be expected, the Mormon clergy's attitudes toward drug laws are much more restrictive than those of other clergy. In a survey of Catholic, Protestant, and Mormon clergy, Jolly (1972) found that a higher percentage of Mormons thought possession of such drugs as marihuana, amphetamines, LSD, and heroin should be punished as a serious crime. Non-Mormon clergy were more likely to choose either legalization or misdemeanor penalties.

The conservative character of the Mormon faithful is reflected in the Utah state government. Jonas (1961, 1969) reported that the Utah legislature is indeed very conservative and typically is 90 to 95 percent Mormon, whereas only 70 percent of the general state population are church members. Three-term governor Calvin L. Rampton has contended that the reason for Mormon over-representation in the state legislature is that Mormons vote as a block for friends, who are always church members. Rampton has also observed that not only are more Mormons elected, but LDS church officials are especially likely to be elected. Thus the Utah legislature is controlled not merely by Mormons but by church officials, who would seem even more likely than other members to follow church teaching.

In 1969 penalties were increased dramatically and took the form of mandatory minimum penalties for most drug offenses (SB143, SB164). One of the exceptions was punishment for first-offense possession of marihuana, which was lowered to a misdemeanor, punishable by 6 months to 1 year in the local jail or by probation. In 1971 penalties were reduced (SB101) for all drug offenses. First-offense possession of any controlled substance, including marihuana, was made punishable by a maximum of 6 months in jail. Punishment for the second offense was reduced from a maximum of 20 years to 1 year of confinement. All these bills passed both houses of the Utah legislature, either unanimously or by wide margins, reflecting the homogeneity of these bodies.

Triggering Events

In 1969 the sponsor of the bill to increase drug penalties argued that the legislation was required because the courts had misused their "broad discretion." Originally the legislation raised penalties for all drug offenses, but the bill ultimately was modified to decrease penalties for possession of marihuana. The question is, Why was the exception made for marihuana?

The head of the Utah Bar Association Committee on Dangerous Drugs and Narcotics opposed the severe marihuana penalty. He said, "We would run the risk of classifying vast numbers of our children as felons, with the extremely serious consequences that brand carries." He noted that a felony conviction would mean loss of civil rights, such as the right to vote, to be admitted to many colleges, and to obtain government employment, or employment in many private concerns. An attorney who lobbied in the Utah senate for reduction in penalties for marihuana possession explained why it was so easy to get the bill modified: "We merely asked the senators if they really wanted to sentence people who are really not criminals—kids and so on. These are your kids after all, we told them." Another attorney involved in the lobbying effort said:

> We sat down with the legislators and said that this would only put kids in the state prison at a youthful age and hurt them. We also pointed out that the courts would be reluctant to convict in marihuana possession cases since the marihuana problem was hitting middle-class families and Mormon youth. For example, I was a federal magistrate judge at the time when a prominent Utah banker's son was arrested for possession of large quantities of marihuana.

And the 1969 bill's LDS senate cosponsor claimed that he finally had been convinced that, with felony marihuana penalties, "we would be punishing kids, and anyway, judges wouldn't enforce it."

Approximately 2 weeks after the amended 1969 drug laws were passed, the Utah governor appointed the Citizen Advisory Committee on Drugs. The main purpose of the committee was to study Utah's drug problem and make recommendations for its control. According to the former governor who appointed the committee: "There was at the time [1969] a growing concern with drugs in Utah among the citizens and their elected representatives, and the 1969 drug legislation reflected this concern. The committee's task was to determine to what extent these concerns were justified." The committee distributed a statewide anonymous questionnaire to high school and college students and also held hearings on the drug-abuse problem in Utah. It issued its report in September 1969. Some of the committee's conclusions were as follows:

> If marihuana is included in a survey, then it can be said that no junior or senior high school in Salt Lake City has not had drugs. The age is lowering when arrests can be made in the sixth grade.
>
> Economic status is no deterrent to obtaining drugs and youngsters of all economic levels are involved.
>
> High school students in Utah report that 33.7 percent of them can obtain drugs quite readily, while 31.6 percent *think* they can do the same thing. (Emphasis added.)

On the basis of testimony from the Salt Lake City chief of police, the committee concluded that the increased penalties (the mandatory minimum penalties) that were in the 1969 drug laws resulted in judges' throwing out cases in some instances. The committee recommended that discretion be returned to the courts by dropping mandatory minimum sentences so that consideration could be given to the "nature and seriousness of the offense, the prior record of the offender and other relevant circumstances." The committee also specifically recommended a further lowering of the penalty for possession of marihuana.

A Utah Bar Association committee studied the state's drug laws at approximately the same time, and in 1971 it proposed legislation that decreased all drug penalties. The committee representative defended the legislation before the Utah legislature as follows: "It was the feeling that there are a lot of people and young people who are experimenting and it didn't make a lot of sense to throw 18- and 19-year-old kids who are merely experimenting in prison for terms where they may come out hardened criminals." The senate sponsor of the bill observed: "This bill gives the judges the permission to exercise some discretion in the case of young people who are first offenders."

Throughout the process there was a visible, but not critical, concern with drugs, at least as reflected in the Utah press. During the year before the 1969 legislation, the LDS church newspaper, the *Deseret News*, published 74 articles on drugs, and the *Salt Lake City Tribune* published 18. In the year before the 1971 legislation, the *Tribune* printed 23 such articles; the *Deseret News*, 26. A constant theme throughout these stories was the high social class and youth of drug users.

The LDS church could have justified a strong stand against lower drug penalties, but it did not take one. Indeed, as early as March 10, 1969, the *Deseret News* gave editorial support to changing long mandatory jail sentences to protect "youthful first offenders." The triggering events for the 1969 amended marihuana penalty reductions and the 1971 across-the-board drug penalty reductions centered, instead, around lawmakers' recognition of the characteristics of local drug users. The statewide drug survey clearly illustrated the type of drug-law violators in Utah. In turn, the characteristics of drug users were, as in Nebraska, a consequence of the homogeneity of the state's population. The numerical and political domination by Mormons provided the essential structural foundations for the legislation. Again, one would anticipate a diametrically opposite situation in any jurisdiction where severe marihuana penalties are maintained.

THE FEDERAL MARIHUANA TAX ACT OF 1937

The first federal attempt to control marihuana was the Marihuana Tax Act of 1937. Like other federal drug controls at the time, the law was enforced by the Federal Bureau of Narcotics (FBN), a branch of the Treasury Department. Punishment was for failure to register one's possession of the controlled substance and to pay the prescribed tax, which in most cases was a prohibitive $100 per ounce. The maximum penalty for failure to pay the tax was a $2,000 fine, 5 years in prison, or both. Why did the federal government pass such a law at that time? Becker (1963) claimed that in the early 1930s, neither the public nor law enforcement officials considered the use of marihuana a serious problem. Indeed, he has shown that in 1930 only 16 states had passed laws prohibiting the use of marihuana; yet by 1937 all states had passed such legislation. What was the reason for this apparently sudden change in attitudes and the consequent federal legislation?

Triggering Events

Becker (1963) and others blamed the passage of the act on a publicity campaign waged by the FBN under Director Henry Anslinger's leadership. Bonnie and Whitebread (1974) provided convincing evidence that the bureau instigated in the early 1930s an "educational campaign" on the evils of marihuana, which undoubtedly contributed to the general definition of marihuana as evil and to its widespread prohibition in the states.

Anslinger and Clinton M. Hester, of the Treasury Department, spoke on behalf of the Marihuana Tax Act during public hearings in the House and Senate (U.S. Congress, House, 1937). They used two main techniques during the public hearings: unverified case histories of the purported tragedy caused by marihuana use, and newspaper editorial opinion cited as fact. Anslinger provided lurid case histories from a variety of regions: "It is only in the last two years that we had a report of seizures anywhere but in the Southwest. Last year New York State reported 195 tons seized, whereas before that I do not believe that New York could have reported one ton seized. . . . Last year the state of Pennsylvania destroyed 200,000 pounds." Anslinger offered opinion as fact to enliven his long list of cases: "I believe in some cases one cigarette might develop a homicidal mania, probably to kill his brother [sic]." During the House hearings (U.S. Congress, House, 1937), Hester quoted from an editorial in the *Washington Times*:

> The marihuana cigaret [sic] is one of the most insidious of all forms of dope, largely because of the failure of the public to understand its fatal qualities. . . . The nation is almost defenseless against it, having no Federal laws to cope with it and virtually no organized campaign for combatting it. . . . The result is tragic. . . . Schoolchildren are the prey of peddlers who infest school neighborhoods. . . . High-school boys and girls buy the destructive weed without knowledge of its capactiy for harm, and conscienceless dealers sell it with impunity. . . . This is a national problem, and it must have national attention. . . . The fatal marihuana cigarette must be recognized as a deadly drug and American children must be protected against it.

Hester then quoted similar editorials from the *Washington Post* and the *Washington Herald*.

Given the apparent propaganda effort of the FBN, what was the actual impact of the campaign on the American public? Surely, were the campaign totally effective, its consequences would be visible in the press. In the *Los Angeles Times*, for example, between May 31, 1936, and June 1, 1937, the 12-month period preceding the passage of the bill, only seven articles concerning marihuana appeared; in the *Dallas Morning News*, 11 such articles appeared; in the *Denver Post*, 18; in the *New York Times, 19; and in the Washington Post*, there were 6. These figures make an overall average of one article a month in each newspaper (Galliher and Walker, 1977). Aside from the limited number of articles on marihuana, their location in the newspapers is instructive: only two appeared on the front page. But despite the small evidence of a marihuana panic, these articles always characterized marihuana as a dangerous narcotic.

Structural Foundations

Assuming that the FBN made some effort at public education, in what type of structural environment did this campaign take place? As discussed in chapter 6, Musto (1973) claimed that to understand the creation of the Marihuana Tax Act, one must recognize that during the economic depression of the 1930s, hatred toward Mexicans and their habits escalated because of the competition they created for scarce jobs. Musto interviewed Anslinger to explore what he recalled of the specific pressures behind the legislation. Anslinger stated that it was political pressure generated from these southwestern states that was the crucial factor in the passage of the new law (Musto, 1973:220, 225):

> Southwestern police and prosecuting attorneys likewise protested constantly to the federal government about the Mexicans' use of the weed. . . . In the summer of 1936 it therefore became obvious that there would be no law to placate the Southwest unless some federal legislation under traditional legal powers was enacted.

In this case, the structural foundations of an intentionally punitive drug law stemmed from ethnic heterogeneity, whereas the homogeneous populations of Nebraska and Utah provided the environment, or structural foundations, for reductions in marihuana penalties.

NEVADA'S MARIHUANA LAW

During the 1960s and 1970s, all American states except one reduced the crime category for possession of small amounts of marihuana from a serious crime involving many years in the state prison, to a minor infraction involving less than a year in the local jail. That one exception was Nevada (Galliher and Cross, 1982; 1983). Long after all other states had altered their laws, Nevada law still required 1 to 6 years' confinement for conviction of possession of the slightest amount of marihuana. The question to ask is, Why would a state with a history of easy moral standards—with respect to legalized gambling and prostitution, divorce laws that require only a 3-week waiting period, and laws permitting the sale of liquor 24 hours a day, including Sunday—why would this same state have a law requiring the most severe marihuana penalties in America?

Triggering Events

In 1968 a Las Vegas newspaper lamented the fact that marihuana use by young people was rising rapidly. That year the Carson City Parent-Teacher Association started a drug prevention program that included kindergarten children, and a candidate for sheriff claimed that drugs were being sold to third graders. Frequent news reports of massive drug raids involving large numbers of suspects and massive amounts of illegal drugs appeared in Nevada's newspapers. The situation was seen as so serious that a U.S. senator from Nevada asked the U.S. Bureau of Narcotics and Dangerous Drugs to send agents to assist the Las Vegas school district in fighting drug abuse.

In 1969 a legislative study of the Nevada drug problem found an epidemic of drug use among middle- and upper-class youths and clung to the belief that future research ultimately would prove the addictive qualities of marihuana (Nevada, Legislative Commission, 1969). During this period of intense concern, a candidate for sheriff in Las Vegas was arrested on two occasions for marihuana possession. In 1970 a candidate for the state legislature was arrested for marihuana possession. In the same year, the sons of two Nevada state legislators were arrested, and one was convicted for possession of drugs including marihuana.

A 1969 Nevada legislative study determined that outsiders ultimately were responsible for the drug problem in the state. "It appears that drugs are introduced into Clark County from Los Angeles and Mexico, while the Washoe County, Ormsby County, and Douglas County problem stems from the Lake Tahoe, Sacramento and San Francisco areas" (Nevada, Legislative Commission, 1969:6). However, the newspaper reports of the residential location of persons arrested for drug offenses in 1967–1968 and 1970–1971 demonstrate that most were not from California, nor even from out of state. Fifty-nine percent of those arrested in 1967–1968 and 65 percent in 1970–1971 had a Nevada address. In 1975 a comprehensive research report based on official arrest and conviction records was prepared by the state government to assess the magnitude and nature of crimes committed in the state by nonresidents (Nevada Department of Adult Probation and Parole, 1974–1975). The study demonstrated, as does the tally of news reports, that nonresidents made up a minority of those charged and convicted of crimes, including drug offenses. But the mere fact that such a research project was ever conducted reflects the concern in Nevada regarding the criminal behavior of nonresidents.

Interviews, the legislative records, and statements in the press show that

Nevadans continued to blame outsiders for their drug problems. Many of those interviewed said that severe drug penalties in Nevada were designed to keep out drug traffickers from California:

DISTRICT ATTORNEY: California is only 13 miles away. There is the conscious thought that Nevada has stiff drug penalties to give Californians a warning to stay on your side.

CIRCUIT COURT JUDGE: We do have a serious problem with California people around the lake [Tahoe] area [which is half in Nevada]. There is no law enforcement around the lake in California and so we have a constant problem with pushers.

A Las Vegas narcotics officer said: "We don't have local kids using drugs; we mainly are making arrests on transients." The director of legislative research said: "Most drug offenders aren't Nevadans but are Californians, since this is a tourist state and California has so many people, so close."

Arrest records from Nevada's two major population centers, Reno and Las Vegas, indicate that between 1972 and 1977, less than 8 percent of those arrested in Las Vegas for narcotics offenses were ultimately convicted as charged. Although Reno keeps no conviction data, it records the type of drug involved in each narcotics arrest. These records indicate that although the total number of drug arrests remained fairly constant during the 6-year period from 1972 through 1977, the proportion of marihuana arrests decreased from 75 percent in 1972 to 15 percent in 1977.

Information from the Nevada Department of Parole and Probation indicates that of 214 persons convicted of possession of marihuana in 1974, only 14 were sentenced to prison. In 1978, there were only 13 prison sentences for marihuana possession, and these were the result of "special cases" involving other criminal charges.

Some of those interviewed mentioned that severe drug penalties gave the state a more respectable image than it might have had otherwise, because of its notorious reputation for gambling and prostitution.

DISTRICT ATTORNEY: We are scared to death that we might look so wide open and permissive to outsiders with our gambling, and all, that the federal government might outlaw everything here. High drug penalties, even though we don't use them, make us look better.

LAS VEGAS NEWSPAPER EDITOR: I was once a public defender and what is important here is law and order rhetoric, but most drug possession cases are dropped by the cops and the law is not enforced.

STATE LEGISLATOR: The rest of the nation is always looking at us. Being a gaming state we must keep a high profile. The federal government is always looking into gaming.

LAS VEGAS NARCOTICS OFFICER: Las Vegas has had a bad image and so the penalty has been kept high so our image won't be hurt and business won't be damaged.

RENO CIRCUIT COURT JUDGE: The state is subject to criticism for open drinking and gambling and so we try to fight the image as a wide open state and so we are tight on drugs. This need for image management in Las Vegas, of course, fits with the conservatism in the state.

The head of the legislative research department stated: "High drug penalties are a relief valve for not being able to deal with other moral issues with force." A member of the legislature agreed: "There is a collective guilty conscience associated with gaming. The attitude is that, yes, we have gaming but we control it and we have no other sins." Severe marihuana penalties serve a symbolic or image-management purpose whether or not the law can be effectively enforced.

Structural Foundations

Nevada has kept its severe marihuana penalties because of the type of actors blamed for the drug problem. News reports of arrests indicated that most drug violators were local and often high-status individuals, although the opinion was expressed in interviews and legislative reports that outsiders, or "transients," were responsible for Nevada's considerable drug problem. Thus Nevadans have an ambivalent attitude toward visitors to their state. These tourists are essential for the state's economy but are considered responsible for many of Nevada's social problems. As Musto (1973) demonstrated, the most repressive drug control laws typically are aimed at some threatening "outsiders" or minority—blacks, Mexicans, or Chinese. In this case the outsiders are tourists.

The heavy marihuana penalties serve as a symbol that Nevadans are not totally without moral standards. Blaming outsiders for the local crime problem also helps Nevadans avoid moral responsibility. Nevada maintains the symbol of severe marihuana penalties for public consumption but seldom enforces the law, which would require severe action against local citizens. In fact, the actual punishment of marihuana users in Nevada is not greatly different from that in other states with much lighter penalties. In recent years, while penalties have been lessened drastically in other states, there has been a corresponding decline in marihuana arrests and convictions in Nevada.

The importance of symbolism for a group obviously depends on who it believes is watching; in Nevada many of those interviewed claimed that the whole nation watches activities in their state. As noted in chapter 6, in the case of antitrust legislation, the producers of the symbols attempted to manipulate others whom they saw as potential consumers of these symbols. Nevada lawmakers recognized that the maintenance of a law-and-order image could protect their gambling industry from external controls. The severe marihuana penalty in the state has both a symbolic and an instrumental role even if the law is seldom enforced.

LEARNING A LESSON: A NOTE ON THE DEBACLE IN NEW YORK

The threat of many types of drugs in New York State is very real and is undoubtedly associated with the large and threatening group of blacks living in New York City. Thus in 1973 the New York State legislature passed a new and comprehensive drug control package that the governor recommended. Penalties were dramatically increased for drug offenses by instituting severe mandatory minimum penalties, with the possibility of a life sentence for sale. If and when a person sentenced under this law was eventually released, after serving a sentence for selling illegal drugs, he or she was to remain on parole for life. As could be imagined, there was considerable opposition to this new law. Some New York judges and defense attorneys argued that these prison terms amounted to cruel and unusual punishment (*Columbia (Mo.) Daily Tribune*, 1974). One New York City judge maintained that the law was a "menace to individual freedom." And another agreed: "How can you rehabilitate a man with a life sentence? Are you rehabilitating him for the undertaker?"

What is most interesting about this law, however, is that it appears to have had no impact on illegal drug use in the state (National Institute of Law Enforcement and Criminal Justice, 1978). Three years after its passage, heroin use seemed to have been as common as before the law was passed. Evidence of an ample supply of heroin is seen in relatively stable heroin prices in New York and in the consistent number of heroin overdose deaths before and after the new law was passed. Indeed, the same prices and the same heroin death rates are found in other eastern states that passed no new drug control laws. One reason contributing to this lack of success is that the police, prosecutors, and judges saw the law as being not only of questionable moral value but as impossible to enforce even if they tried.

They all agreed that sufficient resources to implement this law were not available. Therefore, once this law was in effect, a lower percentage of arrests resulted in indictments and a lower percentage of indictments resulted in convictions. The mandatory sentences made it very difficult for prosecutors to bargain with defendants for information about the source of their drugs. And without any possibility of plea bargaining because of the mandatory sentences, the prosecutors feared that the courts would become hopelessly clogged. The severe penalties made convictions difficult because, as with the death penalty for theft in early England, such penalties caused judges and juries to rebel and refuse to convict obviously guilty parties. But perhaps most important, the heavy drug penalties are hazardous to narcotics agents because the penalty for murdering one of these agents would probably not be any greater than for many drug convictions. Thus a suspect might attempt to murder an officer during an attempted apprehension. Because of all these problems, this law was significantly amended in 1975 and in 1976.

SUMMARY

Over a decade ago, while the famous journalist Stewart Alsop (1974) was dying of cancer, he understandably became sensitive to the fact that heroin could not be used in the United States to kill the agonizing pain of terminal cancer. Unlike the United States, Britain has never banned heroin, and the drug is routinely given to such patients. British physicians have found that heroin is a far superior painkiller to morphine, and because heroin is legally used, it is very inexpensive—about the same cost as aspirin. Surprisingly these injections are given without creating drug intoxication or addiction (CBS News, December 2, 1984). Apparently the extreme pain suffered by these patients somehow overrides the addictive quality of the drug. Of course, even if these patients did become addicted in the last phases of their lives, addiction would seem preferable to unremitting pain. At least patients should have this choice. But American cancer patients do not have such a choice. In this country we cannot use heroin in a rational fashion because of symbolism—because the drug is associated with lawless urban blacks. This association has never existed in Britain. The inability to use certain drugs for legitimate medical purposes has also been true in the case of marihuana. It is well established that marihuana use can relieve the nausea associated with chemotherapy for cancer and can also relieve the symptoms of glaucoma. Yet only approximately half of the states have legalized its use in these instances.

Because marihuana is illegal, the strength and purity of the drug cannot be controlled and there is no age limit for purchase from the many illegal sources. Moreover, many of the illegal sources of marihuana have other, more dangerous types of drugs to sell. If marihuana becomes a "stepping-stone" to the use of other types of drugs, as is sometimes claimed, the common source of these drugs must surely help account for this pattern. In addition, outlawing marihuana or any other type of drug ensures that its use can be a method of rebellion and gives it a glamor that it would not otherwise have. Across the country, people have grown accustomed to pulling down their shades, bolting the door, and getting the incense ready to cover the telltale smell of marihuana in case anyone should come by unannounced.

In fact, our attempts at drug control have been totally futile. For example, in 1971 the Nixon Administration put pressure on Turkey to cut off the supply of opium poppies to the United States, and Turkey complied (Silberman, 1978). As a consequence, more of these drugs began to come into the United States from Southeast Asia. Thus there was never any shortage in the supply of opium. Later, Turkey attempted to regain some of its original markets. The new competition between Turkey and Southeast Asia drove down the price of heroin, with the result that more and more people could afford it, and the glut drove the purity of heroin up, thus making it more addictive and more lethal. This illustrates the difficulty of attempting to use the law to control drug trafficking, as does the routine practice of using narcotics agents to make drug purchases. The numerous buys of drugs by narcotics agents pumps millions of dollars annually into drug dealing, helps make it more profitable for racketeers, creates a larger market than would otherwise exist, and therefore stimulates production (Browning and Gerassi, 1980). After having purchased these drugs, the narcotics agents often recirculate the drugs to informers who are addicts, who will exchange information helpful in making other drug arrests in return for the drugs the police have confiscated. Any attempts to reform these insane and self-defeating laws, which cannot be enforced, are typically blocked successfully by two large occupational groups stimulated by these laws. First, a large army of state, federal, and local narcotics agents can usually be counted on to oppose any reforms because of the threat to their occupation. The problem is that they are often prominent among the "experts" called on to testify before legislative bodies when legal reforms are being considered. Second, a large number of people make a fine living by providing illegal drugs. These people can be counted on to use their considerable money and influence to ensure that drug reform laws do not drive them out of business. Recently it was reported (Royko, 1985) that the federal government claims that 14,000 tons of marihuana are consumed each year in this country. Mike Royko estimated that these 448,000,000 ounces of marihuana, at 20 cigarettes per ounce, would provide 40 joints each year for every man, woman, and child in the country—almost one joint per week per person. Law violation on this scale is clearly impossible to control. As indicated earlier, the national survey on drug abuse in 1979 (Fishburn et al.) found that 68 percent of persons 18 to 25 years of age had used marihuana. Kelsen (1945:436–437) claimed:

> Any legal order, therefore, to be positive, has to coincide in some measure with the actual conduct which it seeks to regulate. . . . The tension between norm and existence, between the "ought" and the "is," must not sink below a certain mimimum. . . . Actual conduct must not completely contradict the legal order which regulates it.

Himmelstein (1983:143) claimed that because of the massive increase in middle-class marihuana use, the imagery surrounding marihuana has been softening: "They appeared as 'someone's kids,' not as anonymous users; as fundamentally normal persons who happened to commit deviant acts, not as deviant persons. . . . Harsh penalties for marihuana users were opposed on the grounds that users were not 'really' criminals." Himmelstein found that the most strident opponents of less severe marihuana penalties do not want actual imprisonment of marihuana users but prefer a de facto decriminalization in which the existing penalties are not imposed. This has the advantage, they argue, of not implying that marihuana use is acceptable, as actual reductions in the penalties would seem to do. Perhaps this de facto decriminalization explains why no state has decriminalized marihuana since 1978. We examined in what ways the situation in Nevada was similar to the problems faced by American lawmakers in the 1930s, when the Marihuana Tax Act established severe federal penalties, and in what ways it was different from the experience of Nebraska and Utah, both of which drastically reduced marihuana penalties. Our study of these marihuana control laws provides the means by which we can assess the capacity of the concepts of structural foundations and triggering events to contribute to the isolation of empirical detail and to guidance in theoretical explanation.

REFERENCES

Alix, E. K.
  1978 Ransom Kidnapping in America, 1874–1974: The Creation of a Capital Crime. Carbondale: Southern Illinois University Press.
Alsop, S.
  1974 "The right to die with dignity." Good Housekeeping, August:69, 130, 132.
Becker, H. S.
  1963 Outsiders: Studies in the Sociology of Deviance. New York: Free Press.
Bonnie, R. J. and C. H. Whitebread II
  1974 The Marihuana Conviction: A History of Marihuana Prohibition in the United States. Charlottesville: University Press of Virginia.
Browning, F. and J. Gerassi
  1980 The American Way of Crime. New York: G. P. Putnam's Sons.
Carson, W. G.
  1974 "The sociology of crime and the emergence of criminal laws." Pp. 67–90 in P. Rock and M. McIntosh (eds.), Deviance and Social Control. London: Tavistock.
CBS News
  1984 "60 Minutes" (Just what the doctor ordered"), December 2.
Chambliss, W. J.
  1974 "Functional and conflict theories of crime." Pp. 1–23 in MSS Modular Publications, Module 17. New York: MSS Information.
Clausen, J. A.
  1961 "Drug addiction." Pp. 181–221 in R. K. Merton and R. A. Nisbet (eds.), Contemporary Social Problems. New York: Harcourt Brace and World.
Columbia (Mo.) Daily Tribune
  1974 "Tough drug law controversial." September 24:18.
Erikson, K. T.
  1966 Wayward Puritans: A Study in the Sociology of Deviance. New York: John Wiley & Sons.

Fishburne, P. M., H. I. Abelson, and I. Cisin
  1979 National Survey on Drug Abuse: Main Findings. Rockville, Md.: National Institute on Drug Abuse.
Galliher, J. F. and L. Basilick
  1979 "Utah's liberal drug laws: structural foundations and triggering events." Social Problems 26:284–297.
Galliher, J. F. and J. R. Cross
  1982 "Symbolic severity in the land of easy virtue: Nevada's high marihuana penalty." Social Problems 29:380–386.
  1983 Morals Legislation Without Morality: The Case of Nevada, New Brunswick, N.J.: Rutgers University Press.
Galliher, J. F., J. L. McCartney, and B. E. Baum
  1974 "Nebraska's marihuana law: a case of unexpected legislative innovation." Law and Society Review 8:441–455.
Galliher, J. F. and A. Walker
  1977 "The puzzle of the social origins of the marihuana tax act of 1937." Social Problems 24:367–376.
  1978 "The politics of systematic research error: the case of the Federal Bureau of Narcotics as a moral entrepreneur." Crime and Social Justice 10:29–33.
Gibbs, J. P. and M. L. Erickson
  1975 "Major developments in the sociological study of deviance." Pp. 21–42 in A. Inkeles, J. Coleman, and N. Smelser (eds.), Annual Review of Sociology, vol. 1. Palo Alto, Calif.: Annual Reviews.
Goode, E.
  1970 The Marihuana Smokers. New York: Basic Books.
  1972 Drugs in American Society. New York: Alfred A. Knopf.
Governor's Citizens Advisory Committee
  1969 Report on Drug Abuse Utah (September).

Hagan, J. and J. Leon
  1977   "Rediscovering delinquency: social history,
          political ideology and the sociology of law."
          American Sociological Review 42:587–598.
Hall, J.
  1952   Theft, Law and Society. Indianapolis:
          Bobbs-Merrill.
Himmelstein, J. L.
  1983   The Strange Career of Marihuana: Politics
          and Ideology of Drug Control in America.
          Westport, Conn.: Greenwood Press.
Jeffery, C. R.
  1956   "Crime, law and social structure. I. Meth-
          odology." Journal of Criminal Law, Crimi-
          nology and Police Science 47:423–435.
Johnston, L. D., P. M. O'Malley, and J. G. Bachman
  1985   Use of Licit and Illicit Drugs by America's
          High School Students, 1975–1984. Wash-
          ington, D.C.: National Institute on Drug
          Abuse.
Jolly, J. C.
  1972   "Clergy attitudes about drug abuse and
          drug abuse education: a case study." Rocky
          Mountain Social Science Journal 9:75–82.
Jonas, F. H.
  1961   "Utah: crossroads of the West." Pp.
          273–302 in F. H. Jonas (ed.), Western Pol-
          itics. Salt Lake City: University of Utah
          Press.
  1969   "Utah: the different state." Pp. 327–379 in
          F. H. Jonas (ed.), Politics in the American
          West. Salt Lake City: University of Utah
          Press.
Kaplan, J.
  1970   Marihuana: The New Prohibition. New
          York: World Publishing.

Kelsen, H.
  1945   General Theory of Law and State.
          Cambridge, Mass.: Harvard University
          Press.
Musto, D. F.
  1973   The American Disease: Origins of Narcotics
          Control. New Haven, Conn.: Yale Univer-
          sity Press.
National Institute of Law Enforcement and Criminal
Justice
  1978   The Nation's Toughest Drug Law: Evaluat-
          ing the New York Experience. Washington,
          D.C.: U.S. Government Printing Office
          (March).
Nevada Department of Adult Probation and Parole
  1974–1975 Non-resident Offender/Victim Im-
          pact on Crime in Nevada.
Nevada Legislative Commission of the Legislative
Counsel Bureau
  1969   Illegal Narcotic and Drug Use in Nevada.
          Bulletin No. 80 (January).
Platt, A. M.
  1969   The Child Savers: The Invention of Delin-
          quency. Chicago: University of Chicago
          Press.
Royko, M.
  1985   "Pot supply, demand too big for law."
          Columbia Missourian, March 14:4A.
Silberman, C. E.
  1978   Criminal Violence, Criminal Justice. New
          York: Random House.
U.S. Congress, House of Representatives
  1937   "Taxation of marihuana." Hearing before a
          subcommittee of the Committee on Finance.
          Seventy-fifth Congress, First Session on
          H.R. 6385, April 27.

8
ADMINISTRATION OF CRIMINAL LAW: THE POLICE

This chapter is based on the assumption that the most important data in the study of crime are details related to the development of laws and their administration rather than studies of the behavior of those persons designated as criminals. While it is essential to know the origins of written law to understand the nature of the crime problem in any society, it is also necessary to study how these same written statutes are enforced to fully comprehend this issue. Showing that criminal laws, as written, reflect the interests of powerful groups points to only a small portion of the total argument. The most consistent complaints from economic and racial minorities concern the administration of laws rather than the laws themselves. Because the first steps in the process of administering the criminal laws are taken by the police, this chapter will explore police activities and behavior in modern America.

DELIVERY OF POLICE SERVICES

In the American colonies law enforcement initially was the responsibility of all able-bodied men, and, as volunteers, they only periodically assumed this responsibility. According to Parks (1970), a specialized modern police department became necessary in the United States as it grew more and more difficult to

Part of this chapter was taken from J. F. Galliher, "Explanations of Police Behavior: A Critical Review and Analysis," Sociological Quarterly 12(Summer 1971):308–318.

control the increasing numbers of poor. In referring to the police, Bordua and Reiss (1967:277) observed: "Increasing social differentiation, heterogeneity, and stratification of the population led to lowered consensus on major values and the necessity to develop formal controls if a heterogeneous community was to have at least a minimum of order."

Historically, in England, all adults had some responsibility for making arrests in certain situations. For example, every citizen had the responsibility of raising the "hue and cry"—assisting in the capture of a thief or other person absconding after committing a crime (Puttkammer, 1953:29–31). Failure to arrest a felon when in a position to do so was, in fact, a separate crime in itself. Today this is no longer recognized socially or legally as a real civilian responsibility. In 1964 in New York City, a woman named Kitty Genovese was attacked and stabbed to death. This assault did not occur in a lonely alley but in front of a large apartment building and in full view of at least 38 adults. The assault lasted about 30 minutes, yet none of the observers intervened or even called the police during that period (Rosenthal, 1964). This is an example of what Mayer (1967:176) called "that attitude of an age of specialization: let the cop do the dirty work; what else are we paying him for?"

However much we might condemn this lack of willingness to help the police, it is true that there are some convincing arguments against direct citizen intervention to stop the commission of a crime. Whereas in many jurisdictions police officers are covered by hospitalization and life insurance for any injuries sustained in the line of duty and by false arrest insurance, the civilian who encounters problems while trying to enforce the law is not similarly covered (Ratcliffe, 1966). Rather than view this attitude as merely a reflection of the breakdown, in a sense, of the community or moral fabric of our society, one can see the legal and social attitude of reliance on police officers for crime control as just one example of a broader societal trend toward greater and greater occupational specialization. Two hundred years ago, most American men performed the tasks of farmers, carpenters, and butchers, whereas today a leaking faucet or roof generally prompts modern homewners to consult the telephone directory for assistance. Most American families now require occasional assistance from specialists in accounting, plumbing, electronics, carpentry, catering, and marriage counseling, among others. Sometimes specialists in law enforcement are needed as well.

Although today the police are expected to do the job of law enforcement by themselves, they are not efficiently organized to accomplish this task. In the United States, there are thousands of federal, state, and local police departments. These various departments usually do not cooperate completely with one another and sometimes work at direct cross-purposes. In every state in the United States, there are myriad municipal and county police departments, most of which have only a handful of officers—usually far too few to offer adequate police coverage. Even at the federal level, a host of police agencies, including the Federal Bureau of Investigation (FBI), the Secret Service, narcotics agents, border patrols, and postal inspectors, are sometimes working on the same case without a fully coordinated effort. A narcotics case can lead several federal police agencies along parallel lines while working independently of each other. Even more striking are the many federal agencies attempting to police organized crime. These include the U.S. Customs Service, Drug Enforcement Administration (DEA), FBI, Immigration and Naturalization Service, Internal Revenue Service (IRS), Securities and Exchange Commission (SEC), U.S. Postal Service, U.S. Marshals Service, and U.S. Secret Service (Comptroller General, 1977:5–6).

In a directory of federal law enforcement agencies (Torres, 1985) 61 separate federal police forces were listed including the FBI, Immigration and Naturalization, Secret Service, IRS, Customs Service, DEA, postal inspectors, U.S. Marshals, SEC, Bureau of Alcohol, Tobacco, and Firearms, and Environmental Protection Agency (EPA). In 1984 these agencies had the following number of special agents or enforcement officers: FBI, 8555; Immigration, 3694; Secret Service, 2802; IRS, 2400; Customs Service, 1900; DEA, 1900; Postal Inspectors, 1850; Marshals, 1786; SEC, 70; Alcohol, Tobacco and Firearms, 60; EPA, 25. It is clear from this distribution of personnel that controlling the stock market, firearms, and land, water and air pollution have very low priorities.

The excessive decentralization of police departments in the United States is sometimes held to be necessary to avoid a police takeover of our government; yet Great Britain, which had only 158 forces in 1962, has not been taken over by a police junta (Banton, 1964:88). Assuming that the goal is efficient police operations, consolidation of police departments is required. The fact that there has not been consolidation of departments suggests that there have been no effective demands for more efficient police services from the persons who set government policy. As explained in the discussion of American crime rates in chapter 5, elite policymakers apparently have no reason to demand more effective police to limit street crime.

One famous case of poor coordination of the police effort involves the murders committed by the Charles Manson family (Bugliosi, 1975). In this instance both the Los Angeles city and county police departments were working on the investigation, and both desired sole credit for its solution. During the investigation each department had some facts that would have been useful to the other in solving the case, but they would not share information. Even within the Los Angeles city police department itself two groups of detectives who were both investigating the case sat in the same office but did not share any information because of internal jealousies. Consequently, Manson and his followers nearly escaped detection.

Another organizational problem is found in large metropolitan areas where the chief of police is typically a political appointee, whereas all the other officers on the force are civil service employees. The chief can be replaced as the political winds shift, whereas the other officers have much more permanent positions (Puttkammer, 1953:34). Those officers who report directly to the chief know that a given incumbent will not last long and that if they attach themselves too closely to any one chief, giving that incumbent complete support, they may be punished later for their identification with the ex-chief. For example, recently Andrews (1985) reported that Chicago has had seven police superintendents and nearly as many acting superintendents in 24 years. These statistics are similar to the national average of 2.8 years of service by police chiefs in cities with more than 1,000 officers. So chiefs are handicapped by both their own inexperience and a lack of wholehearted support from the other officers. Yet a police chief is greatly dependent on the cooperation of the other officers. Unlike most other organizational structures where information flows mainly from the top down, in police departments information about events in the community that the chief needs to perform in a leadership role comes into the organizational structure from the police officers at the bottom who are patrolling the streets (Banton, 1964:107–118).

However, despite these organizational problems, most of the complaints about the police do not concern their inefficiency but rather their brutality, prejudice, and cynicism in performing their job. Opinion surveys have repeatedly shown blacks to be more negative than whites in their evaluations of the police (Bayley and Mendelsohn, 1969; Ennis, 1967; Boggs and Galliher, 1975). Only by exploring the combined impact of racial and class conflict on police behavior can a complete understanding of these findings be achieved.

EXPLANATIONS OF POLICE BEHAVIOR

Perhaps because of these recurrent complaints about police activities, for several decades many social scientists have attempted to explain why police behave the way they do in performing their duties. The following is a historical review of the development of the dominant themes running through the myriad articles and books that have appeared on this subject. This survey does not purport to offer an exhaustive coverage of all the relevant literature but is intentionally selective to highlight some observable patterns. This discussion will illustrate how social scientists have persistently ignored the effects of social structure on police behavior. That is, they have ignored the influence of community heterogeneity on the behavior of the local police, especially the impact of economic disparity and racial differences.

Psychological Perspective

Over the years several sociologists have focused on the personalities of individual police officers as important in determining how they peform their role. Skolnick (1966:42–70) suggested that police officers have a "working personality," by which he means a set of cognitive tendencies that influence their work. By virtue of enforcing the law, the police become very supportive of the status quo. Skolnick argues that to believe in their task and appear consistent to themselves, police become very politically conservative. Moreover, because of their job, police officers are highly sensitive to signs of danger. Because of the constant threat of violence and because their job is to prevent crime, police often become sensitized to things that civilians are unaware of. In the course of their work, police become suspicious of certain kinds of people whose gestures, language, or clothing have become associated with violence or crime. Skolnick (1966:45–48) referred to people who are viewed in this manner as "symbolic assailants"— persons with long hair or wearing black leather motorcycle jackets, persons showing insolence, black men in all-white suburbs, and well-dressed or poorly dressed blacks. In fact, almost everything is suspicious in the black ghetto (Schwartz, 1967). Of course, persons who attempt to evade the police are suspect as are those who are visibly rattled when approached by the police. On the other hand, persons who display an exaggerated lack of concern are also suspicious, and so is anything that seems out of place, such as a long heavy coat worn on a hot day—possibly for use in concealing shoplifted articles. "A young man may suggest the threat of violence to the policeman by his manner of walking or 'strutting,' the insolence in the demeanor being registered by the policeman as a possible preamble to later attack" (Skolnick, 1966:46). This helps explain the willingness of police to act against some citizens, which might otherwise be interpreted as merely harassment.

Automobiles can also be seen as symbolic assailants. Pin-striped Lincoln Continentals, especially with TV antennas, are often seen by the police as "pimp cars." In fact, an experiment (Heussenstamm, 1971) conducted in California illustrates how suspicious certain cars seem to the police. This study involved 15 college students, all of whom had exemplary driving records, kept their cars in perfect working order, and had pledged to drive safely during the experiment. In case any of them was arrested, there was a $500 violation fund. The crux of the experiment involved placing a Black Panther Party (a black radical political party) bumper sticker on their cars. So quick was the police response that within 17 days the participants had received 33 citations, the violation fund was exhausted, and the experiment was ended.

Other well-known views of the police include their pervasive distrust of lawyers and, especially, judges and the courts. The courts are seen by the police as forever interfering with their work and limiting their discretion in making arrests, which they feel is totally unnecessary (Reiss and Bordua, 1967). Police believe that they, as experts in law enforcement, are the ones to know when specific practices are necessary, not the courts. However, given their views of blacks, for example, if the police were able to exercise greater discretion, they would be especially likely to abuse these ghetto dwellers. The problem for the police is that while they have the task of enforcing the law through arrest, they cannot control the outcome of their efforts, since both prosecutors and the courts intervene in controlling conviction rates. If arrests represent successes for the police, acquittals in court represent their failures. Not only do police see their work as impeded by the courts, but also they believe that they are degraded and dishonored as a result of aggressive and sometimes humiliating interrogation by judges and defense attorneys.

The morale of individual police officers is not merely a consequence of their attitudes toward the courts. Chicago hired a new chief of police in the 1960s as one consequence of a city-wide political reform movement. The new chief imagined that his leadership might improve officers' morale. Therefore a study using questionnaires was executed at the beginning of his leadership and again after several years of his reforms (Wilson, 1967). After several years of his leadership, there was considerable improvement in the quality of the work the police believed they were carrying out, yet surprisingly there was no improvement in police morale. Apparently the reason for the lack of improvement in police morale was that even though the officers knew they were doing a far better job, they saw no improvement in the amount of respect they received from the local community. The lesson in this is that police executives can do nothing to increase the amount of citizen respect for police, which is so important to these officers. Finally, it may be that a better-run police department does not generate greater respect from the public because a better-managed and more efficient police department may well show its efficiency by apprehending more suspects, including not only more bank robbers but also more middle-class speeders and drunk drivers. There is no evidence that Americans routinely have more respect for such vigilance. In any case, police morale to a great extent is determined by the amount of respect officers perceive in the community, which seems largely beyond administrative control.

Niederhoffer (1967:103–151, especially 118–119) speculated that police officers are transformed into authoritarian personalities by virtue of the police role. Included in this authoritarianism is a love of power and toughness and a hatred for weakness. Niederhoffer (1967:90–102) also suggested that police officers develop a cynicism toward the public that is a consequence of performing their job. Because their job throws them into contact with so many dishonest people, police officers begin to see everyone as corrupt. Niederhoffer (1967:95) quoted a detective as follows: "I am convinced that we are turning into a nation of thieves. I have sadly concluded that nine out of ten persons are dishonest." In addition, there is the well-known case of the Florida State University criminology professor who noticed this cynicism develop in himself while serving temporarily as a police officer (Kirkham, 1974). He began to feel less and less sympathy for accused criminals and greater and greater contempt for liberal judges and other critics of the police. He even experienced how easy it can be for police officers to lose control of their own emotions and use unnecessary force.

McNamara (1967:211–212) found an increase in authoritarianism in recruits after police training and a further increase after one year on the job. Police officers with two years of experience were found to be more authoritarian than either of the other groups. This supports the notion that police officers apparently become more authoritarian as a result of their experience as active police officers. McNamara suggested that this increased authoritarianism is likely to lead to disagreement with the courts' emphasis on individual rights.

It should be noted that the significance of McNamara's research is somewhat blunted by Bayley and Mendelsohn's (1969:17–18) finding that police are, in fact, less authoritarian than other citizens. Moreover, even if police are made more authoritarian by their occupational role, this says nothing about the structural determinants of this influence or about why the environment is structured to give officers experiences that increase their authoritarianism and cynicism.

Demands of the Immediate Situation

In considering the demands placed upon police in specific situations one can focus on a constellation of practices involved in the clearance of cases. When a case is designated as "cleared," it simply means that the police believe that they know who committed the crime and usually have the person in custody (Skolnick, 1966). Often the police put immense pressure on the persons they have arrested to convince them to plead guilty to additional offenses, especially if there are a number of serious unsolved crimes and if the press and the politicians are critical of the apparent police ineffectiveness. Indeed, suspects are often told that if they tell of their involvement in these additional crimes, they will not be prosecuted for them. Thus admitted criminality becomes a commodity of exchange, and suspects routinely are pressured into admitting to crimes they never committed.

One famous instance of this coercion involved a young black man in New York City named George Whitmore (Shapiro, 1969). This young man ultimately confessed to three murders and an attempted rape, when in reality he committed none of them and was eventually cleared of all charges, but only after several years of confinement. The story began in 1963 with the murders of two prominent young women in their exclusive Manhattan apartment, which created a great sensation in the New York press. Eight months later a black woman was murdered in another part of the city. Shortly thereafter in the same neighborhood, an attempted rape occurred late at night. Luckily a police officer was on patrol nearby, heard the woman's screams, and gave chase but lost the assailant in darkness. Later the police found a black youth loitering in front of a nearby laundromat. The young man gave the officer his name and indicated that he was waiting to go to work in a nearby factory. The police officer incorrectly recorded this young man's name as Whitman rather than Whitmore. Later when the police checked at the factory and found no one by the name Whitman working there, they assumed that he had lied to them. Therefore they returned to the laundromat the following day on the hunch that he might be there as a matter of routine. Indeed, they found him there again and took him into custody. The rape victim positively identified him through a peephole and also positively identified his voice when he was directed to say "Lady, I'm going to rape you; Lady I'm going to kill you." Using the good-guy, bad-guy routine (where one officer is friendly and one is mean), the police badgered George Whitmore into confessing to three murders and a rape. George's confessions became more credible after he identified a police officer's knife as "exactly like" the murder weapon and after he learned many details of the murders because the police discussed the murders in his presence. Political liberals are often critical of these police practices, yet anyone in the position of police officers and consequently subject to intense pressure from politicians and the press is likely to opt for a similar solution.

Perhaps an even better illustration of the consequence of such pressures on the police to inflate their clearance rates is found in the case of Henry Lee Lucas. In 1983 it was reported that he had confessed to 97 murders in 13 different states (*Time*, 1983). A year later he had confessed to the murders of 360 people (*Newsweek*, 1984). Understandably it was also reported (*Newsweek*, 1984:100,104): "These days Lucas spends much of his time satisfying a six-month backlog of interview requests from police investigating murders across the country. In September, prosecutors in California cleared 15 homicides from the books, saying Lucas had been responsible." By 1985 Lucas had confessed to 600 murders (*Time*, 1985). "On the basis of Lucas' confessions, police closed some 210 previously unsolved homicide cases in 26 states" (*Time*, 1985:50). But it was discovered by two newspaper reporters that many of these murders had been committed in such rapid succession in various distant places that it was literally impossible for Lucas to have committed them. In 1 month, for example, Lucas would have had to have driven 11,000 miles, including 4,100 miles in the last 4 days of that month (averaging 50 miles per hour nonstop during those 4 days). Yet the police were so eager to close unsolved cases that they failed to double check his stories. Lucas had admitted to one of the reporters that in reality he had killed only three people (*New York Times*, 1985a). And then, later he claimed that he had killed only one person, alleging that he was forced into the other confessions by the police (*New York Times*, 1985b). So we are led to believe that Henry Lee Lucas has killed 600 people, one person, or some number in between.

The demands of the immediate situation for honesty from the officer are well known to vary not only across departments but also within given departments in different sections of the same city. In the center city where most traditions of open vice exist, the demands of the most powerful citizens compel a continuance of the illicit practices (Whyte, 1955:124–125; Chambliss, 1971). Here the type of officer that functions the best is the one who is open to some bribery and who can ignore certain illegal practices. Unlike the situation in middle-class neighborhoods, the people who live in the center city and who would like to be rid of such practices have insufficient power to remove these operations. The honest officer, however, functions best when assigned to the more affluent areas where the powerful citizens are homeowners who demand strict enforcement of vice laws.

A study of police in small towns is especially useful in demonstrating the relationship of the police to local elites who seem to make specific demands on these officers (Galliher et al., 1975). Tracing the lines of influence is much easier in small towns than in metropolitan areas of several million people. This study found that the police in such small towns define as their main task the job of "rattling doorknobs" of all the local businesses during the evening hours when the stores are closed. Given their great attention to business owners' needs, predictably, small-town police recognized the local business community as their most important supporter.

The demands on county sheriffs in rural areas have also been shown to be very instructive. One study of the role of the rural county sheriff found, for example, that the typical sheriff had no prior background in police work (Esselstyn, 1953). What each political party looked for in a potential candidate was a mature local person; someone with a long career as a farmer or business owner was perfect. A background in law enforcement was unnecessary. The county sheriff, unlike city police, can exercise great discretion in making arrests because the incumbent has no immediate supervisors. This is precisely why a local trusted person seems so essential. If the sheriff knows everyone in the community and their place in the local stratification system, the sheriff will also know if they are the type of people who should be arrested for certain crimes or the type whose crimes should be ignored.

Historically, a number of articles have emphasized the great amount of discretion police may use in deciding to make arrests. It has been found that police rely heavily on the characteristics of the immediate siuation in making these decisions. For example, Bittner (1967) found that police on skid row make their decision to arrest an individual mainly on the basis of the perceived risk that the person will create a disorder rather than on the basis of the degree of guilt. Black (1970) and Black and Reiss (1970) found that another major component in the decision to arrest is the preference of the complainant. Police usually arrest a suspect if that is the desire of the person making the complaint. But studies have also found that the deference displayed by the suspect has a bearing on the use of discretion by the officer (Westley, 1953; Piliavin and Briar, 1964). Piliavin and Briar (1964:210) suggested that "in the opinion of juvenile patrolmen themselves the demeanor of apprehended juveniles was a major determinant of their decisions for 50–60 percent of the juvenile cases they processed."

However, police officers' use of discretion as well as suspects' behavior are not random occurrences. All occur within a social structural context. Unfortunately, some sociologists are mainly concerned with the demands of the immediate situation and neglect the broader social structure within which this interaction occurs. A social structural analysis would require some interpretation of the observation that black Americans, more frequently than other citizens, seem loath to show respect for the police.

Role Conflict

Some studies of police behavior have located explanations in a social psychological, role conflict model. The basic idea is that officers perceive conflicting expectations from others regarding how they should carry out their job. Preiss and Ehrlich (1966:94–121) reported on police officers' perceptions of conflicting expectations among the various audience groups with which they are involved. One example of these conflicting expectations is the discrepancy the police officers perceived between the views of their spouses and the views of their supervisors regarding the appropriate limitations in the demands of their job (Preiss and Ehrlich, 1966:99–101). That is, police officers perceive their spouses as believing that their obligations to the job should end after 8 hours, whereas their supervisors see the police officers' obligations as continuing 24 hours a day. Wilson (1963:198–199) observed another source of conflicting expectations. In a heterogeneous society, one part of the public may want different kinds of enforcement from the police than do other parts. For example, urban liberals and blacks feel differently about the use of force by police than do other citizens.

Skolnick (1966:1–22) discussed the police officer's "dilemma" of enforcing the law while at the same time maintaining order. The police believe that they are expected to do both, but maintaining order may at times require the officer to work outside the law, ignoring a suspect's constitutional rights. Wilson (1963:199) suggested that this conflict between achieving order or catching a suspect and operating within the limits imposed by the law is especially intense when a "crusade" is launched by a department to solve an important case. The rules of law require respect for civil liberties, but during times of crisis, police feel compelled to forget this and consider only the efficiency of the means used to catch a suspect.

Law and order may conflict in yet another way. By enforcing the law among a population, the police officer may destroy the type of social relations necessary to serve as a mediator of their disputes and thereby assisting them in maintaining order (Banton, 1964:38). For example, city police have continuing contact with male youths on the streets in slum areas. The police keep a close watch on their activities for signs of illegal activity (Werthman and Piliavin, 1967). While the police are charged with both enforcing the law and maintaining order, they find, however, that when they attempt to enforce the law, maintaining order sometimes becomes impossible—all hell breaks loose. Attempting to use their legal authority to restore order by clearing the sidewalk or quieting noisy music is more easily ordered from headquarters than it can be implemented on the streets.

It is well known, for example, that in center-city areas young male gang members often transform a city block into a private piece of property that they will defend with force. Since they typically have no other place for private activities, they often engage in behavior on the street corner that other youths confine to a house or car. This list of such behaviors includes playing cards, shooting dice, dancing with unseen partners, singing in a falsetto voice, holding private conversations, and combing their hair in front of store windows. The street corner serves as a corporate dwelling unit where the gang members attempt to maintain some degree of privacy. But the very spot the gang members define as a private place, the police are forced to define as a public place and are compelled to patrol. Police routinely receive complaints from store owners that a gang is loitering near their business and frightening customers away. The police are thus dispatched to the address and demand that the gang members "move on" and leave the area. Assuming that these youths are in an especially good mood, they might even agree to move on to another corner. Then new complaints come in from yet another storekeeper at the gang's new congregating spot. Again the police are dispatched to this new location and repeat their demands that the gang move on, away from yet a second locale. Sooner or later the patience of both the gang members and the police will be worn thin, and verbal and physical conflict becomes likely. This futile scenario illustrates how hopelessly trapped in conflict are both the police and the gang members. There is literally no place where the young men on the street can go and not be an irritant to someone. Yet the police are forced to continually demand that they keep moving. There are no easy liberal reforms, such as increased police training or an increased percentage of black officers, that can make a difference and bring an end to this continual conflict.

Given such police tasks, it should not be surprising that the better qualified and better-trained police departments have had just as serious police-minority relations problems as have other lower-rated departments (Terris, 1967). It apparently does not matter how well trained the police are as long as their essential tasks remain so conflict ridden. The implication in all of this literature is that because of such role conflicts, officers may be forced to make certain compromises, accommodations, and choices. Unfortunately, no theoretical models are offered to help predict the specific choices made. Perhaps this is true because insufficient attention has been given to the structural bases of the role conflict.

Subcultural Approach

Other studies have sought to explain police behavior by using what is essentially a subcultural approach. The argument is that police officers are a unique group. As such, they are subjected to special strains and make collective rather than individual adjustments to these problems.

In an early study of police, Westley (1953) found evidence of a police subculture in a code justifying the use of violence to coerce respect.

> The most significant finding is that at least 37 percent of the men believed that it was legitimate to use violence to coerce respect. This suggests that policemen use the resource of violence to persuade their audience (the public) to respect their

occupational status. In terms of the policeman's definition of the situation, the individual who lacks respect for the police, the "wise guy" who talks back, or any individual who acts or talks in a disrespectful way, deserves brutality. (Westley, 1953:39.)

Westley (1956) also found that this code forbids police from informing against fellow officers. Typically, officers indicated that they would adhere to this rule of secrecy that functions to protect the police against attacks from the community. "However, policemen cannot and do not employ sanctions against their colleagues for using violence, and individual men who personally condemn the use of violence and avoid it whenever possible refuse openly to condemn acts of violence by other men on the force" (Westley, 1953:40). Later research by Stoddard (1968), Savitz (1970), and Reiss (1968) support the notion of a code of secrecy.

Skolnick (1966:53–58) suggested that the dangerousness of the police mission as well as the requirement that officers use authority against civilians contributes to this solidarity. The reasoning is that the more hostility the police receive from the public, the more isolated they become, and consequently, the more dependent they become on one another. Moreover, the more isolated they become from the rest of the community, the less information about department operations gets out into the community. One study during the 1960s found that groups of police officers routinely stood by and did not intervene or report cases where one of their fellow officers was using more force than necessary to control a suspect (Reiss, 1968).

Additionally, it is not merely the rank-and-file officers that have been dependent upon one another; perhaps of all the police, the chief is most dependent on other officers (Banton, 1964:109). The chief, unlike executives of other organizations, needs the respect of those in the lower ranks; otherwise they will not supply the chief with the necessary information to carry out the job. As indicated earlier, police departments are unique in that information more typically flows upward from the cop on patrol to headquarters. In other organizations those at the top have the most information, and therefore information typically flows downward. If the officers on patrol do not trust or respect the chief, they will not forward the information on what is happening in the community that the chief needs to perform adequately. For this reason police executives often respond in a defensive fashion when one of their officers is accused of using excessive force or verbal abuse in dealing with a citizen. The chief is simply in no position to chastise the officers, and moreover, may not even desire to do so since these abusive behaviors are often seen by chiefs as useful in arrest and interrogation and in other crime control situations (Goldstein, 1967). However, a more recent study (Reuss-Ianni, 1983) suggested that what many officers see as the "good old days" of police solidarity may be coming to an end as many big-city police departments become racially and sexually integrated. In New York City, for example, police can no longer count on their fellow officers or on superiors to keep their racism and brutality a secret.

Another subcultural practice of the police is the widespread use of informers. Most major police departments rely heavily on the services of informers, especially the vice squads (Skolnick, 1966). In vice cases, including prostitution, illegal gambling, and narcotics trafficking, there are typically no complaining witnesses. Therefore the police often must rely on informers to supply them with information about present and future illegal transactions. Addicts and prostitutes recognize that they will have a continuing series of contacts with the police because of their lifestyle on the streets. Since the police can make life miserable for addicts and prostitutes, they must accommodate the demands of the police for information.

Although these studies have used sociocultural variables in their analyses of police behavior, they have erred in defining the environment of the police as constant across all communities. Clearly not all American police departments rely on the same corrupt clearance practices as described above—just those communities where there is intense pressure to do so. In addition, we have recently seen the development of police departments with an increasing number of minorities and women represented where the "old-boy" subcultural system is a thing of the past. One problem with such a subcultural approach to police behavior studies is that it is impossible to use it to explain the variations in police attitudes and behavior that are found in different communities. If differences in law enforcement practices exist in various communities, then it seems reasonable to expect differences in the nature of the subculture and related structural strains.

Departmental Characteristics Approach

The problem of explaining differences in policing styles has received some attention from those focusing on departmental characteristics as independent determinants of police behavior and attitudes. The argument is that police behavior is a result of the particular situation found in each department. Whatever the subcultural similarities among police departments, there are clearly differences among them as well. When a very professional, well-trained, efficient, honest, and even-handed force was compared to one that was lacking in all these qualities, both some expected and unexpected differences were found (Wilson, 1966). The professional police were usually therapeutic in orientation and typically explained crime as a consequence of various social problems. Nonprofessional police relied more on moral condemnation and moral explanations of crime. As expected, the nonprofessional police were likely to discriminate against black juveniles in enforcing the law. By contrast, the professional police treated white and black youngsters exactly the same; juveniles of either race who were known to have violated the law were arrested. Meanwhile the nonprofessional police arrested only the black lawbreakers. The consequence of this difference was that among professional police, their therapeutic orientation notwithstanding, the overall rate of arrest was much higher than was true for the nonprofessional police.

In *Varieties of Police Behavior*, Wilson (1968) isolated three types of law enforcement style displayed by various departments. One style emphasizes service to the community, another emphasizes strict enforcement of all laws, and the third is mainly oriented toward the maintenance of order. An important item to note for this discussion is that Wilson pictured police departments as having some independence—as not being directly controlled by the community. As one reflection of this independence, he claimed that it is not always possible to predict the style of law enforcement from the characteristics of the community (Wilson, 1968:227–277).

Gardiner (1969:72) attributed much of the difference in traffic law enforcement in two communities to the differences in the desires of their respective police chiefs. One problem with this type of analysis is that it implicitly assumes that the recruitment of police chiefs is random—at least, not significantly affected by the local social structure or the desires of local community leaders. While neither Gardiner nor Wilson claimed that the law enforcement style is completely independent of the community, they nonetheless, are unable to develop a conceptual model to handle these social structural relationships.

More recently, two veteran observers of police behavior, Skolnick and Bayley (1986) described police operations in Denver, Detroit, Houston, Oakland, Newark, and Santa Ana, California. They concluded that in explaining the quality of police services in any local community "most important of all is the *chief's abiding, energetic commitment to the values and implications of a crime prevention-oriented police department*" (Skolnick and Bayley, 1986:220; emphasis in original). As in other research of this type, there is no discussion of the structural linkages between police departments and the local community. Focusing on such linkages would allow researchers to explain why such cities as San Francisco and Minneapolis typically have had quite different types of police chiefs than such cities as Mobile, Alabama, or Jackson, Mississippi. Clearly the prospective leaders for these departments have quite different orientations and skills that can only be understood by analysis of the local social structure. Police chiefs are never selected in the random process implied by a total focus on the individual characteristics of the chief.

Sociocultural Approach

Over the past several decades a few attempts have been made to describe how societies or communities seem to determine the characteristics of local police.

In comparing European police with those in the United States, Berkley (1969:197) found the latter much more prone to violence. This, he claimed, is a direct reflection of American values. "If the American police are prone to use violent and repressive tactics, American society offers them the means and the climate to do so. No other democratic nation compares to the United States in the acceptance and even glorification of violence as a way to solve problems."

Banton (1964:86–126) attributed many of the differences he found between British and American police officers to the greater social integration that exists in Great Britain. Since Britain is a more homogeneous society with citizens holding more consistent values, it is predictable that British police would be exposed to less violence. This allows the police to operate differently. There is less reason to smother all internal strains within a department and less reason for departmental solidarity (Banton, 1964:118–119).

Bayley (1976) found great differences in the role of Japanese police compared to that found in the United States. Police in Japan are much less likely than their American counterparts to be involved in corruption, are far less likely to use weapons on civilians, and must deal with a crime rate many times smaller than that found in the United States. Thus police in Japan understandably have greater pride in themselves than American police do.

Stinchcombe (1963) compared urban and rural differences in the structural conditions that affect policing. In cities large numbers of people are concentrated into relatively small amounts of public space. This makes police control of public places more economical. Moreover, in the cities informal controls are weakest, and patrol is most necessary. According to Stinchcombe, the fact that police in the cities can, and do, frequently act on their own initiative in making arrests makes sense. Since it is both less economical and less necessary to patrol public places in rural areas, rural police initiate fewer arrests and rely more on citizen complaints to attract their attention to a problem (Stinchcombe, 1963:152).

The relationship of police to our society is also reflected in the results of surveys of attitudes toward the police. Again and again such studies have found that black Americans are more negative toward the police than other Americans (Boggs and Galliher, 1975). Other surveys of citizen perceptions routinely find that police have roughly what can be called a working-class occupational status (Reiss et al., 1961:263–275). Therefore it is not likely that when police behave in a racist or brutal manner it is a policy they have developed on their own. It is much more likely that social policy has been developed by community leaders and not by the working-class operatives—the police.

Although the sociocultural approaches take greater account of social structural influences than do any of the approaches discussed earlier, on the whole they still offer an incomplete conceptual framework. *The fundamental problem in many of the social science explanations of police behavior is that they take no systematic account of the influence of class conflict on law enforcement.*

EMPIRICAL EVIDENCE FOR THE VARIOUS CONCEPTUAL MODELS

We have just seen that if the psychological characteristics of officers are studied, the implication is that this is important in understanding police behavior. It is also sometimes assumed that by studying the demands of the immediate situation facing the officers or their role conflicts, we can better understand their method of operation. Some researchers point to a police subculture or police department leadership to explain officers' behavior. However, only studies that emphasize the social structural environment of policing have the potential of directing attention to social class as a determinant of law enforcement style. All others, of necessity, would miss the importance of class conflict because they direct attention away from the social structure toward a low-level description of the action in immediate law enforcement situations.

Much of police behavior seems most easily explained if one considers that whenever there is a conflict of interests between the dominant classes in a society and the less powerful groups, the police protect the interests of the stronger classes and regulate the behavior of the weaker groups. If the police role attracts authoritarian individuals and their authoritarianism increases once they are on the job, perhaps this happens because of the demands made on the police to suppress economic and racial minorities. Such tasks are most attractive to the authoritarian personality, and undoubtedly any of an officer's initial doubts about those tasks are lessened by an increasingly authoritarian orientation. The literature indicating that police are free to follow the demands of the immediate situation in making arrests also shows that this discretion is used to the disadvantage of minority groups (Skolnick, 1966:85; Goldman, 1963; Wald, 1967:139–151; Wilson, 1966). Wilson's (1963:198–199) observations regarding the differing demands of blacks and urban liberals compared to other citizens as a source of role conflict for the police can be interpreted in class conflict terms. Officers can be seen as experiencing role conflict in part because of different and conflicting demands from various social classes in the community. There is some evidence that police subcultures develop in a department to both legitimate and keep secret brutality toward economic and racial minorities (Reiss, 1968; Westley, 1970). Department leadership and methods of operation can be interpreted as a response to the demands of powerful interest groups (Walker, 1968:13–14). Simple descriptions of police personalities or specific situations faced by the police take no account of class interests and class conflict. Many social scientists have been busy collecting disparate "facts" about policing and have been either unable or unwilling to develop related conceptual frameworks that take into account the social structure, including a consideration of social class. Newman (1966:181–182) claimed that sociological treatment of the legal system, including the police, lacks a theoretical framework and that the theoretical concern of most criminologists has been the social psychological issue of the causation of criminal behavior. As a consequence of this theoretical naiveté, the sociological study of the legal process is empirically simplistic, for without an integrated theoretical framework even intelligent fact gathering is impossible.

Without considering class and class conflict, one cannot accurately interpret the arrest patterns in the United States. It is well established that in most areas of the United States the majority of those people arrested are poor and/or black. As indicated earlier, some observers of arrest practices who emphasize that police can exercise great discretion show that in those cases where this discretion can be most easily exercised, the bulk of those arrested are poor and black (Skolnick, 1966:85; Goldman, 1963; Wald, 1967:139–151; Wilson, 1966). There is also an awareness of other discriminatory treatment given to economic and racial minorities by the police, such as verbal and physical harassment (Reiss, 1968; Schwartz, 1967:446–447). Kitsuse and Cicourel (1963:136–137) maintained that since official rates of deviant behavior are compiled by specific organizations, these rates reflect organizational methods of operation. Using this reasoning, one readily available pool of information regarding police behavior is arrest data.

Curiously, these patterns found in arrest practices and other police treatment of minorities have not usually influenced the theoretical models used in explaining police behavior. If they were used, social class and class conflict would necessarily be incorporated into explanations of police behavior. Cook (1967:120) observed "there is no recognition that the processes of law enforcement serve the interests of dominant groups in the society and either ignore or oppose the interests of those in lower social strata." Perhaps the reason for this is that social scientists have been misusing arrest data. They have been using it as a basis for generating theories of criminal behavior and have been neglecting its use as a reflection of police behavior.

Occasionally some cursory recognition of class does appear. Quite early in *Behind the Shield,* Niederhoffer (1967) introduced the notion of class and its effects on law enforcement. He quoted Joseph Lohman, the late dean of the School of Criminology of the University of California at Berkeley, who was himself a police officer at one time: "The police function [is] to support and enforce the interests of the dominant political, social, and economic interests of the town, and only incidentally to enforce the law" (Niederhoffer, 1967:12). But if Niederhoffer mentioned class quickly, he dropped it even more quickly in favor of "the principle of equilibrium," meaning that police are mainly concerned with protecting themselves from all criticism from whatever source (Niederhoffer, 1967:13–15).

Wilson (1963:213) suggested in passing that a professional police force that applies the law equally to all citizens is impossible in a highly stratified community. Elsewhere in the same paper, he said:

> Property owners, for example, may want maximum protection of their property and of their privacy; slum dwellers, however, may not like the amount of police activity necessary to attain the property owners' ends. Negroes and urban liberals may unite in seeking to end "police brutality"; lower-middle class homeowners whose neighborhoods are "threatened" with Negro invasion may want the police to deal harshly with Negroes or to look the other way while the homeowners themselves deal harshly with them. (Wilson, 1963:198–199.)

Even though class is introduced, Wilson either cannot or will not follow through with any analysis. All he can bring himself to say is that this presents the police with an inconsistency. He says nothing about how this inconsistency is resolved.

Westley (1970) cited statements indicating that police respond differently to different social classes. One police officer is quoted as saying that "in the better districts the purpose is to make friends out of the people and get them to like you. If you react rough to them, naturally they will hate you" (Westley, 1970:98). On the other hand, it seems just as obvious to the police that they can only elicit respect and obedience from slum dwellers by resorting to force (Westley, 1970:99). Westley (1970:96–99) suggested that part of the difference in the police perception of the affluent and the poor is due to the differences in the political power of these groups. Police are afraid to brutalize the wealthy because of their political influence. Moreover, the poor are seen as more disposed to law violation and conflict with the police because of their great economic need. Just as it appears that Westley is on the verge of a thorough structural analysis of police behavior, he tells the reader that police attitudes and behavior have subcultural roots, and surprisingly, he ignores the effects of class conflict on this subculture.

But more recently social scientists are beginning to recognize the impact of social structure and social stratification on the police. One study found that police arrest specific individuals and place them in jail not so much on the basis of the seriousness of their offenses, such as the difference between murder and disturbing the peace, but rather on the basis of the degree of offensiveness of their acts. The degree of offensiveness of acts is increased as a consequence of the offenders being members of disreputable groups, such as racial or ethnic minorities and the poor (Irwin, 1985). Dannefer and Schutt (1982), for example, found considerable racial bias among police in decisions to send juveniles to court, especially in areas with a high percentage of black residents. Another study (Smith and Klein, 1984) found that police tend to ignore and discount complainants' requests in poorer neighborhoods. There also has been a higher per capita police expenditure in cities with a relatively high percentage of black residents and in those cities with a highly mobilized black community that has conducted boycotts or elected militants to political office (Jackson and Carroll, 1981). This militancy and mobilization has apparently been perceived as a threat and thus has created a need for a massive law enforcement presence. In addition, as recent studies of the police have demonstrated, the amount of inequality in an area is important in determining both police behavior and the size of police departments. Correspondingly, Jacobs (1979) found that by 1970 in metropolitan areas with the greatest economic and racial inequality there were typically more police and other law enforcement personnel (see also Liska et al., 1981). There is also a positive relationship in cities between the arrest rate for selected violent crimes and the percentage of black residents, as well as between such arrests and economic inequality, even when the victimization rate is controlled (Williams and Drake, 1980). Moreover, in states with the greatest economic inequality there are typically the greatest number of police-caused homicides (Jacobs and Britt, 1979). Collectively these studies demonstrate that *inequality* is of greater importance than absolute poverty in an area. That is, inequality appears in these studies to be the most significant aspect of social structure in determining the nature of police behavior.

Dirty Work at Home and Abroad

In any society there are certain thankless, and often morally contaminated, dirty jobs that nonetheless must be done. Handling household trash and excrement of hospital patients are two examples. Such tasks are extremely unpleasant and are therefore performed by certain low-status individuals in a way that will not violate the delicate sensibilities of the citizens being served. The garbage collector is usually instructed not to litter middle-class neighborhoods with trash from the truck. In collecting human waste the hospital orderly must be similarly circumspect so as to avoid upsetting patients or their relatives. There are also elements of dirty work in policing. Police officers are required to work undesirable hours in the most deteriorated parts of communities; they may have to intervene in vicious family quarrels, inspect corpses, arrest skid row drunks who reek with various odors and sometimes vomit when moved, and keep masses of the unemployed poor from disturbing the peace of the more affluent.

The fact that social scientists have not always recognized the dirty nature of police work is perhaps in some ways similar to the German citizens' unfamiliarity with the operation of the SS (Schutzstaffel), the Nazi party's elite military arm, which was responsible for the execution of Jews. Hughes (1962) described the apparent ignorance of Germans regarding the systematic extermination of the Jews. He contended that the SS was used by the German people to solve their "Jewish problem." Most Germans felt that a Jewish problem did exist, and once the SS was created, it not only took care of the problem but allowed most German citizens to remain uninvolved in the solution. Since the SS was sworn to secrecy, German citizens could claim ignorance of what this group was doing. One of Hughes' major assumptions is that the public does not accurately perceive the morally outrageous nature of some dirty work and that keeping unpleasant facts from the public is indeed a function of dirty work.

Some immediate similarities appear between the SS role in wartime Germany and the police role in the United States. Many white Americans would doubtlessly agree that our society has a problem controlling ghetto dwellers. The police, like the SS, are highly secretive (Westley, 1956; Reiss, 1968; Savitz, 1970; Stoddard, 1968), which keeps their morally questionable acts shielded from most Americans. This situation permits controlling poor, black Americans in any way necessary, while other citizens can continue to believe that this is a free democratic society and still have their property protected. In fact, the dirty work of policing American slums is so well hidden from the middle classes that even middle-class sociologists sometimes fail to understand that the function of this dirty work is to maintain a highly economically stratified and racist society.

The words of the Bronx borough commander of the New York City police department are instructive in this regard (Bouza, 1978):

> To the degree that I succeed in keeping it cool—in keeping the ghetto cool—to the degree that I can be effective, to that degree, fundamentally, am I deflecting America's attention from discovering this cancer? And the longer it is

deferred—the discovery—as in Vietnam, the greater the moral dilemma, the greater the moral problem when it is ultimately discovered. So maybe I would be better off failing. . . . And that way America would be confronting the problem as it had to do during the urban riots of the '60s. . . . The fact of the matter is that we are manufacturing criminals. We are manufacturing brutality out there. We are very efficiently creating a very volatile and dangerous subelement in our society. And we are doing it simply because we don't want to face the burdens and the problems and the responsibilities that their existence imposes on any society with conscience. So rather than awaken your conscience to the problem, you're far better off just ignoring it. And that's what we are doing. And I am very well paid, almost, to be the commander of an army of occupation in the ghetto.

Earlier, the chief of police in Boston agreed (*Washington Post*, 1976):

We are not letting the public in on our era's dirty little secret: that those who commit the crime which worries citizens most—violent street crime—are, for the most part, the products of poverty, unemployment, broken homes, rotten education, drug addiction and alcoholism, and other social and economic ills about which the police can do little, if anything. Rather than speaking up, most of us stand silent and let politicians get away with law and order rhetoric that reinforces the mistaken notion that the police—in ever greater numbers and with more gadgetry—can alone control crime. The politicians, of course, end up perpetuating a system by which the rich get richer, the poor get poorer and crime continues.

As indicated earlier, the police are not a part of the dominant classes of American society, and they are usually recruited from the working class or lower middle class (Preiss and Ehrlich, 1966:12; Niederhoffer, 1967:36–9; McNamara, 1967:193; Bayley and Mendelsohn, 1969:6). It is predictable, however, that largely working-class individuals would perform the "dirty" police tasks because middle-class and upper-class citizens probably would not comfortably shoot a looter or harass black youngsters but are apparently not bothered by hiring other people who cannot afford to be so choosy about doing the job. For this reason Rainwater (1967) observed a deep-felt American ambivalence toward the police. Most white Americans believe that what Rainwater referred to as the "separate nation" of ghetto blacks must be controlled but are simultaneously somewhat uncertain and ashamed about how they are controlled. Moreover, in the ghetto this control mission is not true of the police alone. Social workers find that in this context their profession has been perverted from a helping profession to one that is designed to spy and to punish. Additionally, the ghetto schools have become custodial institutions and the teachers more like prison guards than educators; consequently little education takes place in these schools. According to Rainwater these functionaries are caught between the upper classes who want them to continue this dirty work in silence and the lower classes who consistently chafe under the controls carried out by these dirty workers.

Social scientists studying the police have typically assumed that individual police officers or departments are free to implement social policy much as they see fit—even though America is recognized as a highly stratified society, and the police officers themselves are known to be from the lower classes or the marginally middle classes at best. Because the police are near the bottom of the stratification system, they are only free to resign their positions if they do not wish to do the bidding of powerful citizens and interest groups. Yet the assumption of the police's freedom to use great discretion is reflected in much of the literature reviewed here; this literature stresses the importance of police personalities, subcultures, or police chiefs as determinants of law enforcement style. If social scientists are unable to understand the place of law enforcement in class conflict, then it should not be surprising that other well-educated political liberals, radical students, and many black Americans see the police as a main source of trouble. Their criticism lends public credence to the social science research that implies that the police are somehow individually or collectively responsible for the way in which laws are enforced. To the degree that the police are seen as independent, they will, of course, be held solely responsible for the manner in which they operate.

CONCLUSION

The absence of references to class conflict in the literature dealing with police behavior is surprising because both the origins of modern police as well as the paramilitary form of modern police bureaucracies have been explained in class conflict terms.

Bordua and Reiss (1967:282) suggested:

> the paramilitary form of early police bureaucracy was a response not only, or even primarily, to crime per se, but to the possibility of riotous disorder. Not crime and danger but the "criminal" and "dangerous classes" as part of the urban social structure led to the formation of uniformed and militarily organized police. Such organizations intervened between the propertied elites and the propertyless masses who were regarded as politically dangerous as a class.

During the late nineteenth century labor was plentiful and therefore very cheap. As more immigrants arrived in this country, the class distinctions grew sharper. Because of the fear of the poor, whole sections of cities were off limits to them (Harring, 1983). Therefore it should not be surprising to learn that during the 1800s American police carried guns and clubs and made at least as many arrests as today. Between 1850 and 1900 there were massive increases in the size of urban police departments. The St. Louis police department, for example, was started in 1846 and by 1861 had 150 officers; in 1880, 489 officers; and in 1905, 1451 officers. The rapid growth in the size of police departments can be attributed to the increasing poverty of the working class and the use of the police as strikebreakers. In St. Louis there were 256 strikes between 1881 and 1900, and there were 92 strikes in Chicago during 1904 alone, with over 300 strike-related deaths. During these strikes the police always sided with the factory owners against workers. Aside from strikes, great effort was put into police control of working-class recreation (Harring, 1983:173). Sixty to 70 percent of all urban arrests were liquor related and directed at controlling the working class and had nothing to do with liquor per se since there were few arrests of tavern owners for violations of liquor license ordinances.

It is sometimes said that if the police were better organized, this would help them do a better job and would reduce police-community tensions (Wilson, 1968; Berkley, 1969). The suggestion is also made that better-trained police would solve many of the problems they encounter (Berkley, 1969:87; Skolnick, 1969:290–291; Task Force Report: The Police, 1967:36–37). However, as Terris (1967:63–64) showed, some cities with well-trained police still have major police-minority problems. As long as police are used for the purpose of containing economic and racial minorities, police-minority conflict will not subside. If police are better educated and better organized, they could just as well become more efficient oppressors.

Since there are obvious differences in law enforcement styles across communities and countries, students of police behavior have recently profited by analyzing how the presence of large groups of economic and racial minorities affects the style of law enforcement in a given jurisdiction. This research involves the relationship between the scope of class conflict and the behavior of the police. The analysis should ideally include a description of the structural linkages between the community and local police departments and a description of the theoretical models that would allow us to predict these linkages.

If it is assumed that "the processes of law enforcement serve the interests of dominant groups in the society and either ignore or oppose the interests of those in lower social strata" (Cook, 1967:120), one might make certain predictions for police behavior. For example, one might predict that in heterogeneous communities with large numbers of economic and racial minorities, police would behave in an oppressive fashion toward minorities because of the threat they symbolize to the rest of the community. Following this reasoning, such police behavior seems less likely to occur in more homogeneous communities. This is precisely what recent research has found.

● ● ●

The basic argument found in this review of police behavior was developed in 1970. In the intervening years, of course, much more research on police behavior has been conducted, but sadly the same shortcomings of earlier studies can be found in some of the work published since 1970. One edition of the Annals of the American Academy of Political and Social Science (November 1980) devoted to the police, for example, showed the same tendency toward a microscopic focus on detail that existed before 1970. Across all the articles in the issue, there was no discussion of concepts or theories that could further our understanding of police behavior. Every article focusing on police behavior offered a different ad hoc piecemeal explanation. One article even claims that the above review of explanations of police behavior, can be discredited because it (1) is "radical," (2) reduces "functions of the police in the United States to nothing more than acts of capitalist oppression," and (3) is a "denial of the legitimacy of the entire police function" (Klockars, 1980:42). Readers can judge for themselves whether this is true. In any event, such allergic reactions to social structural analysis help explain the lack of theoretical advances in the study of police and law enforcement.

REFERENCES

Andrews, A. H., Jr.
  1985 "Structuring the political independence of the police chief." Pp. 5–19 in W. A. Geller (ed.), Police Leadership in America: Crisis and Opportunity. Chicago and New York: American Bar Foundation and Praeger Publishers.

Banton, M.
  1964 The Policeman in the Community. New York: Basic Books.

Bayley, D. H. and H. Mendelsohn
  1969 Minorities and the Police. New York: The Free Press.

Bayley, D. H.
  1976 Forces of Order: Police Behavior in Japan and the United States. Berkeley: University of California Press.

Berkley, G. E.
  1969 The Democratic Policeman. Boston: Beacon Press.

Bittner, E.
  1967 "The police on skid-row: a study of peace keeping." American Sociological Review 32(October):699–715.

Black, D. J.
  1970 "Production of crime rates." American Sociological Review 35(August):733–748.

Black, D. J. and A. J. Reiss, Jr.
  1970 "Police control of juveniles." American Sociological Review 35(February):63–77.

Boggs, S. L. and J. F. Galliher
  1975 "Evaluating the police: a comparison of black street and household respondents." Social Problems 22(February):393–406.

Bordua, D. J. and A. J. Reiss, Jr.
  1967 "Law enforcement." Pp. 275–303 in P. F. Lazarsfeld, W. H. Sewell, and H. L. Wilensky (eds.), The Uses of Sociology. New York: Basic Books.

Bouza, T.
  1978 "An army of occupation." St. Louis Post-Dispatch, February 19:2C.

Bugliosi, V.
  1975 Helter Skelter: The True Story of the Manson Murders. New York: Bantam Books.

Chambliss, W. J.
  1971 "Vice, corruption, bureaucracy, and power." Wisconsin Law Review 4:1150–73.

Comptroller General of the United States
  1977 Report to Congress: War on Organized Crime Faltering—Federal Strike Forces Not Getting Job Done. Washington, D.C., March 17.

Cook, W.
  1967 "Policemen in society: which side are they on?" Berkeley Journal of Sociology 12(Summer):117–129.

Dannefer, D. and R. K. Schutt
  1982 "Race and juvenile justice processing in court and police agencies." American Journal of Sociology 87(March):1113–1132.

Ennis, P. H.
  1967 Criminal Victimization in the United States: A Report of a National Survey. National Opinion Research Center, University of Chicago, Washington, D.C.: U.S. Government Printing Office.

Esselstyn, T. C.
  1953 "The social role of a county sheriff." Journal of Criminal Law, Criminology, and Police Science 44(July–August):177–84.

Galliher, J. F., L. P. Donavan, and D. L. Adams
  1975 "Small-town police: troubles, tasks and publics." Journal of Police Science and Administration 3(March):19–28.

Gardiner, J. A.
  1969 Traffic and the Police: Variation in Law-Enforcement Policy. Cambridge, Mass.: Harvard University Press.

Goldman, N.
  1963 The Differential Selection of Juvenile Offenders for Court Appearance. New York: National Research and Information Center, National Council on Crime and Delinquency.

Goldstein, H.
1967 "Administrative problems in controlling the exercise of police authority." Journal of Criminal Law, Criminology and Police Science 58(June):160–172.

Harring, S. L.
1983 Policing a Class Society: The Experience of American Cities, 1865–1915. New Brunswick, N.J.: Rutgers University Press.

Huessenstamm, F. K.
1971 "Bumper stickers and the cops." Transaction (February):32–33.

Hughes, E. C.
1962 "Good people and dirty work." Social Problems 10(Summer):3–11.

Irwin, J.
1985 The Jail: Managing the Underclass of American Society. Berkeley: University of California Press.

Jackson, P. I. and L. Carroll
1981 "Race and the war on crime: the sociopolitical determinants of municipal police expenditures in 90 non-southern cities." American Sociological Review 46(June):290–305.

Jacobs, D. and D. Britt
1979 "Inequality and police use of deadly force: an empirical assessment of a conflict hypothesis." Social Problems 26(April): 403–412.

Jacobs, D.
1979 Inequality and police strength: conflict theory and coercive control in metropolitan areas." American Sociological Review 44(December):913–925.

Kirkham, G. L.
1974 "What a professor learned when he became a cop." U.S. News and World Report, April 22:70–72.

Kitsuse, J. I. and A. V. Cicourel
1963 "A note on the uses of official statistics." Social Problems 11(Fall):131–139.

Klockars, C. B.
1980 "The Dirty Harry problem." Annals of the American Academy of Political and Social Science 452(November):33–47.

Liska, A. E., J. J. Lawrence, and M. Benson
1981 "Perspectives on the legal order: the capacity for social control." American Journal of Sociology 87(September):413–426.

Mayer, M.
1967 The Lawyers. New York: Harper & Row.

McNamara, J. H.
1967 "Uncertainties in police work: the relevance of police recruits' backgrounds and training." Pp. 163–252 in D. J. Bordua, (ed.), The Police: Six Sociological Essays. New York: John Wiley & Sons.

New York Times
1985a "Reports of bogus murder confessions stir inquiry." April 18:A17.
1985b "Mother is only victim, killer in Texas asserts." April 24:A16.

Newman, D. J.
1966 "Sociologists and the administration of criminal justice." Pp. 177–187 in A. B. Shostak, (ed.), Sociology in Action. Homewood, Ill.: Dorsey Press.

Newsweek
1984 "The random killers." November 26:100, 104, 106.

Niederhoffer, A.
1967 Behind the Shield: The Police in Urban Society. Garden City, N.Y.: Doubleday.

Parks, E. L.
1970 "From constabulary to police society: implications for social control." Catalyst 5(Summer):76–97.

Piliavin, I. and S. Briar
1964 "Police encounters with juveniles." American Journal of Sociology 70(September): 206–214.

Preiss, J. J. and H. J. Ehrlich
1966 An Examination of Role Theory: The Case of the State Police. Lincoln: University of Nebraska Press.

Puttkammer, E. W.
1953 Administration of Criminal Law. Chicago: University of Chicago Press.

Rainwater, L.
1967 "Revolt of the dirty-workers." Transaction 5(November):2, 64.

Ratcliffe, J. M. (ed.)
1966 The Good Samaritan and the Law. Garden City, N.Y.: Anchor Books.

Reiss, A. J., Jr.
1968 "Police brutality—answers to key questions." Transaction 5(July–August):10–19.

Reiss, A. J., Jr. and D. J. Bordua
1967 "Environment and organization: a perspective on the police." Pp. 25–55, in D. J Bordua (ed.), The Police: Six Sociological Essays. New York: John Wiley & Sons.

Reiss, A. J., Jr., (with O. D. Duncan, P. K. Hatt, and C. C. North)
1961 Occupations and Social Status. New York: The Free Press of Glencoe.

Reuss-Ianni, E.
1983 Two Cultures of Policing: Street Cops and Management Cops. New Brunswick, N.J.: Transaction Books.

Rosenthal, A. M.
1964 Thirty-eight Witnesses. New York: McGraw-Hill.

Savitz, L.
1970 "The dimensions of police loyalty." Amer-

ican Behavioral Scientist (May–June, July–August):693–704.

Schwartz, H.
1967 "Stop and frisk (a case study in judicial control of the police)." Journal of Criminal Law, Criminology, and Police Science 58(December):433–464.

Shapiro, F. C.
1969 Whitmore. New York: Bobbs-Merrill.

Skolnick, J. H.
1966 Justice without Trial. New York: John Wiley & Sons.
1969 The Politics of Protest. New York: Simon & Schuster.

Skolnick, J. H. and D. H. Bayley
1986 The New Blue Line: Police Innovation in Six Cities. New York: The Free Press.

Smith, D. A. and J. R. Klein
1984 "Police control of interpersonal disputes." Social Problems 31(April):468–481.

Stinchcombe, A. L.
1963 "Institutions of privacy in the determination of police administrative practice." American Journal of Sociology 69(September):150–160.

Stoddard, E. R.
1968 "The informal 'code' of police deviancy: a group approach to 'blue-coat' crime." Journal of Criminal Law, Criminology, and Police Science 59(June):201–213.

Task Force Report: The Police
1967 Washington, D.C.: U.S. Government Printing Office.

Terris, B. J.
1967 "The role of the police." Annals of the American Academy of Political and Social Science 374(November)58–69.

Time
1983 "Catching a new breed of killer." November 14:47.
1985 "A mass murderer reconsidered." April 29:50.

Torres, D. A.
1985 Handbook of Federal Police and Investigative Agencies. Westport, Conn.: Greenwood Press.

Wald, P. M.
1967 "Poverty and criminal justice." Pp. 139–151 in Task Force Report: The Courts. Washington, D.C.: U.S. Government Printing Office.

Walker, D.
1968 Rights in Conflict. New York: Bantam Books.

Washington Post
1976 "U.S. police chiefs accused of failure of leadership." April 15:A3.

Werthman, C. and I. Piliavin
1967 "Gang members and the police." Pp 56–98 in D. J. Bordua (ed.), The Police: Six Sociological Essays. New York: John Wiley & Sons.

Westley, W. A.
1953 "Violence and the police." American Journal of Sociology 59(July):34–41.
1956 "Secrecy and the police." Social Forces 34(March):254–257.
1970 Violence and the Police: A Sociological Study of Law, Custom, and Morality. Cambridge, Mass.: MIT Press.

Whyte, W. F.
1955 Street Corner Society: The Social Structure of an Italian Slum. Chicago: University of Chicago Press.

Williams, K. R. and S. Drake
1980 "Social structure, crime and criminalization: an empirical examination of the conflict perspective." The Sociological Quarterly 21(Autumn):563–575.

Wilson, J. Q.
1963 "The police and their problems: a theory." Pp. 189–216 in Public Policy: A Yearbook of the Graduate School of Public Administration, Harvard University, vol. 12.
1966 "The police and the delinquent in two cities." Pp. 9–30 in S. Wheeler (ed.), Controlling Delinquents. New York: John Wiley & Sons.
1967 "Police morale, reform, and citizen respect: the Chicago case." Pp. 137–162 in D. J. Bordua (ed.), The Police: Six Sociological Essays. New York: John Wiley & Sons.
1968 Varieties of Police Behavior. Cambridge, Mass.: Harvard University Press.

9
ADMINISTRATION
OF CRIMINAL LAW:
THE COURTS

Journalists, social scientists, and most citizens (even the most cynical persons) refer to American courts as the American criminal justice system. We have become accustomed to using these words in an unthinking fashion. Indeed, in my earlier book (Galliher and McCartney, 1977) the police and courts were referred to again and again as the criminal justice system. The question raised here is whether this is an appropriate way to refer to these institutions. Justice is typically defined as involving the practice of treating people impartially, with moral rightness or equitableness and fairness. Defined in this way justice is available in the United States, but it must be purchased like education, medical care, and automobiles. The quality of any of these products depends on the amount of money one can spend. With unlimited funds one can purchase an Ivy League education, with less funds the student must settle for public education, and with still less one may not even be able to afford vocational training programs. As will be shown here, justice must be purchased in precisely the same way.

There is widespread agreement in the United States that legal justice should be available to all Americans regardless of financial position. Even persons who believe equality in education, medical care, and transportation smacks of communism agree. This belief in equal justice is an important part of the American myth system. Indeed, as a citizen in a democracy, justice is given, not purchased. Having to purchase justice is a degradation of the meaning of the word. Yet in American society justice must be purchased. Nowhere is this free enterprise system more apparent than in American bail practices where freedom while awaiting trial must be purchased. The routine and unreflective use of the phrase "American criminal justice system" probably leads even the most cynical people to overlook the injustice in this system. Political liberals have traditionally seen the bail system, like other constitutional guarantees, as good and fair. Perhaps this is true because it is so often referred to as a part of the justice system. The words we use make us sensitive to some things around us and lead us to ignore others. The ancient Greeks had a number of different words to signify different types of love: the love of a man for a woman, of a man for another man, and of an adult for a child. On the other hand, in our society we tend not to see many types of relationships as really constituting love because of our relatively imprecise terminology. Just so, our use of the phrase "criminal justice system" tends to blind us to injustice in our courts.

While liberals have traditionally admired our bail system, conservatives are angered by it. Shortly after President Reagan was elected (September 28, 1981), he spoke before the International Association of Chiefs of Police: "We will push for bail reform that will permit judges, under carefully limited conditions, to keep some defendants from using bail to return to the streets, never to be seen in court again until they're arrested for another crime." That same year (February 8, 1981) in his Annual Report to the American Bar Association, U.S. Chief Justice Warren Burger agreed: "Any study of the statistics will reveal that 'bail crime' reflects a great hole in the fabric of our protection against internal terrorism." Reagan's Attorney Gerneral's Task Force on Violent Crime (1981) also continued this choreographed conservative attack on traditional bail procedures.

Today Americans take it for granted, and it is seen as natural that individuals should be prosecuted by the state for any crimes they allegedly have committed. Yet under colonial law when one citizen was accused by another of stealing his or her property, the law enforcement authorities, including the sheriff and judge, only served to adjudicate the fairness of the claims and counterclaims between citizens. By the early 1800s, however, the alleged thief stood accused by his or her neighbor and the government as well (Browning and Gerassi, 1980). The reason for this relatively swift and dramatic legal change is that crimes against property increased greatly after the war for American independence. During the colonial period most crimes involved behavior that we today refer to as morals offenses, including fornication, adultery, and not keeping the Sabbath. But shortly after the Revolution a severe depression occurred, and economic inequality increased greatly. Thus, this abrupt change in the focus of legal concerns occurred. In this context government policymakers decided to enter into these disputes on the side of property owners.

As Americans, we are told that we enjoy a court system unique among modern nations, its hallmarks being the equality of all citizens appearing before the courts and the existence of explicit constitutional rights that all citizens may use to defend themselves against government prosecution. These constitutional rights guarantee a speedy public trial, protection against compulsory self-incrimination, and a trial by a jury of our peers. Clearly, dictatorships have never bothered with such formalities. The question is, How does this description of the ideal functioning of the system square with what is known about the actual operation of American courts?

COURT PROCESSES

Shortly after a person is arrested, the accused is brought before a lower or magistrate court either for trial if charged with a misdemeanor punishable by less than one year in the local jail or if charged with a felony, for a hearing to determine whether the suspect should be released or held for a preliminary hearing. If the suspect is held,

> the case then is turned over to a prosecuting attorney who charges the defendant with a specific statutory crime. This charge is subject to review by a judge [the same or another magistrate judge] at a preliminary hearing of the evidence and in many places if the offense charged is a felony, by a grand jury that can dismiss the charge, or affirm it by delivering it to a judge in the form of an indictment. (President's Commission, 1967:7.)

The preliminary hearing is somewhat similar to actual criminal trial proceedings in that the defendant can be represented by legal counsel and call witnesses on his or her behalf. However, at the preliminary hearing it is only necessary for the magistrate judge to be convinced that there is "probable cause" to suppose that the person may be guilty, not to be convinced of guilt beyond a reasonable doubt as in criminal trials. Also at preliminary hearings, unlike criminal trials, the defendant has no right to be heard by a jury. If the defendant is held for trial, the magistrate sets the amount of the bail.

> [The magistrate] is entitled to inquire into the facts of the case, into whether there are grounds for holding the accused. He seldom does. He seldom can. The more promptly an arrested suspect is brought into magistrate's court, the less likelihood there is that much information about the arrest other than the arresting officer's statement will be available to the magistrate. Moreover, many magistrates, especially in big cities, have such congested calendars that it is almost impossible for them to subject any case but an extraordinary one to prolonged scrutiny. (President's Commission, 1967:10.)

After an individual is arrested on a felony charge, the prosecutor must decide whether the person should be prosecuted and on what charges. If the person is prosecuted, a document called the information is drafted by the prosecutor. In some jurisdictions the grand jury is also involved in criminal prosecutions. The grand jury is a group of citizens who, for a specific period of time, are required to investigate in closed sessions charges coming from preliminary hearings in magistrate courts and to initiate proceedings if the facts it uncovers warrant such action. When a grand jury is used, charges against the defendant are presented in a statement called an indictment rather than in the information. Since the grand jury merely determines whether there is probable cause to believe that the accused is guilty, only the prosecution's evidence is heard. After hearing the evidence, the grand jury must decide whether probable cause has been shown to support the charges in the indictment.

Originally the secrecy of the grand jury in England was intended to exclude representatives of the Crown from the proceedings to protect private citizens from unfounded government charges and to enable the grand jury to look into misconduct among government officials (Katz et al., 1972:11–17). However, the grand jury no longer serves this function. Now it is essentially limited to reviewing whether a prosecutor has presented sufficient evidence and testimony to warrant a trial. Usually the grand jury is merely a rubber stamp for the prosecutor and seldom investigates cases on its own. Even when the grand jury does not return an indictment, this may be at the prosecutor's own request. This requested nonindictment is a means of protecting the prosecutor from losing a marginal case in court or from looking cowardly by dropping charges and refusing to bring a case to trial. Because of these manipulations more people are questioning whether the grand jury system is really necessary if the preliminary hearing accomplishes the same general purpose of establishing probable cause.

Whether prosecution is by information or by indictment, when the accused is to be tried for a felony, the first step prior to the trial is the arraignment in the trial court. At this step in the proceedings there are generally three things defendants can do: (1) They can seek a delay before trial for such reasons as obtaining legal counsel or consulting further with their legal counsel; this happens very frequently, in part because defense lawyers do not want the case to go to trial before they have been paid in full. (2) The defendant can plead guilty, not guilty, or no contest—called nolo contendere—which secures the usual advantages of a guilty plea in exchange for a reduced criminal penalty without actually admitting guilt that could leave the defendant liable if later sued for civil damages. (3) The defendant can attempt to have the entire case thrown out of court and the trial process stopped by claiming improper procedure in the arrest or preliminary hearing or by claiming insufficient evidence. At least according to legal theory, the judge does not have to accept a guilty plea from a defendant if, for example, the judge has reason to believe that the guilty plea is the result of coercion of the defendant. But as we will soon see, most of these guilty pleas are a consequence of some degree of coercion. If the case is not delayed and if the judge does not throw it out, the trial process begins. The popular belief in America is that more than any other nation in the world, we go out of our way to give every advantage to those accused of crimes. Yet there is some doubt about this assertion when the actual pattern of events in a typical American trial is reviewed.

The State has the first and the last word in the trial. The prosecution makes the opening statement, outlining its case. The opening statement by the defense follows; then the State submits its evidence and calls its witnesses. The defense then presents its witnesses and contrary evidence; thereupon defense and prosecution may take turns in offering rebuttals, in cross-examining opposing witnesses, and in re-examining its own witnesses. At the end of this rebuttal period, the State summarizes its case and is answered by the closing argument of the defense. The State then presents its closing arguments. (Korn and McCorkle, 1963:111–112.)

This typical order of events normally gives the state four opportunities to address the court compared with three opportunities provided for the defense. The state not only has more opportunities to present its case, but since it has the first and last word, it has the advantage of what are called the primacy and recency effects. Social scientists have documented that the first argument and the most recent argument that people hear have a greater impact on their beliefs than do other arguments (Miller and Campbell, 1959).

After receiving instructions from the judge about what facts they must believe to find the defendant guilty as charged, the jury retires to attempt to reach a verdict. This usually requires complete consensus of the jurors. If the jurors do find the defendant guilty, then the judge usually begins to consider a sentence, although in some states the jury participates to varying degrees in the sentencing. If the jurors cannot agree, the result is a hung jury, and the prosecutor must decide whether the case is worth a second trial.

Having outlined the events leading up to and including the criminal trial, the roles of the various actors and organizations in this process will be discussed in the following sections.

THE BAIL SYSTEM

Bail Bondsmen

Traditionally the bail system in the United States has allowed accused individuals to be released from custody before trial if they have posted with the court funds that the judge considers sufficient to insure their appearance for trial. Perhaps the most outrageous feature of the American bail system is that in most cases the ultimate decision about a defendant's freedom while awaiting trial is not made by the judge or the prosecutor but by someone in a private profit-making business—the bail bondsman. While prosecutors typically determine at what level bail will be set, the bail bondsman decides whether the suspect is a good enough risk to do business with and also decides how much, if any, collateral is required to protect the bondsman's investment. At times, the bondsman demands collateral in the amount of the bond. This forces those accused to act as their own surety. Here the bondsman merely converts the value of the collateral into ready cash that the court will accept (Ryan, 1967). Bail is easily available for those persons involved in large-scale racketeering who have organizational backing or for those who know or are known by bail bondsmen, such as professional thieves. It is the amateurs, often likely to be innocent, and especially poor people who must wait in jail until trial (Goldfarb, 1965:4).

Wice (1974) found that there are six different means through which defendants contact a bondsman. Listed in order of frequency, they are (1) family and friends, (2) the defendants themselves, (3) the defendant's lawyer, (4) court officials—including the court clerk or bailiff, (5) police and jailers, and (6) by prearrangement (professional criminals ask friends to notify a bondsman in the area where they intend to commit a crime in case there is a slipup of some kind and they are arrested).

One abuse of the bondsman's role occurs when bondsmen change their minds about clients after learning something new and discrediting about these people. In such instances, bondsmen may no longer be willing to risk their investment, which could force their clients' return to jail, and they may even fail to return their clients' initial payments (Wice, 1974:40–41). From the bondsman's point of view, the best risks are professional criminals and those involved in illegal gambling. The bad risks are first offenders who might panic and run away. Indeed, bondsmen turn down many defendants whom they consider poor risks (Wice, 1974:38–41). In most areas if bondsmen can convince a judge that they did their best to recapture a defendant who did not appear for trial, the judge will set aside all or part of the amount to be forfeited.

The bondsman's concern is understandable because the defendant who jumps bail and fails to appear for trial loses nothing, since the bondsman charges the defendant a nonreturnable premium (Ryan, 1967). Although insurance companies provide much of the money that bail bondsmen use, if a bondsman's customer forfeits his or her bond, then the bondsman must pay the insurance company and absorb the loss (Goldfarb, 1965:97).

Corrupt Practices

In most jurisdictions bondsmen are governed by formal regulations, but these regulations are not effectively enforced. Rates of interest are formally regulated in most areas, but these rates are often circumvented by charging minimum fees or extra fees for night service (Goldfarb, 1965:100).

In 1961 a grand jury in Kansas City, Missouri, found that most bondsmen were business partners of certain police officers (Goldfarb, 1965:109–115). Some police, after making arrests, would refer defendants to specific bondsmen who would, in return, kick back a percentage of their fees to that police officer. In St. Louis in 1973 bondsmen were operating in the city courts even though the judges did not require them to forfeit the bonds of nonappearing defendants, and it was alleged that here, too, some fee splitting was involved—in this instance between bondsmen and judges (*St. Louis Post-Dispatch*, 1973:9A). "In St. Louis, for example, records of the circuit court reveal that of the 318 forfeitures in felony cases in 1970, 304 were set aside" (Wice, 1974:40). From coast to coast bondsmen owe many millions of dollars to the courts but never have to pay off the debt, because judges are being bribed (NBC News, 1982). The leader of one of Florida's largest cocaine smuggling operations indicated that he told his bondsman when and where big loads were coming in so that the bondsman would be nearby if he was needed. In this case it is clear that bondsmen have some prior knowledge of the crime before it occurs and are very close to being involved in a criminal conspiracy. These bondsmen often never pay the courts the required bond when their client fails to appear for trial and even help these drug dealers escape to South America (NBC News, 1982).

Bondsmen are also at times in collusion with defense attorneys. The bondsman may insist that the defendant use a specific lawyer who in turn splits the legal fees with the bondsman. In such cases, the quality and character of the defendant's legal aid are determined by the bondsman. Finally, the bond system in America has at times resulted in kidnappings and beatings of defendants who jump bail and do not show up for their trial. Bondsmen have been known to hire goons to kidnap, drug, and beat up persons who have jumped bail and then return them to the state court with jurisdiction in the case, thereby ignoring the existence of legal processes providing for extradition (Katz et al., 1972:162). Indeed, recently two American bounty hunters kidnapped a prominent Canadian land developer in Toronto after he had jumped bail while charges were pending against him in a Florida court involving some of his land sales (*Time*, 1983). The Canadian government was outraged that normal legal procedures for extradition were not followed. As Dill (1975:667) observed: "Law-enforcement officials can informally borrow the bondsman's legal authority to avoid having to comply with expensive and cumbersome procedures necessary for interstate extradition of fugitive defendants."

In some cities there is a system of collusion among select bondsmen and jail officials that gives some bondsmen a monopoly on bail services (Dill, 1975). When such a monopoly occurs, those few favored bondsmen refuse to extend any services to those accused of minor crimes whose bail will be very small. The small fees are not worth the risk to them when they can get all the large cases they want. Thus people arrested for major crimes can make bail, while those arrested for minor crimes must wait in jail. As with other court officials, the bondsman is interested in court efficiency. The faster the cases are concluded, the faster the bondsman's money can be turned over (Dill, 1975). To protect this investment it is sometimes necessary to guide a defendant through the entire court process. Court officials will occasionally help certain bondsmen by moving cases forward on a day's court calendar to speed up the release of a client. The help provided to the courts by bondsmen leads court officials to attempt to neutralize the regulations designed to govern bondsmen (Dill, 1975).

The Courts and the Bail System

The magistrate judge's power to set the amount of bail is awesome. Although these decisions are subject to appellate review and reversal by higher courts, they are seldom overturned (Katz et al., 1972:158). Bail is usually set on the basis of severity of the offense with which the suspect is charged. Nevertheless, there is only a slight relationship between the severity of the offense and either the probability of flight to avoid prosecution or the commission of later crimes (Ryan, 1967).

In 1978, 23 states and the District of Columbia had laws that considered defendant danger as one aspect of bail and pretrial detention decisions, but by 1984 the list included 34 states (Goldkamp, 1985). In 1984 new Federal legislation for the "first time in peacetime history . . . explicitly authorized detention without bail of allegedly dangerous defendants in cases other than murder and a few other crimes that have traditionally been punishable by death" (Taylor, 1984:B6). But traditionally the theory of the bail system is that the accused person has given over enough money to the court to satisfy the judge that the defendant will be present for the trial rather than forfeit the money. If this theory is true, then the amount of bail set should be based in part on the wealth of the accused, because this will determine how much money is required to deter the person from fleeing (Ryan, 1967). In fact, as already noted, if the suspect deals with a bondsman, only the bondsman—not the suspect—stands to lose money by the suspect's nonappearance. Since wealth is usually not considered by judges in setting bail, obviously poor people suffer. They typically go to jail to await trial and usually lose whatever employment they have—often forcing their families to go on welfare. All this happens before the trial and any determination of guilt.

Moreover, the bail system can be used intentionally as a political weapon to punish certain groups of people in advance of trial. A defendant can be arrested frivolously in a manner certain not to result in conviction but which nonetheless forces the person to obtain the bail money or remain in jail (Goldfarb, 1965). During the civil rights demonstrations in the South in the 1960s, bail was often set very high, which forced demonstrators to await trial in jail. Moreover, sometimes people are arrested and charged with a number of crimes, and then because a separate high bail is set for each charge, even nonindigent defendants cannot raise the full amount. However, the bail system was never intended as a denial of justice or, in fact as a sentence before trial. It was merely intended as a means to ensure that a person charged with a crime would be available for trial—and at this it fails.

Being a prisoner before and during a trial seems to prejudice the jury and judge against the defendant. If the defendant is in jail before and during the trial, then the accused comes to court in the custody of a guard, which makes it appear that this person is guilty. Therefore, it is not hard to convince the jury that this is indeed so. Defendants in jail during trial experience a higher conviction rate than do those free on bail during trial (Goldfarb, 1965:38–40)—irrespective of the seriousness of the charge, the magnitude of the evidence, and their prior record (New York Legal Aid Society, 1972; see also Rankin, 1964). Aside from the stigma of being a prisoner during the trial, which may prejudice the judge and jury, there are other possible explanations for these results. For example, a person released on bail can claim a good work and family record while awaiting trial, which may influence the judge and jury favorably. The jailed defendant does not have this opportunity (Katz et al., 1972:151–152).

Alternatives to the Bail System

Other Countries   In England bail can be provided only by the accused person or by some friend or relative who will post bail for the defendant. There are no professional bondsmen, and in fact, furnishing bonds for profit is a criminal offense (Goldfarb, 1965:215). Bail is set lower in England than in the United States so that in only 1 percent of the cases in which bail is set are people detained for being unable to raise the money.

In Sweden those freed before trial are ordinarily released on their word that they will return for trial (Goldfarb, 1965:218–222). In Denmark the same practice is used. Both countries also rely heavily on the summons instead of on arrests and bail. The use of summons to appear in court for misdemeanor and felony cases has the advantage of freeing the defendant awaiting trial from the stigma of arrest. In many cases of extreme violence there is little risk to the community. For example, a wife takes years of physical abuse from her husband and finally decides that her only escape is to kill him. In such a case the community is not endangered by using a summons much like a traffic ticket to bring her to trial rather than relying on the arrest and bail procedure. It is unlikely that, while awaiting her trial, this woman would marry another abusive man and decide again that her only escape was murder.

New U.S. Programs   In 1961 the New York University Law School started the Manhattan bail project (Katz et al., 1972:164). Law students interviewed people in jail, focusing on their residential stability, occupational history, and prior criminal record. The more stable and permanent members of the community were recommended to the judge for release on their own recognizance, that is, on their own promise to return for trial. With this program, judges tended to release four times more accused than they did before, and approximately 98 percent of those released showed up for trial.

Another idea to circumvent the problem of bail was first developed in Illinois (Goldfarb, 1965:198–203). With this system the defendant can post directly with the court an amount equal to the premium, or interest, for the bond set (for example, $10 premium on a $100 bond). If defendants show up for trial, they get back the money minus only a small administrative fee (1 percent of the bond). If the defendant does not appear for the trial, the total bond set—not just the premium—is forfeited. Although this cuts out the bail bondsman, some defendants are so poor that they cannot even post the premium for the bond with the court. Also, it may be impossible to collect the full bail amount from poor defendants who do not appear for trial.

There is some evidence that the Illinois system was pushed through the legislature by defense attorneys (Katz et al., 1972:169). Apparently everyone who had anything to do with the bail system was getting paid off. Then to increase the bail fee available for the payoffs, bail was being set at exorbitant levels, leaving the defendants with no money for attorneys. As a convenience and a guarantee for defense attorneys, the Illinois statute now permits defendants to sign over to their attorneys 90 percent of the sum to be returned to them by the court when they appear for trial. This feature, of course reflects the influence of defense attorneys on the legislation. It shows how some apparently humane and progressive innovations can have exploitative origins. Defense attorneys wanted their pound of flesh.

During 1973, in Oregon a sweeping reform movement put bondsmen out of business, but now law enforcement authorities are saying it was a big mistake (Snouffer, 1974; NBC News, 1982). Instead of the bondsman, Oregon relies on county employees called custody referees or release assistance officers. These custody referees interview those who have been arrested and decide who should be released pending their trial. But unlike bondsmen, custody referees do not go after those who leave the area and do not show up for their trials. In fact, there is some evidence that employees in custody referees' offices tell those arrested that if they leave Oregon no one will come after them. Thus many people in Oregon never show up for their trials, and even when they are caught in other states, Oregon will not spend the money to bring them back. An Oregon prosecutor concluded (NBC News, 1982): "The government has no person who looks for and apprehends the person who flees. The crooks know that. Why not flee?" Here is an excellent example of a liberal reform that does not seem to work as intended. The reason that it does not work is that Americans are among the most mobile people in the world. The Statistical Abstracts of the United States (1982–1983:14), for example, showed that almost half of all Americans moved between 1975 and 1980. In most European countries this is the exception rather than the rule. European families often have lived in the same county and even in the same village for hundreds of years. For such people the thought of leaving the area to avoid trial is not a possibility. Therefore relatively lax bail procedures are more workable there than in a society where people have little or no commitment to any given geographical region.

But in spite of the practical problems associated with American mobility, one might still wonder why the courts have made no effort to abolish or control the corrupt bail system, since the system seems so blatantly undemocratic. The reason is that bondsmen help manage defendants during the time between arrest and sentencing (Dill, 1975). Bondsmen remind customers of future court dates and help them find courtrooms. Morever, bondsmen have an interest in guilty pleas, which, as will be shown later, is also true of other court officials. The bondsman's liability for each bond he or she posts only ends when the case is cleared from the docket, and therefore the bondsman often counsels customers to plead guilty. Morever, in many places—not just in St.Louis—most bail forfeitures are set aside by judges. Judges remit bail forfeitures usually because they sometimes want favors from bondsmen, such as refusing to post bail when the judges actually do not want certain defendants released. This was often the case with civil rights demonstrators in the South during the 1960s. Finally, as indicated above, the bondsman has broader legal powers in retrieving defendants who have absconded then does any criminal justice official; they need no warrants for arrest, and unlike the police, they are not restricted by interstate extradition laws (Dill, 1975). If a defendant is not in court on the trial date, the bondsman can often convince the judge and prosecutor to reschedule the case for a later time (Feeley, 1979), which will give the bondsman an interval of time to seek the defendant and bring him or her into court. Yet at times a bondsman is allowed to withdraw from a case when a defendant does not appear for trial, and therefore the bondsman does not have to forfeit any money. In other cases the bond may be reduced to a very small amount when a defendant does not appear. All these favors are afforded to bondsmen because they are so helpful in the operation of the court.

CRIMINAL LAWYERS

To understand the routine practice of criminal law in America, it is important to recognize that criminal lawyers usually have lower social class backgrounds than do lawyers in civil practice (Wood, 1967). Moreover, criminal lawyers as a group have attended less prestigious law schools than did lawyers in civil practice, and criminal lawyers generally make less money than do lawyers in civil practice. Most criminal lawyers did not plan to have this kind of practice, rather this was the only alternative available to them. Attorneys' apparent lack of enthusiasm for the practice of criminal law is understandable. Contrary to the mass media stereotype of the highly paid, brilliant criminal defense counsel, criminal lawyers not only earn less but also have less attractive working conditions than do their counterparts in civil practice. Working largely out of the city drunk tank is not as inherently satisfying as conducting business over a two-martini lunch. Thus most defendants must select counsel from this group of second-class citizens of the legal profession, who may also have received something less than a first-rate legal education.

Yet, Alschuler (1975) found that attorneys recognized several ways to earn a high income in the practice of criminal law. The most obvious—and also the most difficult—way is to gradually develop the reputation of having special skills as a trial defense attorney. A quicker and surer method of achieving financial success involves handling a large number of cases and pleading them all guilty to save time. Yet a third possibility is to combine these two approaches by taking a few highly publicized cases to trial and pleading all the rest guilty. An attorney explained, "One never makes much money on the cases one tries, but they help to bring in cases one can settle." Another attorney explained that "a guilty plea is a quick buck" (Alschuler, 1975:1182). Those lawyers who always plead their clients guilty get fewer concessions from the prosecutor for their clients in return for a guilty plea because the prosecutor knows that no matter what the defense is offered, the attorney will plead the defendant guilty.

One might well wonder how such attorneys attract paying clients. Such "pleaders" stay in business in part because of referrals from bail bondsmen who, as noted earlier, expect a split of the attorney's fees in return. These attorneys enlist a defendant's family to help put pressure on the defendant to plead guilty to avoid the risk of greater punishment. Sometimes they claim that their special connections enabled them to work out a special deal. Moreover, the attorney may intentionally lie about the great strength of the prosecutor's case or even misrepresent the deal struck with the prosecutor in return for the guilty plea.

Public defenders do the same things as private attorneys but for different reasons. Public defenders are grossly understaffed. In 1970 the average caseload per public defender in New York City was 922 cases. In Philadelphia it was nearly 800 cases per year and up to 40 to 50 cases per day, while in Oakland there was a mere 300 cases per public defender per year. Private attorneys who are "pleaders" have been known to handle between 5 and 25 cases per day, charging between 50 and 500 dollars per case. One such attorney earned $400,000 per year (Alschuler, 1975).

The criminal lawyer must be able to work with the prosecuting attorney to arrange agreements on reduced charges in exchange for guilty pleas. In addition, a criminal lawyer must be able to work with the police to keep the number of charges down and to help arrange speedy bail at the police station. In dealing with police, the frequent similarity of social class background between the criminal lawyer and the police may be an important asset.

Criminal lawyers are more politically active than most other members of the legal profession are (Wood, 1967). One may interpret this activity as showing a strong humanitarian orientation because these attorneys are so often involved in liberal politics. But there are other less lofty explanations of this political activity. One possibility is that this involvement can and does lead to opportunities to be nominated for a position as a judge or as a prosecutor—two avenues out of the practice of criminal law. In addition, liberal politics in particular can bring a lawyer's name before massive numbers of poor people; then even if the lawyer does not win the election, these people may remember that name when they need a lawyer.

Legal Counsel for Indigent Defendants

Until recently most jurisdictions in the United States made no allowance, or at best only a small allowance, for the compensation of court-appointed lawyers representing indigents (Tappan, 1960:368). In areas in which indigent defendants were provided with some legal aid, one traditional method of doing so was for the court to use some type of rotation system for assigning indigent cases to members of the local bar. Typically the attorneys assigned to such cases received reimbursement only for minor costs of travel or a modest payment for the time spent on the case. The problems with such a system are all too obvious. Most members of the bar do not practice criminal law and are not qualified for the task. At most these lawyers have had only a couple of courses on criminal law, and they may have been many years in the past. In addition, the typically inadequate compensation places pressure on the court-appointed lawyer to persuade a client to plead guilty and thus save the lawyer time that could be spent on paying clients.

Two Supreme Court decisions made this method of providing legal aid to indigents unworkable. One was the decision in *Gideon* v. *Wainwright* (1963), which required that all indigent defendants accused of a felony be provided with legal counsel. More recently, this provision was expanded (*Argersinger* v. *Hamlin*, 1972) to require legal aid for anyone accused of a crime punishable by imprisonment. Since legal aid in all parts of the United States was now to be routinely offered to indigent defendants, some more systematic method of offering this service became necessary. It seemed desirable to vest this responsibility in a full-time office—the public defender's office. Yet in rural areas it is not efficient to have a public defender system because of the small caseload of indigent defendants. Instead, these areas use the assigned counsel system or another method called the contract system, whereby a local firm makes a bid to handle all indigent cases in the county for a specified period of time (Houlden and Balkin, 1985).

In any case, the public defender, as a result of working daily with the judge and prosecutor, may begin to share their definition of the trial and courtroom situation. The pressure on the public defender is especially intense because, unlike the public defender, both the judge and the prosecutor are elected officials and are therefore much more politically powerful than is the public defender. Sudnow (1965) studied the operation of the public defender's office and observed that the main job of the public defender is to convince a client that the chances of acquittal are too slight to warrant the risk of pleading not guilty. The public defender tries to convince clients to see the reasonableness of pleading guilty to a reduced offense or to the actual offense but in exchange for a reduced penalty. This standard operating procedure has the full cooperation of the prosecuting attorney. Both the public defender and the prosecuting attorney are permanent employees of the court, and both realize that the only way they can prevent a great backlog of cases is to have most defendants plead guilty. They share the same assembly-line orientation toward the court system, one in which efficiency and speed rather than full justice is seen as the measure of success.

The question is, What types of reduced charges are usually used in these plea bargains? Often plea bargains are based on some lesser crime, but one that is statutorily included in the original charge (Sudnow, 1965). For example, a case of manslaughter is included in the statutory definition of first degree murder. Manslaughter is a *statutorily designated* crime that is included in the crime of murder. If it can be shown that a defendant (1) killed another person, (2) that this act was premeditated, and (3) that there was an intent to kill, then a case can be made for first degree murder. The point is that it is impossible to prove a crime of murder without also proving the case for manslaughter; the latter is included in the former's statutory definition. But for the crimes of public drunkenness and child molesting there are no lesser crimes included in their statutory definitions. Thus in these cases there are other crimes selected with lesser penalties that are *typically situationally included*. That is, there are other crimes that usually occur when an individual commits the greater offense. Those arrested for being drunk in public often disturb the peace and those arrested for child molesting often are also guilty of loitering around school yards. Therefore these crimes are used as reduced charges, for it is reasoned that even if for example, one particular person arrested for public drunkenness did not disturb the peace, most people arrested for public drunkenness do.

However, burglary charges are usually reduced to petty theft even though it is not part of the statutory definition of burglary. Petty theft requires actual stealing, while burglary requires only the *intent* to steal another's property by breaking and entering. Nor is it typical of burglars to also commit this other lesser crime. Thus the reduced charge that is negotiated is not necessarily a part of the statutory definition nor is it typically committed by people arrested for the more serious offense. The prosecutor and the public defender usually determine the nature of the reduced charge on the basis of what they see as a reasonable difference between the expected punishments for the two charges (Sudnow, 1965). Their common orientation is to reduce the charge just to the point that the defendant will not get off too easily yet enough to ensure the defendant's cooperation. The prosecutor and public defender also consider what the judge and influential community interest groups desire (Rosett and Cressey, 1976:85–92). Therefore the public defender's activity is seldom geared to securing acquittals for clients. The public defender and the prosecuting attorney take it for granted that the persons who come before the court are guilty of crimes and treat them accordingly. The public defender assumes that every client is going to lose the case even if he or she does not plead guilty. Thus even when a defendant does not agree to plead guilty, the public defender does not prepare the case properly for trial, that is, in a way sufficient to win. The public defender often just glances at the defendant's file immediately before the trial begins (Sudnow, 1965). Indeed, the public defender helps speed the indigent defendant through the court system and, as the defendant's attorney, offers advice to the accused that helps control the defendant and keeps the court system operating as smoothly as possible (Barak, 1975).

Unlike the prosecutor's office, which can merely drop the charges on cases when its backlog of cases gets too great, the public defender must accept all cases. Therefore being typically overworked, public defenders recognize that their office does not provide high-quality service to clients. As might be expected, clients are often hostile toward public defenders and may view the public defender as a government agent. For their part, public defenders usually do not believe in their clients' innocence, have mixed emotions about securing acquittals for clients, and have difficulty in identifying with poor, unattractive clients accused of crimes. It is easier for them to identify with fellow lawyers, including prosecutors and judges (Rosett and Cressey, 1976:122–126)

In our courts, due process requires, among other things, a presumption of innocence and a truly adversary proceeding in which a person receives a full, fair, and open judicial hearing or trial. The hearing must be real, not a contrived pretense. The proceedings must be free from any taint of coercion. Nevertheless, the courts in fact now have an overriding goal of assembly-line guilty pleas. This assembly-line system of criminal law is incompatible with traditional due process. Due process no longer influences the determination of guilt; now plea bargaining serves this purpose (Blumberg, 1967a:4–5). Recent discussions about Supreme Court decisions on the rights of due process against wiretapping, unlawful search, and police coercion and the right to legal counsel have led attention away from the actual operation of the courts. Due process protection for the defendant is meaningless in a system in which defendants are presumed guilty and pressured to plead guilty. If the defendant pleads guilty, the question of whether the police used constitutionally correct means in collecting their evidence is never raised in court. Moreover, the right to legal counsel is meaningless if this legal counsel helps pressure the defendant into pleading guilty as the prosecution desires.

In a small number of cases the public defender may actually mount an aggressive defense for a client. Sudnow (1965:274) indicated that this happens in some "murders, . . . multiple rape cases, large scale robberies, dope ring operations, those cases that arouse public attention and receive special notice in the papers." The public's concern causes both the public defender and the prosecutor to realize that some public airing of these charges is a political necessity. Since so much public attention is given to such cases, the public's stereotypical view of trials is reinforced. While such cases may be insignificant in statistical terms, symbolically they are important (Silberman, 1978:282). These truly adversarial cases attract considerable press attention, certainly much more than the humdrum masses of cases with guilty pleas. By covering only sensational cases, the press reinforces the mistaken notion that public defenders typically operate this way and thereby reinforces a belief in the essential equity or fairness of the system.

A skeptic might well wonder that while this description of the public defender system may apply to public defenders in general, surely it does not apply to public defender offices that are rated highly. Therefore a study of a highly ranked public defender office in Oakland, California (Platt and Pallock, 1974), becomes especially interesting. In Oakland the public defender's budget was found to be dependent on maintaining good working relations with other government agencies, including the prosecutor's office. Whether a given public defender's office receives its finances from the city, county, or state government, the same rule of thumb applies. Given the importance of maintaining these good relations, it should not be surprising that public defenders, including those in Oakland, are typically conservative and attempt to avoid controversy. Public defenders' offices typically do not want to recruit attorneys who are politically controversial or identified with liberal or left-wing politics. This public defender's office in Oakland also recognized that it could not retain most assistant public defenders more than approximately 2 to 3 years, or until these attorneys had gained enough trial experience to start their own private practices. And in fact only 5 of the 58 lawyers in this office planned to make a career of being a public defender, and most do resign after a brief stint. The average length of service in this office was 2½ years.

Usually the idealism of the young attorneys when they first come into the public defender's office quickly turns into cynicism when they learn the sad truth that poor people, just like wealthy people, can lie, cheat, and steal. These young attorneys, who initially are morally concerned with the problems of their clients, soon learn that they cannot trust their clients and begin in this way to share the views of the prosecution. Even in the best public defender offices the attorneys are chronically overworked, inexperienced, and increasingly cynical about the character of their clients and only remain in the office until they have enough experience to get paying clients.

Notice how different the practice of law is from the practice of medicine. Brain surgeons do not begin to practice on their own until they have had a great deal of experience assisting in surgery. But lawyers begin to handle criminal cases on their own with almost no supervision, right out of law school where they may have had only a couple of courses on criminal law. The consequence of plea bargaining by court-appointed attorneys can be seen in a case from Mississippi (*Time*, 1979:49). In 1979 a 14-year-old black youth, four feet seven inches tall and weighing 75 pounds, was convicted of the armed robbery of two fireworks stands and was sentenced to 48 years in prison without parole as a result of a plea bargain by his court-appointed attorney.

Private Defense Attorneys

Even defendants who have sufficient finances to retain private legal counsel usually get something quite different from the public's image of a defense attorney as epitomized by such courtroom fighters as F. Lee Bailey or Clarence Darrow. And only a few major felony cases drawing great public attention follow a true adversary model. Yet, however few in number, such lawyers and such highly publicized cases support the fiction of an adversary system, which we are told, distinguishes American courts from those of totalitarian regimes.

Some nonindigent defendants have insufficient funds to purchase a large amount of a defense attorney's time, only having enough money to arrange a guilty plea. If a case should go to trial it could consume several days or even several weeks of an attorney's time—a guilty plea will consume only several hours. Blumberg (1967b) observed that in the case of persons charged with some type of property crime, such as burglary or shoplifting, there is a close relationship between the proceeds of the alleged crime and the attorney's fee. Defense attorneys try to convince their clients that they must be paid in full before they can exercise their professional expertise and use any of their special political connections with the prosecutor to get the charges reduced. The reasoning of most defense attorneys seems to be that they must be paid in full before the case goes to trial because should their client be found guilty, payment would be unlikely if the client blames the defense attorney or is imprisoned. Even if defendants are not convicted, they may still refuse to make payment at a later time once their freedom no longer hinges on the quality of their lawyer's efforts.

The larger the attorney's fee, the more impressive the attorney's performance must be in terms of not a real attack but of generating a stage-managed image as a person of great influence and power in the courtroom. The judge and prosecutor are aware of the extent to which a lawyer's stock-in-trade involves this stage-managed impression, and for this reason alone the lawyer is bound to the court's authority (Blumberg, 1967b). Therefore if the attorney is well liked and considered reasonable, to some degree the court personnel will aid the attorney in maintaining this impression. The judge and prosecutor will not object to having such an attorney use the courtroom to stage-manage an impression of an all-out performance for the accused to help justify the legal fee. The point is that even if a defendant can afford the financial costs of a not guilty plea, something far different from an adversary, combative proceeding is often purchased. In most areas there is a cadre of lawyers who handle the bulk of all nonindigent criminal cases. These attorneys have greater professional and economic ties to the court system than to their own clients. Criminal lawyers know that they will have a continuing relationship with the other members of the court and that they are expected to be reasonable rather than abrasive (Blumberg, 1967b).

The legal profession is responsible in part for one of the major chronic problems of the modern court system in America—the long delays in bringing a case to trial. Defendants have waited months and even years to be brought to trial. One reason for the delays in criminal trials is that defense attorneys request such delays until they have been paid in full. Very often the client may be free on bail working to get sufficient money to pay the lawyer. Although it is true that in some cases fees from clients are often hard to collect, it is obvious that the court, in granting delays with knowledge of the reason, becomes a collection agency. This need for court assistance in fee collection also serves to make the defense attorney dependent on the authority of the court (Katz et al., 1972:77). Another reason for delays in trials also involves attorneys. In most areas only a few lawyers handle the bulk of all nonindigent criminal cases. These lawyers are simply too busy to handle all cases promptly. For example, one study reported that in Cleveland 12 lawyers were the attorneys of record in one half of all pending felony cases with privately retained counsel (Katz et al., 1972:76).

Some believe that defense attorneys consider the common practice of prosecutors charging defendants with more serious offenses than the evidence supports beneficial because this makes it easy to get a charge reduced and thus enables defense attorneys to show their clients that they are effective. For their part, prosecutors bring more serious charges to bargain down to charges they really want (Katz et al., 1972:74). Thus the privately retained defense attorney, while subject to many of the same pressures as the public defender, has one decided advantage. When a client has considerable resources, the prosecutor will probably recognize that if a plea bargain is to be struck with the defendant, the state will have to give considerably more ground than with the average indigent defendant because the prosperous accused can insist on and receive the full attention of a staff of experienced attorneys for the duration of a trial of whatever length.

In counties with small populations there is considerable variation in the percentage of cases settled by guilty pleas, depending on the idiosyncratic working relationships between prosecutors, judges, and defense attorneys (Skolnick, 1967). In large cities, however, the massive number of cases appears to limit the range of variation, and thus the percentage of guilty pleas is always very high—around 80 to 90 percent. Those private defense attorneys who have the reputation of being the most successful plead most of their clients guilty but get greater reductions in exchange for this guilty plea than do most other attorneys (Skolnick, 1967). A small percentage of privately retained attorneys—known as "gamblers"—usually do not plead their clients guilty. They usually either "win big" or "lose big" (Skolnick, 1967:59). But most defense attorneys prefer not to take such risks.

At times the local jail is used to encourage defendants to plead guilty. Blumberg (1967a:59, 68–69) observed that crowded conditions become extemely useful to the courts. If bail is set at a level that the defendant cannot meet and the accused remains in jail, the worse the jail conditions—such as extreme filth and sexual assaults by other prisoners—the greater the pressure felt by the defendant to opt for a guilty plea. Awaiting an actual trial may take many months or even years, during which the person remains in jail. If the person pleads guilty and is quickly sentenced to the state prison, conditions there are likely to be much better. Political liberals often exhort their fellow citizens to become more aware of the horrible conditions in American jails, assuming that once citizens and policy makers are aware of these conditions they will demand an immediate change. But in fact America could do much better than our festering jails, and ignorance of the situation is not responsible for the problems. Many of those in government are quite aware of the situation yet make no demands for change and seem to feel that these conditions serve law enforcement very well.

It has often been noted that large organizations, such as the court system, usually can use time to their advantage in dealing with defendants. As Littrell (1979:194) noted: "Jails are especially well suited to this purpose." For their part, prosecutors can merely recommend a specific sentence to a judge if a defendant agrees to plead guilty. Judges may agree with the prosecutor's recommendation, but they are not bound by law to do so. "Therefore an element of uncertainty surrounds every guilty plea, and in this respect all defendants must plead in the dark" (Littrell, 1979:199). Therefore sometimes after a defendant pleads guilty and believes that an agreement is reached, he or she is surprised by the judge and given a much longer sentence than the prosecutor had discussed.

Guilty pleas are associated with yet another problem. These pleas protect the leaders involved in conspiratorial crimes and racketeering. James Earl Ray, the man who pleaded guilty to the killing of Dr. Martin Luther King, after his arrival in prison claimed to have been a part of a large conspiracy. But since there was never any trial, evidence on this point was never produced.

Political liberals have made a big issue of the grandness of American constitutional guarantees, including the right to an attorney and to protection from police interrogation unless defendants are informed that they have a right to remain silent and to have an attorney present during their interrogation. These constitutional rights reflected in U.S. Supreme Court decisions rest on the assumption that the trial is an adversarial or combative proceeding where the defense attorney does everything possible to defend the accused. Obviously this does not fit with reality. Since approximately 90 percent of all criminal convictions are the result of guilty pleas, we see just how insignificant the actual trial process has become.

The prosecutor has a number of levers to pressure the defendant into pleading guilty (Cloyd, 1979:456):

> He can: (1) charge the highest crime that evidence will allow; (2) recommend the amount of bail, if any, to be granted, although the judge has final discretion; (3) get access to more investigative resources than are available to the defense; and most importantly, (4) determine what lesser charge to offer the defendant in exchange for cooperation.

Thus in areas where there is a high percentage of guilty pleas, there are extreme differences between the severity of sentences given to those who do and those who do not plead guilty (Brereton and Casper, 1981–1982).

JUDGES

When speaking before various civic groups, judges often proclaim the importance of the jury trial as a keystone of American democracy (Blumberg, 1967a). These very judges, however, give much harsher sentences to those defendants who do not plead guilty and exercise their right to a jury trial. Judges routinely deny probation to defendants convicted by juries who might otherwise merit probation. Therefore the warnings from defense attorneys and the defendants' usual fears of harsh treatment if they do not plead guilty are not groundless

(Blumberg, 1967a:58, 129). Defendants who do not plead guilty receive considerably more severe sentences than do those who plead guilty, and this difference induces the vast majority of defendants to plead guilty. The data indicate that the possibility of probation for a defendant is far greater if the accused has pleaded guilty to a lesser offense rather than having been convicted at a jury trial (Brereton and Casper, 1981–1982). Therefore defendants are usually ready to bargain for a reduced charge or a reduced penalty rather than risk a greater penalty with an actual trial (Maynard, 1984). If the defense attorney and the prosecutor fail to reach agreement on a case, the judge may sometimes become involved in the negotiations, but it has been found that judges usually merely "rubber stamped decisions made by the attorneys" (Maynard, 1982:349).

When a defendant does plead guilty, the defendant must at least pretend to show remorse. This allows the judge to also pretend that the defendant deserves special consideration and leniency for being truly sorry for his or her past crimes. Everyone involved is aware of the total insincerity, especially the defendant. Once the defendant pleads guilty, the judge can presume that the accused is now a repentant individual who has learned a lesson and deserves lenient treatment.

> [The guilty plea is, in fact, an act,] during which an accused must project an appropriate and acceptable degree of guilt, penitence, and remorse. If he adequately feigns the role of the "guilty person," his hearers will engage in the fantasy that he is contrite and thereby merits a lesser plea. One of the essential functions of the criminal lawyer is that he coach his accused-client in this performance (Blumberg, 1967a:89).

Judges can be elected or appointed, and in either case there is no sure protection from corruption and incompetence. The assumption seems to be that merely by virtue of being an attorney, a person is competent for any judgeship. Among the obvious problems caused by selecting judges in partisan political elections is the fact that favors are owed to political backers. The appointment of judges, whether by governors or presidents, carries the same risks.

There have been attempts, however, to withdraw judges from the traditional pressures of partisan politics. One such scheme is called the Missouri Nonpartisan Plan for selecting judges (Watson and Downing, 1969). A list of possible judge candidates is compiled by a commission made up of prominent citizens, including lawyers. Three names selected by the commission are submitted to the state governor, who selects one of them. Typically, after the person has served one year, his or her name appears on the ballot with the question "Shall Judge _____ be retained in office?" If the judge receives a majority of yes votes, he or she remains in office a full term, however long that is for the particular judicial position. This process purportedly takes the selection of judges out of partisan politics, at least to a degree, and ensures at least a minimal competence, which the commission—if not the voters—would presumably require. The plan was adopted by the Missouri electorate in 1940, and since then several other states have initiated similar programs. The disadvantage to the Missouri plan is that since judges run unopposed, their election is virtually guaranteed. Thus to a great extent these judges are not accountable to the public.

Collectively, however, judges are perhaps best known by the nature of their decisions. This discussion now turns to the sentencing decisions of judges. Several studies have found that the courts deal more severely with blacks than with whites. On the average, blacks as compared to whites are required to put up greater amounts of bail money (Farnworth and Horan, 1980). For the same offenses, blacks are more likely to be sentenced than whites are, and of those sentenced, blacks are often given longer terms (Axelrad, 1952; Bullock, 1961; Farnworth and Horan, 1980). Later research found that judges discriminate against blacks in deciding between probation or incarceration even after controlling for all other differences in legal and extralegal factors (Spohn et al., 1981–1982). Another study found similar results: "Whites have an 18 percent greater chance in the predicted probability of receiving probation than blacks when all other things are equal" (Unnever et al., 1980:204). Therefore it should come as no surprise that imprisonment rates are higher in states having the greatest amount of economic inequality (Jacobs, 1978).

For skeptics, the racial distribution of executions provides a dramatic demonstration of these claims of discrimination. Among persons convicted of criminal homicide and sentenced to execution, a significantly higher proportion of blacks than whites were actually executed, whereas a higher proportion of whites had their sentences commuted to life in prison (Wolfgang et al., 1962). From 1930 through 1967, 55 percent of the approximately 4,000 people executed and an astonishing 90 percent of the 455 men executed for rape were blacks (Greenberg and Himmelstein, 1969; see also Bowers, 1974, for evidence of racial discrimination in executions). One could expect that a racist and class-biased society, such as the United States, would produce a similar legal system and that discrimination would be reflected in the sentences handed down by judges. While some researchers have claimed that these differences are a consequence of more serious and more frequent previous criminal acts committed by blacks rather than of racial discrimination, others note that these so-called previous behavioral measures (previous arrests and convictions) also reflect the racism of court officials rather than just the prior behavior of these black defendants (Farnworth and Horan, 1980).

JURIES

If a defendant does not plead guilty, a trial jury must be selected unless the defendant waives the right to a jury trial and accepts trial by a judge. In such cases, the judge not only rules on matters of law but also fills the jury's role of deciding on the facts of the case. Some states restrict the right to waive a jury trial to exclude cases with possible capital punishment or permit that right to be exercised only with the consent of the court. Some defendants feel that waiving a jury trial may help them because they fear the prejudice of local citizens against their race, religion, or type of crime. A person being tried for child molesting may believe, for example, that a group of jurors will be outraged merely by the nature of the charges. Therefore the defendant may decide that a seasoned judge, who has undoubtedly heard all these charges in many prior cases, might be more evenhanded in determining the facts of the case.

Picking jurors is more time consuming in the United States than in England. In England there is less pretrial newspaper publicity to bias jurors. American law gives an extreme amount of freedom to the press to discuss upcoming trials. Jurors tend to be more alike in England's relatively homogeneous culture. The United States is probably the most heterogeneous society in the world, and of course, both the prosecution and the defense are sensitive to how the social characteristics of the defendant—such as race, ethnicity of name, and social class—mesh with those of prospective jurors. Moreover, judges are not elected in England, and so they are not afraid to antagonize lawyers by refusing to release a juror. Reviewing courts in England do not usually reverse decisions on the basis of a judge's refusal to release a juror, whereas there are reversals for this reason in the United States (Puttkammer, 1953:180–181).

In selecting a jury, the lawyers generally ask each prospective juror whether he or she has already read about and formed an opinion about the case. Those persons who admit to having already made up their minds are excused from the jury by the judge. Some critics feel that only citizens who do not read newspapers will not have read about and formed some opinion about most major felony cases, and that juries in such cases are therefore made up primarily of nonreading, nonthinking, marginally intelligent people (Barnes and Tetters, 1959:272).

The trial of a political radical in Oakland, California, demonstrates the degree to which the very process of selecting a jury essentially made an impartial jury an impossibility and gave the prosecutor a great advantage (Wellman and Fitzgerald, 1978). The case involved a Japanese-American woman, Wendy Yoshimura, who was allegedly involved along with Patty Hearst and assorted self-proclaimed radicals, in what was called the Symbionese Liberation Army, in a series of robberies. In Oakland, jurors are selected from lists of registered voters, which tends to underrepresent people who are poor, young, poorly educated, and who belong to racial minorities. In Oakland, only 43 percent of those who are 18 to 24 years old are registered to vote compared to 70 percent of those people who are 45 to 64 years old. Only 47 percent of those people with less than 4 years formal education are registered, while 84 percent of the college graduates are registered. Such lists also exclude the conscientious nonvoter. Moreover, poor people cannot live on the $5 a day paid for jury duty and thus are excused for reasons of financial hardship. As a consequence of these patterns, the jury that was finally selected for the Yoshimura trial was older than the average age in the Oakland area and had only one black member.

When political radicals are tried, as in this case, it is in the interest of the government to locate jurors who accept all of the positive mythology about the legal system, such as the notion that everyone is equal before the law (Wellman and Fitzgerald, 1978). Once a jury is filled with people who believe in this ideology, the government is nearly assured of a conviction. Jurors are sitting in judgment of those people who refuse to believe all that the jurors themselves hold to be true. Jurors are also assumed by the court to be impartial when they say that they are impartial, as demonstated by the case of the juror who claimed he could be fair and yet made a reference to "Jap boys." The prosecution challenged and removed 5 of the 6 blacks among the original 12 jurors called and had the only Asian-American removed as well. The prosecution wanted white jurors because they typically accept the positive myths of the legal system because they are relatively inexperienced with the criminal courts. When the poor people or people from minority groups are asked whether they believe in the essential fairness of the court system, they are faced with a dilemma. If they answer truthfully on the basis of their own experience, they will be removed from consideration for having a negative bias. To serve on a jury they are forced to deny the validity of their own experience.

However, in a criminal trial, many defense attorneys seek well-educated jurors who are believed to be more difficult for the prosecution to convince beyond a reasonable doubt and more likely to be opposed to criminal punishment of any kind. Psychological research tends to support the notion that persons with a good deal of formal education need more information to be convinced about any particular issue (Hovland et al., 1974). For example, the juror with a Ph.D. in philosophy is unlikely to believe that an accused person is guilty as charged simply because he or she has beady eyes. They need much more information to reach a decision. Other research demonstrates that those with more education are most likely to oppose punishment as retribution (Warr and Stafford, 1984). Correspondingly, studies of child rearing indicate that those persons with more education are at least slightly more opposed to physical punishment as a means of controlling behavior (Erlanger, 1974). For the same reasons, the prosecution often wants less highly educated jurors and seeks to eliminate jurors with a good deal of formal education.

Generally, professional people are excused by the court from jury service because of the pressure of their occupational responsibilities. Lawyers do not serve on juries, and it is uncommon for other professional people, such as physicians, business executives, college professors, or ministers, to serve. In cases involving the death penalty people opposed to executions are always excused because of their bias, yet those who are totally and enthusiastically in favor of the death penalty are not similarly excused. Some people argue that systematically excluding jurors who oppose capital punishment but not jurors who strongly favor such punishment, injects an unfair bias into the jury composition in capital punishment cases.

It is interesting to note what types of persons escape jury service. Equally interesting are the methods used to select potential jurors. In various areas, names of potential jurors are obtained from voting records and property tax rolls. These methods of drawing up lists of potential jurors systematically exclude poor people because they seldom own property and vote less often than other people do. Poor people tend to have little faith in the electoral process and believe that their lives will remain unchanged by election results. Because most defendants in criminal trials share the characteristic of poverty, it appears that they are systematically deprived of the constitutional guarantee of a jury of their peers.

Thus a composite picture of the typical American jury shows people who do not have professional jobs, are not highly educated, and are neither terribly poor nor wealthy. "The overwhelming conclusion . . . is the pervasiveness of the bias in jury selection in favor of those characterized as 'Middle Americans' and, conversely, the underrepresentation of racial minorities, . . . [and] lower and upper socioeconomic classes" (Alker, et al., 1976:38). This is not to suggest, however, that there is no variation in social class among American jurors, for Strodtbeck et al. (1957) found that during jury deliberation it was the high-status people who did most of the talking and ultimately became opinion leaders for the other jurors. Therefore jury members who are most unlike the typical defendant in social class characteristics have the biggest impact on juror decisions.

In defense of existing systems for securing the names of potential jurors, it is sometimes argued that voter registration records or tax rolls, while not perfect, are the most representative lists available. Ideally the best list would be a list of all local citizens, but these lists almost always tend to overrepresent the more affluent people. However, there are other easily available public lists of local citizens that are not biased in a way that overrepresents affluent people. The local roster of those dwelling in public housing could provide many potential jurors, as could a list of those receiving unemployment benefits or aid to dependent children. The fact that these types of lists are never used in selecting potential jurors demonstrates the degree to which we have become accustomed to the overrepresentation of more affluent people on our juries. If we were really concerned with providing largely lower-class defendants with a jury of their peers, we would surely use these lists rather than tax rolls or voter registration lists.

It is also sometimes argued that welfare lists are not a satisfactory substitute for voter registration lists because people have registered to vote who have demonstrated that they have a commitment to local government, while this commitment cannot be inferred from being listed on the welfare rolls. Therefore registered voters have demonstrated by their past civic involvement that they will probably perform the role of juror with some commitment. Yet there is no reason why the refusal to exercise one civil right, such as voting, should cause a person to forfeit another civil right, such as jury service. Such reasoning is illogical. Suppose it were to be proposed that those citizens who did not exercise their right to use a city swimming pool would be denied a driver's license and prohibited from driving on the city streets. The logic would be that if a person did not care enough to swim, then that person should not be allowed to drive.

No matter what the problems of jury trials may be, their use has declined over the past 100 years (Feeley, 1979:274–275). Observers claim that this reflects the increasing use of specialists rather than amateurs, such as jurors, in the court process. One type of specialist in the courts—the psychiatrist—will be discussed in the next chapter.

CONCLUSION

Shortly after a suspect is arrested for a felony, the case is brought before a judge for a preliminary hearing in a magistrate court and/or is presented to a grand jury for action. If probable cause is found to indicate that the accused is guilty, the person is bound over for a criminal trial in a higher, circuit court. Magistrate courts try cases involving lesser crimes or misdemeanors. While awaiting trial, and during the trial itself, accused persons may be released on bail if they can negotiate their release with a bail bondsman. The bail bondsman has frequently been found to be a corrupting influence on the judicial process. Alternatives to the traditional bail system have been and should continue to be explored. Criminal lawyers are relatively powerless, have relatively low status within their profession, and frequently are co-opted by the court organization. This description applies particularly to public defenders and to a lesser degree to most privately retained criminal lawyers. The methods used to select judges and juries, although alleged to be democratic, are not in fact representative of every class interest.

The court process seems to work to the disadvantage of people who are poor and powerless. This discrimination is also true of criminal laws and police operations. The protection against excessive bail and the right to defense counsel and trial by jury are so distorted in actual practice as to make a mockery of these constitutional guarantees. Yet there seems to be no movement for radical reform of these processes because the people most affected are poor and from racial and ethnic minorities.

REFERENCES

Alker, H. R., Jr., C. Hosticka, and M. Mitchell
  1976 "Jury selection as a biased social process." Law and Society Review 11(Fall):9–41.
Alschuler, A. W.
  1975 "The defense attorney's role in plea bargaining." Yale Law Journal 84:1179–1314.
Argersinger v. *Hamlin*
  1972 407 U.S. 25.
Attorney General's Task Force on Violent Crime
  1981 Final Report. Washington, D.C.: U.S. Justice Department.

Axelrad, S.
  1952 "Negro and white male institutionalized delinquents." American Journal of Sociology 57(March):569–574.
Barak, G.
  1975 "In defense of the rich: the emergence of the public defender." Crime and Social Justice 3(Summer):2–14.
Barnes, H. E. and N. K. Tetters
  1959 New Horizons in Criminology. 3d ed. Englewood Cliffs, N.J.: Prentice Hall.

Blumberg, A. S.
1967a Criminal justice. Chicago: Quadrangle Books.
1967b "The practice of law as a confidence game: organizational cooptation of a profession." Law and Society Review 1(June):15–39.

Bowers, W. J.
1974 Executions in America. Lexington, Mass.: Lexington Books.

Brereton, D. and J. D. Casper
1981–1982 "Does it pay to plead guilty? Differential sentencing and the functioning of criminal courts." Law and Society Review 16:45–70.

Browning, F. and J. Gerassi
1980 The American Way of Crime. New York: Putnam's.

Bullock, H. A.
1961 "Significance of the racial factor in the length of prison sentences." Journal of Criminal Law, Criminology, and Police Science 52(November–December):411–417.

Burger, W. E. (Chief Justice of the United States)
1981 "Annual report to the American Bar Association." Houston:February 8.

Cloyd, J. W.
1979 "Prosecutors power, procedural rights, and pleading guilty: the problem of coercion in plea bargaining drug cases." Social Problems 26(April):452–466.

Dill, F.
1975 "Discretion, exchange, and social control: bail bondsmen in criminal courts." Law and Society Reveiw 9(Summer):639–674).

Erlanger, H. S.
1974 "Social class and corporal punishment in childrearing: a reassessment." American Sociological Review 39(February):68–85.

Farnworth, M. and P. Horan
1980 "Separate justice: an analysis of race differences in court processes." Social Science Research 9:381–399.

Feeley, M.
1979 The Process is the Punishment: Handling Cases in a Lower Criminal Court. New York: Russell Sage Foundation.

Gideon v. Wainwright
1963 372 U.S. 335.

Goldfarb, R.
1965 Ransom. New York: John Wiley & Sons.

Goldkamp, J. S.
1985 "Danger and detention: a second generation of bail reform." Journal of Criminal Law and Criminology 76(Spring): 1–74.

Galliher, J. F. and J. C. McCartney
1977 Criminology: Power, Crime, and Criminal Law. Homewood, Ill.: The Dorsey Press.

Greenberg, J. and J. Himmelstein
1969 "Varieties of attack on the death penalty." Crime and Delinquency 15(January): 112–120

Houlden, P. and S. Balkin
1985 "Quality and cost comparisons of private bar indigent defense systems: contract vs. ordered assigned counsel." Journal of Criminal Law and Criminology 76(Spring): 176–200.

Hovland, C. I., I. L. Janis, and H. H. Kelly
1974 Communication and Persuasion: Psychological Studies of Opinion Change. New Haven, Conn.: Yale University Press.

Jacobs, D.
1978 "Inequality and the legal order: an ecological test of the conflict model." Social Problems 25(June):515–525.

Katz, L., L. Litwin, and R. Bamberger
1972 Justice is the Crime: Pretrial Delay in Felony Cases. Cleveland: Press of Case Western Reserve University.

Korn, R. R. and L. W. McCorkle
1963 Criminology and Penology. New York: Holt, Rinehart & Winston.

Littrell, B. W.
1979 Bureaucratic Justice: Police, Prosecutors, and Plea Bargaining. Beverly Hills, Calif.: Sage Publications.

Maynard, D. W.
1982 "Defendant attributes in plea bargaining: notes on the modeling of sentencing decisions." Social Problems 29(April):347–360.
1984 "The structure of discourse in misdemeanor plea bargaining." Law and Society Review 18:75–104.

Miller, N. and D. T. Campbell
1959 "Recency and primacy in persuasion as a function of the timing of speeches and measurements." Journal of Abnormal and Social Psychology 59(July):1–9.

NBC News
1982 "Nightly News," March 15.

New York Legal Aid Society
1972 "The unconstitutional administration of bail: Bellamy v. The Judges of New York City." Criminal Law Bulletin 8(July–August): 459–506.

Platt, A. M. and R. Pallock
1974 "Channeling lawyers: the careers of public defenders." Issues in Criminology 9:1–31.

President's Commission on Law Enforcement and Administration of Justice
1967 The Challenge of Crime in a Free Society. Washington, D.C.: U.S. Government Printing Office.

Puttkammer, E. W.
1953 Administration of Criminal Law. Chicago: University of Chicago Press.

Rankin, A.
1964 "The effect of pretrial detention." New York University Law Review 39(June): 641–655.

Reagan, R.
1981 "Remarks of the President to the International Association of Chiefs of Police." New Orleans: September 28.

Rosett, A. and D. R. Cressey
1976 Justice by Consent: Plea Bargains in the American Courthouse. Philadelphia: Lippincott.

Ryan, J. V.
1967 "The last days of bail." Journal of Criminal Law, Criminology, and Police Service 58(December):542–550.

Silberman, C. R.
1978 Criminal Violence, Criminal Justice. New York: Random House.

Skolnick, J. H.
1967 "Social control in the adversary system." Journal of Conflict Resolution. 11(March): 52–70.

Snouffer, W. L.
1974 "An article of faith abolishes bail in Oregon." Oregon Law Review 53:273–337.

Spohn, C., J. Gruhl, and S. Welch
1981–1982 "The effect of race on sentencing: a re-examination of an unsettled question." Law and Society Review 16:71–88.

St. Louis Post-Dispatch
1973 "Judge Brown said to have faced move for contempt citation." June 7:9A.

Statistical Abstracts of the United States
1982–1983 103rd ed.:14.

Strodtbeck, F. L., R. M. James, and C. Hawkins
1957 "Social status in jury deliberations." American Sociological Review 22(December): 713–719.

Sudnow, D.
1965 "Normal crimes: sociological features of the penal code in a public defender office." Social Problems 12(Winter):255–276.

Tappan, P. W.
1960 Crime, Justice and Corrrection. New York: McGraw-Hill.

Taylor, S., Jr.
1984 "New crime act a vast change officials assert." New York Times, October 15: A1, B6.

Time
1983 "Putnam County vs. Canada." August 8:58.
1979 "Rough justice in Mississippi." February 26:49.

Unnever, J. D., C. E. Frazier, and J. C. Henretta
1980 "Race differences in criminal sentencing." The Sociological Quarterly 21(Spring): 197–205.

Warr, M. and M. Stafford
1984 "Public goals of punishment and support for the death penalty." Journal of Research in Crime and Delinquency 21(May):95–111.

Watson, R. A. and R. G. Downing
1969 The Politics of the Bench and the Bar: Judicial Selection under the Missouri Nonpartisan Plan. New York: John Wiley & Sons.

Wellman, D. and R. Fitzgerald
1978 "The appearance of justice and the advantages of the state: the process of voir dire in political trials." Contemporary Crises 2:373–405.

Wice, P. B.
1974 "Purveyors of freedom: the professional bondsmen." Society 11(July–August): 34–41.

Wolfgang, M. E., A. Kelley, and H. C. Nolde
1962 "Comparison of the executed and the commuted among admissions to death row." Journal of Criminal Law, Criminology, and Police Science 53(September):301–311.

Wood, A. L.
1967 Criminal Lawyer. New Haven, Conn.: College and University Press.

10
ADMINISTRATION
OF CRIMINAL LAW:
PSYCHIATRISTS

Besides lawyers, defense attorneys, prosecutors, judges, and juries, psychiatrists have become increasingly important in the court process in a few highly visible cases because the commission of a crime that is especially heinous is proof to many people, including many psychiatrists, that the accused is mentally ill. Still the public apparently wants punishment for criminals, but they usually cannot have it both ways. Under American law the accused traditionally is defined as either mentally responsible and punishable for a crime or mentally ill and therefore not responsible or punishable under the law.

The difficulty in these not guilty by reason of insanity judgments can be seen in the case of John Hinckley, Jr., who was tried in 1982 for attempting to kill President Reagan. Hinckley apparently believed that he was a character in a movie in which the actress Jodie Foster had played a teenage prostitute. His plan was to protect Jodie Foster by kidnapping her, kill President Reagan, and move into the White house with her. Understandably, the jury found him not guilty by reason of insanity. This verdict was widely condemned by American political leaders as a travesty of justice. It was clear to everyone that although Hinckley had attempted to shoot the president, he now seemed to be on the verge of avoiding any criminal punishment. Americans apparently wanted criminal punishment imposed on John Hinckley, and technically he avoided such punishment by being found not guilty by reason of insanity. He was not imprisoned but rather was committed to a mental hospital for an indefinite term—presumably until he was cured and no longer a menace to the community.

There was also considerable dispute as to whether Patty Hearst was mentally ill. She was kidnapped by the Symbionese Liberation Army in 1974 and held for an extended period of time in a closet before she began to identify with her kidnappers and apparently converted to their radical politics. Ms. Hearst was judged to be sane and served a prison term for her participation in their activities. In addition, how about Sirhan Sirhan, the killer of Senator Robert Kennedy? In this case the psychiatric community was deeply divided on the issue of his mental competence. This case demonstrates that a problem exists in the psychiatric definition of mental illness.

Even at the present time psychiatrists do not seem to agree on the definition of mental illness. For example, there is considerable disagreement within the American Psychiatric Association, (APA) on how homosexuality should be defined (Conrad and Schneider, 1980:204–214). In 1974 homosexuality was officially dropped from the APA list of mental diseases after intense lobbying from the gay community. But there was considerable opposition to this action and there continues to be a belief among at least a large minority of psychiatrists that homosexuality is indeed a disease.

A clear and dramatic demonstration of the degree of psychiatric confusion is found in a study of admissions practices at mental hospitals (Rosenhan, 1973). A group of researchers decided that they would feign mental illness in attempts to be admitted into various mental hospitals with the plan of studying these hospitals from the inside as participant observers. All the pseudopatients claimed at the hospitals' admission offices that they heard voices saying "empty," "hollow," and "thud." The researchers imagined that psychiatrists would reason that this symptom indicated that the patients believed that their lives were empty. Otherwise they did not alter their usual behavior. They feared being exposed as fakes and not being admitted, However, they all were admitted— most with a diagnosis of schizophrenia. Once admitted, they stopped displaying any symptoms; yet none of the professional staff recognized that they were faking or were anything but mentally ill. Only the other patients recognized the ruse. All the pseudopatients were ultimately discharged with schizophrenia in remission. Not one was cured according to the psychiatric staff members.

Since psychiatrists have no clear definition of what is and what is not mental illness, they merely see everything that a mental patient does as mental illness. When these participant observers were seen taking field notes, this activity was defined by the staff as compulsive note-taking behavior while the other patients realized precisely what these researchers were doing. Psychiatry, this research found, locates problems in the individual personality and ignores problems that are obvious in the environment. Thus when patients were observed to be half an hour early for meals, this was defined by the psychiatric staff as oral-acquisitive behavior rather than behavior indicating boredom caused by the sterile environment of the institution. This same search for internal causes of behavior and attitudes has obvious implications for dealing with the common rage of black Americans.

The staff members at another hospital heard about these results and understandably doubted their validity. Thus, to prove their point, the research team informed this hospital's staff that at some time in the following 3 months one or more pseudopatients would request admittance there. Out of the 193 patients who applied for admission at the hospital during that period, 41 were strongly believed to be pseudopatients by at least one staff member. In fact, no pseudopatients were sent. The first task of any science is to define its objects of study, which still has not been done for psychiatry. This situation is the equivalent to geologists not agreeing on the definition of rock.

Whatever the shortcomings of their profession, psychiatrists become involved in two distinct phases of the court process and in two separate questions about accused persons. One question deals with whether the accused is psychologically fit to stand trial. The other question involves whether the alleged act was the product of a psychologically diseased mind.

PRETRIAL PSYCHIATRIC EXAMINATION (FITNESS TO STAND TRIAL)

It sometimes happens that an individual is judged by psychiatrists to be psychologically unfit to stand trial. Competence to stand trial generally means that the defendant understands the criminal charges and the nature of the trial proceedings and can assist the defense counsel in developing a defense against the charges. A person bleeding from a recent gunshot wound would not be tried until the wound was dressed and the bleeding stopped. Similarly an individual suffering from a virus with an extremely high temperature would not be tried until the fever had subsided. In other words, the law requires that no one should be put on trial who cannot perform the role of defendant (Szasz, 1965). Although the law requires the ability to help defend oneself, it does not require perfect physical or mental health. If the court can consider the question of the defendant's mental capacity to stand trial, it seems reasonable that the defendant should be allowed to question the competence of the judge, the prosecutor, and jury (Szasz, 1965). This questioning never happens because only the defendant is thought to have committed a crime that is widely believed to result from mental illness.

Individuals who are unwilling to cooperate with the defense attorneys will not competently assist in their own defense according to the court rules. But they are not necessarily mentally ill, they merely choose not to perform the defendant's role properly. If competence to stand trial is not necessarily a medical question, then medical experts should not make this decision. Rather, the decision could be made by a judge or a panel of judges, a lawyer or a panel of lawyers, or a jury of lay people. In fact, as human beings, we all evaluate the performance of actors in the various roles they play.

The case of David Berkowitz, the Son of Sam killer who claimed that a German shepherd dog had ordered him to commit numerous murders, raised issues of competency to stand trial (Steadman, 1979). During a hearing on the issue of his competence, one psychiatrist claimed that Berkowitz was incompetent to stand trial and another psychiatrist claimed that he was competent. The judge sided with the latter psychiatrist, and Berkowitz was tried for his crimes. This decision by the judge was undoubtedly made more on political, rather than scientific, grounds. The public would have been outraged if no trial had been held.

The reason psychiatry survives in the courtroom is that, similar to the bail bond system, it has some utility. For example, if a prosecutor has plenty of evidence for a conviction, he or she will be anxious to go to trial. But if the prosecutor has little evidence, a ruling of incompetency to stand trial will hold a defendant until a more effective case can be prepared. Although it is no longer possible to indefinitely confine those persons found to be incompetent to stand trial, in some minor cases the person may be held as long as they would have been if they had been sentenced to prison. Understandably, judges only rarely disagree with the psychiatric recommendations they receive (assuming the psychiatrists agree among themselves). Because in reality few trials are held in criminal cases, the question should not be whether a person is mentally competent to stand trial but rather whether they are mentally competent to negotiate a guilty plea. A number of courts now recognize this distinction.

Even though competence to stand trial is not necessarily a medical-psychiatric question, individuals who are found incompetent to stand trial for the crime or crimes of which they are accused are committed to a mental hospital until such time as they are judged by psychiatrists to be well enough to stand trial. If and when they are certified as recovered, they are subject to trial and penal commitment. If they are subsequently convicted and sentenced to a penal institution, the time spent in the mental hospital is usually not credited against the period of penal commitment. In such cases our system deals more harshly with those persons thought to be mentally incompetent than with others accused of crime. Many observers suggest that there should be no prosecution following release after commitment for incompetence (Rubin, 1965).

Having psychiatrists determine a defendant's competence to stand trial could raise some questions about infringement of constitutional rights. Szasz (1968) claimed that the Sixth Amendment to the U.S. Constitution guarantees the right to a speedy and public trial and that this right is not contingent on a defendant's capacity to prove his or her sanity to government psychiatrists. In addition, the Fifth Amendment guarantees that people cannot be made to testify against themselves. Wiretap evidence is often inadmissible for this reason, as well as because it violates the guarantees against unreasonable searches and seizures provided by the Fourth Amendment. Therefore the logic of Fifth and Fourth Amendments would seem to extend to "mindtapping" by psychiatrists, who are experts at digging information out of people, but the courts have not accepted this inference.

The Fifth Amendment also protects defendants against being tried twice on the same charge. This constitutional protection against double jeopardy appears to be violated when a person is found unfit to stand trial and is committed to a mental hospital, yet is tried later after recovery and sentenced to a period of imprisonment. In such cases incarceration in a hospital is a punishment directly attributable to the offense with which the defendant is charged. Incarceration in excess of the prison term that defendants would have had to serve had they originally been tried, sentenced, and not hospitalized is clearly a case of double punishment. Usually it is indigent persons who are denied the right to trial by being forced to undergo a pretrial psychiatric examination (Szasz, 1968). The defendants' court-appointed lawyers typically do not care; if no trial is held, their time is not consumed, which is an even more expedient outcome than they could hope to obtain from a guilty plea.

DETERMINATION OF CRIMINAL RESPONSIBILITY

Although an individual may be judged competent to stand trial, psychiatrists testifying before the court may argue that because of some mental disease or defect the defendant should not be held criminally responsible for the act of which the person has been accused. Sometimes the defendant is urged by legal counsel to enter a plea of not guilty by reason of insanity or mental defect. Such a plea does not contest the facts of the case but rather claims that the defendant should not be held criminally responsible and should not be punished. Those defendants found not guilty under such pleas are typically not released but instead they are judged to be still dangerous and are confined for an indeterminate period in a mental hospital. Such civil commitment can result in long-term institutional stays. Civil commitment resulting from being found not guilty by reason of insanity is open-ended and therefore potentially may be a life sentence, for there is no mandatory release date as with most prison sentences.

Several models have been used to assess criminal responsibility in the United States. Over 100 years ago, an important precedent set in England became a guide that is still often used to some degree in assessing ciminal responsibility. This was the M'Naghten case (1843:719). It stated that "to establish a defence on the ground of insanity, it must be clearly proved that at the time of committing the act the party accused was labouring under such a defect of reason, from disease of the mind, as not to know the nature and quality of the act he was doing, or as not to know that what he was doing was wrong." This rule is often simply called the right-wrong test of criminal responsibility.

A different rule was established in a precedent set by the U.S. Court of Appeals in Washington, D.C., in which the defendant, Monte Durham (*Durham* v. *United States*, 1954), was convicted of housebreaking. A psychiatrist testified that the defendant heard voices, suffered from psychoses, and had a psychopathic personality. The Appeals Court rejected the right-wrong test and held instead "that an accused is not criminally responsible if his unlawful act was the product of mental disease or mental defect" (*Durham* v. *United States*, 1954:874–875). In other words, even if defendants knew that what they did was wrong, they are not held responsible if this act was caused by mental defect or disease.

One central difference in the effect of the two rules is that more defendants are covered by the Durham rule than by the M'Naghten precedent (Rubin, 1965). It is argued that the Durham rule is more humane and moral because it excludes more people from criminal prosecution than does the M'Naghten rule, and it is also argued that the Durham rule is scientifically more sound because it relies heavily on the advice of psychiatrists. Psychiatrists usually do have a larger role in jurisdictions where the Durham rule has been used because the issues raised by the Durham rule are more complex than the issues raised by the M'Naghten rule. But according to Rubin (1965), it is untrue that excluding people from criminal punishment under the Durham rule is more humanitarian. Whether a person is sentenced to a prison or committed to a mental hospital, that person is still deprived of freedom. More often than not, the conditions and daily routine in the mental hospital are similar to those in a prison, only the name of the institution has been changed, which camouflages the true nature of the situation. Any notion of superior treatment of patients in public mental hospitals must vanish in those locales where public mental hospitals can be used to control especially unruly prisoners. Prisoners essentially become mental patients as punishment. Under the Durham rule some individuals have been committed to mental hospitals, even though the offenses with which they were charged were very minor. Moreover, individuals found not guilty by reason of mental incompetence are subject to more, not less, stigma as a result of this decision. In fact, there is a double stigma: they are both "mad and bad." The reasoning in civil commitment usually is that a person is helpless or is dangerous to themselves or to others. The Durham rule, however, only requires that an individual's crime be caused by mental illness. Ordinarily mental illness in and of itself is not grounds for civil commitment.

A further problem of the Durham rule concerns the issue of crime being *caused* by mental illness (Rubin, 1965). The fields of criminology, sociology, and psychiatry are filled with studies that show criminal behavior to be *correlated* with specific psychological conditions as well as certain social conditions, including slums, poverty, and racial discrimination. However, correlations do not prove causes. Moreover, if individuals can escape criminal responsibility due to psychiatric or psychological conditions, it seems logical that their experience of social problems should also provide the same escape from criminal liability. Clearly American courts are not about to entertain the notion that blacks' experience of racism should qualify them for exclusion from criminal liability. Because of all these problems, the Durham rule was largely unworkable and is no longer used in assessing criminal responsibility. The same circuit judge in Washington, D.C., who originated the Durham rule later discarded his own earlier reasoning (Bazelon, 1971).

Another test of criminal responsibility is referred to as the irresistible impulse rule (*United States* v. *Pollard*, 1959). According to this reasoning, a person can have the understanding required by the M'Naghten rule but still will not be held criminally responsible if it can be demonstrated that the person suffered from such a diseased mental condition as to create in his or her mind an uncontrollable or irresistible impulse to commit the offense. The irresistible impulse rule argues that a person may realize what he or she is doing is wrong but nevertheless is impelled to commit the act with which he or she is charged. Obviously this rule emphasizes an individual's passions and instincts and tends to de-emphasize his or her reasoning power.

Another rule that was used in California until recently is called the diminished responsibility rule. The idea here is that a given defendant should be held only *partially* responsible for a crime if he or she suffers from mental incapacity to some extent. To the same degree that they are mentally ill, they should be immune from criminal responsibility. The advantage to this rule is that it allows some recognition of mental illness while at the same time allowing criminal punishment to proceed. This became know as the "Twinkie defense" used by Dan White in 1979 to answer to double murder charges for killing the San Francisco mayor and another prominent local elected official (*Newsweek*, 1982). White's lawyers argued that his steady diet of Twinkies and other junk food impaired his mental faculties and led to his violent outburst. Apparently the jury believed this defense and found him guilty only of manslaughter—not murder. The public outrage in California following his relatively lenient sentence undoubtedly led to the later repeal of the law that allowed such a finding. The loss of this legislation probably should not be mourned. If psychiatry cannot distinguish mental health from mental illness, then psychiatry is even further removed from being able to distinguish different degrees of mental illness or incapacity.

More recently, in some states another attempt is being made to integrate both punishment and recognition of mental incapacity. These new laws allow the defendant to be found "guilty but mentally ill." While this is a profound alteration of the reasoning of both the M'Naghten and Durham rules, which only allowed mental incapacity *or* criminal responsibility, there seems to be widespread support for such legislation at this time, perhaps because of the outrage associated with the Hinckley case. This legislation allows a judge to sentence a defendant found guilty but mentally ill exactly as a sane defendant found guilty of the same offense. The only difference is that in guilty but mentally ill cases defendants would begin their sentences in a mental hospital and would only be transferred to a prison to complete their sentences when they had been certified as cured.

Whatever rule is used in assessing criminal responsibility, any conflict in expert testimony essentially throws the whole question of mental illness back upon the jury—an awesome responsibility that makes a further mockery of the notion of psychiatric expertise. Lay people become in a sense the last court of appeals when psychiatrists cannot agree. Court-appointed psychiatrists offer one more way of short-circuiting the trial process and one more way to deny poor and powerless defendants the rights guaranteed them in the U.S. Constitution.

There is yet another way in which psychiatrists, and sometimes social workers, are used in the trial process. Their expertise is needed if the judge requests a presentence investigation of a convicted defendant supposedly as a help in determining an appropriate sentence. However, in reality, judges typically pick over the report selectively to justify the sentence they have already decided on. Because these reports are not taken seriously by judges, it is not surprising to discover that the people who prepare such reports take various shortcuts, such as the use of stereotypes to describe defendants. Moreover, the reports describe defendants in a way that is consistent with their new status. The defendants' positive characteristics are rarely mentioned; the descriptions consist mainly of negative and unsupported cliches. A further problem with such reports is that they follow an individual from the court to a correctional institution if the person is incarcerated and may later be used to influence the prisoner's future release (Blumberg, 1967:157–161). Psychiatry plays a coercive role in the court process, in part because it is not recognized by defendants and others as potentially destructive of human dignity and freedom.

ROLE IN DETERMINING PUNISHMENT OR TREATMENT PROGRAMS

Psychiatric judgment of mental abnormality enters into the criminal law in three ways. Aside from fitness to stand trial and criminal responsibility, if an individual is convicted, psychiatry is often consulted in designing a custodial or treatment program for him or her. Answers must be obtained for questions, such as should the defendant be sent to a mental hospital or to a prison or should the person be placed on parole and compelled to participate in a specific program, such as Alcoholics Anonymous?

Confusion in the Roles Played by Psychiatry and the Law

One problem in the use of psychiatry in the legal system is that there are vast and irreconcilable differences in the legal and the mental health systems' approaches to crime. According to legal standards, fairness is achieved by responding to a specific act with a specific type of reaction while ignoring a mass of details about the accused (Aubert, 1965). On the other hand, in the mental health approach of psychiatry the whole personality of the accused is relevant in determining the state's response to criminal behavior.

Psychiatry is an applied science, but legal practice makes no such claim. Clearly, as long as a judge and jury have such important roles in the court process, convicted criminals cannot be treated primarily according to scientific standards. While it is customary for a judge and jury to participate in the legal process, we would find their dealing with matters of mental health bizarre. Aubert (1965) also argued that while the legal process is typically open to scrutiny by all people affected, the procedures of psychiatry are almost never made public.

The types of accountability of the legal and mental health systems are quite different. If a court correctly describes the facts of a case and chooses the correct legal response to these facts, the court is never held accountable for any negative consequences flowing from its actions, such as the suicide of a convicted offender. What ultimately happens to the convicted offender or whether the offender's family must go on welfare is not the court's concern. The judge is not bound to such utilitarian considerations. However, the judge is bound by law to a specific range of responses. Psychiatry, on the other hand, is responsible for how its decisions affect the individual in the future. If a psychiatrist's patient commits suicide, the therapist cannot escape responsibility. Legal practice is more oriented to past legislation and legal precedents, while psychiatry is more oriented to the future.

Even with these considerable contradictions, the legal system is sometimes used as a vehicle for delivering psychiatric and social services (Allen, 1964). Three problems result: (1) the psychiatric services are not effectively delivered by the legal system, (2) the legal system diverts its resources in attempting to deliver these services, making it impossible to operate effectively, and (3) the effort to deliver psychiatric services may lead to the corruption of the legal system.

Clearly psychiatric services are not effectively rendered when alcoholics are arrested for vagrancy, as is so often true. Alcoholics are arrested again and again on the same charges. They spend a short period in jail, sober up, and then are released to the streets, only to immediately get drunk and thus continue the cycle. Middle-class alcoholics are seldom arrested in this way. Thus the courts attempt to deal with psychiatric problems by selecting these people for special treatment—not on the basis of the degree of their mental problems but on the basis of their poverty. This example demonstrates that psychiatric services cannot be rendered effectively by the legal system.

Secondly, attempting to use the legal system to deliver psychiatric services diverts legal resources, making it impossible for the legal system to offer any services adequately. No one really believes that the routine arrest of alcoholics actually deters habitual drunkenness, since some alcoholics have been arrested hundreds of times. In fact, this action consumes valuable court and police time to no useful end.

Finally, attempts by the legal system to deliver psychiatric services can lead to law enforcement corruption. In the case of the medical problem of drug addiction there is usually a willing seller and a willing buyer with no complaining witnesses. This situation contains the seeds of police corruption because the police can often be bought off when no one is forcing the issue by bringing a complaint. Whether an individual is arrested is solely a matter of police discretion.

Effects of Indeterminate Sentencing

Psychiatrists seem to agree that a truly civilized legal system is not solely or even primarily concerned with the crime allegedly committed but focuses instead upon the needs of the accused (Allen, 1964). Rather than supporting the notion of the classical criminologists that the punishment should fit the crime, psychiatrists and other therapists would have the state's reaction, which they feel should be rehabilitation, not punishment, fit the needs of the defendant. However, before we can know individuals' problems, we must first know the nature of their acts. Psychiatrists tend to assume, without any detailed examination, that all people who are incarcerated are guilty of a crime and therefore require therapy. But surely some prisoners who have been recipients of psychiatric services are in prison for crimes they did not commit. As will be demonstrated later in this chapter, the most concern about who needs psychiatric therapy is seen in the juvenile court where there is a corresponding lack of concern about strict legal procedures. The main concern allegedly has been with the needs of the child, not with the fine points of law.

It is sometimes claimed that individuals are committed to mental hospitals or prisons because they are dangerous, even if only to themselves. Yet some types of dangerous behaviors are ignored, and some are even rewarded, such as race car driving and the behavior of trapeze artists, astronauts, and Green Berets (Szasz, 1968:45–46). Moreover, much of the behavior that is most dangerous to society may reflect a normal adaptation to conditions of life that the courts cannot control (Allen, 1964:52). Since courts cannot control these conditions, the whole notion of rehabilitation is a farce. In such cases the court processes individuals not to offer them therapy but because they represent a threat to the community. Moreover, the results of anonymous questionnaires show that most middle-class Americans have committed crimes; yet these crimes seldom result in commitment.

Another problem with the myth of psychiatric treatment or therapy is that this ideology has led to longer sentences. If it is believed that crime is a result of mental illness, then as in the case of physical illness, it is not known initially how long the treatment process will require. A treatment for cancer may take 1 year or perhaps 2 years or even the rest of the patients's life. Initially, the therapist simply cannot make any guarantees on the length of therapy required. Applying this medical model to the treatment of crime, therapists have been staunch supporters of indeterminate sentences such as 1 to 10 years, 2 to 5 years, and even 1 year to life (Cullen and Gilbert, 1982).

Under these laws the exact length of confinement is typically determined not by a judge at the time of initial sentencing but by parole and prison officials based on their judgment of the speed of the person's rehabilitation process while in prison. Before these indeterminate sentences were enacted, offenders were typically sentenced to a specific length of time for punishment. A problem has developed, however, because parole boards, who must determine the prisoner's release date, have been much more conservative than legislators may have imagined. Thus with the indeterminate sentences prisoners serve more years than they did with the old specific term sentences (Rubin, 1966). Parole officials appear to determine readiness for release on the basis of how close a person is to the maximum sentence. For example, rather than serving 2 years of punishment for auto theft the person may now serve 3½ years for his or her rehabilitation under a sentence of 2 to 5 years. Every American state, those with and without the indeterminate sentencing structure, has a parole system that releases prisoners prior to their serving their full sentence.

The long prison sentences mandated by American legislators have been met with several objections (Rubin, 1966). Long prison sentences are applied to all individuals convicted of certain types of offenses. Such blanket treatment does not necessarily provide the community with protection from the most dangerous people. Not all people who have committed these specific offenses are terribly dangerous. Moreover, some very dangerous individuals have not committed these crimes that carry the very long sentences. These long prison sentences also seem to be associated with a loss of deterrence. The available literature on the deterrence of crime indicates that certainty of arrest and punishment is more important in deterrence than severity of the prescribed penalty. As noted in chapter 6, as the severity of a penalty increases, the certainty of its imposition typically decreases.

Yet another problem in indeterminate sentencing is that such sentencing helps a prison staff maintain a reign of terror. Prisoners recognize that the only way they can possibly hope for an early release is to bow to every staff whim, since a bad recommendation can scuttle their parole chances (Mitford, 1973). After serving the minimum term of a sentence, prisoners typically at least have the right to an annual review of their case for possible parole. Many prisoners, however, do not insist on such hearings because they regard them as shams that only raise false hopes of release. The prospect of being potentially very close to freedom yet still facing the possibility of serving many more years is very tantalizing and torturous for the prisoner.

Rehabilitation and Political Coercion

Political liberals, who have been steady supporters of the rehabilitation ideology, usually attribute inadequate efforts at rehabilitation to a disinterested, uncivilized, or uneducated public. While a lack of funds is certainly a contributing factor, the failure of rehabilitation is more directly caused by a lack of information and ignorance of human behavior. Laws that call for rehabilitation of prisoners assume that psychiatrists know how to rehabilitate such people when in fact this knowledge does not exist. These laws also assume that there are facilities and professional staff available to use this knowledge. These assumptions are false (Rubin, 1966). All the liberals' good intentions do not alter the fact that what is called treatment in correctional institutions deprives people of their freedom largely on the basis of information that does not exist.

Szasz (1968) observed a massive redefinition: what are in truth moral and political values have been transformed into matters of public health. On this basis, many people can justify the use of coercion to themselves and to others.

> The redefinition of moral values as health values will now appear in a new light. If people believe that health values justify coercion, but that moral and political values do not, those who wish to coerce others will tend to enlarge the category of health values at the expense of the category of moral values. (Szasz, 1968:5–6.)

Forcing a given set of moral values on other people would be seen as autocratic, while compelling good health is not seen in the same negative way.

Some psychiatrists claim that they have never found a single law violator who was not mentally ill (Hartung, 1965). This is obviously a ridiculous claim given the massive amount of illegal marihuana smoking among American youth, estimated at over two thirds of those between 18 and 25 years old (Fishburne et al., 1979). Based on that claim it could be concluded that the late Rev. Martin Luther King and his followers were mentally ill because they often violated southern states' statutes. Currently, the protesting black Africans in South Africa who often violate local laws could also be dismissed as mentally ill.

The confusion in the definition of mental illness, as well as its relationship to crime, should lead us to ask precisely what is meant by the idea of rehabilitation in prisons. Surely few people would suggest that the goal of rehabilitation should be to help the prisoners adjust to prison life more fully. Indeed, some people have observed that complete adjustment to life in prison often makes adjustment to life outside of prison impossible. Rather, proponents of prison rehabilitation programs argue that they are primarily interested in helping the prisoners make a better adjustment to their life in society. That sounds sensible at first blush, but is this a just, fair or moral goal? Should black prisoners be taught to adjust to ghettos? Should chronically poor people be taught to adjust to unhealthy diets? Moreover, should those people who inhabit American slums, where rats as large as puppies gnaw on babies' fingers, be taught by therapists to live with the rats and like it? Clearly the answers to these questions have more to do with politics and morality than with mental health. It reflects an obscene professionalism when behavioral scientists recommend that their clients adjust to conditions that the therapists themselves would find unendurable.

Often psychiatrists confuse their upper-class conception of decent, upper- or upper-middle-class behavior with a scientific definition of mental health (Hartung, 1965). Much of the behavior considered to be the result of mental illness is judged as such because it is contrary to middle- and upper-class practices. Only a small portion of this behavior would be considered the result of illness by lower-class people. The lower-class transient who claims to be Jesus or Napoleon, and acts accordingly, is clearly recognized by other poor people as crazy. Much of the rest of what is called mental illness is simply lower-class behavior, which explains why researchers have found many types of mental illness to be most common among the lower classes. Hollingshead and Redlich (1958), for example, found higher rates of psychoses and mental hospitalization among the lower classes than among the higher social classes. All this suggests that the designation of mental illness represents a type of cultural imperialism foisted upon largely lower-class prison inmates. The angry outbursts of ghetto blacks, for example, are defined by most whites, including most white psychiatrists, as evidence of "irrational" rage and psychological "maladjustment." Also, it should not be surprising that Linsky (1970) found the highest ratio of involuntary to voluntary admissions to mental hospitals among nonwhites and persons with the least education.

Throughout Western law a central question often asked involves what a "reasonable person" can be expected to do or to believe. If a reasonable person can be expected to believe a certain thing or behave in a certain fashion, then when someone acts or behaves in this same way, they are not held criminally liable. The problem is that what seems reasonable varies quite a lot among different people. Great hatred and distrust of American society is not seen by middle-class, white psychiatrists as a healthy or reasonable response by lower-class black prisoners.

Perhaps the imperialistic nature of mental illness designations can be seen more clearly by looking at another time and place. Prior to European colonialization, death was the prescribed punishment for witches in Africa. But because European governments by the time of colonialization no longer recognized the validity of witches, they abolished these punishments in their colonies as well (Seidman, 1965). Nonetheless African belief in witches continued. Thus the African who believed in witches was faced with a serious dilemma. According to the local traditional beliefs, the fear of witches was intense, and there was local cultural support for the killing of witches. But the colonial law did not recognize these beliefs and did not permit such executions.

Colonial courts, therefore, felt forced to define the killing of witches as murder, but the courts typically recommended some clemency for persons convicted of murdering suspected witches. Usually the colonial courts recognized the inadequacy of judicial solutions to these problems. Seidman (1965) described some cases to illustrate this point. One case involved a man who beat an elderly woman to death because he believed her to be a witch. His argument of self-defense was not successful. Another person killed a witch doctor because be believed that the witch doctor's spirit was threatening him. Once again the argument of self-defense was rejected by the colonial court. A husband believed that his wife was being bewitched and killed the suspected bewitcher. The court admitted that such beliefs were common among Africans, but these beliefs were none the less unreasonable. The critical question in all of these cases is, Whose standard shall be used to determine what is reasonable? The standard used by the courts was what the average European believed, not what the average African believed.

In another case an African relied on the expert advice of a witch doctor who told him that his brother was being controlled by a witch. On this advice he killed the witch and was convicted of murder. Compare this case with the case in the 1930s of an English physician who performed an illegal abortion on a 15-year-old girl who had been raped because a psychiatrist had said that if she carried the baby to term she would suffer severe psychiatric harm. The courts held this abortion to be justified based on the expert opinion. Both the African man and the British physician relied on expert opinion, but only the African man was convicted of a crime.

These cases all demonstrate that Africans had to act not as reasonable Africans but as reasonable Europeans, and if they did not, criminal intent was presumed by colonial courts. African beliefs and morality were ignored. Much the same type of bias is built into the American court system. If black Americans do not see the world in much the same manner as middle-class whites, this is typically deemed to be an unreasonable perception, and these judgments are often supported by the testimony of middle-class psychiatrists. Black rage is typically not considered a reasonable response to American racism—this is pronounced as a medical or scientific fact.

The Soviet Union has raised the use of the medical model and rehabilitation as political coercion to a high art (Stone, 1972; Medvedev and Medvedev, 1971). The Soviet logic seems to be that anyone criticizing the existing political regime is insane, since life in that Soviet socialist country is obviously a paradise for the masses. Political dissidents are often hospitalized. The Soviet government denies that they are punishing such political dissidents, rather the government is only attempting to help and rehabilitate them. Many of these dissidents request exit visas to leave the country permanently. Apparently the Soviet government reasons that it cannot in good conscience let one of its citizens engage in international travel if they are mentally or physically ill to avoid contaminating people in other countries. Many such "patients" in hospitals in the Soviet Union can establish their sanity—this is the catch—only by ceasing their criticisms of the government and dropping their requests to leave the country.

Finally, it may be useful to distinguish between punishment and treatment because they often seem to be confused in actual practice (Galtung, 1966). Treatment is an effort to change people and is administered, of course, only until the desired change in the person has occurred. Punishment on the other hand is given regardless of whether rehabilitation or personal reformation has occurred. Treatment, therefore, is more concerned with the state of mind of the person accused, while punishment is more concerned with the attitudes of other people in the society including, but not limited to, the victim. In mental hospitals it is especially easy to observe how this distinction between punishment and rehabilitation has become confused; electroshock therapy has at times been administered for both treatment and punishment. In prisons inmates are sometimes placed in solitary confinement and on a restricted diet, allegedly for purposes of their rehabilitation.

The Myth of Rehabilitation

Duster (1970) noted society's inconsistent attitude regarding the relationship between crime and mental disease. Criminals are often seen as being responsible for their acts yet at the same time are viewed as being mentally ill and in need of therapy, for most serious crime is commonly considered the work of madmen. "One must be mentally healthy in order to commit a crime, but the commission of a crime reflects an unhealthy mental state" (Duster, 1970:277). The way this inconsistency is usually resolved is to consider the accused criminal to be mentally responsible during arrest, trial, and conviction. Just prior to the trial, the defense attorney and the prosecutor usually attempt to bargain with the accused, assuming that he or she is a rational person. Once incarcerated, the convicted person is described as being mentally ill and therefore in need of a prison rehabilitation program.

During the 1950s and 1960s there seemed to be an ever-increasing amount of verbal and written discussion by professional social scientists, journalists, and government officials about the rehabilitation of criminals that served to perpetuate the fiction that something called rehabilitation was taking place in American prisons. One initial indication that this is a fantasy may be found in the personnel breakdown and budgets of most correctional institutions. Typically no more than 5 percent of most prison budgets is spent directly on therapists and other social scientists who could participate in a therapy program. An interesting practice that supports the fiction of rehabilitation is a name change in many institutions. Prisons become training centers, and reformatories become youth camps. All this helps foster the myth at no added cost and with no organizational change.

The lack of professional skills of psychiatrists has already been noted. Much the same problem exists in any plans for rehabilitation programs whether directed by psychiatrists, social workers, or sociologists. Thus the discussion of the inadequate funding of rehabilitation or therapy programs should not be construed as a suggestion that well-funded and fully implemented programs are a panacea for crime control. California has made the greatest effort to develop and maintain a well-financed therapy program, but evidence shows that the program has had little or no effect on the target population (Mitford, 1973). In defense of rehabilitation programs it has been observed that the evaluation of the success or failure of any given program ideally requires a more precise measure of successful prisoner change than merely the usual use of recidivism rates (Bowker, 1982:255). There is nonetheless considerable evidence that social scientists, including psychiatrists, do not have sufficient information to develop a useful rehabilitation program, even when funds are made available. The evidence indicates that the types of institutions, therapy programs, or staffs and the length of sentence appear to have no impact on recidivism rates (Martinson, 1974; Bailey, 1966; Wilkins, 1969:78).

Community-based treatment, such as confining convicted criminals in halfway houses at night and allowing them to work by day in the community, is more humane and less costly than institutionalization but is no more effective in altering recidivism rates (von Hirsch, 1976:15). In fact, many of these community-based programs, including the deinstitutionalization of mental patients, were legitimated as liberal reforms and liberal victories but really were a product of the growing fiscal crisis of the state (Scull, 1977). At least in the case of some mental patients, their release from institutions without other support has often resulted in a confused life on the streets, which often ends in death through starvation or exposure to the elements.

Limits of Psychiatric Knowledge: Psychopaths and Goblins

The experiment by Rosenhan (1973) who sent pseudopatients into mental hospitals was discussed earlier in this chapter. Everything that researchers did while in the mental hospitals was defined by the professional psychiatric staff as mental illness because psychiatrists had no independent or objective definition of mental illness. This research clearly demonstrates the severe limits of psychiatric knowledge. Given these severe limits in psychiatric or treatment knowledge, the impact of a given rehabilitation program can be unpredictable. As one researcher noted (Andrews, 1980:456): "Within one of the institutions, the presence of volunteers was associated with more open and frank discussion, according to the prisoners; the effect was exactly the opposite within the other institution." Thus a given correctional program may have a positive impact, a negative impact, or no impact at all. Often the success of an entire program depends not so much on the elements of the program as on the leadership of charismatic individuals (Bowker, 1982:255). In addition, sometimes the fact that the programs are new and the participants (both staff and prisoners) know the program is expected to have positive results temporarily effects a positive outcome (Bowker; 1982:255). This is a type of self-fulfilling prophecy often referred to as the Hawthorn effect.

The sexual psychopath laws, whose passage and content have been influenced by psychiatrists, are a good example of legislation designed to control crime by reliance on scientific information about mental disease that does not exist (Sutherland, 1950). Sutherland saw in these laws a potential threat to civil liberties and viewed the passage of these laws, which were passed in a number of states during the 1930s and 1940s, as a part of a more general social movement involving the medicalization of deviance. He was one of the first social scientists to express concern about this social movement that he believed was beginning during his lifetime. Tappan (1960) showed that Sutherland's concern about these laws was well founded:

> By statutory definition in a number of the states, sexual psychopaths are individuals who are neither insane nor feeble-minded but who lack the capacity to control their sexual impulses. . . . Since the concept of psychopathy is so vari-

ously defined by the specialists, it is not surprising to discover a wide disparity in the definitions that have been formulated in these statutes. The states obviously look to quite different qualities as evidence of dangerous sexual psychopathy (pages 411 and 412).

Some states' laws even refer to something called a sociopath. In reality, none of these laws have any clinical support. The problem is that people who are certified as psychopaths or sociopaths under these laws are subject to indefinite civil commitment in a state mental hospital. This provides a clear illustration of persons losing their freedom as a consequence of scientific information that does not exist.

There is no agreement as to the syndromes or aberrations that justify special treatment. According to Tappan (1960):

> Hospital authorities handling cases of alleged sex psychopaths committed to them by the courts discover a wide spread of psychological types—many who are normal. . . . Psychopathology is defined in the statutes by such terminology as "impulsiveness of behavior," "lack of customary standards of good judgment," "emotional instability," or "inability to control impulses" (pages 412 and 413).

Indeed, it is argued by some psychiatrists that these laws do not accurately describe the psychological characteristics of those persons charged with sex offenses (Tappan, 1960:413).

The extreme has been reached in the use of this pseudoscientific term by Alan Harrington (1972:45–46), who puts almost everyone into the psychopath category:

> We are now confronted by a band of psychopaths . . . in their various ways evil and sometimes beneficent, headlong and magical, louts and schemers, children unrestrained and charged with energy . . . drunkards and forgers, addicts, flower children, Mafia loan shark battering his victim who can't pay up, charming actor who makes crippled little boys and girls laugh, charming orator, murderer, the prophet who makes us love life again, gentle, nomadic guitarist, hustling politician, hustling judge, writers and preachers coming back with a vengeance to visit retribution on the middle classes that rejected them, whore and pimp, cop on the take, chanters filling the multitudes with joy, prancing Adonis of rock concerts, the saint who lies down in front of tractors, and student rebel, icily dominating Nobel Prize winner stealing credit from laboratory assistants, the businessman who then steals the scientist's perception, turning it into millions . . . all, all doing their thing, which is the psychopathic commandment.

As indicated earlier in this chapter, psychiatrists are called on by the courts to make professional judgments about the competence of people to stand trial or whether defendants are not guilty by reason of insanity. On the advice of these psychiatrists, those people determined to be incompetent to stand trial or not guilty by reason of insanity are often confined to mental hospitals because of their alleged future dangerousness. But there is some question about the accuracy of these predictions of future dangerousness.

In the first place there is no psychiatric definition of dangerousness that is not tautological (Cocozza and Steadman, 1978). People are judged to be dangerous because they act dangerously. Definitions of present and future dangerousness are based on past actions and thus shift from case to case: "He or she is dangerous because they did _____." Thus it can be seen that a psychiatrist's judgment of the future dangerousness of a person is dependent mainly on the crime the person is accused of, and it appears that there is no need for psychiatrists to make these judgments. Indeed, most of the reports psychiatrists make to the courts explaining their judgments are very brief, sometimes just one sentence, which explain almost nothing. An example of such a report predicting future dangerousness defends this statement as follows: "Because of his admitted numerous fights with people" (Cocozza and Steadman, 1978:270). These reports are almost never longer than two sentences.

In over 80 percent of cases where psychiatrists testify on future dangerousness the judge follows the psychiatrists' advice. When judges diverge from psychiatric testimony, they are more likely to feel that the defendant is not dangerous. In other words, it appears again that psychiatrists judge more things to be reflective of mental illness or dangerousness than would most other people. In fact, by reviewing hospital readmission records and later arrest records, Cocozza and Steadman (1978) found no difference in the behavior of people psychiatrists said were dangerous and of those people considered not dangerous.

There appears to be some confusion between physical disease and mental disease. Because physicians have made great strides in gaining knowledge about physical disease, it is assumed by some people that this is also true of physicians' knowledge about mental disease. That is, the tendency is to apply the same standards of competence to both areas of practice, even though this is hardly warranted. Notice also that the distinction between crime and mental illness is unclear. Some writers assume that nearly all criminal behavior is a manifestation of mental disease. It seems that the reason for both of these ambiguities is that we really do not know what mental illness is, and that is the reason we cannot distinguish between mental illness and physical illness on the one hand, and mental illness and crime on the other. Nowhere has there been a more persistent attempt to use psychiatry, illness, and therapy than in the juvenile courts, and therefore juvenile courts will be discussed next.

MENTAL HEALTH AND JUVENILE JUSTICE

Treatment Goals

Rehabilitation or treatment ideals are still very much alive, especially in the case of juveniles. While there is evidence that the rehabilitation of prisoners in general is of secondary importance to most citizens (Warr and Stafford, 1984), the rehabilitation of juveniles continues to find support among much of the public, as well as among judges, lawyers, and corrections administrators (Cullen et al., 1983). The alleged goals of the juvenile court, unlike those of the criminal court, are not to punish or control but to diagnose and treat the problems of the young people who are brought to its attention. A new vocabulary is used in the juvenile court to symbolize the difference between its proceedings and criminal proceedings. Examples of this new terminology include the following: *petition* instead of *complaint, summons* instead of *warrant, initial hearing* instead of *arraignment, finding of involvement* instead of *conviction*, and *disposition* instead of *sentence*. Presumably the goals are to investigate, diagnose, and prescribe treatment—not to fix guilt or blame, as in criminal courts. It is just assumed that the child committed the act being considered (Haskell and Yablonsky, 1974:30–31); therefore his or her background becomes more important than the facts of the given incident. In this setting, lawyers are considered unimportant by court officials because the proceedings are not adversarial and everyone is supposedly trying to help the child. The hearing is informal and private, including only the immediately involved parties. Since the hearing is allegedly not an adversary proceeding, no juries are used.

Constitutional Rights of Juveniles

In spite of all the fine prose about the juvenile courts' goals of caring for and treating young people, it has gradually become clear that in the name of treatment these courts in fact have a highly coercive potential (Cullen and Gilbert, 1982). For one thing, because young offenders brought before juvenile courts were allegedly there for help and not punishment, they were originally not accorded any of the constitutional rights provided citizens in criminal courts.

The U.S. Supreme Court's first attempt to specify the constitutional rights of juveniles is embodied in a 1967 decision (*In re Gault*, 1967). This case involved a 15-year-old Arizona youth, Gerald Gault who was taken into custody by a county sheriff because a neighbor complained that she had received a "lewd and indecent" phone call from him. No notice of the specific charges to be made in court was given to the boy's parents, nor was notice given of any right to counsel or privilege against self-incrimination. The hearing was held in juvenile court 1 week after the boy was apprehended, and the boy's accuser was not required to be present. Gault was sentenced to a state juvenile institution. In 1967 the U.S. Supreme Court ruled that the handling of this case was unconstitutional and that juveniles are guaranteed the following rights under the constitution:

1. The right to notice of the charges.
2. The right to counsel.
3. The right to face prosecution witnesses and cross-examine them.
4. The right to refuse to answer questions that might tend to be incriminating.

The Supreme Court, however, did not rule in this case that juveniles have the right to bail pending disposition of their case, the right to trial by jury, the right to a public trial, the right to a transcript of the proceedings, or the right to appellate review—all of which are rights that are accorded to adults (Shireman and Reamer, 1986).

Defense attorneys in the juvenile court are often confused about what role they can play in the proceedings. This confusion arises because the rights of juveniles are unclear and in a state of flux due to the combination of constitutional and treatment concerns. The vagueness of delinquency laws also contributes to the confusion (Platt, 1969:168, 173). As seen in chapter 3, the phrase "Immoral or indecent conduct" is often part of state juvenile codes, yet no one can really be sure what this phrase means. In addition, the rules of evidence in the juvenile court are unclear. There is much reliance on such information as reports that are the result of interviews with a child's teacher or neighbors, which are legally only hearsay—or secondhand evidence—and inadmissible in criminal trials of adults. Because of this confusion, attorneys in juvenile courts often do nothing (Lemert, 1967). Their inactivity causes juvenile court judges to look down on them for contributing nothing to the process.

In juvenile courts the offense alleged does not allow a prediction of the kind of response the court will make. The juvenile court considers not only the offense but also the youth's overall behavior, personality, family, and social circumstances (Emerson, 1969:89). Essentially, the court wants to know what type of youth is being processed, and this is in turn essentially a question of moral character (Emerson, 1969:90). Three types of moral character are distinguished by the court: normal, hard-core or criminal, and disturbed (Emerson, 1969:91). But the disposition depends on more than judgment of moral character; family background is also important. A hardcore boy from a stable family may be released to his parents, whereas a hard-core boy with a different home situation may go to reform school (Emerson, 1969:97).

The court presentation by the lawyer or probation officer can depict the youth's character in a favorable light and keep a youth with a long record out of an institution. That is, a *pitch* can be made for the youth. On the other hand, a more severe disposition than usual may be sought by presenting an argument to discredit the youth's character—in other words—a *denunciation* of the youth can be made (Emerson, 1969:102–106). A denunciation will show that the act is part of a hopelessly criminal career, whereas a pitch will claim that the act is part of growing up into normal adulthood. Both presentations claim a general pattern of behavior, and both relate the actor to wider social factors, the most important of which is the delinquent's family situation. A pitch can use a bad home life as an excuse, whereas a denunciation may cite the family situation as the cause of this and other potentially serious delinquency.

Defense strategies include claims of innocence, justification, excuse, or counterdenunciation. A justification advances some higher competing value against that violated by the act, such as an "appeal to higher loyalties." A youngster might claim, "I had to rob the liquor store because my brother asked me to help him, and I had to help my brother even if it was against the law." An excuse does not challenge the values violated by the act but merely mitigates the actor's responsibility for misconduct, as, for example, youths who claim that they were forced to commit crimes by older and bigger boys. Complete defenses, such as claims of innocence, are not usually accepted by the court. Counterdenunciations, especially of court officials, are also usually unacceptable (Emerson, 1969:142–143).

The courtroom ceremony is structured to intimidate young people and saddle them with the role of wrongdoer, denying them any opportunity to express a lack of commitment to that role. Sometimes the court dramatizes the delinquent's powerlessness by announcing a disposition and then at the last minute suspending it and placing the youth on probation (Emerson, 1969:172–215).

Demeanor regarded as meriting leniency from the court includes expressions of remorse, deference, and appreciation to the court. This involves displaying verbal as well as nonverbal signs of respect, such as facial signs of remorse. The youth, in short, must fully submit to the role of wrongdoer. Normal rules of social interaction do not apply to court personnel, for the judge can stare at the youth, ridicule the youth's appearance, and ask intimate and embarrassing questions. Poise and coolness on the part of a youth, which are normally rewarded in other social situations, are punished in the court. The judge may be more matter of fact with a youth, rather than harsh, if the judge feels that the youth is not responsible for the delinquent behavior or that a youth is hopeless and that a routine commitment is the only alternative. However, once a judge commits a youth, the court's potential sanction has actually been used, and control of the youth's demeanor may become more difficult (Emerson, 1969:172–215).

CONCLUSION

This chapter has described how psychiatry is utilized to determine questions of fitness to stand trial, criminal responsibility, and treatment alternatives for persons either found not guilty by reason of insanity or convicted of crimes. In each instance the potential for psychiatric coercion seems apparent. Psychiatrists have some role in this political process as the gatekeepers deciding who is mad, who is bad, and who is both. This massive power seems all the more objectionable both because it is based on an incorrect assessment of the degree of knowledge of the psychiatric profession and because America's youth have been the special target of this domination. Despite all the inequities in the criminal legal process routinely suffered by adults, the juvenile legal system possesses even fewer qualities of decency and democracy.

REFERENCES

Allen, F. A.
1964 The Borderland of Criminal Justice: Essays in Law and Criminology. Chicago: University of Chicago Press.

Andrews, D. A.
1980 "Some experimental investigations of the principles of differential association through deliberate manipulations of the structure of service systems." American Sociological Review 45(June):448–462.

Aubert, V.
1965 The Hidden Society. Totowa, N.J.: The Bedminster Press.

Bailey, W. C.
1966 "Correctional outcome: an evaluation of 100 reports." Journal of Criminal Law, Criminology and Police Science 57 (June):153–160.

Bazelon, D. L.
1971 "New gods for old: 'efficient' courts in a democratic society." New York University Law Review 46(October):653–674.

Blumberg, A. S.
1967 Criminal Justice. Chicago: Quadrangle Books.

Bowker, L. H.
1982 Corrections: The Science and the Art. New York: Macmillan.

Cocozza, J. J. and H. J. Steadman
1978 "Prediction in psychiatry: an example of misplaced confidence in experts." Social Problems 25:265–276.

Conrad, P. and J. W. Schneider
1980 Deviance Medicalization: From Badness to Sickness. St. Louis: C. V. Mosby.

Cullen, F. T. and K. Gilbert
1982 Reaffirming Rehabilitation. Cincinnati: Anderson.

Cullen, F. T. Cullen, K. M. Golden, and J. B. Cullen
1983 "Is child saving dead? Attitudes toward juvenile rehabilitation in Illinois." Journal of Criminal Justice 11:1–13.

Durham v. United States
1954 C.A.D.C. 214 F.2d 862–876 Federal Reporter.

Duster, T.
1970 The Legislation of Morality: Law, Drugs, and Moral Judgment. New York: The Free Press.

Emerson, R. M.
1969 Judging Delinquents: Context and Process in Juvenile Court. Chicago: Aldine Publishing Co.

Fishburne, P. M., H. I. Abelson, and I. Cisin
1979 National Survey on Drug Abuse: Main Findings. Rockville, Md.: National Institute on Drug Abuse.

Galtung, J.
1966 "Prison: the organization of dilemma." Pp. 107–145, in D. R. Cressey (ed.), The Prison: Studies in Institutional Organization and Change. New York: Holt, Rinehart & Winston.

Gault, In re
1967 387 U.S. 1.

Harrington, A.
1972 Psychopaths. New York: Simon & Schuster.

Hartung, F. E.
1965 Crime, Law and Society. Detroit: Wayne State University Press.

Haskell, M. R. and L. Yablonsky
1974 Juvenile Delinquency. Chicago: Rand McNally College Publishing.

Hollingshead, A. B. and F. C. Redlich
1958 Social Class and Mental Illness: A Community Study. New York: John Wiley & Sons.

Lemert, E. M.
1967 "Legislating change in the juvenile court." Wisconsin Law Review 1967(Spring): 421–448.

Linsky, A. S.
1970 "Who shall be excluded? The influence of personal attributes in community reaction to the mentally ill." Social Psychiatry 5(July):166–171.

Martinson, R.
1974 "What works—Questions and answers about prison reform." Public Interest(Spring): 22–54.

Medvedev, Z. A. and R. A. Medvedev
1971 A Question of Madness. New York: Knopf.

Mitford, Jessica
1973 Kind and Usual Punishment: The Prison Business. New York: Knopf.

M'Naghten's Case, D.
1843 8 English Reports 718–724.

Newsweek
1982 "The insanity plea on trial." May 24:56–61.

Platt, A. M.
1969 The Child Savers: The Invention of Delinquency. Chicago: University of Chicago Press.

Rosenhan, D L.
1973 "On being sane in insane places." Science 179(January):250–258.

Rubin, S.
1965 Psychiatry and Criminal Law. Dobbs Ferry, N.Y.: Oceana Publications.
1966 Crime and Juvenile Delinquency. New York: Oceana.

Scull, A. T.
1977 Decarceration, Community Treatment and the Deviant: A Radical View. Englewood Cliffs, N.J.: Prentice Hall.

Seidman, R. B.
1965 "Witch murder and mens rea: a problem of society under radical social change." Modern Law Review 28(January):46–61.

Shireman, C. H. and F. G. Reamer
1986 Rehabilitating Juvenile Justice. New York: Columbia University Press.

Steadman, H. J.
1979 Beating A Rap?: Defendants Found Incompetent to Stand Trial. Chicago: University of Chicago Press.

Stone, I. F.
1972 "Betrayal by psychiatry." New York Review of Books 18(February 10):7–8, 10, 12, 14.

Sutherland, E. H.
1950 "The diffusion of sexual psychopath laws." American Journal of Sociology 56:142–148.

Szasz, T. S.
1965 Psychiatric Justice. New York: Collier Books.
1968 Law, Liberty, and Psychiatry. New York: Collier Books.

Tappan, P. W.
1960 Crime, Justice and Correction. New York: McGraw-Hill.

United States v. *Pollard*
1959 171 Supp. 474 (E.D. Mich. 1959).

von Hirsch, A.
1976 Doing Justice: The Choice of Punishments. New York: Hill & Wang.

Warr, M. and M. Stafford
1984 "Public goals of punishment and support for the death penalty." Journal of Research in Crime and Delinquency 21(May):95–111.

Wilkins, L. T.
1969 Evaluation of Penal Measures. New York: Random House.

11
CONTROL
AND PREVENTION
OF CRIME

CONTROL OF CRIME THROUGH PUNISHMENT

Morality of Punishment

The view that the current crime crisis in the United States can be controlled by punishment is widely accepted by Americans. Some people argue that our prisons have been turned into country clubs for criminals and that the police have been handcuffed by the Supreme Court, which historically has been excessively concerned about equality and citizens' constitutional rights. The argument continues that if, as a society, we really get tough with criminals through longer sentences and more executions and if we show less concern about suspects' constitutional rights, a sense of safety now lacking can be restored to American cities.

Basically, this argument suggests that punishment can be used as deterrence. Implicit in this argument is Bentham's (1823) notion that people are pleasure-seeking, pain-avoiding creatures. As noted in chapter 1, after a long dormancy, a new interest in deterrence has developed recently. This dormancy is understandable because of the long history of positivism in criminology. If the positivist belief that people are forced to commit crime is accepted, then studying deterrent techniques becomes a fruitless activity (von Hirsch, 1976:37). According to Bentham, however, crime can be controlled if the penalties are no greater, but also no less, than necessary to deter the individual offender in the future.

This is sometimes referred to as primary deterrence. Bentham's rationale for punishment implies taking stronger measures against poor law violators because their poverty gives them stronger motives to commit many types of crimes. Price-fixing business executives need only be fined, or at the most, fired from their jobs to deter similar offenses in the future, whereas the knife- and pistol-wielding poor people must be imprisoned to deter a repetition of their offenses (von Hirsch, 1976:147).

Punishment may have differing effects on offenders depending on whether they believe the punishment is legitimate or not. If the law violator believes the legal system to be fundamentally unjust, as many do, then the criminal punishment cannot rehabilitate them but will only serve to make them bitter. Greater bitterness can be expected when people are punished to make an example of them and thus help restrain other potential law violators. This is called secondary deterrence. Secondary deterrence is often criticized as unjust because it requires the infliction of pain on some individuals for the benefit of others (Grupp, 1971). However, primary deterrence has also been characterized as unjust. Morris (1974b), for example, suggested that it is unjust to imprison people for long periods because of their alleged *future* dangerousness, since this is punishment in *advance* of criminal behavior.

Incarceration for alleged future dangerousness is also unjust because, as Morris (1974a) recognized, the concept of dangerousness is vague and imprecise. Consequently, attempting to incarcerate individuals who would commit future dangerous or violent acts could result in the mistaken incarceration of a large number of people who would not commit such acts if released. Indeed, Morris reviews research which indicates that therapists are unable to make accurate predictions of future dangerousness, which was also demonstrated in chapter 10. Since it is not possible to predict such future behavior accurately, many prisoners who would not have committed dangerous acts if released are held in prison longer because their sentences have been influenced by such incorrect predictions (von Hirsch, 1976:21). But even if reasonably accurate predictions of future dangerous behavior were possible, the problem of injustice would remain as long as people are essentially punished for the crimes that they have not yet committed (von Hirsch, 1976:125).

Thus the efficacy of punishment and its morality raise distinct but interrelated questions (Zimring, 1971:20–25). Random selection of parking violators for execution is an example of what would likely be an effective but clearly unjust punishment. Legal threats probably have a greater impact on some types of people than on others, but it generally would be considered unjust for the law to specify punishment only for those people most likely to be deterred.

Effectiveness of Punishment

During the 1950s Janis and Feshback (1953) conducted an important study of fear-arousing communication. Three randomly selected groups of high school students heard three different types of lectures on dental hygiene. One group heard a lecture intended to provide a strong fear appeal, with frequent references to pain and tooth disease. Another group was given a lecture with a lesser amount of fear appeal, and a third group heard a lecture providing other reasons why dental hygiene was a good idea. A higher percentage of those in the first, high-threat group indicated that they had worried about dental hygiene, but a lower percentage reported conforming to the hygiene recommendations than the other two groups did. A later follow-up of their dental hygiene behavior found no differences among the three groups experiencing the three different threat intensities. It seems possible that the same generalization applies to criminal law and that the threats contained in the law have little influence on criminal behavior.

For a threat of criminal punishment to deter, people must be aware of the legal threat and also believe that law enforcement agents really wish to punish them for committing the threatened act (Zimring, 1971). If a threat has generally not been enforced over the years, people will tend to believe that the threat is insincere and that the law is really meant to punish people other than themselves. Middle-class college marihuana smokers have reason to feel this way about law enforcement as do most antitrust violators. In addition to being seen as willing to punish the law breaker, the law enforcement agency must be seen as capable of apprehending the offenders. Since both marihuana smoking and antitrust violations are so widespread, there is little belief among violators that the law can really be enforced because of the sheer numbers of violators.

One tactic in deterrence is to make the widest possible distinction between criminal and noncriminal behavior by threatening nearly all criminal behavior with severe criminal penalties. The idea here is to attempt to prevent potential law violators from committing any crime. The high penalties for relatively minor property crimes that were found in eighteenth-century England illustrate this legal strategy (Zimring, 1971). Another possibility is to provide for a considerable variation in criminal penalties to emphasize the differential seriousness of various types of crime. The philosophy here seems to be that if total conformity is not possible, then at least the law can pressure offenders to choose less serious offenses. This implies less concern about the corruption of the offender who commits a less serious offense.

A group of young males in their late teens and early twenties were asked their perceptions of effective crime deterrents (Walker, 1971). Most of these respondents felt that their chance of getting away with a serious crime like burglary was about 50/50, when in fact the police do not apprehend that high a percentage of these types of law violators. However, the more experience the respondents had with committing offenses, the more optimistic and realistic they tended to become. They were also asked what they feared the most about ever being apprehended by the police and being forced to appear in court. Possible criminal punishment ranked fourth behind concern about the reactions of their immediate families and their employers and general loss of face in the community.

While the fear of criminal punishment does not seem paramount, we do know that a sudden and well-publicized removal of police efficiency leads to dramatic increases in some types of offenses. For 7 months in 1944 the Danish police force was under arrest by the Nazi occupation troops with the result that robberies escalated (Walker, 1971). The massive looting that occurred during the New York City blackout was discussed in chapter 2. The same pattern also generally occurs during police strikes (Clark, 1969).

Aside from the moral problems inherent in using punishment as deterrence, it has been demonstrated, contrary to the rantings of some American politicians, that merely increasing the penalties prescribed in the criminal statutes will not effect an increase in obedience to law. Recent research comparing different political jurisdictions has found that the severity of punishment for specific types of crimes is not usually associated with lower rates of these offenses (Gibbs, 1968; Tittle, 1969). But certainty of punishment is associated with lower crime rates and therefore does appear to have some deterrent effect. Earlier, in chapters 6 and 7, in the discussions of the Nebraska marihuana law (Galliher et al., 1974) and property crimes in England (Hall, 1952), we demonstrated that prescribed penalties have been reduced, rather than increased, to enhance the likelihood that the law would be enforced. In both instances the prescribed penalties were so severe that judges, prosecutors, and juries often allowed law violators to escape any punishment. The consequences of a 1955 Connecticut crackdown on speeders can be understood in the same terms. The prescribed penalties were increased dramatically, but there was also a sharp rise in the percentage of speeding violators judged not guilty (Campbell and Ross, 1968).

At times the punishment of law violators may even encourage some people to violate the law. One study indicated that some people claimed that they had begun minor falsifications of their tax returns after hearing that others had been convicted of tax evasion. These respondents said that the convictions, which involved blatant violators, had inadvertently made them aware of safe or moderate offenses, which they then committed (Schwartz and Skolnick, 1962).

Folklore About Crime Control

There is no shortage of commonly accepted ideas about the consequences of the threat of punishment by the state. Some people believe that the threat and administration by the state of criminal punishments indicates to citizens that the society they respect views such behavior as morally wrong. Thus the threat and example of punishment may aid in moral education, primarily as an attention-getting mechanism, and in this way play an important role in the general socialization process (Zimring, 1971). In addition, it is believed that at first people may obey the law because of the threat of punishment but that later this obedience becomes a habit and that people then obey the laws without really thinking about the threat.

Public officials also have some unfounded beliefs about the deterrence of crime through punishment. One traditional belief of many public officials is like "Aunt Jane's cold remedy" (Zimring, 1971). Every time you have a cold you take this remedy, and as the proponents of the remedy promise, in 2 weeks your cold symptoms disappear. Of course, the cold remedy may have had no effect on your cold, and the symptoms would have disappeared in 2 weeks whether or not they were treated. However, if you always return to this remedy every time you are ill, you will never know the difference and will remain convinced of its effectiveness. The same pattern appears in the use of crime remedies. First the crime rate spurts upward. Next, some immediate government countermeasure is taken. The particular measure taken varies from case to case and from city to city. Sometimes the police are equipped with larger revolvers, sometimes with trained attack dogs, and other times with cruisers having massive, high-powered engines. In any event, soon afterward the crime rate recedes. Government officials from a variety of agencies rush to take credit for these reductions, citing the new guns, dogs, or cars as the reason for the successes. But it is arguable that these reductions would have occurred even without these countermeasures.

In Connecticut during the 1950s the state-wide crackdown on speeding was a response to increased auto fatalities. After the crackdown began, there was an immediate reduction in fatalities. These apparent swift results created a great public sensation until it was discovered that the fatality rates had also decreased in neighboring states where no similar countermeasures had been taken (Campbell and Ross, 1968). The same pattern of rapid increase occurred in the number of armed robberies of taxi cabs in New York City in 1966. Police officers were authorized to take jobs moonlighting as taxi drivers, and the robberies decreased (Zimring, 1971). The problem is that we have no way of knowing what the rates of either auto fatalities or armed robberies would have been if the corresponding countermeasure had not been introduced. Officials are typically stimulated to begin new programs during periods when the rate of crime is high, and thus the officials can take credit when the crime rate returns to its previous level. Moreover, when the rate stays at its exceptionally high level, law enforcement officials sometimes argue that crime rates would have been even higher were it not for the new programs or that more of the new program is in fact required to get noticeable results: more guns, more police dogs, or even bigger patrol car engines. What is missing in all of these arguments is some measure of the amount of crime to be expected if the government had made no response.

It has also been observed (Zimring, 1971) that crime control is somewhat like the old story about "tiger prevention." The story involves a man running around the streets of New York City snapping his fingers and moaning. Finally, he is stopped by the police, and officers ask the man what he is doing. The man responds by claiming that he is keeping tigers away. The officer says: "Why that's crazy. There aren't any wild tigers within 5,000 miles of New York City." Thoughtfully the man concludes, "Well then, I must have a pretty effective technique" (Zimring, 1971:17). Similarly, in crime control it is often assumed that the existence of high criminal penalties is the only reason a crime wave does not occur. Yet as indicated earlier in this chapter, it has often been found that high criminal penalties are difficult to impose and therefore may actually encourage law violation. And studies comparing the murder rates in states with different penalties for homicide reveal no relationship between the presence of the death penalty and murder rates. Even if a relationship were to be found between the severity of the penalty structure and rates of homicide, this may simply mean that the citizens in the area with the higher penalties feel more strongly about these offenses and that informal community controls keep the crime rate down rather than the formal criminal penalties.

A third unfounded belief is sometimes found in prison wardens' surveys of prisoners on death row (Zimring, 1971). Some prison wardens have said that their interviews with men on death row show that deterrence is a myth. None of these men on death row indicate that they have been deterred from committing their crimes by the threat of criminal penalties. But there are two problems with this type of survey: (1) It is clearly not in the present interests of those on death row to demonstrate the effectiveness of the death penalty. (2) Even more importantly these men clearly have not been deterred from committing crimes by the existing penalties, and if penalties deter any individuals, it is among people almost everywhere else than on death row. The point in this discussion of the folklore among law enforcement officials regarding crime control is that much of what passes for expert knowledge is in reality nearer fantasy than fact.

It is sometimes suggested that punishing law violators will in some way be good for them, that it will rehabilitate them or be therapeutic for them by teaching them a new respect for the law and the rights of other people (Grupp, 1971). Such an argument may seem sound when the analogy of the punishment of a child by a parent is used, but it is widely recognized that American prisons do not teach new respect for the law and the rights of others (American Friends, 1971). Long-term isolation from family and friends in decaying and barren institutions, combined with the brutal treatment commonly received from guards and other prisoners, can hardly be character building.

Punishment as Retribution

Punishment as retribution is much easier to defend on logical grounds than on moral grounds. Punishment produces the pain that citizens believe the criminal deserves. It is sometimes argued that it is desirable to provide for an orderly collective expression of society's disapproval of criminal acts. Indeed, Durkheim (1933:70–110) argued that a certain amount of crime is functional for a society because the society's punitive response increases each member's identification with the norms of the society. Punishment of deviance reaffirms and clarifies the normative boundaries of the group. When a certain behavior is punished, people see clearly that this behavior is outside the acceptable limits. In fact, it has been argued that one function of crime waves and the consequent punishment of deviance in society is to give meaning to a group when it needs it most—at the time of a group identity crisis (Erikson, 1966). By punishing law violators a society indicates quite clearly that this type of behavior and this type of individual are beyond the moral boundaries of the group and that neither will be tolerated.

In pressing charges against an offender, the victim and those who identify with the victim are able to express hostility against the offender in a socially acceptable manner (Grupp, 1971). The size of this group of observers sympathetic to the victim varies with the type of crime. Such groups are generally large in cases of murder but smaller, for example, in the case of blackmail where there is some obvious victim complicity. Without the opportunity to perform some legal action against the law violator, the possibility of a loss of faith in the legal system is likely, as is the possibility of vigilante action.

Punishment is not required to prevent the bulk of the population from committing a crime because the socialization process prevents most deviant behavior. But without such punishment of law violators, the law-abiding citizens in a society would become indignant and ultimately demoralized. They would see people who apparently suffer no ill effects and who perhaps even prosper from violating the law leading lives that seem to compare favorably with their own humdrum conventional existence. There is another way, however, in which deviant behavior can be useful to social groups, aside from making punishment possible. It has been suggested that deviant behavior serves to keep the norms down for what is taken to constitute a satisfactory performance, making it easier on other group members to engage in satisfactory levels of achievement (Dentler and Erikson, 1959). Without these low performers, the norms for satisfactory achievement would necessarily increase, which helps explain why groups often attempt to keep deviant performers in the group rather than expelling them. People never feel so good as when they are talking about other group members who just do not measure up in some way—morally, intellectually, or physically.

The moral indignation associated with punishment as retribution may be seen in seventeenth-century England among the middle-class entrepreneurs who accepted puritanical rules for living (Ranulf, 1964). These people were interested in worldly success, but they saw success as something that should be obtained only by great self-discipline. They could see, however, that the lower classes and the nobility were enjoying life more than they did. Many of these people did not seem to suffer for their revelry, as the middle class's puritanical religion suggested would necessarily follow such behavior. The members of the nobility imposed no discipline on themselves but still managed to get along well. Even the lower classes appeared reasonably happy in their debauchery. Members of the middle class felt that their rewards for denying themselves worldly pleasures were inadequate and that others who were living it up still had more than they did. This created strain for the middle class. It was important to the middle class that these immoral people should be punished, and during this period brutal punishments for law violators emerged at the urging of middle-class merchant groups.

This violent reaction to the transgressions of others served to protect the value system of the middle class. Through severe punishments the middle class reassured itself of the worthlessness of these law violators. Convicts were punished publicly and held up to public ridicule to emphasize that people who lived as they did were socially degraded even if they were financially successful; and in this way the middle class could still stand out as God's elect even though it was not as wealthy as the nobility. This need for vicious punishment would not have occurred if success had been distributed solely on the basis of morality, but it was not. Thus another means was required to dramatize the middle class's adherence to a godly way of life. The influence of affluence, power, and class interests is clearly evident in this example of middle-class moral indignation.

PUNISHMENT BY DEATH

In England during the 160 years prior to 1820 the number of capital crimes rose from 50 to over 200 (Cooper, 1974). During Elizabeth I's reign (1558–1603) the preamble to a law on theft read: "Whereas persons in contempt of God's commands, and in defiance of the law, are found to cut pockets, and pick purses, even at places of public execution, while execution is being done on criminals. Be it therefore enacted that all such persons shall suffer death" (Cooper, 1974:11). Just prior to, and during public executions large crowds would press together near the scaffold, providing an excellent opportunity for pickpockets to steal others' belongings unnoticed. The fact that pickpockets often plied their trade during the execution of other pickpockets is often used as anecdotal evidence indicating that the death penalty does not deter. But the death penalty was avoided by juries. Between 1803 and 1810, of 1,872 people convicted of the capital crime of stealing from dwellings, only one was actually executed. Many people objected to these extreme penalties because property crimes were never punished, which appeared to be responsible for increases in the crime rates. Therefore by 1836 hanging for forgery and burglary had been abolished, and capital punishment was used almost solely for murder. The executions that did take place at this time were public, and the *London Times* defended public executions as the only way to prove to the average citizen that wealthy people were actually executed. But by 1868 the upper classes became less afraid of the masses, and Parliament outlawed public executions and their grisly spectacles.

From 1967 until Gary Gilmore's 1977 death by firing squad in Utah, no person was executed in the United States. The hiatus in executions was due to both shifts in public opinion and Supreme Court decisions. In 1966 only 42 percent of Americans supported the death penalty (Gallup Poll, 1966). Also, in 1972 in the *Furman* v. *Georgia* decision (408 U.S. 238) the Supreme Court ruled that since mainly blacks and poor whites had been executed in this country, capital punishment was so "arbitrary" and "capricious" in practice that it violated the Eighth and Fourteenth Amendments, which prohibit cruel and unusual punishment. Fifty-five percent of those executed in the United States between

1930 and 1967 were black, as were 90 percent of those executed for rape (Greenberg and Himmelstein, 1969). But by 1976 the states had found a legislative formula for drafting death penalty laws to meet the Supreme Court's objections, as shown when the Court upheld the death penalty laws of Florida, Texas, and Georgia in *Gregg* v. *Georgia* (429 U.S. 875). Most states quickly passed new death penalty laws that met these requirements. And by 1985, 72 percent favored state executions (Gallup Poll, 1985). In an apparent effort to sanitize the death penalty and make it acceptable to a broad range of people, in recent years several states have changed the prescribed method of execution from electrocution or gasing to lethal injection. Given these shifts in public opinion and the new state laws, it should not be surprising that by the 1980s executions had become a more common event. The number of those awaiting execution on American death rows is increasing rapidly, especially in southern states where all but a few of the recent executions have been carried out.

Morality and Science of the Death Penalty

The arguments for and against the death penalty often confuse the issues of effectiveness and morality. Often the debate is heated, and those involved move back and forth between moral and scientific arguments, making logical debate impossible. If a person believes that the death penalty is a moral necessity for responding to murder, such as an "eye for an eye and a tooth for a tooth," then scientific evidence about the lack of deterrent effect of the death penalty will not sway them. But if they hang their moral beliefs on arguments regarding the effectiveness of the death penalty in controlling crime, they have moved from the realm of morality to that of science. Those opposed to the death penalty also often attempt to move from morality to science and back again, making a hopeless muddle of the issues involved.

Thus the question becomes, what in fact is the deterrent effect of the death penalty? Among social scientists there is deep division on this question, apparently associated with their moral or political predispositions. The reader may recall that in chapter 1 an economist was quoted who concluded that "an additional execution per year over the period in question may have resulted, on average, in 7 or 8 fewer murders" (Ehrlich, 1975:414). But opponents of the death penalty argue that because many murders are crimes of passion committed on the spur of the moment, those committing such crimes do not reflect on the existence of a death penalty. In addition, research has found no consistent differences in the number of murders committed in culturally similar states, though some have and some do not have the death penalty, and no differences in the murder rates over time in those states that repealed the death penalty and then later restored it (Sellin, 1967). There are great differences across American states in the rate of murder, but these differences seem more related to cultural and economic differences than to the presence or absence of a death penalty.

Investigating the deterrent effect of the death penalty involves studying the nature of secondary deterrence. For example, will the execution of a convicted murderer keep others from committing similar crimes? Given the American constitutional rights of trial and appeal, only a small proportion of those convicted of murder are actually condemned to die, and those who are actually put to death are executed long after they committed the crime. Both the low percentage of executions of murderers and the long delays violate what psychologists have long known about the principles of negative reinforcement and human learning. To extinguish undesirable behavior among people observing others being punished and to have a maximum impact on these observers, punishment must be reasonably consistent and closely tied in time to the undesired behavior. Both these principles are violated in the imposition of the death penalty in America. The only possible means of instituting a potentially effective death penalty would require major alterations in American constitutional freedoms.

But even people most opposed to the death penalty must recognize that under some conditions the death penalty can control human behavior. During the German occupation of Norway during World War II the Nazis instituted the death penalty for Norwegians trafficking in illegal newspapers. This new penalty largely stopped the lively circulation of these publications. The previous penalty of imprisonment did not work well because the Norwegians recognized that the Nazi occupation could not last (Grupp, 1971:142). Indeed, the truth about the deterrent effect of the death penalty is possibly that it deters those of some social classes and some races better than it does others. As discussed in chapter 1, one deterrence researcher found that "lower status" and "nonwhite" people are most easily deterred by criminal penalties (Tittle, 1980:301, 304). Perhaps it also deters people with certain educational levels and those in some types of communities better than it does others. However, it is clearly unjust to have a death penalty only for specified types of people, for example, lower-class, native-American women in small towns.

A Note About Death Row

Finally a word should be said about the experience of living on death row. We can only imagine the horror of living in a death row cell watching one appeal after another slip by without sucess over a period of months and years, knowing that you are getting closer and closer to your date with the executioner. Americans like to think of their country as unusually civilized and humane, but the fact is that the United States is the only Western democracy to still have the death penalty. In addition, some people might argue that our particular process of implementing the death penalty is more brutal than found in most dictatorships. In totalitarian governments executions are generally carried out swiftly, avoiding the protracted agony of anticipation. Of course, the reason for the delays in the United States is to provide for all possible court appeals, but this produces agony nonetheless.

The adaptations of prisoners condemned to die are similar to those found among terminally ill patients (Johnson, 1981). Among the latter, five stages of adjustment have been discovered after the patients learn they have an incurable disease. These stages are shocked denial, followed by anger and fear, then bargaining ("God, if you let me live another year, I promise to . . ."), depression comes next, and finally acceptance. Among prisoners condemned to die by execution these stages take the following form. When new prisoners initially come to death row, they often experience a sense of disbelief about being there and have a feeling of general optimism about their case. Gradually, however, it dawns on death row prisoners that their case is not going to be quickly overturned. At this stage anger and fear develop, and prisoners begin to accept the "domino theory" of capital punishment, which is that a few executions will eventually open a tidal wave of executions. Then prisoners attempt to bargain with the appeals courts or perhaps with the governor. For some prisoners this stage lasts for years. Next, condemned prisoners become depressed about such things as opportunities lost in their lives, as well as about their impending death. Finally they reach the last stage in the process and feel neither depressed nor angry. In fact there is a void of feeling now; thus most prisoners walk to their executions with surprising calmness. Moreover, most prisoners do not break down at the time of their executions because they typically fear such loss of control more than the execution itself (Johnson, 1981).

For people who would argue that this is the simple justice of an eye for an eye and a life for a life, it is sometimes maintained that the state is actually more brutal because those convicted and sentenced to death for murder experience not only death as did their victims but also protracted anticipation of death (Pepinsky and Jesilow, 1984). Imagine getting to know the man in an adjacent cell who is scheduled for an execution date before your own. His date of execution comes, and he is given his last meal of his choice and is then led away to his death. In such a situation living is undoubtedly harder than dying. This is a type of organized torture that street criminals almost never use on their victims.

Speaking of torture, during ancient history, as well as in the Middle Ages, courts did not hesitate to impose *physical* torture and mutilation (van den Haag, 1975). Torture has been used legally for most of written history both to secure confessions and to punish crimes. Whether legal or not, some people argue that torture can be justified in some cases, such as when a prisoner is the only person who knows the location of a bomb set to go off that will surely kill many innocent people (van den Haag, 1975). Hence, a curious attitude has developed: physical torture is abhorrent, but the death penalty is acceptable. Although we cannot countenance cutting off one finger of an individual convicted of a heinous crime, most Americans do support the death penalty.

LEGISLATION LIMITING CONSTITUTIONAL RIGHTS

Constitutional change is yet another method of attempting to control crime. In 1968 the U.S. Congress, in near hysteria over the series of political assassinations, riots, and demonstrations that occurred earlier in the decade, passed the Omnibus Crime Control Bill and Safe Streets Act (Harris, 1968). The act specifically provided that information obtained from clandestine police wiretaps could be used as evidence in court cases involving national security and organized crime, which is contrary to the Fifth Amendment's protection against self-incrimination and the Fourth Amendment's limitations on legal police searches. To the degree that Americans feel that their only chance of surviving the siege of violent crime is to turn over more power to the state, they will likely do so, and do so gladly.

CRIME PREVENTION

The idea of preventing crime rather than punishing the offender sounds attractive at first glance. It is only when specific proposals for preventing crime are put forward that we see how frightening this idea can be. Four methods of controlling crime, including punishment, rehabilitation, limitation of constitutional rights, and legalization, are also ways of approaching prevention.

      Punishment before trial of those considered crime prone may seem ridiculous, yet it was suggested in 1969 by the Nixon administration (Graham, 1969). It was called preventive detention and would have involved denying bail to those awaiting trial if the judge felt that there was a likelihood of their continuing to commit crimes. Later, a number of states adopted just such a policy. Rehabilitation might also be used in crime prevention. When certain personality characteristics or genetic patterns are linked to crime, as they are by some researchers, these findings suggest that it would be useful if such traits were spotted in school children so that they could be given special help—perhaps special medication or specifically designed training—before they get into trouble with the law. Such a policy suggests as well the necessity of mandatory screening among school children, including mandatory blood tests. Limitation of constitutional rights might involve giving the police and courts greater freedom to arrest and incarcerate individuals considered most predisposed to crime. Legalization or decriminalization of certain behaviors would, of course, prevent the label of criminal being attached to those predisposed to such acts. People in the gay community and drug addicts would obviously benefit from the change.

      At times political liberals urge social reforms, such as slum clearance, with the promise that taking such steps will prevent crime. These promises were made during the 1960s in support of various social welfare programs, as Moynihan (1969) observed, yet no decreases in crime occurred. One problem with such promises is that bad living conditions are not the only causes of crime because, as evidence from anonymous questionnaires and the White House Watergate tapes indicate, all types of crime occur in all social classes. When even the leaders of our nation are implicated in burglaries, it is time to reconsider the importance of slums as a direct or exclusive cause of crime. Such social changes as slum clearance must be justified in their own right as morally compelling without the empty promise that they will necessarily prevent crime. When these programs are justified as a type of crime control, yet lower crime rates are not produced, the entire social welfare program is jeopardized, as it has been in the 1970s and 1980s.

CRIME CONTROL THROUGH REHABILITATION

As will be explained in chapter 12, Rothman (1971) demonstrated that in nineteenth-century America the belief grew that convicted criminals could be rehabilitated by incarceration in prisons. This optimism about the reformative potential of incarcerating offenders did not exist during the colonial period in the eighteenth century. This faith in rehabilitation has been bolstered in the twentieth century by the development of the behavioral and social sciences, whose practitioners typically support this view of reforming human behavior. Currently, the typical liberal position on crime and its control is that convicted criminals should not be punished for their crimes but should be treated and rehabilitated so that they can lead law-abiding and useful lives after their release from prison. At first glance this may sound both humanitarian and enlightened, but the argument is not without its problems.

Social workers, psychologists, and psychiatrists generally agree that a progressive legal structure pays little attention to the crime alleged, but rather focuses attention on the needs of the defendant. Instead of taking the old neoclassical position of making the punishment fit the crime, they argue for making the state's reaction fit the needs of the individual. However, this position overlooks the possibility that before we can know an individual's problems we must first know the nature of his or her acts. After all, some persons mistakenly convicted of crimes have been subjected to many years of unnecessary rehabilitation. The problem is that the concern with rehabilitation has encouraged procedural laxity and irregularity, since its emphasis on the individual's needs results in a lessened concern with the exact facts of a case. This procedural laxity is especially true of the juvenile courts, which were discussed in chapter 10, where the treatment ideology has been especially pronounced.

The rehabilitative ideal began in the eighteenth century and lasted through most of the twentieth century but declined in less than 10 years during the 1970s (Allen, 1981). The rehabilitative ideal accepted the position that behavior is caused by forces other than free will. Almost all innovations in the criminal justice system in this century are reflections of this ideal: the juvenile court, the indeterminate sentence, rehabilitation programs in prisons, and probation and parole programs that release individuals under supervision to see if they can adjust to the community. Everyone seemed to accept this ideal, including politicans, and lay people, and especially scholars. While scholars gave considerable attention to the causes of criminal behavior, they traditionally have rejected the deterrence efficacy of penal sanctions. A signal of the beginning of the end of this ideology came in the early 1970s with the publication of *Struggle for Justice* (1971) by the American Friends Service Committee, which condemned the rehabilitative ideal while noting that it was widely accepted even by those who were most humanitarian. Unquestioning acceptance of the rehabilitative ideal was no longer true by the mid 1970s. As will be shown in chapter 14, prison rehabilitation programs were being developed and refined in the 1950s, 1960s, and 1970s, but not thereafter. Thus as noted in chapter 2, the liberal idealism of the 1960s had clearly vanished by the 1980s. It is significant therefore that in 1976 the California legislature revised its criminal code, moving away from the older ideas of rehabilitation to legislation explicitly designed for punishment. About the same time most American states scrambled to pass death penalty bills, which were congruent with this movement (Allen, 1981).

Out of the Vietnam War and the radical politics of the 1960s came the radical criminology of the 1970s. Rehabilitation efforts were seen by these scholars as merely another example of class oppression. Still other scholars on the right such as Wilson (1975) and van den Haag (1975) rejected rehabilitation in favor of achieving greater public order through increased law enforcement power. *The Child Savers* (Platt, 1977), an excellent illustration of the protests against the rehabilitative ideal, saw an allegedly humanitarian social movement as fundamentally an effort at class oppression. Solitary confinement has been called "constructive meditation," and such a cell is referred to as "the quiet room." The use of cattle prods on prisoners has been termed "aversion therapy"; turning a powerful water hose on juveniles has been called "hydrotherapy," and incarceration without treatment of any type has been called "milieu therapy" (Allen, 1981:51). Moreover, this rehabilitation ideology is found in other cultures. Prisoners in the People's Republic of China realize that if they expect lenient punishment, they must confess and show remorse when accused of crimes and not insist on their legal rights (Allen, 1981).

The rehabilitative ideal presupposes that dominant groups have a great deal of confidence in their values and that there is a widespread belief in the malleability of human character and behavior, as well as a consensus on what it means to be rehabilitated (Allen, 1981). But in fact there is increasing pessimism about such changes, perhaps brought about in part by the obvious failure of the liberal reforms of the 1960s. Watergate, the Vietnam War experience, and the civil rights movement all challenged the legitimacy of the dominant social institutions that the rehabilitation ideal requires as an article of faith. For example, there was a dilemma of what to do with war resisters convicted during the Vietnam War. And in the case of abortion there is no agreement on what constitutes a criminal. The vastly differing views of terrorism further illustrate this point.

From 1950 to 1975 the number of male youths 15 to 17 years old doubled. This is the highest-crime age group, and as a consequence of the growth of this age cohort, the overall crime rate increased greatly. The growth in the crime rate placed a significant stress on the rehabilitative ideal, and at the same time the number and proportion of nonwhites in prisons increased (Allen, 1981). In 1978 black men made up 5.4 percent of the general population but 45.7 percent of all prisoners (Christianson, 1981). In recent years this disparity between blacks and whites has been increasing. These figures are significant because confidence in rehabilitation decreases as the difference between liberal supporters of rehabilitation and potential clients increases. With nearly ideal timing Martinson in 1974 found that no rehabilitation programs seemed to work. It is in this context that a sociobiology movement began that also denies a rehabilitation potential. Moreover, the political right wing feels that sentencing discretion of judges must be removed, although it has been seen as essential for rehabilitation (Allen, 1981). The remaining support for rehabilitation is only a pale reflection of its earlier promise. Cullen and Gilbert (1982) provided the following arguments for rehabilitation:

1. Rehabilitation is the only justification of criminal sanctioning that obligates the state to care for an offender's needs or welfare (page 247).
2. The ideology of rehabilitation provides an important rationale for opposing the conservative's assumption that increased repression will reduce crime (page 253).
3. Rehabilitation still receives considerable support as a major goal of the correctional system (page 257).
4. Rehabilitation has historically been an important motive underlying reform efforts that have increased the humanity of the correctional system (page 261).

The significance of these points is that they defend the rehabilitation ideology on political grounds rather than on the grounds that convicted felons either can be or should be rehabilitated. Thus these points leave the impression that the rehabilitation ideology is at most a useful tool in liberals' political maneuvering against the right wing to keep prison conditions from deteriorating even further.

Further light can be shed on the increase in the percentage of black prisoners by noting that in 1970 black unemployment was 8.2 percent, while in 1982 it had risen dramatically to 18.4 percent (Ball-Rokeach and Short, 1985). Among blacks 16 to 19 years old the unemployment rate in 1986 was an incredible 42.7 percent (U.S. Census, 1986). Yet it is sometimes argued that poverty is not the cause of crime because black Americans have more money than do citizens in most third world countries. But there is no reason to suppose that black Americans compare themselves to black Africans rather than to American whites. In a futile attempt to deal with alienation, between 1980 and 1982 an additional 50,000 adults were imprisoned in the United States, but with no noticeable effect on the crime rate (Currie, 1985a). Significantly, among industrialized countries American incarceration rates are only lower than those in the Soviet Union and South Africa (Curtis, 1985). Instead of incarceration, some people argue that there must be an expansion of the Affirmative Action program—giving job preferences to minorities—combined with greater educational opportunities for America's black lower class (Ball-Rokeach and Short, 1985). In this way we can at least begin to reduce racial and economic inequality, which as noted in chapter 3 is strongly associated with high levels of violent crime.

FULL EMPLOYMENT

If Americans have finally had their fill of crime of all types and really want to get serious about locating workable solutions, we should perhaps start by considering employment as a basic and inalienable right of citizenship. Even a passing glance at historical cultures should tell us of the wisdom of this idea. Anthropologists have long known that in preliterate societies all people capable of working were supplied with labor that made some meaningful contribution to the society. In contemporary socialist societies we also find that employment is both a right and an obligation of citizenship. But in the United States unemployment is all too common—in recent years typically between 5 and 10 percent of the available workforce. This figure usually does not incude those who are so discouraged that they are no longer seeking employment. Among racial minorities the figures are even higher, and among teenage black males the figure is often around 50 percent unemployed. In addition, those in this demographic category have the highest rates of most types of street crime. One recent study has found a strong relationship between unemployment among black men and family disruption on the one hand, and family disruption and violent crime on the other (Sampson, 1987). As with the relationship between cigarette smoking and the incidence of lung cancer, while the correlations do not necessarily prove causes, at the least they should make us suspicious.

However, it is often heard that the reason people do not work is because they are too lazy to work. The jobs are there, it is claimed, but poor people simply are unwilling to work and prefer a life on welfare, cheap wine, and ultimately, prison. The question really involves whether people, and especially lower-class Americans, are at the core of their being naturally active or naturally idle. Some hint about the real desires of human beings can be discovered in the complaints of prisoners. In American prisons we find that one of the most persistent complaints is that there is not enough work to occupy all prisoners— not that the labor is too hard. If convicted criminals were as lazy as is often claimed, they should be quite content with years on end with no constructive work of any kind, but they are not. Rather than concocting convoluted explanations of why lower-class people commit so much armed robbery and appear so alienated from American society, perhaps the armed robbery, as well as non-violent property crime, has much of its origin in the lack of any other income prospects. In this sense armed robbery may be a rational solution to people who see no other income prospects. Correspondingly, a study of the effect on arrests of economic payments to ex-felons for a 12-month period immediately after release from prison found that such payments did reduce the number of arrests (Berk et al.) If for no other reason than self-interest, surely this nation has waited long enough to begin thinking seriously about providing employment for all those who are able to work. The improvement in our safety and the recipients' material situation and self-concept seem to be compelling reasons for such a national commitment. It should not be surprising that there is a positive statistical relationship between a high incidence of serious crime and unemployment (Cantor and Land, 1985). Thus in 1985 the Massachusetts state legislature made Massachusetts the first American state to pass the following amendment to the U.S. Constitution:

> To enact legislation presenting to the states a proposed constitutional amendment wherein the right to employment shall be guaranteed to every person in the United States in accordance with his or her capacity, at a rate of compensation sufficient to support such individual and his or her family in dignity and self-respect (Humanist Sociologist, 1986:5).

And it is not simply that more jobs are needed, but more jobs are needed that provide an "adequate living" and "self-respect" (Currie, 1985b:265). Because of competition with third-world countries most new jobs created in America are at the minimum or subminimum wage level and will not offer a real alternative to street crime.

LEGALIZATION AND DECRIMINALIZATION

Legalization and decriminalization are the most efficient methods for eliminating a crime problem and, applied to much behavior now classified as criminal, would pose no threat to society. Decriminalization, unlike legalization, might control the activity through civil fines rather than through arrests. It is sometimes suggested as an approach to handling prostitution. Decriminalization might involve medical treatment rather than arrest, as is often recommended in dealing with public drunkenness. On the other hand, legalization was used when prohibition was repealed. Americans who were routinely committing alcohol-related offenses could then legally continue their sale and distribution of alcohol. Similar changes in our nation's current vice laws are sometimes recommended in this context. Homosexual relations between consenting adults could be legalized, with no increased physical threat to the community. Prostitution could be legalized, as has been done in some parts of Nevada. The same applies to gambling, which has been legalized in some forms in Nevada, New Jersey, and a growing number of other states. As one Nevada judge said years ago: "If people want to do it, legalize it and put a tax on it, and everybody will be happy."

Perhaps the most pressing crime problem in modern America is the sale, possession, and use of various illegal drugs. Much of the total resources of the police, courts, and prisons are devoted to this problem. As a consequence, Alfred Lindesmith (1965) urged the adoption of the British system in the control of drug addiction. This system decriminalizes drug addiction by enabling addicts in Great Britain to obtain drugs legally and maintain their habit at a small cost through prescriptions from physicians. This not only legalizes what is, in fact, a physical state (addiction) but also reduces other crimes, because it is estimated that many property crimes are committed by addicts who steal to obtain the money required to support their addiction (Schur, 1965:140). Addiction is expensive only because the drugs are illegal and the risk in selling them is high, which forces the price up. If the drugs could be obtained from physicians, the price would plummet, forcing most clandestine drug dealers out of business. This happened to many bootleggers when prohibition was repealed.

Since decriminalization forces clandestine dealers out of business, we could anticipate their opposition to such legal changes, as well as opposition from narcotics control agencies whose existence and need for being are also threatened by such changes (Schur, 1965). Opposition also sometimes comes from moral conservatives, such as fundamentalist Protestant groups. Concerted opposition from such diverse groups has made legalization difficult to achieve. Yet such an approach to crime control seems especially well suited to victimless offenses, such as prostitution, gambling, and drug use. A similar decriminalization plan would be in order for the handling of public drunkenness, traditionally prosecuted as vagrancy.

In chapters 6 and 7 it was shown that repressive drug laws are based on racial prejudice and misinformation and that they are often designed as a means of excluding minorities from the job market. We should also remember that American alcohol prohibition is now recognized as a total failure in its effort to impose a rural middle-class Protestant morality on all Americans. But we have learned precious little from history. Our local, state, and federal governments continue to pump many millions of dollars into futile attempts to prohibit marihuana, cocaine, and heroin while at the same time physicians freely prescribe equally or more dangerous drugs, such as amphetamines and barbiturates. It is clear that the use of drugs associated with racial or economic minorities is legally proscribed, while the addiction of the affluent is not. It is often alleged that certain drug users must be given prison or jail sentences if only for their own welfare to help convince them to stop using dangerous drugs. The hypocrisy of this claim is apparent when it is recognized that this is never suggested for the good of barbiturate addicts, alcohol users, or cigarette smokers. Since much violent crime and property crime is associated with illegal drugs, it may be instructive to give special attention to alternatives to our current impotent attempts at drug control.

Policy Alternatives for Drug Control

1. Perhaps the best-known policy is that of criminalization of both sale and possession. This is the current practice in much of the world in attempting to control marihuana, heroin, and cocaine.

2. Another possibility involves continued criminalization of production and sale only, not of simple possession. Possession of drugs would be punished by a civil fine. Possession of small amounts of marihuana is handled in this fashion in 11 American states, while sale of these drugs is still subject to severe criminal penalties in these same states.

3. There is also the possibility of legalization of possession of specific substances while retaining criminal penalties for manufacture and sale. This is precisely the option used during the nationwide prohibition of alcohol in this country. The experience with prohibition of alcohol does not speak well for this option. The essential problem with either of these last two options is that it is an attempt at control, which is inconsistent. Possession is more or less ignored, while sale and manufacture are subject to criminal punishment. Such contradictions in the law make law enforcement more difficult because the authorities must determine who is essentially a user and who is a seller. Moreover, such inconsistent legislation breeds disrespect for the law.

4. A final solution calls for the legalization of possession, manufacture, and sale of all drugs including marihuana, cocaine, and heroin. Decriminalization of possession and sale represents a useless alternative because small civil fines cannot serve as a deterrent and large fines are uncollectable and may encourage a continued high price charged by dealers to offset these business expenses. By legalizing all drugs, governments can control, as they do with alcohol, their purity and strength and can determine the prices of these substances, as well as the age limits for legal purchase. While the possibility of legalized drugs may seem frightening to some people, once it is recognized that drug usage is largely a cultural phenomenon beyond the reach of law, people should be less concerned.

CONCLUSION

The various justifications for the punishment of crime are readily recognized and easy to understand. Ironically, the alternative of treatment or rehabilitation has even greater potential for repression than punishment, mainly because its coercive nature is not usually recognized. Political conservatives often deride the notion of rehabilitation as senseless sentimentality and argue instead for swift and sure punishment of convicted criminals as a means of controlling crime. The late J. Edgar Hoover (1958:1–2), the longtime head of the Federal Bureau of Investigation, aptly represented the conservative position:

> It is therefore imperative that law enforcement and the general public recognize and re-evaluate the rehabilitation procedures which allow ill-advised leniency to criminals. . . . In addition, moreover, soft-hearted leniency, coddling of juvenile criminals . . . should be brought out in the open.

However, political liberals typically support programs labeled as rehabilitation and oppose punishment. They see punishment as heartless as well as ineffective in controlling crime and argue that treatment is morally and intellectually superior. This continuing dialogue, and especially the liberals' claims that rehabilitation is an effective and humane method of crime control, seems to have diverted public attention from the coercive characteristics of rehabilitation programs. As will be discussed in chapter 14, the only just rehabilitation alternatives are those that attempt to open up new opportunities to people convicted of crime. Legalization is another noncoercive solution to crime control. It seems especially useful in cases of crimes without victims, such as prostitution, gambling, drug use, and vagrancy. Recently, we Americans, our elected representatives, and our Supreme Court have been so cowed and frightened by the specter of crime that we have allowed limitations to be imposed on our constitutional freedoms under the banner of crime control. In recent years a more conservative U.S. Supreme Court has seemed intent on giving those accused of crime fewer legal protections, and this, of course, affects the freedoms of all Americans. Only time will tell where this new national mood in crime control will lead.

REFERENCES

Allen, F. A.
  1981 The Decline of the Rehabilitative Ideal: Penal Policy and Social Purpose. New Haven, Conn.: Yale University Press.
American Friends Service Committee
  1971 Struggle for Justice. New York: Hill and Wang.
Ball-Rokeach, S. J. and J. F. Short, Jr.
  1985 "Collective violence: the redress of grievance and public policy." Pp. 155–180 in Lynn Curtis (ed.), American Violence and Public Policy: An Update of the National Commission on the Causes and Prevention of Violence. New Haven, Conn.: Yale University Press.
Bentham, J.
  1823 An Introduction to the Principles of Morals and Legislation. Reprinted 1948. New York: Hafner.
Berk, R. A., K. J. Lenihan, and P. H. Rossi
  1980 "Crime and poverty: some experimental evidence from ex-offenders." American Sociological Review 45(October):766–786.
Campbell, D. T. and H. L. Ross
  1968 "The Connecticut crackdown on speeding: time series data in quasi-experimental analysis." Law and Society Review 3(August):33–53.
Cantor, D. and K. C. Land
  1985 "Unemployment and crime rates in the post-World War II United States: a theoretical and empirical analysis." American Sociological Review 50(June):317–332.
Christianson, S.
  1981 "Our black prisons." Crime and Delinquency 27(July):364–375.
Clark, G.
  1969 "What happens when the police strike." New York Times Magazine, November 16:45, 176–196.
Cooper, D. D.
  1974 The Lesson of the Scaffold: The Public Execution Controversy in Victorian England. Athens, Ohio: Ohio University Press.
Cullen, F. T. and K. E. Gilbert
  1982 Reaffirming Rehabilitation. Cincinnati: Anderson.
Currie, E.
  1985a "Crimes of violence and public policy: changing directions." Pp. 41–62 in Lynn Curtis (ed.), American Violence and Public Policy: An Update of the National Commission on the Causes and Prevention of Violence. New Haven, Conn.: Yale University Press.
  1985b Confronting Crime: An American Challenge. New York: Pantheon.
Curtis, L.
  1985 "Introduction." Pp. 1–13 in Lynn Curtis (ed.), American Violence and Public Policy: An Update of the National Commission on

the Causes and Prevention of Violence. New Haven, Conn.: Yale University Press.

Dentler, R. A. and K. T. Erikson
1959 The Functions of Deviance in Groups, Social Problems 7(Fall):98–107.

Durkheim, E.
1933 The Division of Labor in Society. (George Simpson, trans.) Glencoe, Ill.: The Free Press.

Ehrlich, I.
1975 "The deterrent effect of capital punishment: a question of life and death." American Economic Review 65:397–417.

Erikson, K. T.
1966 Wayward Puritans: A Study in the Sociology of Deviance. New York: John Wiley & Sons

Furman v. *Georgia*
1972 United States Reports 408 U.S. 238, June 29.

Galliher, J. F., J. L. McCartney, and B. Baum
1974 "Nebraska's marihuana law: a case of unexpected legislative innovation." Law and Society Review 8(Spring):441–455.

Gallup Poll
1966 No. 13, (June):16.
1985 Nos. 232–233 (January–February):4.

Gibbs, J. P.
1968 "Crime, punishment, and deterrence." Southwestern Social Science Quarterly 48(March):515–530.

Graham, F. P.
1969 "Preventive detention studied as method of curbing crime." St. Louis Post-Dispatch (January 30):1, 4.

Greenberg, J. and J. Himmelstein
1969 "Varieties of attack on the death penalty." Crime and Delinquency 15(January): 112–120.

Gregg v. *Georgia*
1976 United States Reports 429 U.S. 875, October 4.

Grupp, S. E. (ed.)
1971 Theories of Punishment. Bloomington: Indiana University Press.

Hall, J.
1952 Theft, Law, and Society. 2nd ed. Indianapolis: Bobbs-Merrill.

Harris, R.
1968 The Fear of Crime. New York: Praeger.

Hoover, J. E.
1958 "Statement of Director J. Edgar Hoover." FBI Law Enforcement Bulletin, XXVII (November):1–2. (Reprinted in David Dressler (ed.), Readings in Criminology and Penology. New York: Columbia University Press, 1964.)

Humanist Sociologist
1986 "Massachusetts urges constitutional guaran-

tees for employment and income." 11(April):5–6.

Janis, I. L. and S. Feshback
1953 "Effects of fear-arousing communications." Journal of Abnormal and Social Psychology 48(January):78–92.

Johnson, R.
1981 Condemned to Die: Life Under Sentence of Death. New York: Elsevier.

Lindesmith, A. R.
1965 The Addict and the Law. Bloomington: Indiana University Press.

Martinson, R.
1974 "What works—questions and answers about prison reform." Public Interest (Spring): 22–54.

Morris, N.
1974a The Future of Imprisonment. Chicago: University of Chicago Press.
1974b "The future of imprisonment: toward a punitive philosophy." Michigan Law Review 71(May):1161–1180.

Moynihan, D. P.
1969 Maximum Feasible Misunderstanding. New York: The Free Press.

Pepinsky, H. E. and P. Jesilow
1984 Myths That Cause Crime. Cabin John, Md.: Seven Locks Press.

Platt, A. M.
1977 The Child Savers: The Invention of Delinquency. 2nd ed. Chicago: University of Chicago Press.

Ranulf, S.
1964 Moral Indignation and Middle Class Psychology. New York: Schocken Books.

Rothman, D. J.
1971 The Discovery of the Asylum: Social Order and Disorder in the New Republic. Boston: Little, Brown.

Sampson, R. J.
1987 "Urban black violence: the effect of male joblessness and family disruption." American Journal of Sociology 93(September):348–382.

Schur, E. M.
1965 Crimes Without Victims. Englewood Clifffs, N.J.: Prentice Hall.

Schwartz, R. D. and J. H. Skolnick
1962 "Two studies of legal stigma." Social Problems 10(Fall):133–142.

Sellin, T. (ed.)
1967 Capital Punishment. New York: Harper & Row.

Tittle, C. R.
1969 "Crime rates and legal sanctions." Social Problems 16(Spring):409–423.
1980 Sanctions and Social Deviance: The Question of Deterrence. New York: Praeger Publishers.

United States Bureau of the Census
1986   Statistical Abstract of the United States. 106th ed. Washington, D.C.: U.S. Government Printing Office, p. 394.

van den Haag, E.
1975   Punishing Criminals: Concerning a Very Old and Painful Question. New York: Basic Books.

von Hirsch, A.
1976   Doing Justice: the Choice of Punishments. New York: Hill & Wang.

Walker, N.
1971   Sentencing in a Rational Society. New York: Basic Books.

Wilson, J. Q.
1975   Thinking About Crime. New York: Basic Books.

Zimring, F. E.
1971   Perspectives on Deterrence. Washington, D.C.: National Institute of Mental Health, Center for Studies of Crime and Delinquency.

12
HISTORY OF INCARCERATION

In modern America we take it for granted that the primary response to serious law violation will be incarceration. It seems logical that the state will take away the freedom of those who violate the criminal laws both to protect society and to punish the law violator. But, in fact, in the history of the world incarceration as a response to law violation is the exception rather than the rule. For example, during the Middle Ages when most offenses of any magnitude were punishable by death and corporal punishment, the only use of imprisonment was to detain individuals while they awaited trial or, after a trial and a guilty verdict, while they awaited execution or flogging. One practice was to have a judge ask the local landed nobility to keep the individuals locked in their castles in return for some payment. Since custody served only a limited purpose, there was no need to develop large institutions for confinement.

ANCIENT AND MEDIEVAL PENAL PRACTICES

Even earlier, in ancient Athens, flogging was the usual punishment for slaves, who were not considered citizens of the state (Sellin, 1976). Most of these offenses by slaves were settled between the slave's owner and the victims. In Athens, which is still associated with justice and democracy, there was more severe punishment for slaves than for foreigners and more severe punishment for foreigners than for citizens of Athens. Slaves could be killed at will by their owners, and they were routinely tortured during trials to determine whether they were telling the truth. No one except a slave could be tortured. In ancient Rome, initially citizens were not subject to the same punishments as were slaves, but during later phases of the empire citizens lost all advantages and were punished the same as slaves. The reason for the change was that initially citizenship was a privilege enjoyed by only a few people, but by AD 200 citizenship was common.

In medieval England physical punishment was widely used, including mutilation and death. Later, with the growing mercantile expansion of Europe, punishment by sentencing to galley slavery and transportation developed for economic reasons but were rationalized as merciful (Orland, 1975). Transportation was used to enable business people to locate the vast amount of cheap labor necessary to develop the New World, while galley slavery was a critical means of powering merchant ships. Thus galley slavery and slavery on public works, such as fortifications, were to a great extent a consequence of a growing reluctance in the thirteenth and fourteenth centuries to use the death penalty. And this reluctance to use the death penalty in turn was a consequence of economic needs. In England, where there was wide use of convicts as galley slaves, a problem developed involving what should be done with old, sick, or invalid oarsmen (Sellin, 1976).

By the close of the sixteenth century, galley ships were no longer considered effective and were replaced by sailing ships (Tappan, 1960). Many of the slaves no longer needed to power the galley ships were detained on the old unused ships anchored in the harbors until transportation began to be widely used in the 1700s (Sellin, 1976). Transportation to the American colonies ended with American independence in 1776, but transportation to Australia lasted until the 1860s. In a similar fashion, even before the Revolution in Russia, Siberia was used as a location to deposit law violators. Some offenders were sent to Siberia for a specific period of time, while some were given life sentences. Depending on their sentence, some prisoners had a much greater degree of freedom than did others.

In 1599 Holland gave its prison system a monopoly on the grueling task of chopping wood to be used in making dyes for its cloth industry, which was booming at the time (Sellin, 1976). This shows a close resemblance to the current practice of allowing prisoners to learn trades impossible to use elsewhere, such as making license plates for automobiles. In fact, it was common for the early houses of correction in Europe to supply merchants with laborers, with no effort made at reforming the prisoners.

For economic reasons an institution called the Bridewell was established in London in 1552. Essentially it was a workhouse for destitute individuals (Tappan, 1960). The feudal system was breaking up, causing great unemployment for many of the former serfs and mercenary soldiers, who were wandering in the cities. These vagrants, even if not guilty of any offense other than idleness, were incarcerated in the Bridewell to get them off the streets. (See the discussion in chapter 6 on how the first vagrancy laws emerged.) In the Bridewell the length of incarceration was generally longer than in the early jails, and in this sense it was a forerunner of the modern prison. For the first time prisoners were in an institution for control, not merely awaiting punishment. Later the workhouse came to be used for petty offenders such as alcoholic vagrants whose stay was generally rather short in duration and where prisoners were forced to perform various types of productive labor. These later workhouses were generally run by county or city governments. Today jails are run by city and county governments and are still used to detain people awaiting trial and punishment, but also, of course, to incarcerate individuals for minor offenses.

EFFECT OF ECONOMIC DEVELOPMENT

Another interpretation of the class origins of punishment is that of Rusche and Kirchheimer (1939), who observed that specific forms of punishment are associated with given stages of economic development. In support of their argument, they provided numerous examples. They asserted that generally conditions in prisons are determined by the living standard of the lowest classes of free people; the living standard of prisoners must be lower, or else prisons hold no threat. Rusche and Kirchheimer (1939:8) also traced the development of punishment through the Middle Ages: "Penance and fines were the preferred methods of punishments in the early Middle Ages. They were gradually replaced during the later Middle Ages by a harsh system of corporal and capital punishment which, in its turn, gave way to imprisonment about the seventeenth century." Initially, the lot of the workers was quite good, but in the later Middle Ages conditions deteriorated "and the inability of lower-class evildoers to pay fines in money led to the substitution of corporal punishment in their case" (Rusche and Kirchheimer, 1939:9).

> In practice, it [the fine] was reserved for the rich, whereas corporal punishment became the punishment of the poor (page 17). . . . The constant increase in crime among the ranks of the poverty-stricken proletariat, especially in the big towns, made it necessary for the ruling classes to search for new methods which would make the administration of criminal law more effective (page 14). . . . The creation of a law effective in combating offenses against property was one of the chief preoccupations of the rising urban bourgeoisie (page 15). . . . The poorer the masses became, the harsher the punishments in order to deter them from crime (page 18).

At this time, according to Rusche and Kirchheimer (1939:19–20), mutilation became quite common, and "the whole system of punishment in the later Middle Ages makes it quite clear that there was no shortage of labor."

In short, the inability of the poor to pay fines led to corporal punishment for them, and the brutal system of punishment in the later Middle Ages reflected a plentiful labor supply. The working masses were expendable as far as the elites were concerned. The transition to a capitalist economy in fourteenth- and fifteenth-century Europe led to the development of harsh criminal punishments directed at the lower classes because of the rising crime rate among this increasingly poverty-stricken group that had no place in the emerging capitalist economy. The punishment imposed was determined not by the crime committed but by the economic status of the criminal. It was harsher if the culprit was poor. However, when a labor shortage developed in the seventeenth century, poor convicted criminals were no longer executed or mutilated but were put to work in prisons to help ease the shortage.

AMERICAN PENAL PRACTICES

Early Prison Systems

Historians have documented that in the eighteenth century new concepts about the rights and dignity of human beings began to develop. This new attitude about the nature of people helped spawn numerous revolutions, including those in the United States, France, and Russia. People in Europe and the New World began to see themselves as possessing a right to more freedom than they previously had. It is no coincidence that at this time the concept of punishment through confinement developed. Punitive confinement only makes sense when people place a high value on what they believe to be their inherent right to freedom. Obviously it is impossible to threaten to punish a slave with imprisonment. Those who are not free cannot have freedom taken from them. It is in this historical context that the writings of both Beccaria and Bentham emerged, which were discussed in chapter 2. Recall that Beccaria (1775) demanded equality under the law for all people, and Bentham (1823) called for limitations on criminal punishments to the minimum necessary for deterrence.

The first institution specifically designed for youthful offenders was developed in Rome in 1703 (Tappan, 1960). But it was not until the 1800s that similar institutions began to be opened in the United States. At the outset it was hoped that such institutions would be especially nonpunitive and emphasize the education of the young. However, more often these institutions, often called reformatories, have gravitated simply to a concern with preventing escapes of prisoners and have become merely prisons for young people. Institutions for adult prisoners also developed during the 1700s and 1800s, and in this the United States was something of a leader. The origins of such institutions are found in the efforts of the Quaker William Penn. Penn and his followers were successful in erecting the first jail in Philadelphia in 1682. In 1776 a new prison was opened in Philadelphia, and in 1790 it became the first state prison in Pennsylvania.

In 1829 another prison was begun in Philadelphia. This prison was established on two principles: total separation of prisoners from each other and punishment by hard labor. Each prisoner was confined in a separate cell and was never let out for the duration of the prison sentence. Generally the individuals spent their time working at some handicraft in their cells. Adjacent to the cells was a small private walled courtyard where the prisoners were allowed to exercise for short periods of time. There were 400 cells in seven cell blocks radiating out from a central rotunda. The only person the prisoners ever saw was the guard who brought them their food, but the guard was forbidden to speak. No letters or visits from friends were ever permitted. The advantages to this system were (1) that it made it possible for the prison staff to totally segregate the prisoners from each other and thus avoid the possibility that they would further contaminate each other with their evil thoughts and (2) that it made control of prisoners easy. The disadvantages of this type of prison were that it was expensive to build and operate and moreover that it often led to madness among prisoners. But the ease of operation of this prison system, sometimes called the Pennsylvania or separate system, attracted a great deal of international attention and admiration.

A somewhat different type of prison system, often called the congregate or silent system, was developed in Auburn, New York, in 1816. The goal of this system also was to prevent prisoners from contaminating each other, but the means to this end were different than those used by the Pennsylvania system. Those people confined in the Auburn prison left their cells to work in the prison shops during the day. But they were not allowed to speak to each other. When moving to and from their work assignments and meals, they were required to march in "lock step," each prisoner being required to put his head down and to put one hand on the shoulder of the prisoner ahead of him. Most prisons in the United States originally followed the basic ideas of the Auburn system, perhaps primarily because it made possible industrial production in prison shops, which was impossible under the Pennsylvania plan. Those advocating the Pennsylvania system claimed that the Auburn plan really did not keep prisoners from communicating, but proponents of the Auburn system brought up the embarrassing problem of the systematic creation of madness by the Pennsylvania plan. There was intense debate between the proponents of each type of system until around 1860. Both types of systems have long ago fallen into disuse. As will be shown in chapter 13, dealing with the organization of prisons, while prisoners may be regimented in prisons today, they are still allowed many more freedoms than were found in either the Pennslyvania or Auburn systems.

Theoretical Explanation of Incarceration

Most historians view the development of prisons and mental hospitals as something of a reform over previous practices, which included many types of corporal punishment and the widespread use of the death penalty (Rothman, 1971). But this explanation does not address the issue of why this particular type of reform emerged, nor why this particular reform emerged at this particular time in the United States. David Rothman (1971) is well known for tracing the specific origins of our massive reliance on confinement in the United States in our feeble efforts at crime control.

Rothman's view is that the orphan asylum, the reformatory, the penitentiary, the insane asylum, and the almshouse (for the poor) were all developed in the United States at approximately the same time in the hope that they each could help ensure the cohesion of the community at a time when many people were alarmed by the speed of the social changes that were occurring. Many citizens in the young American nation around 1820 to 1830 recognized that rapid changes were occurring and felt this carried with it possible dangers and opportunities (Rothman, 1971). Colonial attitudes toward orphans, the poor, and the insane, as well as toward those convicted of crimes, were quite different from those found during the early 1800s. During the 1700s poverty and crime were not considered serious social problems. These problems were not defined as symptoms of social decay but rather were attributed solely to individual responsibility.

Therefore, in the case of crime, colonial policy makers devoted little attention to developing programs aimed at eradicating this behavior or reforming the law violator (Rothman, 1971). In addition, since crime and poverty were not really dreaded, no effort was made to isolate those people involved. According to colonial religious belief poverty was considered inevitable, and traditionally its relief was considered the responsibility of the affluent. The poor people were to be pitied but not feared. There was somewhat greater apprehension about crime. But crime was not seen as an indication of any fundamental flaw in society, and colonal citizens did not expect to eradicate it. According to Christian thought, mere mortals were born to sin. A wide spectrum of behavior was considered to be crime since sin was often also a crime. Offenses of the time included idolatry, blasphemy, and witchcraft. Even though policy makers were not terribly worried by these crimes, the penalties were severe, because these crimes were not just transgressions against the society but also against God.

In the hope of counteracting the powerful temptations of man, colonial leaders relied on the family, church, and community social relations. Laws were enacted to assist the local citizens who had material needs (others, such as dependent strangers, were excluded). Few communities had workhouses, and most supported the poor in their own homes whenever possible. Similarly, a prison sentence was not likely for those convicted of crimes. Usually jails were simply filled with people awaiting trial. Rather than imprisonment, the two most common colonial punishments were fines and whipping. Typically if citizens could not pay a fine, they received the whip. This shows yet again the way in which economic circumstances determine the nature of penal law. The stocks were also used in some minor cases instead of a fine. The stocks, which held the person up for public ridicule, were a great deterrent in small colonial communities.

But the colonial America just described began to change during the 1800s. Both geographical and social mobility seemed to grow beyond belief (Rothman, 1971). The West was opened, and new fortunes were created overnight. Immediately after the American War of Independence laws were made considerably more lenient to coincide with revolutionary ideals. At this time many in this new nation felt that just as colonial laws had exploited citizens and encouraged crime, the new American laws would discourage crime. Capital punishment for crimes was mostly abolished, which meant that some sort of prison would be necessary to house criminals who would have been executed under the earlier colonial laws.

No thought was initially given to just what these institutions should be like, but by the 1820s it was obvious to American policymakers that more attention would have to be given to these institutions. It was now painfully clear that the belief of the 1790s that crime would disappear after the Revolution had been naive. Thus attention was now given to the life histories of convicted criminals in the hope of determining the proper type of institutions to build to overcome these problems. In New York's Auburn penitentiary, officials developed life histories of hundreds of convicts in an effort to discover the causes of criminal behavior and the necessary remedies. These researchers found, for example, that individuals who committed a crime usually lacked proper discipline during their childhood, no matter how old they were when their first crime occurred. Government policymakers now began to believe that crime was really not natural or inevitable after all and could be curtailed by the proper action of the state—a view that still exists in contemporary America.

During the early 1800s many Americans judged their rapidly changing society according to the relative stability of the colonial period and determined that the new mobility was a central corrupting influence (Rothman, 1971). They were fearful of this rapid change but at the same time had a new optimism about ultimately controlling crime. These beliefs about the causes of crime led to the penitentiary as the solution. Great attention was given to the design of such institutions—their external appearance, internal arrangement, and daily routine—in an attempt to eliminate all those influences that were breeding crime in the community. American prisons, rather than just being afterthoughts as they had been immediately after the Revolution, became famous for creative policies throughout the Western world by the 1830s.

The issue was not whether the penitentiary was a cure for crime, because everyone seemed to know that this type of institution was essential, but whether the Pennsylvania or Auburn system was the most effective in doing the job. Both plans placed great emphasis on preventing prisoners from communicating with, and thereby contaminating, each other. If the offender was isolated from all corrupting contacts, the prison system could instill in convicts the type of discipline that their parents had earlier neglected. The promise of the penitentiary seemed unlimited.

If incarceration had been seen as only a necessary alternative to capital and corporal punishment, then there would have been a minimum of investment in these institutions. But that was not the case. The institutions built at this time were elaborate and expensive, and great attention was given to architecture. The penitentiary was symmetrically arranged to help create the order so long missing in the lives of convicts. The daily routine of everything being done at the same time every day was also designed to reflect this order and stability.

Yet there was a great difference between the theory of how the institution should operate and its actual practice. Prison labor never paid for all prison expenses as had originally been hoped, in part because free laborers and business owners complained and often were successful in pressing for legislation restricting the types of prison industries. But hard labor was still stressed as valuable in and of itself, even if the prisons could make no products and show no profits. Sometimes the work merely involved moving a pile of rocks from one side of the prison yard to the other and back again. Wardens organized the daily life of prisoners in an orderly military style, including a military formation and roll call every morning. The idea of institutional treatment for both criminal behavior and mental illness was that the respective institutions could teach a sense of order and discipline, a sense of one's limits, and a satisfaction with one's position to offset the fluidity of society.

While poverty was not considered a problem during the colonial period, by the 1820s Americans began to see poor people as a source of unrest. Thus the almshouse was established to incarcerate and reform the poor, to remove them from the corruptions of the community. Like the penitentiary and the mental asylum, the almshouse emphasized order and discipline.

Originally all types of institutions that confined people were developed for the purpose of reforming the people confined, but it soon became apparent that this was not working. Even control, much less real reform, within the institution became difficult. But the institutions were still used, despite the difference between theory and practice. Once the earlier idealism was lost, these institutions could harness their incredible discipline and isolation for purposes of political coercion of the endless waves of immigrants who were arriving by the mid-1800s (Rothman, 1971).

Colonial Crimes and Justice

As noted above, originally in the American colonies there was a close association between crimes and sins. The reason for this was that the founders of these colonies looked to the Bible for guidance in drafting their criminal laws (see Nelson, 1967). This similarity of sin and crime lasted until approximately the 1750s, and by 1810 a system of law enforcement similar to that of today had emerged, which emphasized the protection of private property. The question is, What happened between 1760 and 1810 that can account for this change in the basic function of the law from the preservation of morality to the protection of property?

In Massachusetts, for example, prior to 1770 most prosecutions were for offenses against God and religion, incuding fornication, adultery, and violation of the Sabbath. Offenses against private property were less common. In 1770 the person convicted of a crime was not considered an outcast from society, but rather an ordinary person who had sinned. At the time it was felt that crime like sin could strike anywhere and anyone. Correspondingly, government records from this period indicate that citizens from all social strata were among those convicted. Convicted criminals were not isolated from the community, as they are today. Violators were fined or administered some type of corporal punishment or even sold into servitude. None of these punishments isolated the convicted person from the society.

Penal Reform in the New American Nation

During the years following the War of Independence from Britain prosecutions for immorality nearly ceased, and economically motivated crimes and their prosecutions increased greatly. These economically motivated crimes were committed mainly by urban poor people. With the advent of this type of crime, hard labor emerged as a typical punishment. The old colonial practice of a thief paying treble damages was not workable because so many thieves could not pay these fines. Equally important was the fact that during the colonial period victims could sell convicts into servitude but that later there was no market for convict servants, and if a convict could not be sold, he or she went free after 30 days. Meanwhile a reform movement had begun that pressed for prison rather than corporal punishment. Thus at this point hard labor in prison seemed to be the only answer—the hard labor presumably paying the costs of prison construction and the continuing cost of housing and feeding the prisoners.

It is essential to remember that there is a link between the crime control objectives in any society and the development and needs of the local economy (Adamson, 1984). A review of the period after the War of Independence shows that the labor supply and business cycle influenced how convicted criminals were processed by the legal system; convicts were treated either as threats to the economic system or as exploitable economic resources. Between 1790 and 1812 corporal and capital punishment were eliminated except for murder and treason. At this point criminals were not seen as a threat to the economic system, and so the prison policy stressed reforming criminals, not merely deterring them from crime. Prison industries, therefore, were established with this reform in mind.

The prison reformers were composed of wealthy and powerful merchants who viewed prisoners as a resource to be expoited. During this post-Revolutionary War period there was a growing demand for, and great scarcity of, labor. Thus at this time we find that prison industry was geared to the nation's chief industries: housing and shipbuilding (Adamson, 1984). A lot of labor-intensive work was required in these industries to prepare materials for use by skilled tradesmen. This work included making nails, sawing stone, and polishing marble. At this time there was no strong objection to selling prison-made goods on the open market.

After the War of 1812 to 1814, a long recession began that lasted until 1822 (Adamson, 1984). Predictably, convicts began to be seen as more of a threat at this time. While there had been little trading with Europe during the war, after normalization of relations many American firms could not compete with the more efficient British firms and therefore went bankrupt as cheap imports flooded this country. The situation was so severe that one fifth of the population of New York City was on welfare in 1814. This recession effectively killed prison industries. As the surplus labor population continued to grow, the idea of reforming convicts through labor became more and more difficult to defend. There were increasing calls for a more severe disciplinary system to deal with the increasing number of felony sentences at this time. The problem was that the very fact that the felons were provided with a roof over their heads and food made life better for them than for many of the noncriminal poor. Therefore a harsh innovation developed: the treadmill, which was a large wheel with footholds that turned when walked upon. The treadmill was often connected to heavy grindstones. Policymakers feared that if prison conditions were not made more harsh, there would be an uprising of the noncriminal poor.

Beginning in 1825 and through 1837, convicts were seen as a resource once again. A massive amount of cheap labor was needed for road and canal construction, and the shortage of both skilled and unskilled workers was a chronic problem. But by 1837 and through 1860 the tables turned again, and convicts were seen anew as a threat. This was a period of massive immigration, which many felt contributed to the growth of crime, especially in the coastal cities, where many immigrants settled. Predictably, the number of inmates in state prisons tripled from 1850 to 1860.

In the South after the Civil War from 1865 to 1890, state officials developed a prison system that was apparently intended to fill much the same role as had slavery (Adamson, 1984). The convict lease system, sometimes called the contract system, filled this role very nicely. Often the convicts were hired out to planters, mining companies, and railroad contractors. The southern economy was in ruins at the time, and masses of free and restless former slaves roamed the countryside. The question for white leaders was how to control these former slaves at a low cost. This contract system also made money for the state and encouraged northern capitalists to invest in the South because of the availability of cheap labor.

When the southern states leased prisoners to private companies, they gave these companies complete powers of supervision and discipline over the prisoners. State officials by the 1870s and 1880s had no legal power to regulate the living and working conditions in the work camps. Some historians have claimed that the reason the southern states adopted the convict lease system was because of the destruction of southern prisons during the Civil War as well as the fiscal crisis after the war. But this development was not merely because of fiscal problems but was "a political means to re-establish white supremacy in the South" and "a functional replacement for slavery" (Adamson, 1983:556). During the period of slavery "the very idea of imprisonment as a punishment for crimes committed by slaves was a contradiction" (Adamson, 1983:557), because slaves were already prisoners. Thus the typical punishments for slaves were public whippings and executions. Most southern states had contructed prisons by 1850, but these were smaller than those in the North. After the Civil War southern states also relied on informal social control through vigilantism and lynchings rather than professional law enforcement.

After the Civil War there was an acute need for cheap labor to build railroads in the South, and the convict lease system allegedly both punished and deterred crime but also mobilized the required labor. After the war many southern states passed laws that required long sentences for minor theft, which served to greatly increase the size of the convict populations—Mississippi's grew 300 percent in four years and Georgia's tripled in 2 years (Adamson, 1983). These laws not only mobilized labor but "were designed to eliminate the threat posed by a wandering army of propertyless blacks" (Adamson, 1983:562). In most southern states over 95 percent of the convict populations were blacks, but whites and blacks were totally segregated with blacks being leased outside the prison and whites working inside the prison. The convict lease system was very profitable for both the state governments and the private companies. By the 1880s northern states had abolished the contract system of convict labor in part because of the objections of the labor movement, but this did not happen in the South.

This system lasted well into the twentieth century. The chain gang in the southeastern states is somewhat like contract labor, but here the prisoners sleep in confinement and work outside. In Georgia, for example, chain gangs have been used to work on the roads and highways. This is especially degrading because it puts the convicts on public display. One of the unintended functions of the prison is that to some extent it does hide the identity of the prisoner from public view.

It was during the opening decades of the 1900s, called the "progressive" period in American history, that we find the following ideas developing: probation, parole, the indeterminate sentence, and the juvenile court (Rothman, 1980). The idea of order being instilled by institutions was now rejected. At this time authorities assumed the need for individualization of treatment. One offender might need treatment in the community, another might need a short term in a prison, and another a longer term. What was needed was the possibility of discretionary responses to each type of case. Presentence reports with information on the offender's family, home, and work history have their origins in this period.

After the Civil War there was an increased awareness of the problems in prisons occasioned by understaffing, overcrowding, contract labor, and corporal punishment methods such as the "pully," which totally suspended a person in air by just the wrists (Rothman, 1980), or the "water crib," which involved cuffing a person's hands behind his or her back, placing the person face down in a coffinlike box, and then gradually adding water. With this knowledge of past abuses, probation and parole caught on quickly after 1900. In 1900 only six states allowed probation, but by 1920 all states had probation for juveniles and 33 states had adopted this procedure for adults. Few states had parole in 1900, but by 1923 more than half of all releases from prison were through parole. Although probation was widely recognized as ineffective, its use continued because prosecutors, judges, and defense attorneys liked it, since it was used as a reward to entice defendants to plead guilty (Rothman, 1980). However, these progressive reforms did not so much improve conditions for convicted criminals as cause problems of their own. Probation, for example, had the effect of increasing the total number of people brought under the supervision of the criminal justice system.

   Parole was a very unpopular innovation, especially with the police who claimed it was responsible for the failure to control crime. It was well known that parole supervision practices were a farce. It survived, however, because prison wardens believed they needed it, for both the indeterminate sentence and parole made control of the offender more, not less, complete. Prisoners felt forced to bow to staff demands if they ever hoped for release on parole prior to finishing their complete sentences. For their part, the juvenile courts were without rules of evidence and often without the possibility of appeal; a youth was thus totally at the mercy of the judge. Juvenile institutions were supposed to be like a family, with intimate social relations. Moreover, the names of these institutions were often changed from reformatories to boys' schools or training schools, and new facilities often were built around a cottage plan. But in fact it was difficult to distinguish a juvenile institution from a prison in terms of the actual practices used in these institutions (Rothman, 1980).

   The progressive reformers were graduates of universities and were influenced by the new social sciences, which had courses on crime. But these reformers had no quarrel with American capitalism. They merely believed that the government would have to offer some guidance to business interests. These reformers believed there should be recreation and amusements in prisons and no lock step, rules of silence, or restrictions on letters and visits from friends and relatives (Rothman, 1980). In this context, the addition of psychiatrists to the staffs of prisons was merely symbolic because in reality very few were hired (29 full-time psychiatrists in 13 states in 1926), and they really did not have the skills to help prisoners. Educational and vocational programs were also stressed but seldom actually implemented.

Reforms in Juvenile Justice, 1909 to 1948

   The discussions thus far have indicated how economic considerations are responsible for changes over time in the legal system. A different type of economic pressure for custodial institutions for juveniles is that all reforms in the juvenile justice system can cause these institutions to quickly lose their population (Rains, 1984). For example, one institution for juveniles was begun in Montreal in 1912. The population in this institution rose dramatically during the last part of World War I because of the increasing number of children in trouble and unsupervised while their fathers were away at war. Predictably, after the war when the fathers returned, there was increasing use of probation by the courts, and the number of children sent to this reform school declined.

At this crisis point the school and its prominent board of directors asked for public donations, since tax monies were more and more difficult to obtain given the shrinking numbers of children being sent by the courts. The institution also tried to recruit voluntary cases, that is, boys sent by their parents rather than by the courts. Thus in 1922 the number of voluntary cases in the institution increased by more than 300 percent. Also the board lobbied for indefinite sentences in the hope of keeping each boy for a longer period of time and for higher age limits for children to retain the legal status of delinquent. In accordance with these wishes the legal age limit for incarceration in juvenile institutions was raised from 16 to 18 years old. The indefinite commitment, which was a "core tenet" of the movement to reform delinquent children and which held that children should only be released when reformed according to the judgment of institutional staff, can be seen as having essentially an economic basis to ensure survival of the institution. Indefinite commitment also made the children easier to control because, as with adult prisoners, their release date hinged on pleasing the institutional staff.

When World War II ended, the institution's population again fell. The courts were increasingly reluctant to send younger boys there because of concern about the effects on these younger boys of exposure to older hard-core delinquent boys. Therefore the institution was increasingly used as a place of last resort for the hard-core older juvenile, which was not at all the original intent. Financial survival required that the institution modify its goals or cease operation entirely (Rains, 1984).

CONTEMPORARY PRISONS

Types of Prisons and Prisoners

Modern prisons are typically classified on the basis of the type and the number of precautions that are taken to control the behavior of inmates, especially to limit their possibility of escape.

1. Minimum security institutions generally have no fence around their perimeter and no towers for armed guards. Usually none of the staff carry firearms. Institutions for juveniles and women are typically minimum security.
2. Medium security institutions may have a fence or wall and perhaps even a few guard towers on the perimeter. Even so, most staff members are not armed.

3. Maximum security prisons usually have high walls, with many armed guards on the walls to prevent escape, no matter how great the expense in salaries.

These classifications represent only very rough distinctions, and in fact, there is some disagreement about which specific institutions qualify for each category. Part of the basis for this disagreement is that these categories only deal with perimeter security and say nothing of internal security within the institution. In some institutions, for example, great emphasis is placed on perimeter security with few resources devoted to control within the prison—to protect prisoners from each other. However, it is less common, but not unheard of, for the prison staff to devote most of their resources to internal controls, leaving the perimeter relatively unnoticed and giving the casual observer the false impression of a minimum security institution.

It should also be mentioned that within most institutions inmates experience differing degrees of freedom based on the degree to which the staff believe the inmates can be trusted to control themselves without supervision. The two extremes in freedom range from solitary confinement to the trustee status. Inmates in solitary confinement are alone in their cells 24 hours a day, except for a brief exercise period in some cases. Often these cells do not have even the minimim of conveniences that are found in other cells, sometimes not even having a bed, chair, or light fixture. Also prisoners in solitary confinement may not be given the full ration of food provided to other prisoners and may lose the privilege of seeing visitors. There are three reasons why a prisoner may be in solitary confinement: (1) Those on death row are held in solitary confinement. (2) Some are in solitary confinement as punishment for violation of institutional regulations. (3) Finally, some are in solitary confinement for their own protection from other prisoners. This last alternative is sometimes called administrative segregation. Only the second type of solitary confinement, which is used as a type of punishment, typically entails all the elements of the spartan existence described immediately above.

On the other extreme is the trustee status, which is generally only given to those in whom the staff have the greatest confidence. Many times these prisoners are so close to finishing their sentence that the staff is sure they will not try to escape. Trustees are generally allowed to work outside the walls of the prison without immediate supervision.

Another method of classifying institutions relies on the types of routines and central goals developed in differing prisons (Fenton et al., 1967:13). Considering a prison's routines and goals we can locate the following distinctions:

1. *Confinement-oriented institutions* are those where the chief concern is with discipline and control of prisoners. In such a setting there is little communication between the prisoners and the staff and a maximum of social distance between the two groups.
2. *Training-oriented institutions* specialize in academic and vocational training. Those in charge of such institutions usually believe that discipline combined with hard

work will lead to good adjustment after release from the institution. In such institutions there is still very little communication and great social distance between the staff and the prisoners.

3. *Treatment-oriented institutions* stress individualized psychotherapy for the prisoners. Even in these settings there is often considerable social distance between the staff and the prisoners.

As was noted in the discussion of organized crime, in any organization commands are followed for at least two reasons, because of either the expertise or the power of the person issuing the commands. That is, people may voluntarily obey commands because of a belief in the technical competence of the person issuing the orders, for example, a physician telling a patient when to take a prescribed medicine. Orders may also be obeyed because of the power or authority of the person issuing the commands, as in the case of a shop foreman ordering the other workers to speed up their production or in the case of a military officer telling lower-ranking soldiers to charge the enemy. In these latter two examples obedience is less voluntary than in the first illustration.

This distinction is mentioned here because in traditional institutions oriented to custody, prison inmates comply with the rules in less than a voluntary fashion (Johnson, 1974). The guards merely tell the prisoners what to do, and their commands are backed up by guns. To change an institution from a custodial type of orientation to an institution with a less rigid routine where a real attempt at treatment or rehabilitation is made, requires that persuasive controls be substituted for coercive controls. However, for persuasive controls to work prisoners must voluntarily believe in the treatment staff's technical competence to offer them leadership and sound advice. But since the idea of rehabilitation in prisons is of doubtful merit it becomes difficult to convince prisoners to cooperate with such programs.

Prisons for Women

Special mention should be made of prisons for women because they present a much different set of circumstances than do prisons for men. Reviewing the history of the incarceration of women indicates that women have consistently made up less than 5 percent of the total prison population in this country (Additon, 1951; Simon, 1975). Originally women were confined in prisons for men but in separate quarters, and this is still the practice in some institutions. Where there were separate prisons built for women, the older institutions were built on a traditional prison plan; but all new institutions are composed of a collection of cottages. Thus many institutions for women are not prisonlike in appearance, and inmates have individual rooms in these cottages rather than barred cells.

There are at least two possible reasons why prisons for women are different. Since the numbers of women to be confined are so small compared to the numbers for men, the expense in building high-quality institutions for women is small. But the fact of fewer female prisoners might just have the opposite effect, for the small numbers could just as easily make any allocation of funds for institutions all that much harder to secure. Thus, there is accumulating evidence of a more influential factor: as a society we are not as fearful and as obsessed with revenge in dealing with female offenders as we are in dealing with male law violators. We are therefore less concerned with prison security and the prevention of escapes and more amenable to the idea of minimum security facilities (Adler, 1975). It is often true that even those women who have been convicted of murder are housed in minimum security institutions.

In the less populous states where there are too few female prisoners to justify having a separate facility for them, combining resources with neighboring states is sometimes recommended (Tappan, 1960). But even with such regional institutions there is not likely to be sufficient funds to build different institutions to isolate various types of female offenders from each other, as is usually attempted with men. Moreover, this idea of regional institutions has the decided drawback of placing the institution at such a great distance from most prisoners' friends and family that visits to the prison become almost impossible.

Vocational training for women in prisons has traditionally been even more inadequate than in most prisons for men (Tappan, 1960; Simon, 1975). It is sometimes seen as an inefficient use of tax money to set up schools and vocational training programs to service a relatively small group of female offenders. This same argument, citing the small numbers, is used to justify little expenditure for recreation and entertainment for these women as well. In addition, since women are not feared, the recreational facilities and vocational training programs in women's institutions can be ignored without anyone feeling any great risk (Adler, 1975; Simon, 1975). Moreover, traditionally women have not been seen as a part of the labor force, and thus vocational training is not viewed as so essential for them. Yet over the past several decades an ever-increasing percentage of women have entered the labor market; and, now the majority of American women work full time outside the home (U.S. Department of Commerce, 1985). But the largely lower-class women in prisons have always been forced into the labor market. Thus if this stereotype of nonworking women applies to any American women, which is doubtful, it certainly does not apply to them. In line with the obviously incorrect and sexist stereotypes of the occupational needs of female offenders, we find that the training programs that are available are typically courses is cosmetology, typing, or nurse's aide training.

Microhistory of a New Institution*

The stated goals of the administrators of most new prisons emphasize the education and rehabilitation of their charges. However, it often happens that after the new institution has been in operation for awhile several escapes occur,

*The information in the following section of this chapter was taken from J. F. Galliher, "Change in a Correctional Institution: A Case Study of the Tightening-up Process," Crime and Delinquency 18(July 1972):263–270.

and consequently the priorities of the staff begin to shift to a primary concern for control of the prisoners. The old saying used by prison staff that "you can't treat 'em, if you can't keep 'em" obviously applies here. Education and rehabilitation pay off only in the long run, if at all, while escapes attract immediate negative attention. During crisis situations involving escapes, prison administrators are often under intense pressure to place more emphasis on security.

What follows is the story of a midwestern state prison built and opened during the early 1960s that changed from a minimum security institution to a maximum security prison during its first few years of operation (Galliher, 1972). Funds were originally allocated for construction of this facility in 1954 after a serious prison riot had occurred in the old, crowded state penitentiary. This penitentiary, originally built in 1836, housed nearly 3,000 inmates—about twice its intended capacity. The voters of the state passed a bond issue to build a new prison, which would help relieve congestion at the penitentiary. Unfortunately all the construction bids received were in excess of the available bond money. The original plans called for four, 300-man housing units and eight guard towers. But because of the limited funds two of the housing units were deleted from the building plans, as were all of the guard towers. According to the revised plans, the only perimeter security for the new institution would be two parallel chainlink fences. Since the new institution would have no guard towers, of necessity, it could only be used to house model prisoners.

To make sure that the policy worked, the head of the state department of corrections appointed a committee of staff members from the new institution to handpick prisoners to be sent to the new facility. This committee reviewed the records of prisoners at the state penitentiary and selected the ones to be transferred. As one committee member recalled, "Originally we handpicked the inmates to be sent here after reviewing their files. At first the idea was to send up inmates who wouldn't escape." For their part prisoners were not forced to transfer to the new institution but were only transferred at their own request. With such a trusted group of model prisoners, it was not necessary to have a list of rules for prisoners to memorize and follow, as do most prisons. Indeed, the front gate of the institution was not even locked until about a month after the institution opened. One staff member explained: "At first we had an inmate population that could be handled without tight security. We handled the men with respect and tried to help them."

But in spite of these hopes, not all of the prisoners could be trusted. During the first 7 months of operation, there were six escapes. The warden of the new prison persuaded the local county prosecutor not to press charges against any of these men for attempted escape, as provided under state law. Instead they were simply sent back to the old prison. Solitary confinement was not used to control the prisoners at the new institution. In the few cases where staff members thought severe punishment was required, the inmates were merely subject to return to the old prison. Some simply could not be trusted to live in an institution offering so much freedom, and, moreover, did not deserve to live there.

By the end of the first year of operation, the prisoner population had expanded to 445 or approximately three fourths of the institution's capacity. As the number of prisoners increased, the committee was unable to be as selective in choosing new inmates as it had been before. "Making the institution's population larger," one employee observed, "forces you to dig deeper into the barrel." Thus forcing the institution to fill to its capacity made certain types of operational methods at the new prison impossible. All employees agreed that as the new prison received more and more prisoners who could not be trusted, it became necessary to tighten security, including assigning personnel to guard the fences.

In the meantime more trouble was brewing at the old prison. In less than 3 months, four inmates were killed by other prisoners, and a near riot occurred in a severely crowded dormitory. As a result, the situation at the old penitentiary became a hot political issue in the state. It was often criticized by a candidate for governor who promised to straighten out the situation if he was elected, which he was. To help calm the situation at the old prison some of the troublemakers were transferred to the new prison. But now another problem developed at the new prison. Twelve escapes occurred at the new institution in a 4-month period. To the staff and local community this seemed like an epidemic when compared with the previous 11 months without escapes. The staff members at the new prison indicated that this rash of escapes could have been expected given the changing character of the prisoner population. The local community, a town of approximately 13,000 people, was outraged. The local newspaper published at least one article a day on the local escape problem.

The rash of escapes was topped off by the escape of three men who kidnapped a local woman and her two small children. The fear among the local citizens was undoubtedly aggravated by the kidnapping. The townspeople claimed that the prison staff had lost control and demanded that some action be taken. A petition (printed by the local paper) demanding a grand jury investigation of the institution was signed by 1,500 citizens of the town and was given to the governor and the leaders in both houses of the state legislature. Two weeks later funds were approved by the legislature to build guard towers at each corner on the front side of the institution. The placement of guard towers on the front, which was the part of the institution most visible to the general public, was nicely suited to solve the problem of public relations. Construction began immediately, and the demand for a grand jury investigation was dropped.

The practice of handpicking prisoners for the new prison was stopped. Once the new guard towers were completed the department of corrections felt justified in sending prisoners to the new institution who were causing trouble at the old prison. "To make room for these prisoners," one staff member recalled, "inmates who were rated as good security risks were transferred to the mini-mum-security state prison farm." Later, increased crowding at the penitentiary forced the building of another 300-cell dormitory at the new prison, which in turn required the building of yet two more guard towers on the rear corners of the institution. Additional security measures included an around-the clock roving patrol, development of a long list of formal rules, frequent shakedowns of prisoners, and the use of isolation cells for unruly prisoners.

The metamorphosis was now complete. The institution had gone in the space of 3 years from a minimum security institution for a small select group of trusted prisoners to a much larger maximum security prison for inmates of all types. Political pressures exerted on both the old prison and the new prison served to make it essential and inevitable that the new prison tighten its security to a considerable degree. Given the common nature of these pressures the wonder is that anything less than maximum security prisons can ever be maintained.

To Build or Not to Build New Prisons?

The debate over whether to build new prisons rages among liberals and conservatives. Political liberals often argue that in the name of common decency we cannot allow prisoners to sleep six men to a two-man cell, where four must sleep on a concrete floor. John Conrad has been quoted as saying that old prisons are not "fit for civilized habitation" (Sherman and Hawkins, 1981:16). The political conservatives on the far right often disagree. They adhere to the old adage, "If you can't do the time, don't do the crime." Translated, it means that since these prisoners have been convicted of crimes, often serious crimes, there is no reason for us to feel sorry for them. Other political liberals are not so sure about the wisdom of building new prisons. Building these new institutions perpetuates the concept of imprisonment, and additional prison capacity generates an increased number of prisoners because old prisons are seldom closed. There is abundant evidence that as soon as new prisons are completed they are almost immediately as seriously crowded as were the old prisons. The total number of prisoners immediately increases, and thus there is no reduction in prison crowding (Mullin, 1985). The only accomplishment of the new prison is that for a short time local judges and prosecutors increase the number and severity of prison sentences. Thus the issue remains, What should be done about genuine suffering? Should people of good conscience move to solve the short-term problems of human misery found among today's prisoners even if this will surely complicate the possibility of ever abandoning the use of prisons at some time in the future for those convicted of nonviolent crimes, for example?

There is some evidence of support among the public for longer sentences. In any event in recent years sentences have been getting longer (Sherman and Hawkins, 1981). Imprisonment rates are rising even while there is a growing understanding of its ineffectiveness. In 1968 American prisons held 200,000 inmates, and at that time 63 percent of the public surveyed said that the courts were not harsh enough with criminals. In 1978 the number of prisoners had risen by 50 percent, and still 88 percent said that the courts were too lenient (Sherman and Hawkins, 1981:46). Obviously the public is not responding to the harshness of the sentences. Because of these hard-line public attitudes, a cutback in the use of incarceration and a moratorium on prison building is unlikely. A strong argument for construction of new prisons can be made by citing the fact that many state prisons built far back into the nineteenth century are steadily deteriorating. Alternatively, the federal courts have sometimes allowed no new admissions into a state prison system if it is too crowded, as in the case of Mississippi (U.S District Court, 1972). The dilemma is that then prisoners are merely kept in local city and county jails for years on end where conditions are generally even worse than in state prisons. In 1982 there were 8,200 held in local jails because of prison overcrowding (Bolduc, 1985). Sometimes it is argued that what are considered horrible prison conditions vary considerably from time to time. For example, when the Alcatraz Island prison in the San Francisco bay was first opened, both its location and design were considered ideal by the experts of the period. Years later it was condemned. The fact that standards have changed over the years does not make the human misery of inmates currently in American prisons any less real.

It is not surprising that the United States outranks most nations in the rate of imprisonment. Recently, the *Wall Street Journal* has reported that 169 new American prisons were under consideration at an estimated cost of over $5 billion (1981). At least 37 states have enacted new mandatory sentencing laws to ensure longer sentences. In 1983 there were 438,830 convicts confined in state and federal prisons which represented a doubling in one decade. In 1970, 96 criminals per 100,000 total population were incarcerated, but by 1982, 169 per 100,000 were incarcerated (Funke, 1985). Between 1972 and 1977 23,000 bed spaces were added in American prisons, but 81,000 additional prisoners. From 1978 to 1980 there were 7,000 additional bed spaces but 61,000 additional prisoners. From 1981 to 1985 there were 21,000 additional bed spaces but 39,000 additional prisoners. Thus, based on these figures we are left with nearly 500,000 prisoners occupying space for 350,000. Consequently, in 1980 Texas had over 1,000 prisoners sleeping on floors until a court order brought this to a halt. Ninety-six percent of these prisoners were male, and 48 percent were black. Nearly half of these prisoners were incarcerated in the southern states, and in 1983 seven states had their entire prison system under court order to limit the number of offenders confined (Austin and Krisberg, 1985).

Faced with such court orders there are three strategies for a department of corrections to use (Austin and Krisberg, 1985). (1) There are "front-end options," which involve reducing the number of prisoners sentenced to institutions, as well as giving shorter sentences. (2) There are also "back-end options," involving early releases of prisoners to lower the prison population. (3) And finally the state can expand the capacity of the prisons. One problem with adding prison space is that the costs of these additions varied in 1985 from $40,000 to $100,000 per inmate (Mullen, 1985). It is widely agreed by experts that each prisoner requires at least 60 square feet of space in which to live—the size of the average bathroom. Even by this meager standard 66 percent of all state prisons failed to measure up in 1978 (Mullen, 1985).

SUMMARY

It should be clear from this review of punishments, including incarceration, from ancient times through the Middle Ages, the colonial period in what would become America, and finally into the twentieth century that economic forces typically determine the type of options selected in responding to crime. Modern minimum security prisons are inherently unstable and have a tendency to gravitate toward maximum security because of likely community pressures and because the payoff from minimum security institutions is poorly defined and comes only in the long run. Currently Americans must make an economic, political, and social decision involving whether bulding billions of dollars worth of new prisons is a just response to the threat of crime. How this question is finally resolved will likely hinge on other key economic considerations, not the least of which are the ability of the economy to support the expense of this construction and the degree to which the economy can generate jobs for the type of unskilled workers often in trouble with the law.

REFERENCES

Adamson, C. R.
  1983 "Punishment after slavery: southern state penal systems, 1865–1890." Social Problems 30(June):555–569.
  1984 "Toward a Marxian penology: captive criminal populations as economic threats and resources." Social Problems 31(April): 435–458.
Additon, H.
  1951 "Women's institutions." Pp. 297–309 in P. W. Tappan (ed.), Contemporary Correction. New York: McGraw-Hill.
Adler, F.
  1975 Sisters in Crime: The Rise of the New Female Criminal. New York: McGraw-Hill.
Austin, J. and B. Krisberg
  1985 "Incarceration in the United States: the extent and future of the problem." Annals of the American Academy of Political and Social Science 478(March):15–30.
Beccaria, C. B.
  1775 An Essay on Crimes and Punishments. 4th ed. London: E. Newbery.
Bentham, J.
  1823 An Introduction to the Principles of Morals and Legislation. Reprinted 1948. New York: Hafner.
Bolduc, A.
  1985 "Jail crowding." Annals of the American Academy of Political and Social Science 478(March):47–57.
Fenton N., E. G. Reimer, and H. A. Wilmer
  1967 The Correctional Community: An Introduction and Guide. Berkeley: University of California Press.
Funke, G. S.
  1985 "The economics of prison crowding." Annals of the American Academy of Political and Social Science 478 (March):86–99.
Galliher, J. F.
  1972 "Change in a correctional institution: a case study of the tightening-up process." Crime and Delinquency 18(July):263–270.
Johnson, E. H.
  1974 Crime, Correction, and Society. 3d ed. Homewood, Ill.: The Dorsey Press.
Mullen, J.
  1985 "Prison crowding and the evolution of public policy." Annals of the American Academy of Political and Social Science 478(March):31–46.
Nelson, W. E.
  1967 "Emerging notions of modern criminal law in the revolutionary era: an historical perspective." New York University Law Review 42(May):450–482.
Orland, L.
  1975 Prisons: Houses of Darkness. New York: The Free Press.
Rains, P.
  1984 "Juvenile justice and the boys' farm: surviving a court-created population crisis, 1909–1949." Social Problems 31(June): 500–513.
Rothman, D. J.
  1971 The Discovery of the Asylum: Social Order

and Disorder in the New Republic. Boston: Little, Brown.

1980 Conscience and Convenience: The Asylum and its Alternatives in Progressive America. Boston: Little, Brown.

Rusche, G. and O. Kirchheimer
1939 Punishment and Social Structure. New York: Columbia University Press.

Sellin, T. J.
1976 Slavery and the Penal System. New York: Elsevier Scientific.

Sherman, M. and G. Hawkins
1981 Imprisonment in America: Choosing the Future. Chicago: University of Chicago Press.

Simon, R. J.
1975 Women and Crime. Lexington, Mass.: Lexington Books.

Tappan, P. W.
1960 Crime, Justice and Correction. New York: McGraw-Hill.

United States Department of Commerce
1985 Statistical Abstract of the United States. Washington, D.C.: U.S. Government Printing Office, p. 38.

United States District Court N.D.
1972 Mississippi, Greenville Division, Gates v. Collier, Fed Supp 349. September 13:881–905.

Wall Street Journal
1981 "Life in prison: more riots feared as overcrowding fuels tensions behind bars." August 18:1, 21.

13
EFFECTS OF FORMAL AND INFORMAL PRISON ORGANIZATION

TOTAL INSTITUTIONS

Nowhere have the general effects of confinement been better described than by Goffman (1961). Goffman contended that mental hospitals, prisons, reformatories, as well as monasteries, all have specific characteristics in common, and thus he used the term *total institutions* to refer to all such facilities. According to Goffman (1961:xiii): "A total institution may be defined as a place of residence and work where a large number of like-situated individuals, cut off from the wider society for an appreciable period of time, together lead an enclosed, formally administered round of life." It is typically the case that people work, sleep, and play in different places and with different groups of people. It is also typically true that there is no overall plan for organizing all of these activities of the daily lives of individuals. But in total institutions the usual separation of these various spheres of life is missing. All aspects of individuals' lives in total institutions are carried out in one locale and under one authority. All individuals living in a total institution are required to do the same activities, which are tightly scheduled by rules imposed by institutional officials. In such settings all activities are designed to achieve the explicit goals of the institution. In the free society only a small part of one's daily activities are regimented, such as activities on the job.

Entering a Total Institution

When an individual first enters a total institution, the staff begins a systematic process of degradation and humiliation (Goffman, 1961). The new-comers' clothes are often taken from them, and they are sometimes given an institutional haircut. They are also given institutional numbers that will be used during their incarceration rather than their names. All of these things serve to strip the individuals of their personal identities. If this is not enough, the staff may engage a newcomer in a "will-breaking contest." This will-breaking contest is used on any newcomer who shows the least defiance and involves ever-increasing punishment until the individual capitulates to the authority of the staff. The staff of total institutions can rationalize this exercise of power on the basis of the need to be able to rely on the obedience of all people confined in the institution—for example, in prisons to guard against possible escapes and riots.

Further subordination is forced upon the individual by being required to address the staff as sir and to always show great deference to them. For their part, the staff and others confined in the total institution have no obligation to show any sign of respect to this individual. Inmates may experience humiliation because people who live in most total institutions are forced to live in such close quarters that others learn things about them that are ordinarily concealed, such as embarrassing tattoos, scars, or birthmarks on parts of their bodies ordinarily shielded from public view. The individual's privacy in relationships with others outside the institution is also often invaded by the staff in reading and censoring the inmate's outgoing and incoming mail.

In total institutions Goffman (1961) found what he calls the "looping process." This process occurs when individuals complain about some humiliation or punishment in the institution, only to learn that it is impossible to protect themselves in this fashion because their protests are used by the staff as grounds to justify further punishment. In other words, the reaction to the original situation is looped back into the situation itself. In mental hospitals when patients complain about electroshock therapy, this demonstrates to the staff that the patient needs more of the same for their rehabilitation. In prisons inmates who protest the conditions in solitary confinement are also often seen by the staff as requiring more of this "therapy."

There are also myriad institutional rules that demand specific conduct from the inmate. The infamous Alcatraz federal penitentiary, for example, had hundreds of inmate rules listed on 19 single-spaced pages that the prisoners were required to memorize and follow (Madigan, 1956). If these rules are obeyed, the prisoner becomes eligible for certain privileges from the staff. We should note that many of these privileges are things the person probably took for granted before incarceration, such as a hot meal or a cigarette. Therefore punishment in total institutions often involves simply withdrawing these elementary privileges.

More recently it was observed (Schwartz, 1972) that prisoners are humiliated not only through their lack of having any privacy for themselves but also through being forced to observe the exposure of others. Moreover, not only may the person's letters be invaded by snooping staff, but also the visits from relatives and friends may be defiled through intense public observation throughout the visit.

Some aspects of this exposure are coincidental in that they are not really intended by the staff nor necessary for the goals of the organization but occur merely as a by-product of regimented mass activities (Schwartz, 1972). Unintentional invasions of privacy involve visibility to one's peers—other prisoners or mental patients. There are, of course, intentional invasions of privacy that involve observation by the staff. For example, some institutions forbid inmates from covering their heads while they are asleep to help the staff know with certainty that the person is in fact in the bed and not climbing over the wall during the middle of the night. The staff feel that they must not only know what prisoners are doing, but also what they are planning to do in the future, including such things as future murders, riots, and escapes. To secure this type of information, the staff requires a well-developed system of informers or "rats" among the prisoners.

Reactions to Total Institutions

When confronted with such oppression, the individual in a total institution may refuse to cooperate. Usually, however, this is only a temporary solution because the staff has such great power. Another possible reaction is that the individual may withdraw from all social interaction and even from reality. In mental hospitals this is called regression. Or the inmates may engage in what Goffman called "colonization," that is, they may develop their whole way of life around the institution and may not care to leave. For example, immediately upon release some older prisoners who have lived most of their lives in penal institutions commit another crime that will ensure their return to prison. Finally, the person in the total institution may be begin to accept the staff's definition of proper behavior and attempt to change their lives accordingly. Prisoners who join Alcoholics Anonymous or become born-again Christians while in prison are illustrations of this last adaptation.

During the same period of time that the staff may be confronting the individual in the will-breaking contest and attempting total degradation, the person is probably learning how to "work the system" (Goffman, 1961). For example, prison inmates and mental hospital patients soon realize that if they engage in group therapy sessions—even if they have no intention of benefiting from the therapy itself, they can enlist the help of the therapist in securing better work and cell assignments and even get assistance in building a case for early release. Feigning religious conversion may be acted out with the hope of similar rewards. Learning to work the system involves bending the rules of the organization so that the spirit of the rules are violated without actually violating the letter of the law and risking punishment.

Naming Behavior in Total Institutions

As indicated above, in total institutions, and especially prisons, the staff coerces deference from the prisoners. Traditionally the institutional rule books have begun with exact specifications of the terms of address that will be allowed when a prisoner addresses a staff member (Galliher, 1972). Any verbal impropriety on the part of the prisoner when addressing the staff is considered grounds for swift and sure punishment. The names signify to the inmates what expectations exist for their behavior in this social relationship. Since the prisoners are quickly told the appropriate terms to use in addressing the staff, this helps define the inmate-staff relationship for the prisoner. Addressing someone else as Sir, for example, defines the relationship between the two people conversing as one in which the speaker has the subordinate role. Forcing prisoners to prostrate themselves verbally before the insitutional staff through coerced deference compels them to be most concerned with the feelings of the institutional staff rather than with their own and makes it abundantly clear that the main goal of the institution is control, not therapy.

SOCIALIZATION AND RESOCIALIZATION SYSTEMS

The attempted impact on inmates in an institution depends to a very great extent on whether its goals are primarily socialization, as in the case of military academies, or resocialization, as in the case of prisons (Wheeler, 1966b). Unlike socialization systems that engage in general education, resocialization systems are designed to correct some earlier deficiency in the educational process and to reform deviant actors, whether these actors are criminals, delinquents, or mental patients. In either type of system the training may be to assist in either role or status socialization. Role socialization refers to training in the performance of specific tasks, while status socialization refers to a broader type of education designed to help the individual occupy a general status in life, not a specific role. In a socialization system, such as a university, training in chemical engineering or nursing represents role socialization, while training in liberal arts is status socialization because it prepares the individual not for a specific occupational role but rather for the more general status of being a college graduate, which requires a well-rounded education.

In resocialization settings, such as prisons, vocational training programs are examples of role socialization, while group therapy is an attempt to turn the individual into a generally law-abiding person, that is, status socialization. In resocialization systems these two types of socialization are often seen as complimentary, because those without adequate occupational skills (inadequate role socialization) often tend to develop nonconventional life styles. However, in resocialization settings at times there is some conflict between persons involved in the two types of socialization. Treatment programs in prisons are often in sharp conflict with vocational training programs for both space in the prison and for institutional staff, as well as in competition for the prisoners' time.

Socialization and resocialization systems deal differently with those people under their supervision who are failures and do not benefit from the training offered (Wheeler, 1966b). Socialization systems, such as public schools, fail or expel students who do not succeed, while resocialization systems get rid of their successes. Prisoners who display some evidence of rehabilitation are often released ahead of many other inmates. Thus the longer people are in a resocialization system, the more likely they are to have contact with the failures because the successes are released. These failures tend to accumulate in such resocialization settings as prisons and tend to create an inmate belief system that emphasizes there is little possibility of ultimate success for prisoners.

Finally, socialization systems, such as schools, provide more fanfare and rites of passage when people leave, or graduate, than when they enter. The rites of passage when leaving serve to give the individual a new identity or public status, for example, as a high school or college graduate. In resocialization settings the essential ceremonies, such as criminal trials, are found upon entry rather than departure and are defamatory in character (Wheeler, 1966b). The person's public identity is radically and permanently altered upon entering a mental hospital or prison. When people leave such institutions, their identities are never the same again; they are forever an ex-mental patient or an ex-convict.

PRISON LIFE

Punishment in Prisons

In most correctional institutions staff members have the authority to issue warnings and reprimands for violation of the institutional rules. Such infractions and punishments go into the prisoner's institutional file and may often make early release on parole much more difficult. Examples of minor institutional rule violations that could warrant some institutional punishment include refusal to shave, fighting with another prisoner, or swearing at a staff member. When behavior problems become even more serious, such as perhaps threatening a staff member, most institutions have a disciplinary court made up of a few staff members that meets regularly in the institution to decide what punishments should be given for each infraction. The alternative forms of punishment from which they may choose include loss of various privileges in the prison, being placed in solitary confinement for a period of time, or loss of any possibility of early release on parole. For even more serious types of infractions, such as attempted escapes or a serious assault on another prisoner or a staff member, new criminal charges may be filed, and the prisoner may be tried in the nearest local criminal court.

Psychological Impact of Prison: The Zimbardo Experiment

Nowhere can the punishment inherent in imprisonment be more clearly seen than in an experiment conducted in the early 1970s at Stanford University by the psychologist Philip Zimbardo (1972). This research was "an attempt to understand just what it means psychologically to be a prisoner or a prison guard" (Zimbardo, 1972:4). The experiment required the construction of a simulated prison in the basement of a classroom building at Stanford University complete with metal bars, cots, and buckets for toilets (Faber, 1971) and involved 21 young men who were "intelligent college students" (Zimbardo, 1972:4). They had volunteered for this experiment and were paid $15 per day for the planned 2-week duration of the experiment. None had any criminal record and were selected from a larger group of volunteers as the "most stable (physically and mentally), most mature, and least involved in anti-social behaviors" (Haney et al., 1973:5). By the chance flip of a coin 11 of these volunteers were designated to be guards in the experiment, and 10 were prisoners. "The guards wore khaki uniforms and reflecting sunglasses to make themselves more impersonal" (Faber, 1971:82). They also were equipped with billy clubs, whistles, and handcuffs as symbols of authority, power, and control—although for ethical reasons no physical abuse was allowed.

The guards were informed of their potential vulnerability to many of the possible contingencies they might face, such as prisoner escape attempts, and they decided to make up "their own formal rules for maintaining law, order, and respect and were generally free to improvise new ones during their eight-hour, three-man shifts" (Zimbardo, 1972:4). "During meals, rest periods, and after 10 p.m. lights out, prisoners were forbidden to speak. Every night at 2:30, they were rousted out for a head count" (Faber, 1971:82). Without advance warning the prisoners were picked up at their homes by a city police officer in a cruiser, and they were searched, handcuffed, fingerprinted, and booked at the local police headquarters. Then they were blindfolded and taken to the simulated jail where they were stripped and put into a uniform, given a number, and placed in a cell with two other prisoners. The prisoners were referred to only by a number placed on their uniforms. All of the interaction between the guards and the prisoners was recorded on videotape.

At the end of only 6 days, Zimbardo was forced to prematurely stop the experiment because of unexpectedly frightening results. The problem was that neither the guards nor the prisoners could any longer differentiate between role playing and reality. "We were horrified because we saw some boys (guards) treat others as if they were despicable animals, taking pleasure in cruelty, while other boys (prisoners) became servile, dehumanized robots who thought only of escape, of their own individual survival and of their mounting hatred of the guards" (Zimbardo, 1972:4). Indeed, within 4 days, three of the prisoners had to be released from the experiment because of hysterical crying and severe depression, and another was released when he developed a psychosomatic rash. But by the fifth day the prisoners were so programmed that they no longer recognized that they could quit. Unlike the prisoners, none of the guards attempted to quit, and some remained on duty voluntarily after their shift had ended without extra pay (Haney el al., 1973). About one third of the guards obviously enjoyed their power over the prisoners and became tyrannical. One guard recalled: "I was surprised at myself. I was a real crumb. I made them call each other names and clean out the toilets with their bare hands" (Faber, 1971:83). Even those guards who remained reasonably fair never interfered with any of the abusive guards.

The point of the Zimbardo experiment is that if such traumatic conditions can be so quickly created in this artificial situation among middle-class college students who presumably should know it is an experiment and that they could quit at any time, it must be all the worse for people in real prisons for years on end. As Hughes (1962) observed, it is not that those who do horrible things are awful people, rather the problem is worse than that. Those who carry out acts of cruelty are usually just ordinary citizens placed in a position to do these things, and when requested, they comply.

Surviving in Prison

A study of men in the maximum security wing of a prison found that they were preoccupied with the passage of time and had great fear of their own deterioration and loss of personal identity (Cohen and Taylor, 1972). Many psychologists have studied the effects of stimulus deprivation, which is especially intense in prison. They have found that such deprivation can be caused by covering a person's eyes and placing the person in a closed air-conditioned box or, as in some experiments, suspending a person in a tank of water. Subjects in such studies have been given panic buttons to push when they feel they must get out. These experiments routinely find that stimulus deprivation is associated with suffering from anxiety, hallucinations, and delusions.

Aside from the effects of stimulus deprivation, there is the issue of meaning deprivation whereby subjects know that it is intended that they be deprived of any stimulus. For example, one study found that if subjects like those in other stimulus deprivation studies were given a panic button but put in a room with chairs, water, and a sandwich—that is, the environment was not at all deprived—they still behaved as if it were (Cohen and Taylor, 1972). A control group was placed in the same room but without a panic button. The experimental group in this study experienced more deprivation than did the control group. The point is that the group with the panic button knew that they were supposed to feel deprived and responded accordingly. Prisoners then suffer from a double deprivation. They live in the drabness and uniformity of prisons, and they also know that it is intended that they be deprived. Thus they suffer from both stimulus and meaning deprivation. In addition, prisoners appear to suffer the most if they have a medium amount of contact with the free world in the form of letters and visits. Therefore prisoners typically either attempt to hold on to all of their associations outside of prison or forget about them entirely, since the middle ground is intolerable.

The resistance from these prisoners takes several forms (Cohen and Taylor, 1972). (1) Some prisoners attempt to protect themselves by mind or body building as a type of escape from the prison. Weight lifting in prisons is a major preoccupation for many prisoners, which serves this role of protecting their bodies from the ravages of time. (2) Some prisoners spend a good deal of time complaining about prison conditions, which is only effective in annoying the staff. (3) Some prisoners attempt to confront the staff or go on strike such as the hunger strikers among the Irish Republican Army (IRA) in British prisons. As the example of the IRA demonstrates, there is little that prisoners can typically do to confront the staff except punish themselves. (4) Finally, prisoners can attempt to escape, which some try numerous times—some with incredible success.

Men serving long sentences have no clues from the staff when they will finally be released from prison, and thus they build their own time frameworks or phases of their sentence to give temporal meaning to their lives. An example of this is found in the case of the prisoner who was doing 20 years, 5 years at a time (Cohen and Taylor, 1972). This is not really unexpected because many people try to break large tasks or long trips into more managable portions.

Aging in Prison

For older prisoners, survival takes on a special meaning. The important question is whether they can live long enough to be released from prison. One prisoner saw it this way (Reed and Glamser, 1979:354):

> There's something else funny that happens to some people; they come down here and their age seems to fix at what it was when they came in. And something else: I don't think they age as much in appearance as they do in the free world. Down here I see guys all the time that are 60 or 75 who look like 40 to 45. Physically they stay younger.

Earlier research found this optimistic view of aging in prison to be fairly widespread (Gillespie and Galliher, 1972). Inmates in their twenties were considerably more optimistic about their situation than the rest of the inmate population. These young men believed that prison had actually been beneficial in that it had given them an opportunity to mature and make a better life for themselves after release. One prisoner in his twenties observed; "I haven't aged fast physically; I've aged fast mentally—as far as wisdom and knowledge go. I think I've gotten better as a matter of fact" (Gillespie and Galliher, 1972:469).

Prisoners between 30 and 59 years old, the middle-aged prisoners, while not claiming that they have been improved by prison, at least believed that prison slows the aging process and "preserves" them. The inmates supported their claim in two ways. First, from the standpoint of their physical well-being, they argued that life in prison offers some advantages over life on the streets. Prison they said, removed them from the temptations of liquor, drugs, prostitution, and the other attractions of an active night life. On a more positive side, prison offered regular meals, sleep, and the opportunity to keep physically fit by participating in various sports programs. A prison sentence—even a fairly long one—can be regarded as a temporary state, relative to the same amount of time spent on the streets. It is as if the inmates believed that they can return to the streets unchanged, ready to begin life where they left off. Unlike the younger prisoners, life in an institution neither increases nor decreases the possibility of future success on the streets.

Unlike the other two age groups, prisoners over 60 years old uniformly believed that prison life had aged them greatly. Apparently, watching what little future they have slip away while imprisoned causes them to blame the prison for their physical and mental deterioration. They seemed especially concerned that the prison offered them little or no protection from younger and stronger prisoners, and the consequent anxiety caused them to believe that they had aged more rapidly than they would have if they had been free.

Inmate Leaders Help Staff Maintain Control

The staff members of a prison, especially many of the guards, are in close contact with the prisoners throughout the day, which makes it very difficult for the guard to remain aloof from the prisoners. The prisoners know the guard too well for that (Sykes, 1956). Moreover, the guard is dependent upon the prisoners for the maintenance of order. The guard is so outnumbered that it is impossible to use force in all cases to secure compliance with the institutional rules. Yet guards are usually judged on the basis of how well they can keep order. Thus the best compromise guards can make is to ignore most minor offenses or to make sure they are not in a position to see certain violations of institutional rules. The guards also know that someday there could be a riot at the prison, and they could be taken hostage, and whether they live or die could depend on how well the inmates believe they had been treated by specific guards in the past.

Many of the duties of the guards are boring and time consuming, such as checking cells and making up endless reports, and these duties are often gradually transferred to the prisoners. Once the guards start this practice, it is hard to stop because if the guards attempt to restore their authority, the prisoners may tell the guards' superiors about how the prisoners have been performing the various staff functions. Even a new guard has trouble changing such past practices because of institutional traditions (Sykes, 1956).

But by and large even though the staff is greatly outnumbered by the prisoners, most of the time in most prisons the inmates are kept under at least some semblance of control. Even the strongest, most powerful, and influential prisoners generally do not attempt revolt (McCleery, 1960) because the leaders among the prisoners have a certain stake in the status quo and a position of advantage to maintain. In one prison, for example, the leaders among the prisoners were allowed special privileges by the staff, and in return, these leaders helped the staff control other prisoners. A reform movement at this prison determined that these special privileges were a symptom of staff corruption, and thus these arrangements were terminated. When the inmate leaders lost these special privileges, they lost all motivation to control the situation and helped lead an attempted insurrection (Hartung and Floch, 1956).

One type of inmate leader is the one who is apparently fearless and always willing to defy the staff (McCleery, 1960). At times the staff may even give up attempting to completely control such prisoners, believing that it is easier to try to ignore them. Some inmates have considerable influence over other prisoners because of their special access to information or certain materials. Certain inmate clerk-typists may know in advance when inspections or shakedowns will occur, allowing the clerk who typed the order time to tell all friends what is in the offing and giving them time to make special preparations. Alternatively, some prisoners may work in the institution's bakery and have access to the yeast needed for making home-brewed alcoholic beverages. If you want the yeast, you must be nice to the prison bakers and do what they command. Curiously, many prisons use incredible amounts of yeast, presumably only for use in baking bread. The type of inmate leadership is most strongly influenced by the type of prison it is—custodial or treatment—even though the age and racial composition of the inmate population, as well as the level of inmate criminality also have some influence on the leadership that emerges (Akers, 1977). For example, custodially oriented institutions are most likely to produce abusive and autocratic inmate leaders.

The reliance on inmate leaders to help maintain order can be interpreted as a flaw in the prison organization, but the staff does not necessarily lose complete control even if they must rely on these selected prisoners to help maintain order. The staff still has some control because at times, they can determine which prisoners will be allowed to occupy positions that carry such power in the prison and thus can make demands on them (Cloward, 1960).

Prison Riots

As noted above, it has been believed that when inmate leaders are deprived of their positions, they lose all motivation to help contain the situation, and as a consequence, riots often develop (Hartung and Floch, 1956; Sykes, 1958). Useem's study (1985) of the 1980 New Mexico prison riot used interviews with both prison staff and inmates to attempt to locate the source of this upheaval. Thirty-three inmates were killed and 400 injured. In addition, there was $200 million in property damage, making it the most bloody and expensive prison riot in American history. It all started when several prisoners over-powered several prison guards. The riot spread to other parts of the prison because of carelessly unlocked gates and acetylene torches left in the prison by construction crews that were then used to burn open other gates.

No individual or group of prisoners was in charge of the riot. Control over hostages and negotiations with the authorities were therefore very frag-mented. Inmates alone or in small groups beat, tortured, raped, mutilated, and killed other inmates. One prisoner was decapitated with a shovel; another was killed by a screw-driver pushed through his head. Others were burned to death with the acetylene torches or by lighter fluid thrown on their bodies. There were many independent groups involved in torture, which included cutting off geni-talia and beating on corpses. The assaults, while savage, were selective. All of those attacked were snitches. Twelve guards were taken hostage, but none were killed—although some were sodomized, beaten and threatened with death. Useem (1985) found that they were not killed for two reasons. The prisoners realized that killing the guards would quickly result in the storming of the prison by the authorities, and also if the guards were killed, they could no longer torture them. Not all of the prisoners participated in the riot; 120 black pris-oners, representing 9 percent of the prison population, organized to protect themselves from the riot and eventually escaped.

Both prisoners and guards claimed that the riot occurred because of the deteriorating conditions in the prison after the warden was removed in 1975. After 1975 the prison became so crowded that, as one prisoner recalled, in a 45-man dormitory there had been 120 prisoners and you could step on other inmates and start a fight by just going to the bathroom at night. A U.S. Depart-ment of Justice study after the riot found it to be one of the harshest prisons in the nation. Even the guards agreed that after 1975 the conditions had worsened. Many, however, felt that this was appropriate because the prisoners had been given too much prior to 1975. There had been, for example, many programs for the prisoners, including computer training, a school release program for those near parole, a Bible study class, a Jaycees club, Toastmasters, and frequent outside entertainment. After the warden was removed in 1975, these programs were terminated, and almost no one in the prison had any activity.

In the early 1970s two types of inmates were used by the staff to help maintain order (Colvin, 1982). The prisoners used in this manner included inmate administrators of various prison programs, such as the computer key-punch shop, as well as a group of prisoners who controlled the heroin and other drug trafficking in the prison. (Drug use increased dramatically in the prison between 1971 and 1976.) Both of these groups of prisoners wanted stability in the institution and therefore helped the staff police the prison. Thus there were few escapes and little violence. But because of the apparent flow of drugs into the prison, the warden and much of his key staff were transferred out of the prison. At that time the state attorney general said (Colvin, 1982:454); "The free flow of contraband drugs into the penitentiary is at an alarming level."

The warden was replaced by a strict disciplinarian who disapproved of inmates having so much control. He therefore removed all prisoners from administrative positions of the prison programs, increased drug searches, and clamped down on sources of drugs coming into the prison. Therefore these two types of prisoner leaders no longer had any interest in helping to control the prison. The prisoners soon staged a work strike to protest the new conditions, but the strike was broken with a staff assault of tear gas and ax handles intended to show that there was now more reliance on coercive staff control. In this climate the prisoners who had a reputation for violence seemed to have had the best opportunity for gaining power (Colvin, 1982).

Prior to 1975, prison officials gathered information from prisoners through an elected inmate council and the other prisoner programs—all of which were abolished after 1975. Thus the staff thereafter resorted to reliance on a snitch system whereby prisoners were threatened with disciplinary action unless they told of other prisoners' misbehavior. Another tactic the staff used was the threat to inmates that they would be reported to other prisoners as a snitch if they did not cooperate. These snitches were a major target of violence during the riot that would soon occur. Many snitches were killed during the riot, and rioters apparently made a special point to break into the prison files to determine the identities of these snitches (*New York Times*, 1980).

Prison Subculture

Aside from the prison's formal organization, or written institutional rules that are enforced by the staff, there is also an informal organization among the prisoners called, at times, the prison subculture. If a unique subculture does develop among prisoners, then this should be reflected in a distinct set of values, norms, and rules accepted by the prisoners to guide their own behavior. Indeed research has found that traditionally there has been such a set of normative prescriptions (Sykes and Messinger, 1960). (1) One important norm found among prisoners was that prisoners should not interfere with the interests of other prisoners even if it is clear that they are violating the prison rules; the rule is, don't rat on other prisoners. (2) Apparently there have also been rules against starting arguments with other prisoners in a collective effort to minimize friction within the group. One of the reasons for this collective prohibition is that the whole prisoner population may at times be punished for what just a handful of prisoners have done. For example, after a serious fight the total prisoner population may be locked in their cells for an extended period of time. (3) There are norms against cheating or swindling other prisoners. The issue does not concern morality so much as the fact that if one prisoner cheats another, this could start a fight, and again everyone in the prison could be punished or even drawn into the altercation. (4) There are also norms against showing fear or respect for the staff or fear of other prisoners. Among prisoners there apparently is an exaggerated sense of masculinity, perhaps because without any women around, demonstrating toughness and bravery are the only means of proving this masculinity.

Traditionally in American prisons the inmates are held in high esteem by their peers to the degree they live up to these subcultural dictates. Therefore one of the most despised prisoners is the inmate informer or "rat." The inmate rat who helps the staff can cause great damage to the interests of other prisoners. As noted above, in the recent New Mexico State Prison riot, the prisoners briefly took control of the institution, broke into the staff records, learned who the prison informers were, and promptly tortured, mutilated, and executed them. The point is: the degree to which prisoners follow these subcultural rules is the same degree to which it is possible for the prisoners to lessen the pain of being imprisoned. Clearly if these rules were not followed at all, there would be a continual war within the prison from which no prisoner could escape because of the prison walls. As with any subculture, within the prison subculture prisoners can find at least some social support and some people who do not define them as totally worthless (McCorkle and Korn, 1954).

In one institution the prisoners, the guards, and the treatment staff were asked what the prisoners as a group were really like (Wheeler, 1966a). All respondents reflected great agreement on how they described the prisoners. They all saw prisoners as totally opposed to the staff—total inmate solidarity and support for the prison code or prison subculture. Yet when individual prisoners were asked about their personal values, they were not nearly so opposed to the staff. Perhaps the reason for the difference between what everyone believes about most prisoners and what the individual prisoners really believe is that the most visible prisoner to both the staff and other inmates is the one who makes most of the trouble. This type of prisoner leads both inmates and staff into the false conclusion that the most troublesome prisoners are representative of all prisoners. The origins of these negative staff stereotypes of prisoners are undoubtedly not unlike the origins of other stereotypes of ethnic and racial groups—the most visible members of each collectivity are the ones who are the most difficult to control and who cause observers to falsely assume all of the group are like them.

Prisonization

Because unique attitudes and values exist in the prison subculture, the new arrival in a prison often learns these new ways of behaving. The process of assimilation into a new culture is generally referred to as socialization; therefore this process within the prison setting has been referred to as prisonization (Clemmer, 1958). This process can be impeded by such factors as a relatively short sentence and positive relationships with friends outside the prison. Obviously the person who is anticipating serving 20 years must come to terms with the prison subculture in a different way than an individual serving only a few months does. It is easier to hold yourself aloof from the local prison situation if you anticipate an early departure. If the prisoner has good relationships with people outside the prison and receives numerous letters and visits from these people, then there is some alternative social involvement besides the prison social system.

This description of the prisonization process was originally developed by Donald Clemmer (1958), and the impression he left is that this process is generally progressive: the longer the person is confined, the more complete the process becomes. This description of the prisonization process was based on observations made by Clemmer over an extended period of time. Later an attempt was made to perform an empirical test of Clemmer's observations (Wheeler, 1961). In this test of the prisonization process it was necessary to measure the degree to which prisoners accepted or rejected staff moral judgments. Thus hypothetical situations were developed to measure the degree to which prisoners agreed with staff expectations. One such situation involved whether prisoners believed that it was correct to tell the staff when the inmates were aware that other prisoners were planning an escape. The answers to these questions were then correlated with the degree of association between the respondents and other prisoners. Predictably, the prisoners indicating that they had the most frequent and intense relationships with other inmates expressed the greatest divergence from staff expectations.

This research also found a U-shaped distribution of conformity to staff expectations based on whether the prisoners were in the early, middle, or late phase of their sentence. That is, during the early phase of prisoners' sentences there was relatively high conformity with staff expectations, during the middle phase there was low conformity, and during the late phase high conformity again appeared. So during the early phase of a sentence just after arriving at the prison and just prior to release, the prisoners typically reflected greater conformity to staff expectations than they did during the middle phase. Thus prisonization appears to operate as Clemmer described during the initial part of the sentence. The assimilation is gradual and progressive, but as the inmate nears release, there is a reversal of this process. This reversal of the prisonization process as release from prison approaches can be interpreted as a type of anticipatory socialization. Anticipatory socialization refers to the process whereby the individual accepts new attitudes and values that will be appropriate for a situation they anticipate facing in the future. Apparently the prisoners begin to prepare themselves psychologically for their imminent return to the free world where the subcultural values unique to the prison are no longer completely relevant. It has also been found that a prisoner's specific expectations concerning future adjustment after release from the institution greatly affect the extent to which an inmate will become prisonized (Zingraff, 1975). The less optimistic the prisoner is regarding success after release, the more change there is through prisonization.

Sex and Prison Subculture

It is beyond dispute that homosexual relations, both consensual and coerced, are rampant in prisons for men. The prisoners do not interpret these actions the way most other citizens would. Some prisoners are essentially homosexual rapists; among prisoners this aggressive behavior, ironically, is not condemned, while less aggressive homosexual behavior is apparently condemned merely because it is more passive. For many relatively young and small prisoners there are really only three choices: (1) Find a larger prisoner and become his "woman" in return for his protection from all the other prisoners. (2) Run a high risk of being repeatedly raped by a number of other prisoners. (3) Commit suicide. Some apparently choose the third way out after experiencing the first and second alternatives.

A study of sexual assaults in the Philadelphia prison system conducted from June 1966 through July 1968 demonstrates the scope of the problem (Davis, 1968). During this period, out of approximately 60,000 inmates who passed through this prison system, 3,304 prisoners were interviewed, as were 561 out of 570 guards. The researchers also took 130 written statements from those who gave important information. Some employees and some prisoners were asked to take lie detector tests, and if they refused or failed to pass the test, their statements were not used in the research.

The research found that sexual assaults were epidemic. The most hardened of the men and those who were so frail that they were immediately put in solitary confinement for their own protection were the only ones that escaped homosexual rape. Many of the guards were indifferent to these problems and indicated to the prisoners that they did not want to be bothered with such complaints. One reported case involved a victim who screamed for over an hour while he was being raped in his cell. The nearby guard totally ignored his pleas for help and laughed at him after the attack was completed. The prisoners who reported this attack passed a lie detector test, while the guard identified in this case refused to take the test. This study excluded those homosexual relations that were truly consensual; yet it is impossible to distinguish consensual homosexuality from rape because many apparently consensual liaisons originated from gang rape or its threat.

The typical sexual aggressor in this setting does not consider himself to be a homosexual or even to be engaged in homosexual actions. There is a tendency for these male prisoners to identify as male sexual activity that which is aggressive and, as homosexual, any sexual activity that is passive. Rape appears to serve as a method of asserting manhood and power. Other men do this in dealing with women or by occupational success, but neither is possible in prison. Thus sexual release is not the primary motive of these rapists but rather the degradation of his victim, just as Brownmiller (1975) found is true of heterosexual rape.

This description of sex in prisons for men does not appear to characterize women in prison. There is homosexuality among women in prison to be sure, but no reports of rape or other sexual coercion (Ward and Kassebaum, 1965; Giallombardo, 1966; Heffernan, 1972). Homosexual behavior of any kind, active or passive, is not condemned or despised as a sign of weakness as is passive sexual behavior in prisons for men. Rather, homosexual relations are widely encouraged among female prisoners as a rational solution to the problems encountered during one's life in prison. While homosexual relations among male prisoners mainly serve to establish power relationships, among females such a relationship is used to give the woman a warm and supportive association such as is often provided by families (Ward and Kassebaum, 1965). Here we see a stereotype emerging to the effect that women need such supportive relationships more than men do. But as in prisons for men there are two basic social roles in the homosexual liaison, one more masculine and one more passive. Since the passive role represents the least alteration in traditional female sexual behavior, there are more women choosing the passive than the masculine role. Therefore those women choosing the more masculine role are in great demand in women's prisons. More passive females often attempt to win their favor by giving them presents or running errands for them. The more masculine women sometimes cut their hair very short and dress and talk in an exaggerated masculine fashion.

In addition to these findings, some research claims that women in prison develop pseudofamilies that approximate those found in free society as a means of making their imprisonment less painful (Giallombardo, 1966). This creates a substitute set of social relations similar enough to those in free society that prisoners can preserve an identity relevant to life outside the prison. Again we find the reasoning that social roles involving the family are more important to women in general, and specifically to women in prison, than such roles are to men. It is alleged that a key part of most female prisoner relationships is the homosexual alliance, which is often recognized by the prisoners as a legitimate marriage. All other social relationships in the prison hinge around this homosexual liaison.

As in any family, there are aunts, uncles, nieces, and mothers. Such social roles in the pseudofamily are much more stable than the marriage unit, which may have frequent changes in partners. However, once women are in a prison pseudofamily, they typically remain there until their release from prison. Therefore these roles add considerable stability to the prisoner social system. As in any other family, sexual relations between those who are kin is identified as a deviant activity. It has also been observed that the prison pseudofamily appears to perform an economic function in production and distribution, not unlike families in the wider society, in addition to its role in emotional support (Heffernan, 1972). For example, the members of pseudofamilies often help their prison kin with specially made clothing and special rations of food. Since the prisoner social system is so different among women than among men, it is not correct to claim that the inmate culture is an automatic response to imprisonment but rather appears to depend as well on the differing emotional needs that inmates bring with them into prison.

Finally, while some of the research on women in prison has found pseudofamilies (Giallombardo, 1966; Heffernan, 1972), some has found no evidence of these families (Ward and Kassebaum, 1965). These differing results may mean that there are differences among prisons for women: some having pseudofamilies, while some do not. Since these families do not appear in all institutions for women, we must rethink the typical picture of women as being necessarily so dependent upon the family. And there are some convincing reasons to suspect that many women in prison are not nearly so dependent on families as is sometimes claimed. The women in prisons are not generally recruited from those social strata where women have had the luxury of dependence on their families. Many of these women previously had a life on the streets as drug addicts and prostitutes, and to suggest that these women are dependent on a family is nothing more than a sexist stereotype.

Other Types of Prison Subcultures

Aside from these differences in inmate subcultures among men and women, some research (Irwin and Cressey, 1962) has demonstrated other differences among men. One value system has been referred to as the *thief subculture* and one as the *convict subculture*. Professional thieves are involved in a subculture of sorts whether they are in or out of prison. For example, the value system that thieves learn forbids betrayal of others to the police and places a high value on their remaining levelheaded when confronted with the danger and risks inherent in a career of theft. Since one of the occupational hazards of the trade is that from time to time they can expect to be arrested, the thief subculture provides them with norms to guide their behavior in this situation. Status in this group comes from professional expertise in stealing.

The other subculture among men in prison, called the convict subculture, is one in which all status is achieved as a result of manipulating both the staff and other prisoners to gain special privileges and power in the prison. Such prisoners place a high value on being tough and forming powerful inmate cliques to effectively dominate the cellblock or prison. Generally those oriented to this subculture have a long history of confinement. There are, of course, prisoners oriented toward neither of these subcultures but rather toward more conventional values. Since conventionally oriented inmates and thieves are not so interested in power within the institution, they usually do not expend as much effort in attempting to manipulate the situation there as do the convicts. The former are not so concerned, for example, in gaining access to forbidden supplies (such as yeast from the bakery for use in making home brew) to trade or sell to other prisoners. Generally the thieves and the conventionally oriented prisoners are better behaved than the convicts because they just want to do their time, be released as soon as possible, and return to work in free society—albeit illegal work in the case of the thieves.

The behavior patterns found in most prisons for men are likely to be a combination of these two types of prison subcultures. As thieves are incarcerated longer and longer, they may feel more and more separated from their civilian occupational role and, at least to a degree, begin to attempt to attain some special power or privilege in the prison. Also the convict may admire the thief and his values, and in this way the two distinct subcultures become blended into one. This may account for the fact that many studies of prison subcultures have found only one subculture (Irwin and Cressey, 1962). A major contribution of this research is that we learn from the thieves that people in prison are not only influenced by the *deprivation* in their immediate situation but also by *importation* of their past experiences and values, as was also allegedly true in the case of the subculture found among women in prison.

Correspondingly, Thomas (1973:20) found in a test of the deprivation and importation models of prisoner resocialization that prisoners

> relate to their present situation in a way that reflects their preprison learning experiences [such as age at first conviction], their extra-prison relationships [reflected in letters received], and their post-prison expectations [for success]. These external variables . . . influence their potential receptivity to both prisonization and resocialization.

In an international survey it has been found that the prison subculture is indeed dependent on both the type of prison situation faced by prisoners as well as the characteristics they bring into the prison, "such that the type of prison determines the general level of drug activity which can be expected, but that which inmates will engage in drug use as an adaptation . . . depends on which ones have had prior experience with drugs" (Akers et al., 1977:548).

Race Wars in Prisons

Aside from these traditional divisions among prisoners, racial divisions are obvious to all observers of modern prison life. In most state prisons there is considerable racial segregation in living quarters, originally done intentionally by the staff based on racism, but now perpetuated by both black and white prisoners. These distinctions between white and black prisoners seem even more important than the distinction between convicts and thieves. There is a clear irony that as late as the 1980s there are clear patterns of racial segregation in these state-run public facilities in clear opposition to the spirit of federal law and U.S. Supreme Court decisions regarding the unconstitutionality of racial segregation in public facilities.

A description of life in the California state prison, San Quentin, during the 1970s gives some indication of why this is so (Bunker, 1972). In this prison there was so much racial paranoia that any specific provocation was unnecessary to incite violent behavior between white and black prisoners. Almost any excuse was enough to start the killing. Furthermore, convicts no longer engaged in fistfights. If one prisoner would hit another one, he was likely to be killed in retaliation. Therefore many prisoners realized that if the issue is not worth killing someone for, or possibly being killed, they probably should forget it.

In this prison the black inmates kept themselves segregated whenever possible. The Chicanos were usually closer to the whites than to the black prisoners. And since most of the guards were white, they typically sided with the whites against the blacks as well. Examples of the intensity of feeling were not difficult to locate. Two white prisoners swindled a black prisoner out of $100 worth of heroin with counterfeit money. But an hour later when this was discovered, the black man and some of his friends caught the two whites and stabbed them severely. When the white inmate leaders heard about this situation, they felt that justice had been done.

But the black prisoners were not content. Shortly, other black prisoners stabbed a white prisoner sleeping in his cell. There was no provocation for this stabbing except that the prisoner was white. An hour later another white prisoner was stabbed by three black prisoners merely because they found him alone. The white leaders, of course, recognized that they had to make some reprisal, for if they did not, the blacks would feel that they could stab whites at will. However, before they could respond a 55-year-old white inmate was stabbed by four black prisoners. This was especially ironic because this particular white prisoner had been very generous with black prisoners, sharing tobacco and coffee. Next, yet another white prisoner was killed by three blacks. Though whites outnumbered blacks in this prison 50 to 35 percent, the blacks had greater power within the prison than their numbers suggested because the whites were less united.

In the context of prison violence it must be realized that many blacks feel no hope and nothing but hatred as a consequence of generation after generation of systematic and institutionalized racism. The alienation is so complete that often they have no motivation for any activity except revenge. Some blacks feel that they are political prisoners, that the entire American political system is totally corrupt, and that they have never really been a part of this system but rather were always exploited outsiders.

All of this violence seems to be above the law, and no indictments were filed because none of the prisoners would testify in court. The prisoners would not cooperate with the courts both because they feared retaliation from those against whom they were to testify and because they hated and distrusted the legal system as much as they did the prisoners of other races. But the white guards had a plan of their own. They let the white prisoners know that they would look the other way if the whites should decide to strike back in retaliation. This coalition of guards and white prisoners was based only on a mutual hatred for the blacks. Therefore it was not really unexpected when two black prisoners were soon stabbed, and shortly five more black prisoners were stabbed as well.

One black prisoner immediately rushed to a white guard to show him the open knife wound, but the guard was unconcerned. The guards also refused to investigate any of the cases involving black victims.

As a consequence of this last round of violence, a sort of balance of terror had been restored at San Quentin (Bunker, 1972). For example, black prisoners stopped jumping into lines ahead of whites and stopped intentionally bumping them. For the time being the black prisoners were showing more respect for the whites, but it was a respect based on fear, not tolerance. Clearly there was no evidence in this prison of one unified prisoner subculture and certainly no solidarity across races.

The history of the Stateville penitentiary in Illinois since 1936 also shows how the problem of racial violence has escalated (Jacobs, 1977). Back in the 1930s there were few employees at this prison except the warden, the guards, and a handful of civilian clerks. The prisoners filled all of the other clerical positions, which put them in an ideal position to bargain for special privileges. At that time ethnic gangs, including the Irish and the Italians, dominated the prison, much as black gangs would by the 1970s. In 1936 a new warden took over at Stateville. Based almost wholly on the strength of his personality, he took complete control of the institution and stripped the gangs of their special power and privileges.

The new warden attempted to institute other reforms. By building his own independent base of political support, he attempted to ensure that partisan politics would never again interfere with the prison's operation as it had so often in the past. Thus no one would ever be forced to resign his prison position because of a party change in the governor's office. Also he gained complete control of the prisoners through heavy reliance on a system of informers. But because of the rigid discipline he instituted, combined with low wages, there was a high rate of employee turnover among the lower-ranking staff. Thus the tradition of firm control this warden instituted was carried on by a small number of high-ranking staff members and a group of high-status prisoners, such as inmate clerks and teachers, who benefited from the status quo.

Prisoners were not allowed to talk during meals or while waiting in line, and everything in the institution took place on a tightly organized daily schedule. For their part, the prisoners could be given greater freedom if they supplied information to the staff, and thus the inmate social system put a great deal of effort into identifying and punishing informers.

This strong-willed warden was eventually replaced in 1961 by a more liberal warden. The new warden loosened up the daily routine to a considerable extent, allowing talking at meals and while standing in line. Also in 1962 a new Illinois criminal code was passed that allowed a parole from a life sentence after serving approximately 11 years. As a result of these new parole possibilities, many of the old convicts that had become accustomed to the old routine were released from the prison. The release of these men and an ever-increasing percentage of black prisoners led to the destruction of the old inmate social system, as well as the system of informers. One other change was a new militancy among the black prisoners, especially among the Muslims.

In 1972 the state placed new stricter limits on what the institutional staff could do to control prisoners. This combination of events demoralized the guard staff, and inmate-to-inmate violence escalated, as did the number of escapes. The irony is that the liberal reforms instituted by both the new warden, as well as new state regulations, ultimately resulted in more violence against the prisoners by other inmates. Since the prisoners were now considered to be clients, they could no longer be used as school teachers or as clerks, and thus all the good job opportunities for prisoners vanished. At the same time the courts began giving prisoners at least minimal legal protection.

With the staff under greater and greater legal and administrative control, there developed a power vacuum that was filled by three black gangs and one white gang. Blacks now constituted 80 percent of the prison population. The black gangs have increasingly used the rhetoric of the civil rights movement, and the black gangs' expectations are without doubt influenced by this movement. Now the real power of an individual is determined on the basis of the gang membership, and the gang's power in turn depends on the power it has on the streets of Chicago. In an earlier era the power of the prisoner depended on his position within the institution, such as having a special job as a clerk. But since these special jobs are a thing of the past, there are no longer any grounds for accommodation between prisoners and staff. As a consequence of all these changes, during the 1970s the number of guards injured each year continued to rise. The fear among the guards was palpable, and white guards, especially, often resigned because of their great fear of black prisoners.

A smiliar situation has developed as a consequence of liberal reforms in the Texas prison system (Marquart and Crouch, 1985). A researcher worked as a prison guard for 19 months and observed how the guards used the "rat" system and the techniques used to control the prisoners who, in the institution studied, were all older, hard-core recidivists. In the maximum security prison at Eastham, Texas, each of the 18 cell blocks had one prisoner who was appointed by the staff as the "head building tender." Head building tenders had the job of helping to control prisoners. In exchange they were given special open cells and bathing privileges. At a second level there were three to five building tenders in each cell block who acted as assistants for the head building tender. The third level of the building tender system involved prisoners referred to as runners, strikers, or hitmen. They were not assigned by the staff but by the building tenders to act as informants. Runners also cleaned up around the cell block. Finally, there were approximately 17 turnkeys among the prisoners who also assisted the building tenders.

The building tender system functioned as an information network that divided and controlled ordinary inmates. The turnkeys and building tenders had snitches working for them all over the prison, which made them both useful to the staff in controlling other prisoners, while the building tenders also used direct physical punishment to control unruly prisoners. Thus most building tenders were selected from those inmates serving time for violent crimes, such as armed robbery and murder, who were typically mentally and physically superior to other prisoners. And most building tenders were white because the staff felt that they could most easily trust the whites. (This system is similar to the practices developed in Stateville).

The staff used minor physical assaults in private on prisoners to force them to conform. But when inmates violated "sacred" rules, such as attacking an officer, they received severe beatings that could involve concussions, loss of consciousness, and broken bones. These beatings were always performed in front of other prisoners to serve as a warning but were always justified as necessary for self-defense. The system exploited ordinary prisoners and kept them in total submission. Guards used verbal intimidation on prisoners, such as "You stupid nigger, if you ever lie to me or any other officer about what you're doing, I'll knock your teeth in" (Marquart, 1986:351). Prisoners were sometimes threatened with extreme physical assaults: "Nobody cares if a convict dies here, we'll beat you to death" (Marquart, 1986:351). One type of unofficial physical coercion was referred to by prisoners and staff as a "tune-up" or "attitude adjustment" or "counselling." These were used for minor infractions, such as arguing with an officer, and included slaps, kicks, and verbal humiliation but rarely involved serious physical injury. Inmates who were given official punishment by the institutional court were often given further unofficial punishment in the form of these tune-ups as well. To avoid lawsuits and federal investigations the staff often wrote ficticious reports indicating that the violence was required to subdue a prisoner. Doing so they always managed to avoid legal intervention.

Once the courts ruled that such practices had to be stopped, prisoners began to openly challenge the staff's authority. From 1982 to 1984 inmate threats and attacks on the staff increased nearly 500 percent. More and more the prisoners refused to follow orders from the staff without some show of defiance. No longer was there any fear of physical assaults by guards, and the guards, for their part, no longer had the building tenders to help them control prisoners. This loss was especially crucial because the building tenders had been feared more than the guards.

Although the building tenders had ruled through fear and terror, they did keep down the incidence of violence among inmates. In 3 recent years the inmate-to-inmate prison violence nearly tripled, even though the prison population decreased. As the amount of violence has grown, inmate gangs have emerged to fill the power vacuum left by the building tenders. These changes left the guards totally demoralized, and they now think that the prison has been totally turned over to the prisoners. They in fact no longer feel that they know what is going on in the prison. Although the court intervention was made to enforce constitutional rules of fairness, it is ironic that as the staff's authority has been eroded, life for most prisoners has become much more dangerous (Marquart and Crouch, 1985).

SUMMARY

For any who doubt the systematic horror created by imprisonment, one need look no further than the experiment by Philip Zimbardo at Stanford. Add to this the constant threat and reality of homosexual rape in prisons for men, and we see a situation that can only be characterized as a living hell. Traditionally the pain of imprisonment has been partially mitigated by an inmate subculture. But a unified inmate social system seems to be largely a thing of the past. During this century the percentage of black prisoners has steadily risen, and the level of rage among these black prisoners makes their control and supervision nearly impossible. First, blacks are brutalized in American ghettos and later are further dehumanized by American prisons. Ultimately, everyone around them, both during their incarceration and after their release, will pay the price for this dehumanization.

REFERENCES

Akers, R. L.
  1977 "Type of leadership in prison: a structural approach to testing the functional and importation models." The Sociological Quarterly 18(Summer):378–383.

Akers, R. L., N. S. Hayner, and W. Gruninger
  1977 "Prisonization in five countries: type of prison and inmate characteristics." Criminology 14(February):527–554.

Brownmiller, S.
  1975 Against Our Will: Men, Women and Rape. New York: Simon & Schuster.

Bunker, E.
  1972 "War behind walls." Harpers (February):39–47.

Clemmer, D.
  1958 The Prison Community. New York: Holt, Rinehart & Winston.

Cloward, R. A.
  1960 "Social control in the prison." Pp. 20–48 in Theoretical Studies in Social Organization of the Prison. New York: Social Science Research Council.

Cohen, S. and L. Taylor
  1972 Psychological Survival: The Experience of Long-Term Imprisonment. New York: Pantheon.

Colvin, M.
  1982 "The 1980 New Mexico prison riot." Social Problems 29(June):449–463.

Davis, A. J.
  1968 "Sexual assaults in the Philadelphia prison system and sheriff's vans." Transaction 6(December):8–16.

Faber, N.
  1971 "An unusual experiment at Stanford dramatizes the brutality of prison life." Life (October 15):82–83.

Galliher, J. F.
  1972 "Naming behaviour and social interaction in prisons." British Journal of Criminology 12(April):167–174.

Giallombardo, R.
  1966 Society of Women: A Study of a Women's Prison. New York: John Wiley & Sons.

Gillespie, M. W. and J. F. Galliher
  1972 "Age, anomie, and the inmate's definition of aging in prison: an exploratory study." Pp. 465–483 in D. P. Kent, R. Kastenbaum, and S. Sherwood (eds.) Research, Planning, and Action for the Elderly. New York: Behavioral Publications.

Goffman, E.
  1961 Asylums. Chicago: Aldine.

Haney, C., C. Banks, and P. Zimbardo
  1973 "A study of prisoners and guards in a simulated prison." Naval Research Reviews, U.S. Office of Naval Research (September):1–17.

Hartung, F. E. and M. Floch
  1956 "A social-psychological analysis of prison riots: an hypothesis." Journal of Criminal Law, Criminology and Police Science 47(May–June):51–57.

Heffernan, E.
  1972 Making it in Prison: The Square, the Cool, and the Life. New York: John Wiley & Sons.

Hughes, E. C.
  1962 "Good people and dirty work." Social Problems 10(Summer):3–11.

Irwin, J. and D. R. Cressey
  1962 "Theives, Convicts and the Inmate Culture." Social Problems(Fall):142–155.
Jacobs, J. B.
  1977 Stateville: The Penitentiary in Mass Society. Chicago: University of Chicago Press.
Madigan, P. J. (Warden)
  1956 "Institutional rules and regulations." United States Penitentiary, Alcatraz, Calif.
Marquart, J. W.
  1986 "Prison guards and the use of physical coercion as a mechanism of prisoner control." Criminology 24(May):347–366.
Marquart, J. W. and B. M. Crouch
  1985 "Judicial reform and prisoner control: the impact of *Ruiz* v. *Estelle* on a Texas penitentiary." Law and Society Review 19(4):557–586.
McCleery, R.
  1960 "Communication patterns as bases of systems of authority and power." Pp. 49–77 in Theoretical Studies in Social Organization of the Prison. New York: Social Science Research Council.
McKorkle, L. W. and R. Korn
  1954 "Resocialization within walls." Annals of the American Academy of Political and Social Science 293(May):88–98.
New York Times
  1980 "TV: New Mexico prison riot." September 23:C22.
Reed, M. B. and F. D. Glamser
  1979 "Aging in a total institution: the case of older prisoners." The Gerontologist 19:354–360.
Schwartz, B.
  1972 "Deprivation of privacy as a 'functional prerequisite': the case of the prison." Journal of Criminal Law, Criminology and Police Science 63(June):229–239.
Sykes, G. M.
  1956 "The corruption of authority and rehabilitation." Social Forces 34(March):257–262.
  1958 Society of Captives: A Study of a Maximum Security Prison. Princeton, N.J.: Princeton University Press.
Sykes, G. M. and S. L. Messinger
  1960 "The inmate social system." Pp. 5–19 in Theoretical Studies in Social Organization of the Prison. New York: Social Science Research Council.
Thomas, C. W.
  1973 "Prisonization or resocialization? a study of external factors associated with the impact of imprisonment." Journal of Research in Crime and Delinquency 10(January):13–21.
Useem,B.
  1985 "Disorganization and the New Mexico prison riot of 1980." American Sociological Review 50(October):677–688.
Ward, D. A. and G. G. Kassebaum
  1965 Women's Prison: Sex and Social Structure. Chicago: Aldine.
Wheeler, S.
  1961 "Socialization in correctional communities." American Sociological Review 26 (October): 697–712.
  1966a "Role conflict in correctional communities." Pp. 229–259 in D. R. Cressey (ed.), The Prison: Studies in Institutional Organization Change. New York: Holt, Rinehart & Winston.
  1966b "The structure of formally organized socialization settings." Pp. 51–116 in O. G. Brim, Jr. and S. Wheeler (eds.), Socialization After Childhood: Two Essays. New York: John Wiley & Sons.
Zimbardo, P. G.
  1972 "Pathology of imprisonment." Society 9(April):4, 6, 8.
Zingraff, M. T.
  1975 "Prisonization as an inhibitor of effective resocialization." Criminology 13(November): 366–388.

14
POSSIBILITY OF PSYCHOLOGICAL CHANGE IN PRISONS

PSYCHOLOGICAL AND SOCIAL CHANGES IN EXTREME PRISON SITUATIONS

Presumably the way rehabilitation in prisons works is that while the convicted person is incarcerated the staff has some profound impact on the person that changes this individual forever. Few would deny that the German Nazi concentration camps had a profound and lasting impact on their prisoners, although clearly rehabilitation was not the Nazi intention. The Communist Chinese forces had considerable success in changing the behavior and attitudes of United Nations troops in their custody during the Korean War. This chapter begins with a review of these two historical examples to see what can be learned about the capacity to change human behavior under the most extreme prison conditions. Perhaps from these extreme cases we can learn to what degree the goals of modern prisons are feasible and morally proper.

Nazi Concentration Camps

Bettelheim's Research   Much of what is known about life in Nazi concentration camps comes from the well-known research of psychologist Bruno Bettelheim (1943) who studied the operation and impact of these camps while a prisoner himself. Bettelheim spent one year confined in two different concentration camps. His study reported that in the camps every movement of the prisoners was very strictly controlled. For their part, the prisoners did not know precisely why they were imprisoned nor for how long they were to be held.

The Nazis who ran these camps desired to break the will of the prisoners and to transform them into docile masses who would offer no resistance. For the most part, they were successful. Bettelheim also reported that the camps were used to spread terror among the general civilian population by showing what could happen to enemies of the Nazis. Bettelheim said that his primary reason for conducting the study was to keep his sanity and self-respect under these dehumanizing conditions. By conducting this research and recording his observations—with great secrecy, of course—he could continue to feel some self-respect even as the Nazis attempted to reduce him to a nonhuman object.

The prisoners' reactions, he found, depended on both their social class and political background. Political prisoners, such as socialists and communists, saw in these camps a demonstration of just how dangerous the Nazis really were. This demonstration supported their earlier hatred and fear of the Nazis, and in this sense the Nazis' brutal treatment of the political prisoners did not really surprise them greatly. On the other hand, the nonpolitical, middle-class prisoners never really got over the shock and surprise and could never really comprehend just what was happening to them. The conventional middle-class Jews in these camps had always obeyed the law imposed by the government leaders and assumed that if they did so, they would ultimately be saved from their imprisonment. They had always been supporters of the legal authorities, and up until this time, the authorities had always supported them. The upper-class Jewish prisoners were understandably even more surprised by their incarceration. They assumed that their arrest was the result of an oversight and that when the authorities discovered what had occurred, they would be released immediately because of their importance. Since they believed that they would be quickly released, these upper-class prisoners segregated themselves whenever they could from the other prisoners who they believed would have a longer stay in the camps.

Bettelheim found that a feeling of total indifference swept over many prisoners. They became completely indifferent to acts of brutality and torture by the guards and seemingly no longer cared whether they were shot because it was as if what was going on was not really happening to them—so great was their state of shock. It was as if they had become detached observers, even while watching brutality directed toward themselves. The feeling of unreality about the horrible acts of brutality was so great that often prisoners felt greater anger when the camp guards committed a relatively minor insult or act of hostility. Bettelheim reasons that experiences they might have had prior to their incarceration during their "normal" life history provoked a "normal" reaction.

In this study Bettelheim found considerable differences between prisoners who had been in the camps less than a year and those longer-term prisoners who had spent at least 3 years in the camp. Among the short-term prisoners there was great concern with how they would adjust to life in society once they were released from prison. Long-term prisoners, however, were mainly concerned with surviving within the prison camp. Once prisoners reached this reaction stage in the prison camp, everything that happened to them there became very real. There was no longer a split between being a victim and being a disinterested observer. At this point prisoners stopped speculating about the welfare of their families and no longer attempted to make contact with people outside the camp. Now most of the prisoners' efforts were directed toward improving their living conditions within the camp. These long-term prisoners learned to direct a great amount of aggression against themselves, rather than against the Nazis, to maximize their chances of survival.

This study is important not only because these were extremely brutal prison conditions but also because one of the prisoners was a trained behavioral scientist studying prison life from the inside, which also is quite unusual. Typically, studies of prison life rely on interviews with prisoners by behavioral scientists, or sometimes on direct reports of prison conditions by prisoners having little formal education. The Bettelheim study is especially important because it involves direct prison experiences as seen through the eyes of a trained behavioral scientist.

Knowledge Gained   There is not the slightest doubt that the Nazis completely broke the spirit of those in the concentration camps. History records that millions of prisoners marched to their deaths in relatively orderly fashion without any type of prisoner uprising. We also know from this research that prior background, social class, and length of stay in a prison situation were all critical elements in determining the individual's ultimate response to the massive pressures imposed by the staff of the prison camps.

Bettelheim (1943:421–422) reported that he conducted this research while he was a prisoner in an attempt to maintain his sanity through using his professional skills.

> [The] question arose, namely, "How can I protect myself against becoming as they [other prisoners] are?" The answer was comparatively simple: to find out what had happened in them, and to me. . . . So I set out to find what changes had occurred and were occurring in the prisoners. . . . By occupying myself during my spare time with interesting problems, with interviewing my fellow prisoners, by pondering my findings for the hours without end during which I was forced to perform exhausting labor. . . . I succeeded in killing the time in a way which seemed constructive. . . . As time went on, the enhancement of my self-respect due to my ability to continue to do meaningful work despite the contrary efforts of the Gestapo became even more important than the pastime.

Thus Bettelheim recalls that the main problem was to protect his sanity and that by his systematic plan he was successful in protecting himself from the attempts of the Nazis to destroy his personality. Bettelheim was confined in two concentration camps for approximately one year. Other prisoners who had been confined as long as seven years have indicated that his behavior represented a type of "lone wolf" adaptation that most prisoners went through during their first year of confinement (Foreman, 1959). Thus Bettelheim is not as unusual in this regard as he seems to have imagined. All prisoners ultimately discovered, however, that they could not keep up this "lone wolf" behavior if they expected to survive. Long-term survival under such oppressive conditions required considerable social support from the other prisoners—something that Bettelheim never mentioned.

Bettelheim believed that repelling efforts to destroy one's personality in a concentration camp is largely a matter of self-disciplined individual resistance. It is interesting to note that the code of conduct for U.S. military personnel also demonstrates this attitude to a great degree. It reads as follows (Foreman, 1959:292):

1. I am an American fighting man. I serve the forces which guard my country and our way of life. I am prepared to give my life in their defense.
2. I will never surrender of my own free will. If in command, I will never surrender my men while they still have the means to resist.
3. If I am captured, I will continue to resist by all means available. I will make every effort to escape and aid others to escape. I will accept neither parole nor special favors from the enemy.
4. If I become a prisoner of war, I will keep faith with my fellow prisoners. I will give no information or take part in any action that might be harmful to my comrades. If I am a senior, I will take command. If not, I will obey the lawful orders of those appointed over me and will back them in every way.
5. When questioned, should I become a prisoner of war, I am bound to give only name, rank, service number, and date of birth. I will evade answering further questions to the utmost of my ability. I will make no oral or written statements disloyal to my country and its allies or harmful to their cause.
6. I will never forget that I am an American fighting man, responsible for my actions, and dedicated to the principles which made my country free. I will trust in my God and in the United States of America.

This set of rules seems to have been designed either by a Hollywood movie scriptwriter or by high-ranking officers who will never have to worry about being taken prisoner. In fact, this type of self-discipline and obstinate resistance will not serve a prisoner very well during long periods of confinement. These rules do not consider the possibility that if five people escape from a prisoner-of-war camp, the enemy may have 50 other prisoners shot. Therefore such clandestine activities as sabotage in a prison camp cannot be tolerated by other prisoners, since one explosion could result in 50 executions. The world of the prison camp is not really as simple as the military rules imply.

Often German criminals were released from prisons to work as officials in concentration camps. These criminals brought with them the practices of graft and other schemes that they had formerly used while they were prisoners. They routinely sold standard concentration camp mess kits to the prisoners and even tried to sell the prisoners protection. Some prisoners were ready to purchase this protection, but such an individualistic orientation, while possible in some jails and prisons, did not work in concentration camps. Prisoners in these camps eventually found that they had to consider the problems of the whole group, since none of them knew when, or if, they would be released. Thus the models of behavior held up by the Bettelheim study and by the U.S. military are not possible for those anticipating long-term confinement. Those serving indefinite or long sentences in American prisons must also come to terms with their environment, forget about the free society, and learn to live as best they can with the demands of both the staff and other prisoners. Remaining aloof from one's environment in such a situation is simply not possible. An even more dramatic demonstration of the psychological impact of imprisonment can be seen in the Chinese prisoner-of-war camps.

Chinese Prisoner-of-War Camps

Indoctrination or Brainwashing Methods Interviews with those who had been released from Communist Chinese prisoner-of-war camps at the end of the Korean War gave a fairly detailed description of these camps (Schein, 1956). Many of the United Nations forces were originally captured by North Koreans who were generally brutal and harsh. By contrast, the Chinese were very friendly and rather lenient. Often when new prisoners were first turned over to the Chinese, they were offered "congratulations" for being "liberated." The Chinese explained that the United Nations had entered the war on the side of the South Koreans illegally and that all United Nations (UN) forces were technically war criminals and therefore could be executed. But since these UN soldiers were only carrying out the corrupt orders of higher officials, they would be sent instead to schools and taught the truth about the war. Any captured UN soldier who refused to go to these schools would automatically revert to their war criminal status and be shot. Thus the prisoners found it impossible to refuse to attend the lectures.

After the prisoners were captured in North Korea, they were forced into long marches to prison camps inside China. The stress on the prisoners was so great at this time that the men became increasingly apathetic and disorganized, and the lines of authority among the UN troops tended to break down. During these forced marches the attitude seemed to be one of "every man for himself." Hence there was open competition for food and clothing, which made stable social relations impossible.

Finally, when those men who did not perish en route arrived at the permanent prisoner-of-war camp inside China, they were segregated by nationality, rank, and race. They were then assigned to squads of about 10 to 15 men who lived in the same quarters. The Chinese appointed leaders for each squad without regard to rank—thus a soldier could be put in charge of those with higher military rank, which would weaken the military chain of command.

In addition to ignoring rank in making leadership assignments, the Chinese tried to undermine any group organization found among the men by segregating them according to rank, making military leadership impossible. Convincing the youngest soldiers to collaborate was easier when their leaders were removed. Any time evidence of informal group organization appeared, the Chinese would quickly remove the key figures in this movement. The Chinese also separated black prisoners from the others in an effort to put special pressure on them to recognize their second-class status in the United States. The Chinese believed that the black prisoners would be especially vulnerable to indoctrination. To weaken the bonds of group solidarity, no religious services were permitted. The prison staff withheld prisoners' mail from relatives and claimed that the reason the prisoners were not getting any letters was because their relatives had forgotten about them. All of these practices were instituted to weaken prisoner morale.

Most of the prisoners' time during the first year in the camp was spent in the education or indoctrination sessions. As it became clearer to the Chinese that a truce would be signed, which would end the Korean War and return the UN troops to their homes, more time was allowed for recreation. But at first everything at the permanent camps seemed designed to support the indoctrination program. The Chinese had several indoctrination or brainwashing techniques.

The Chinese prison officials removed all possible support for the beliefs and the values of the prisoners. The prisoners could get no information about the world outside the prison camp except from the Communist newspaper *The Daily Worker* and from Chinese radio broadcasts. In other words, the prisoners' only information came from their Chinese captors.

The prisoners' values came under direct attack as well. In addition to attending a series of lectures, all prisoners were shown films and leaflets comparing the Communist and capitalist systems. The films were reasonably effective in changing prisoners' attitudes because of the sheer lack of any other audiovisual materials to which modern people have become so accustomed. The Chinese used the prolonged idleness in the camps to effectively force prisoners into considering the Communist point of view because reading Communist literature was the only activity available. This technique is similar to the traditional American practice of putting unruly prisoners in a cell by themselves with nothing but a Bible.

But perhaps the most effective attack on the values and beliefs of these prisoners were testimonials from other prisoners who had apparently converted to the Communist philosophy. These testimonials both weakened group solidarity and presented more pro-Communist arguments. If all of the prisoners had continued to defend their nation's ideals, they could at least have had group support for their ideas even though they could not defend them logically. But when just one UN prisoner became convinced of the Communist ideology, it became necessary for other prisoners to reexamine their own beliefs, which made them vulnerable to the highly one-sided arguments of the Chinese.

The Chinese convinced several Air Force officers to make confessions about participating in germ warfare, and a movie was made of two of these officers giving this testimony. Also, the officers went from camp to camp explaining how the UN had used such horrible germ warfare. These confessions were very convincing because the officers did not seem to be under direct coercion and traveled from camp to camp without supervision. Korean women and children also testified about the brutality of the UN forces.

Aside from these direct attacks on the beliefs of these prisoners, the Chinese also used indirect attacks on the prisoners' beliefs. The prisoners were required to break up into their squads following each lecture, go to their living quarters, and discuss the lecture. Psychologists have found that attitudes can be most easily changed through group discussions where people feel that they have taken some active part in the decision-making process (Lewin, 1958).

The prison staff also used interrogations of the men that relied mainly on psychological rather than on physical punishment. So sophisticated were the Chinese that usually only threats of punishment were needed to gain cooperation. The men were required to go through elaborate public confessions even for minor violations of the camp rules. There were lengthy lists of rules that the men were forced to sign when they arrived at the camp. Most of the men did not read the rules carefully because they were too tired and hungry to do so. The Chinese looked carefully for discrepancies in their confessions and required the prisoner to explain them. In some cases the Chinese wanted men to cooperate and did not really care whether they accepted Communism or not. In such cases collaboration was elicited by rewards, including special freedom in the camps.

The principles on which the Chinese indoctrination program are based are worthy of special emphasis:

1. Everything the Chinese did was based on repetition. In other words, they had great patience.
2. The Chinese apparently had given considerable thought to the pacing of commands. Prisoners were asked first to sign trivial confessions and then were gradually forced into more significant confessions.
3. The prisoners were never allowed to listen passively. Some individual or group participation was always required.
4. The situations in the prison camp were always such that the correct prisoner response was followed by some reward, but an incorrect response was followed by some threat or punishment. The psychological principles of reinforcement and learning were deftly applied by the prison staff.
5. Public confessions from Air Force officers were aired based on the principle that a prestigious source of information has tremendous impact.
6. Pleas for peace were also effective among these war-weary soldiers.

Prisoner Reactions   There were a number of different reactions to the extreme stress placed upon these prisoners by the Chinese. Some prisoners withdrew both from the Chinese and from other prisoners. Some men were constant resisters—nothing or no one could get them to conform. They openly defied the Chinese even in the face of severe torture. Many of these men had been unable to conform to the authority of the UN military forces and found they had the same response to prison. Some soldiers were idealists whose moral or political ideology demanded that they resist all pressure from the Chinese. But many prisoners were different. Many worried that they might break and cooperate with the Chinese. Indeed, only a few men were able to avoid collaboration altogether—so effective was the Chinese use of reward and punishment and other human manipulation techniques. Finally, some men fully cooperated with the Chinese. The reasons for this collaboration varied. Some could not resist any authority nor withstand any psychological or physical discomfort. Some were opportunists who collaborated solely for the material rewards. And some prisoners collaborated because in this way they achieved a status that they had never achieved before, either in the Army or in civilian life.

AMERICAN PRISON REHABILITATION PROGRAMS

Given this awesome and frightening legacy from Germany and China, the question is, What have Americans been doing to change the orientations of those in its prisons? The techniques vary in the degree to which they attempt *profound personality changes* or merely *behavioral change*. Several types of rehabilitation programs were developed during the 1950s, 1960s, and 1970s. Some programs will be discussed to demonstrate the coercive potential of such ideas.

Behavior Modification One attractive fad in prisoner rehabilitation is behavior modification. Basic to all behavior modification is that specified changes in an individual's environment are made to alter this individual's behavior. Although there are different types of behavior modification, they all use rewards to reinforce desired behavior and punishment to extinguish unwanted behavior.

Perhaps remembering the Chinese and German experience, psychologist James V. McConnell (1970:74) boasted:

> I believe that the day has come when we can combine sensory deprivation with drugs, hypnosis and astute manipulation of reward and punishment to gain almost absolute control over an individual's behavior. It should be possible then to achieve a very rapid and highly effective type of positive brainwashing that would allow us to make dramatic changes in a person's behavior and personality. I foresee the day when we could convert the worst criminal into a decent, respectable citizen in a matter of a few months—or perhaps even less time than that. . . . *we'd assume that a felony was clear evidence that the criminal had somehow acquired [a] full-blown social neurosis and needed to be cured, not punished.* We'd send him to a rehabilitation center where he'd undergo positive brainwashing until we were quite sure he had become a law-abiding citizen who would not again commit an antisocial act. We'd probably have to restructure his entire personality (Emphasis added).

McConnell's assumption that all crime is somehow related to mental illness is speculative at best and ignores the issue of law violators' rights, denying them even the integrity of their own personality.

Some behavior modification is oriented toward operant conditioning and some toward classical conditioning. Operant conditioning involves the use of rewards that are given to subjects after they produce the required behavior. For example, some attempts at behavior modification in rehabilitation programs in penal institutions use positive reinforcment or rewards, such as special privileges in the institution for conforming behavior (Schwitzgebel, 1971). Another example of rewarding conforming behavior is the "token economy" program often employed in institutions for juveniles. One study of delinquent boys in an institution allowed the boys to earn points for successfully completing specified amounts of educational material. For the first 3 to 5 days in the institution the boys were given attractive rooms and excellent meals. After these first few days the boys could only keep the nice room and have the good meals if they paid for them with the points they earned. The boys could also use these points to pay for snacks, magazines, and private tutoring. When a student did not complete his school work, he was referred to as a "relief" student, lost his private room, and could only eat after all the other boys had eaten. Such relief students were not allowed to see movies or wear civilian clothing (Schwitzgebel, 1971). Most of the boys showed great improvement in the level of their academic performance and decreases in the number of their behavior problems compared with those boys under regular institutional conditions. In other programs a juvenile who enters the institution receives no privileges—is not allowed to go to movies or eat desserts and has only the barest essentials in his room—until, by obeying the institutional rules, the youth earns credits with which to buy such privileges.

Although such programs using positive reinforcement are not frightening, the bizarre degree of control claimed by McConnell does lend itself to abuses, especially in the case of classical conditioning. Classical conditioning utilizes a neutral stimulus such as a bell ringing, an unconditioned stimulus such as an electric shock, and an unconditioned (or unlearned) response such as jumping when shocked. If the neutral stimulus (the ringing bell) and unconditioned stimulus (the shock) are repeatedly paired, the neutral stimulus (the ringing bell) eventually becomes capable of eliciting the response of jumping even when the unconditioned stimulus (the shock) is no longer present. The neutral stimulus becomes the conditioned stimulus, and the response is called the conditioned or the learned response. Classical conditioning has been used primarily with alcoholics and homosexuals. The idea is to produce an unpleasant reaction to alcohol or homosexual activity. The electric shock is paired with the sight and smell of alcohol or, in the case of homosexual child molesters, with pictures of children. Eventually it is hoped that the sight of alcohol or children ceases to become positively valued.

But classical conditioning is at times used for other types of cases. "At the Iowa Security Medical Facility, inmates who lie or swear are injected with apomorphine, a drug that sets them vomiting uncontrollably for from 15 minutes to an hour" (Sage, 1974:17). Another drug, Anectine, which induces sensations of suffocation and drowning, has been used at California's maximum security institution at Vacaville in an attempt to associate the drug with, and extinguish, violent behavior. As could be expected, this drug causes great anxiety among subjects (Mitford, 1973:127–128). These abuses are of special concern because of McConnell's questionable assumptions regarding crime and mental illness, which has spawned or at least legitimated such programs. Such cases are more than curious anomalies. They are natural outgrowths of the total lack of respect for the individual and for human dignity that provides the philosophic foundation for much behavior modification.

Reality Therapy Another psychiatric idea for the rehabilitation of prisoners is reality therapy, developed by William Glasser, which has rapidly caught on in state after state as the approved vehicle for rehabilitation programs. The basic tenets of reality therapy are outlined below (Glasser, 1965).

> In their unsuccessful effort to fulfill their needs, no matter what behavior they choose, all patients have a common characteristic: *they all deny the reality of the world around them.* . . . Therapy will be successful when they are able to give up denying the world and recognize that reality not only exists but that they must fulfill their needs within its framework (page 6). . . . The therapist must teach the patient better ways to fulfill his needs within the confines of reality (page 21).

In other words, reality therapy is an effort to help patients adjust to their situation or station in life, no matter how lowly and debased it is. Furthermore, unlike conventional Freudian therapy, reality therapy lays great stress on abiding by social values and morals. Instead of attempting to reduce concern and anxiety, as does Freudian therapy, it seeks to increase patients' concern regarding the violation of societal norms. Obviously, such an approach is extremely supportive of obedience to the status quo, and it wrongly assumes either that there is a value consensus or that the morality of powerful groups is more reasonable than that of other groups in American society.

In this view, the therapist's problem is to help patients act "responsibly." Correcting the patients' behavior and not their attitudes is the goal of reality therapy. People violate the law, according to Glasser, because they are irresponsible—not because they are angry or bored. In other words, what should be impressed upon law violators is that their violation is entirely their own fault.

After having sanctified obedience to law, Glasser (1965:23) conceded, using Thoreau as an example, that some responsible people do not conform to society's rules. And at times, according to Glasser, to be responsible one must violate the laws of society (1965:14). "In Nazi Germany, a responsible man, by our definition, would have been placed in a concentration camp." Yet almost immediately he swings back and encourages docility in the face of American racism and American poverty (Glasser, 1965:32). "We never encourage hostility or acting out irresponsible impulses, for that only compounds the problem. We never condemn society. If a Negro [sic], for example, feels limited by the white society, he must still take a responsible course of action." In other words, responsible Germans violated the law, whereas responsible Americans must obey the law. "Responsibility, a concept basic to Reality Therapy, is here defined as the ability to fulfill one's needs and to do so *in a way that does not deprive others of the ability to fulfill their needs*" (Glasser, 1965:13). The clear implication is that legal rights could be substituted for needs. The "responsible" person never violates the legal rights of others. Responsible action includes only behavior within the legal boundaries of the society, for "usually the law is psychiatrically right . . . because human beings with human needs have made the law according to their needs" (Glasser,1965:57). What is known about the social origins of law and pressure from special interest groups makes Glasser's optimism seem terribly naive. Even so, Glasser (1965:9) wavers again in admitting that some people, such as blacks in the South, cannot meet their needs because of environmental, not psychiatric, problems. Curiously he says nothing about the needs of blacks in the South Bronx, Newark, or St. Louis.

Since the boundary between environmental and psychological problems is not defined and seems subject to personal whim, reality therapy appears to be no more than intellectually empty moralizing, and the term *irresponsible behavior* appears to be no more than name-calling or labeling. Small wonder that this approach to adjustment is so popular among law enforcement officials charged with the control and rehabilitation of prison inmates, usually without adequate institutional budgets, information, or personnel.

Treatment Techniques with Groups

Group Counseling   One answer to the staffing problems of rehabilitation programs seems to be found in group counseling (Conrad, 1967:237). Here the staff person leading the group need not be a professionally trained behavioral scientist but rather an institutional guard or work detail supervisor. Group counseling differs from group therapy in that group counseling makes no attempt to help the prisoners achieve deep insight into the root of their problems. In group counseling only a discussion of individuals' current problems develops. The effort is not to achieve insight but to place conventional standards on human conduct. The advantage to the state is that such programs provide the appearance of therapy programs, even when funds do not permit hiring professional staff to provide therapy services. The disadvantage is that there is no logical reason to expect that such a technique would have any impact upon prisoners' behavior, nor is there any empirical evidence that it does.

Guided Group Interaction   Another approach to rehabilitation is called guided group interaction. This is a type of group therapy where professional leaders take more active roles than they do in other group therapies. Among other places, this technique has been used in early and well-known experiments in New Jersey (Weeks, 1958) and in Provo, Utah (Empey and Rabow, 1961). Guided group interaction requires that the offenders be involved in frequent, intensive, and prolonged discussions of the behavior and attitudes of individuals in the group. This approach attempts to develop a group culture that encourages those involved to assume responsibility for helping and controlling each other.

It was in New Jersey that guided group interaction was used in what was called the Highfields project. The reasoning of this program, and the one in Utah, was that since crime and delinquency are products of group life and group pressure, any attempt to stop this type of behavior must deal in some way with the group and not with the individual independent of the group. The Highfields project was limited to 20 boys ages 16 and 17 who were assigned by the juvenile court. Boys with prior commitments to correctional institutions were not accepted nor were mentally disturbed youths or sex offenders. The staff had these requirements for participation in the program to ensure the group sessions' maximum possibility of success. There were two 10-member groups that met for 1½ hours every weekday evening. The goal was to effectively rehabilitate the boys in 3 to 4 months. The boys worked in a mental hospital during the day. At night they returned to an old mansion on a large tract of land that had been acquired by the state for this project. Here the boys lived and participated in the guided group interaction. Life for the boys was to be as free as possible. The boys were allowed to go to the local villages with an adult to shop or to see a movie. Also, the boys could get furloughs to go home for short periods.

Unfortunately, some of the boys participating in this program ran away and were then sent to the state reformatory. Also, some of the boys would not honestly participate in the group and they were sent back to the reformatory as well. Some boys had to be removed from this setting because they had a bad effect on all of the other boys participating in the project and on the group culture.

After all of this handpicking of boys to participate and stay in the program, it should be no surprise that the boys from Highfields were more successful in staying out of trouble with the law after their release than was a group of boys at the state reformatory matched according to background characteristics, such as education, previous crimes, and type of home situation. Moreover, all the boys in this program were volunteers; if they met the requirements, they were allowed to choose Highfields or the reformatory. This self-selection for participation introduces yet another bias that confounds the interpretation of the results. Obviously the Highfields boy had above-average motivation to succeed. Finally, the boys from Highfields may have done better after release than the boys from the state reformatory simply because they were not brutalized by being subjected to the reformatory system. In other words, it is not so much what Highfields did for these boys, but what the reformatory did not do to them.

As indicated above, the use of guided group interaction was also used in an early experiment in Provo, Utah (Empey and Rabow, 1961). In this experiment the boys lived at home and spent only part of each day for approximately 4 to 7 months at the project headquarters called Pinehills. Only habitual offenders 15 to 17 years old were assigned, and highly disturbed boys were not permitted to participate. The project could handle 20 boys at once. The first phase of the program used a combination of work, such as in city parks, and the delinquent peer group as the primary vehicles to change the boys. The boys were involved in these activities in this phase 3 hours a day for 5 days a week and all day on Saturday. The second phase of this project was designed to maintain group contact with the boy after release from the program and to help him find employment.

In any case, during the first phase of the program there was no long list of formal rules as found in most institutions. The fact that there were no rules had a tendency to make the boys very uneasy, and they were forced to turn to the group for answers about what they could and could not do. The guided group interaction was used in an effort to get the boys to question the usefulness of their delinquent activities, to make the boys aware of other alternatives, and to give recognition to a boy for his efforts at reformation of himself or others. Before the group would begin to try to help the boy, he was required to tell the group of his total delinquent history—even things not known by the law enforcement authorities. Sometimes, therefore, the boys attempted to avoid telling the group the truth. Notice the similarities to the Chinese program of reform. Both programs used confessions and group discussions.

But it was the group, and not the staff, that had the power to decide when the boy was ready for release. No one in the group could be released until the whole group was honest and until everyone got involved in helping to solve each others' problems. Thus the boy has two choices; he could either become involved with the group or face escalating pressures from the other boys. Ultimately, if the boy did not become involved in the group, he was dropped from the program. And if a boy ran away, he was placed in the state reformatory. The directors of this program believed that attitudes toward employment were critical for these boys and that they must be taught "they can learn to live a rather marginal life" and find employment that will often involve a good deal of "drudgery" (Empey and Rabow, 1961:689). In fact, during their participation in the project the boys were put to work maintaining city parks and streets.

The second phase of this program (the time after the boys' release) involved periodic meetings with their former group for discussions. This phase was designed not only to check on the boys' behavior but also to help them with any new problems that had developed in their life since leaving the program and to keep the influence of the group active. The boys were also given some help in finding employment

Unlike the Highfields program, these boys were randomly assigned to this program, to probation in the community, or to the state reformatory. First the judge decided if a given boy should be sent to the reformatory or given probation, and then he randomly assigned one half of each group to Pinehills. The ultimate test of a successful program is what percentage of the boys avoided recidivism, and results 6 months after release were as follows: 84 percent success for Pinehills, 77 percent for probation, and 42 percent for the state reformatory (Task Force Report, 1967). But the key to the apparent success of this program is that the boys were all helped after release from the program. The group sessions may not have been nearly so helpful as assistance in finding a job.

Based on the experiences of Highfields and Pinehills, many juvenile institutions across the country now have a program that uses "positive peer culture." The theory behind these programs is to produce group pressure that is anticrime and that forces the individual to be honest about all past crimes. Again, as with the Utah program, notice the similarity to the techniques of the Chinese prison camp officials. However, insisting that the individual be attuned to the demands of the group creates a false foundation for rehabilitation. Typically after release the individual will be surrounded by equally compelling social as well as economic pressures to commit crime. Therefore it is little wonder that research has found that rehabilitation programs seem to have little effect on the ultimate success of reform after release.

Along with positive peer culture, there are other recently developed programs that have made claims to considerable success. The Outward Bound program emphasizes experiences in wilderness camping, which most urban delinquents have never had, and yet another involved training in sailing (Roberts et al., 1974; Miner and Boldt, 1981). The rationale behind these programs is that having such experiences and learning skills of almost any kind help develop self-respect, which the law violator previously attempted to gain in illegal ways. Any such programs—no matter how farfetched—can demonstrate convincing results if, as in the Highfields program, they can handpick their participants.

More Reasons Why Rehabilitation Programs Don't Succeed

One problem in attempting individualized treatment in prison is that it may be interpreted by the inmates and some staff as unfairly giving certain prisoners privileges or favors not given to others (Cressey, 1960). This occurs because the rehabilitation-as-treatment rationale would require that inmates judged to have been rehabilitated be released even if they have a poor record of adjustment to the prison, including a lengthy record of prison-rule violations. It can also appear that a prisoner is being transferred to what the prisoners generally consider a good prison job as a reward for misconduct. These types of prison release and assignment practices are felt by some nonprofessional staff and prisoners to be so unfair as to lay the foundation for serious unrest among the prisoners.

The point is that prisoners may resent such individualized treatment dispensed for the purpose of rehabilitation. For example, there is the story of a boy who escaped from a state reformatory (Rubin, 1963:668). While he was free, he committed a series of burglaries. When he was finally recaptured, the juvenile court judge took a special interest in him and went out of his way to set up conditions in the community that would make the boy's adjustment especially easy: finding him a job and a good place to live. From the standpoint of individualized treatment, the judge's behavior was helpful. But the other boys in the reformatory were bitter when they heard about this treatment. This boy had broken the institutional rules by escaping, then had committed a series of burglaries, and now he was free; but they were still incarcerated. The judge's decision may have helped the one boy at the expense of jeopardizing all the other boys' respect for the law, that is, jeopardizing their rehabilitation.

If we are really sincere about rehabilitation of prisoners, it must be recognized that prison is perhaps the worst possible place to try any treatment program. It is doubtful that any trained therapists would recommend small prison cells, as well as stone walls and a drab, humiliating social environment, as the perfect setting for treatment. In fact, because of the chronic shortage of prison treatment staff, rehabilitation in practice may simply be defined as the ability to conform to the institutional rules, which bears little relationship to the ability to adjust after release from the institution (Tappan, 1951:198–201). Moreover, even when professional treatment services are available, the prisoners may not cooperate with such treatment for several reasons. They may believe that participation in the treatment program indicates to others that they are crazy and also that by talking with the therapist they may reveal secrets about themselves or other prisoners that could later be used against them. In most institutions these latter fears are not without foundation.

Since prisons effectively hide their internal operations, it is possible for the public, especially many well-meaning political liberals, to believe that prisons do in fact offer treatment and rehabilitation to prisoners. But one of the reasons that correctional institutions have had difficulty in securing funds for treatment programs and personnel is that they really cannot demonstrate much benefit from such programs (Grosser, 1960:139). Legislators are not likely to spend money on programs that have no proven effectiveness. Even if a prison has sufficient resources to hire trained treatment professionals, there is considerable doubt about whether middle-class, college-trained therapists can communicate with largely lower-class prisoners. Moreover, although many prison administrators accept the principle of rehabilitation as a major function of the institution, that is, helping to change the prisoner's motivation for past crimes such as theft, they usually resort just to punishment if the prisoner steals within the prison (Richmond, 1965:88). After consideration of these factors, the concept of prison rehabilitation seems bizarre and unimaginable.

TRADITIONAL VERSUS DEMOCRATIC TREATMENT ALTERNATIVES*

Traditional Assumptions about Rehabilitation

Much of the original concern for the rehabilitation of prison inmates came from religious groups who believed that through evangelism and isolation they could change convicts and perhaps save their souls. Because of this histor-

*The remaining sections of this chapter were taken from J. F. Galliher, "Training in Social Manipulation as a Rehabilitative Technique," Crime and Delinquency 17(October 1971):431–436.

ical emphasis on the individual soul, we should not be surprised that most contemporary practical and theoretical approaches to the rehabilitation of prison inmates have usually focused on the individual personality as the object in need of change (Cressey, 1955:116–117; 1965:87–88). Cressey attributes this emphasis on the individual personality to the sociologists' neglect of rehabilitation theory; by this neglect, they have left the field to psychiatrists. He also suggests that such an orientation to the rehabilitation of prison inmates is of little practical value, since it is impossible to recruit even the minimum number of professional therapists needed for correctional work (1965:88). In 1966 Cressey (Sutherland and Cressey, 1966:382) reported that there were only 52 psychiatrists, 664 social workers, and 156 psychologists serving over 200,000 adult prisoners in the United States. At that time 36 states had no full-time psychiatrist to serve their prison system.

It has also often been implicitly assumed by many of those involved in correctional research (perhaps as an outgrowth of the religious underpinnings of early rehabilitation ideology) that an overall or general change in the individual personality structure was required to ensure against recidivism (Cressey, 1955, 1965; Ohlin, 1956:29–32; Sykes, 1956). Among many of these same students of corrections, however, there is wide agreement that the harsh environment of the prison is an unlikely place to implement any reformation of the prisoner (Sykes, 1956; Barnes, 1965; Cressey, 1960; Clemmer, 1950). This fact helps account for the popularity of reality therapy, which attempts less than total reformation of individuals' attitudes. Because most contemporary prisons are not only oppressive and antiquated but also fail to provide adequate professional treatment services, it is obvious that the prison is no place to attempt major alterations in the attitudes and orientation of the prisoners—at least not changes toward more conventional attitudes.

Thus there seems to have been some movement away from the individualist psychiatric postition and toward awareness of the role of the group in the development and support of attitudes and behavior, and a similar shift toward the use of techniques that attempt to modify the orientation of the group in which the prisoner is involved. However, even though these techniques work through the social group, the ultimate goal is usually to implement a basic change in the orientation of the individual. It is still often assumed that the successful culmination of these treatment techniques is a subject's rejection of criminal motives and acceptance of new, noncriminal motives. By treating groups rather than individuals, these techniques minimize the problem of insufficient professional staff. However, because these group techniques share the essential goals of the psychiatric approach, they also often share the problem of an unsuitable treatment environment.

It is interesting to note that while the state renders psychological services to prisoners in an attempt to change them, there is an unwillingness to go to extreme lengths to accomplish this goal of reformation. There is seldom an attempt to brainwash prisoners, in spite of McConnell's urgings mentioned above. Using the Chinese or German techniques (which really work) would be seen as both illegal and immoral, probably even by avid supporters of the death penalty. Perhaps they believe that we have no moral or legal right to brainwash a prisoner because this strips the person of his or her identity and replaces it with one designed by the state, while even with executions a new identity is not created—just an old one lost.

Traditional Parole Practices

Again, probably because much of the original concern for the rehabilitation of convicted prisoners came from religious groups, the supervision of convicts after their release from prison has traditionally been very stodgy and decidedly moralistic. Many states have insisted that parolees abstain from alcoholic beverages and extramarital cohabitation, keep regular hours, have regular employment, and not marry without permission (Arluke, 1956). All these requirements seem designed to force the parolee to live a circumspect, rural, middle-class way of life. This is especially inappropriate for the rehabilitation of urban lower-class prisoners who make up the majority of most prison populations. Some parole officers claim, however, that these rules are not usually enforced but that they are useful in revoking paroles when it is believed, but cannot be proved, that a parolee has committed another crime. The injustice of this is obvious. If there is no legal proof of the commission of another crime, the parolee should not be reincarcerated.

The compulsive concern for rigidly conventional behavior as evidence of rehabilitation is, predictably, also reflected in attempts at occupational guidance and training. Anything less than an honest day's work, usually measured in terms of physical labor, is not considered wholly desirable for the rehabilitation of prisoners. Not only the person's leisure-time pursuits but also their work choice must stand the test of puritanical moral guidelines, which even many generally law-abiding citizens would be hard pressed to satisfy. Apparently we have traditionally demanded that the released prisoner lead an even more exemplary life than do most other citizens. It is curious that we should demand greater conformity from those alleged to be least able to conform.

We are forced to recognize that the psychiatric personality-reformation approach to rehabilitation is both incomplete and unworkable with the existing resources. Newer group-related techniques, though avoiding some of the staffing problems of the psychiatric approach, are still usually oriented to the same impossible goals. Moreover, it is also apparent that the demands made upon parolees are equally unworkable and unreasonable. If current correctional practices are not useful, then we might ask what social science can offer as an alternative.

Anomie Theory and Rehabilitation

To provide a sociological and noncoercive alternative to existing correctional practice and theory, it is first necessary to have some idea of current sociological notions about the causes of deviance. Modern anomie theory as formulated by Merton (1957) has enjoyed wide popularity among sociologists as an explanation of deviant behavior. In contrast to psychiatric explanations, anomie theory emphasizes social structural variables in explaining the etiology of deviant behavior. Anomie theory holds that deviance is a consequence of discrepancies between culturally prescribed goals and the socially approved means available to achieve those goals. Some people are in relatively unfavorable competitive positions for using legitimate means to attain goals. Consequently, these people experience frustration and strain and are motivated to resort to deviant or illegitimate means.

If anomie theory is accepted as a reasonable explanation of the social etiology of deviant behavior, then it seems logical to consult it when attempting to modify such behavior. Perhaps anomie theory can offer useful and heretofore untapped leads in efforts to rehabilitate the offender. From this point of view giving prisoners vocational training in conventional occupations, such as carpentry and plumbing, can be seen as opening legitimate avenues for success. However, such programs are effective only among inmates who assume a conventional orientation and reject the notion allegedly prevalent among prisoners that "only fools work" (Sykes and Messinger, 1960:11). Quite obviously, carpentry skills are of little value to the individual who rejects their use in possible future employment.

Social Manipulation Training—a Democratic Alternative

Other useful training, however, can be offered in the prison—training that does not necessarily assume or require a conventional orientation. This seems to be true of the Dale Carnegie "human relations" courses that have been taught in some state and federal prisons and reformatories. One fundamental goal of such programs is to train the inmate in the known techniques of social manipulation. The student in such a course is taught how to control other people by means of consciously affected and skillfully convincing role playing (Carnegie, 1936). The acquisition of these skills appears to open up (1) new legal avenues for achieving success, (2) new illegal avenues, and (3) new avenues that are neither strictly legal nor clearly illegal.

In such courses inmate-students are sometimes taught techniques for manipulating social situations that might arise during interviews for employment. They practice skills useful in handling the responses of employers who are suspicious and leery of ex-convicts. Such techniques may be useful in securing an initial opportunity in many different types of legitimate employment that might otherwise be closed to the individuals because of their criminal records. More specifically, expertise in social manipulation obviously supplies some of the requisite skills for legitimate careers in retail sales positions. This illustrates how possession of these skills opens noncriminal means of achievement that do not generally conflict with the nonconventional belief that only fools work, since prisoners, most of whom have lower-class backgrounds, may often define work as involving physical labor. Also, conventional sales work may not require a basic change in orientation among inmates who are cynical and predatory in their relations with others. The individual can usually perform adequately in legal sales work without necessarily changing this attitude. Like behavior modification, training in social manipulation requires no changes in attitudes but only alterations in activities.

New illegal avenues for achievement might also be opened as a result of training in social manipulation. As Sutherland (1937:21) noted, professional thieves, including successful con men, are generally not recruited from the slums because slum dwellers usually lack the social skills required for such activities. As a consequence of training in social manipulation, however, the lower-class inmate-student may acquire the necessary finesse for manipulating people to obtain illegal goals without resorting to physically aggressive behavior. Artfully executed confidence games and swindles can be accomplished with the individual's new knowledge of human relations (Maurer, 1940). Some would argue that these illegal avenues for achievement have the distinct advantage of involving less likelihood of criminal prosecution than would physically aggressive crimes. The likelihood of detection is lessened because victims of confidence games are either too embarrassed by their own gullibility or too deeply involved in the crime itself to complain to the police. Examples of such involvement are people who, believing they have been given an illegal tip about a stock, invest a large sum of money in it, only to find that both the tip and the investment were frauds and that the individual taking the money has disappeared. Even if the offender is prosecuted, the punishment is likely to be lighter than that for physically aggressive crime.

Finally, new avenues for achievement are opened that are neither strictly legal nor clearly illegal. Such behavior may be prohibited by statute; that is, it is technically illegal, yet seldom or never actually prosecuted. Certain business practices, perhaps best exemplified in a used car enterprise that misrepresents the goods it sells, fall into this category. In more general terms, the ability to use social manipulation techniques allows the individual to take advantge of the fact that in our achievement-oriented society there is a large gap between strictly legal and clearly illegal practices in money matters and business transactions. The kind of behavior that falls between business practices that are considered morally exemplary and those that are clearly proscribed by law is characterized by normative confusion and ambivalence (Sutherland, 1949:45–51; Aubert, 1952). This ambivalence is reflected in the public admiration for the salesperson who could "sell an icebox to an Eskimo" even though the intent of such a sale is obviously exploitative. The traditional laissez-faire orientation to business practices and the caveat emptor admonition (let the buyer beware) furnish other evidence of the relative lack of normative control of business affairs. The caveat emptor legal admonition appears to warn the buyer to be on guard because fair and honest treatment is not guaranteed by the normative structure. As a matter of fact, a case can be made for the argument that in an achievement-oriented acquisitive society like ours, the wide gap between the strictly legal and the illegal in business transactions allows individuals more freedom in their attempts to meet the culturally prescribed demands for success.

The training of prisoners in social manipulation should in most cases be supplemented by instruction in language skills. The required pleasant and conventional facade can be projected most easily if the student commands a passing middle-class knowledge of word meaning, pronunciation, and sentence structure. Undoubtedly, some prisoners will be unable to develop these skills, and others will do so only with great effort. But such training in social manipulation does not coerce prisoners and is designed to help equalize opportunities between the rich and the poor. Clearly, this proposal does not envisage the best of all possible worlds but attempts to bring greater equality to a society so thoroughly based on human exploitation.

PROPOSAL FOR A NEW TYPE OF REHABILITATION PROGRAM

Endorsing prisoner training in social manipulation is not a suggestion that prison or parole authorities openly advocate that inmates resort to nonviolent illegal means of achievement. This would not be tolerated by the public. Rather, the staff should endorse role-playing skills for use only in strictly legal enterprises. Those inmates who are not conventionally oriented are likely to discover for themselves the potential use of such skills in illegal activities.

The programs should be fairly easy to implement in most areas. Unlike prison industrial production or industrial training and apprenticeship programs, which are often opposed by labor and manufacturing groups because they feel that such programs unfairly compete with their economic interests, training in social manipulation meets with no similar outside opposition. In some cases, initial opposition to such programs may come from political and correctional officials who might feel that it encourages immorality. Those involved in the development of these programs can argue that this approach to the rehabilitation of prison inmates would benefit not only the prisoner but also society. Because these programs give former prisoners more alternatives to achieve success, the likelihood that they will choose an illegal solution is probably diminished. Even if acquisition of these manipulatory techniques does not deter individuals from future criminal violations, the probability that they will resort to violent violations of the law seems to be reduced because other illegal avenues of goal attainment are available to them. The person now possesses skills in socially manipulating others and can use those skills in criminal activities. According to

Sutherland (1937:43), professional thieves who are skilled in social manipulation do not find it necessary to resort to physical aggression in following their illegal careers.

Because the traditional rehabilitation programs have not succeeded, more flexible rehabilitation programs that do not demand a display of basic attitude alterations from those who are unconventionally oriented have been suggested. Such programs would include courses in human relations. They would demand less moral rectitude in the occupational choice of the parolees when the facts indicate that this could help them lead a less dangerous, less bothersome, and perhaps even more law-abiding life. If our current attempts to rehabilitate prison inmates are judged to be less than a complete success, one possible reason may be that we have been attempting in a feeble manner to implement more change among inmates than is reasonable or fair.

Not all offenders, however, commit crimes because of a lack of access to legitimate opportunities for income. Those who have committted sex offenses do not usually have this problem. Yet even for this group, the same principle of opening new opportunities without imposing any moral judgments is applicable and has been used. "At Atascadero State Mental Hospital in California, homosexual child molesters are trained to cruise in gay bars so they will not have to resort to children; . . . heterosexual child molesters are taught to pick up women at parties; and rapists are coached in sex techniques to improve their relationship with their wives" (Sage, 1974:16).

CONCLUSION

Considering the awesome potential that exists to alter human behavior under prison conditions, perhaps it is fortunate that most prison systems have given only half-hearted support to rehabilitation programs. Indeed, there is an increasing belief that treatment and rehabilitation of any kind is impossible in prison settings. If prison therapy programs have not made a dent in the American crime problem, perhaps it is because most so-called rehabilitation programs can do nothing about opening new educational and occupational opportunities that arc undoubtedly the root problem for many of these prisoners. These therapy programs do nothing to alleviate the interrelated problems of a lack of education, unemployment, poverty, and racism, which are so much a part of the lives of most prisoners.

REFERENCES

Arluke, N. R.
  1956 "A summary of parole rules." National Probation and Parole Association Journal 2(January);6–13.

Aubert, V.
  1952 "White-collar crime and social structure." American Journal of Sociology 58(November):263–271.

1965   The Hidden Society. Totowa, N.J.: Bedminster Press.

Barnes, H. E.
1965   "The contemporary prison: a menace to inmate rehabilitation and the repression of crime." Key Issues 2:11–23.

Bettelheim, B.
1943   "Individual and mass behavior in extreme situations." Journal of Abnormal and Social Psychology 38:417–452.

Carnegie, D.
1936   How to Win Friends and Influence People. New York: Simon & Schuster.

Clemmer, D.
1950   "Observations on imprisonment as a source of criminality." Journal of Criminal Law and Criminology 41(September–October): 311–1319.

Conrad, J. P.
1967   Crime and its Correction: An International Survey of Attitudes and Practices. Berkeley: University of California Press.

Cressey, D. R.
1955   "Changing criminals: the application of the theory of differential association." American Journal of Sociology 61(September):116–120.
1960   "Limitations on organization of treatment in the modern prison." Pp. 78–110 in Theoretical Studies in Social Organization of the Prison, Pamphlet No. 15. New York: Social Science Research Council.
1965   "Theoretical foundations for using criminals in the rehabilitation of criminals." Key Issues 2:87–101.

Empey, L. T. and J. Rabow
1961   "The Provo experiment in delinquency rehabilitation." American Sociological Review 26 (October):679–695.

Foreman, P. B.
1959   "Buchenwald and modern prisoner-of war-detention policy." Social Forces 37 (May):289–298.

Glasser, W.
1965   Reality Therapy: A New Approach to Psychiatry. New York: Harper & Row.

Grosser, G. H.
1960   "External setting and internal relations of the prison." Pp, 130–144 in Theoretical Studies in Social Organization of the Prison, New York: Social Science Research Council.

Lewin, K.
1958   "Group decision and social change." Pp. 197–211 in E. E. Maccoby, T. M. Newcomb, and E. L. Hartley (eds.), Readings in Social Psychology, New York: Henry Holt and Company.

Maurer, D. W.
1940   The Big Con. New York: Bobbs-Merrill.

McConnell, J. V.
1970   "Criminals can be brainwashed now." Psychology Today 3(April):14, 16, 18, 74.

Merton, R. K.
1957   Social Theory and Social Structure. Rev. ed. Glencoe, Ill.: The Free Press.

Miner, J. L. and J. Boldt
1981   Outward Bound U.S.A.: Learning Through Experience in Adventure-Based Education. New York: William Morrow.

Mitford, J.
1973   Kind and Usual Punishment: The Prison Business. New York: Alfred A. Knopf.

Ohlin, L. E.
1956   Sociology and the Field of Corrections. New York: Russell Sage Foundation.

Richmond, M. S.
1965   Prison Profiles. Dobbs Ferry, N.Y.: Oceana.

Roberts, K., G. E. White, and H. J. Parker
1974   The Character-Training Industry: Adventure Training Schemes in Britain. Newton Abbot, U.K.: David and Charles.

Rubin, S.
1963   The Law of Criminal Correction. St. Paul: West.

Sage, W.
1974   "Crime and the clockwork lemon." Human Behavior 3(September):16–25.

Schein, E.
1956   "The Chinese indoctrination program for prisoners of war: a study of attempted brainwashing." Psychiatry 19:149–172.

Schwitzgebel, R. K.
1971   Development and Legal Regulation of Coercive Behavior Modification Techniques with Offenders. Chevy Chase, Md.: National Institute of Mental Health, Center of Studies of Crime and Delinquency, Public Health Service Publication No. 2067.

Sutherland, E. H.
1937   Ed., The Professional Thief, by a Professional Thief. Chicago: University of Chicago Press.
1949   White Collar Crime. New York: Dryden Press.

Sutherland, E. H. and D. R. Cressey
1966   Principles of Criminology. 7th ed. Philadelphia: J. B. Lippincott.

Sykes, G. M.
1956   "The corruption of authority and rehabilitation." Social Forces 34(March):257–262.

Sykes, G. M. and S. L. Messinger
1960   "The inmate social system." Pp. 5–19 in Theoretical Studies in Social Organization of the Prison, Pamphlet No. 15. New York: Social Science Research Council.

Tappan, P.
1951   Contemporary Correction. New York: McGraw-Hill.

Task Force Report: Corrections
  1967 The President's Commission on Law Enforcement and Administration of Justice. Washington, D.C.: U.S. Government Printing Office.

Weeks, H. A.
  1958 Youthful Offenders at Highfields: An Evaluation of the Effects of the Short-Term Treatment of Delinquent Boys. Ann Arbor: University of Michigan Press.

15

HUMAN NATURE, HUMAN RIGHTS, AND THE DEVELOPMENT OF CRIMINOLOGICAL THEORY

LIBERALS, CONSERVATIVES, AND THE SCIENTIFIC SPIRIT

The simple world of criminology typically is divided into only two groups: criminals and the rest of society. This being true, the criminal actors and society are seen as having different *human natures* as well as specific *human rights*. This chapter will explore the historical development of these notions of human nature and human rights in American criminology. The long liberal tradition of American criminology will be primarily represented in this chapter by the works of the late Edwin Sutherland and will be contrasted to the current conservative challenge found in *Crime and Human Nature* (1985) by Wilson and Herrnstein. The limits imposed by both liberal and conservative analysis will then be explored.

The history of criminology is often traced to Jeremy Bentham (1823) in nineteenth-century Europe. Recall from chapter 2 that Bentham was concerned with establishing a just and fair set of laws that had the additional promise of controlling criminal behavior. While his view of law violators was not highly elaborate, he did have some firm notions about criminal behavior, which included the assumption that society could only be protected if the criminal punishments could overcome the inherent pleasure the actors find in crime. Justice involved establishing penalty structures no more severe than were required to prevent crime. While Bentham's writing has often been used to focus

An early draft of this chapter was read at the annual meetings of the Society for the Study of Social Problems, New York City, 1986.

on this one facet of human behavior, his work in fact attempts to describe the total *collective human nature of society*. But, twentieth-century criminologists have extracted from this work ideas about human nature and the motivation of human beings only insofar as they were potentially criminal actors. There was also an emphasis in Bentham's work on the *collective human rights of society* to be protected from crime.

Later, with the development of biological theories of human behavior in the late nineteenth and early twentieth centuries, one of its eminent American practitioners was Henry Goddard (1917a; 1917b). He was concerned with the human nature of criminal actors, who were in his view made up largely of inferior foreigners, and with the collective human rights of society, which he felt needed protection from these biologically inferior types. Recall also that according to his research, discussed in chapter 2, European immigrants had both lower IQs and higher crime rates than did native-born Americans.

Sutherland and His Legacy

During the early 1920s the famous criminologist Edwin Sutherland, who some believe was largely responsible for the movement of criminology into sociology, challenged this biological analysis. He claimed that immigrants did not commit more crime than others (1924:99), nor were criminals more likely to be mentally defective (1924:109). We will give considerable attention to Sutherland's work because of his importance to the sociological study of crime. Here we see for the first time a primary concern for the human rights of criminal actors—something of only secondary importance to Bentham (found in his rejection of unnecessarily brutal punishments) and totally foreign to Goddard. In Sutherland's well-known book, *The Professional Thief* (1937), there is not the slightest hint of moral outrage on Sutherland's part about the activities of professional thieves, which he felt were both rational and sophisticated. Sutherland established a close, continuing, and nonjudgmental relationship with the professional thief who was the informant he relied on for information about this subject.

If Sutherland could empathize with thieves, he had this same capacity for accused rapists. Indeed, this same primary concern with the human rights of allegedly criminal actors is implied in Sutherland's startling and appalling analysis of rape and rape victims (1950a:545):

> Charges of forcible rape are often made without justification by some females for purposes of blackmail and by others, who have engaged voluntarily in intercourse but have been discovered, in order to protect their reputations. Physicians have testified again and again that forcible rape is practically impossible unless the female has been rendered practically unconscious by drugs or injury; many cases reported as forcible rape have certainly involved nothing more than passive resistance. Finally, statutory rape is frequently a legal technicality, with the female in fact a prostitute and taking the initiative in the intercourse.

Thus Sutherland defended immigrants in 1924, professional thieves in 1937, and finally those accused of sex offenses. Over the years Sutherland seemed to become more bold in defending the cause of less and less attractive minorities. This concern for the human rights of accused criminals has become a central theme in modern criminology as reflected in contemporary criminology textbooks' discussions of the racism and class injustice of American police, courts, and prisons.

Sutherland was also the champion of the cause of rehabilitation of prison inmates as early as the first edition of his criminology textbook published in 1924. And he reasoned that if criminal behavior has social rather than biological origins, control of this behavior through prison rehabilitation programs should be relatively easy by utilizing indeterminate prison sentences, which Sutherland also endorsed (1924). A later generation of criminologists, on both the left and right, would begin to criticize both the justice and efficacy of the indeterminate sentence and the rehabilitative ideal (Platt, 1977; Wilson, 1975); but from the 1930s through the early 1970s, Sutherland's ideas remained dominant.

A correlate of Sutherland's concerns with the *human rights of deviant actors*, to the exclusion of the *collective human rights of society*, is the notion of victim-precipitated crime. According to this perspective, crime victims are alleged to be at least partially reponsible for the crimes committed against them. The idea of victim-precipitated crime has long been recognized by criminologists, and one early analysis includes sex offenses as a possible example (von Hentig, 1948:439). One indirect reflection of what von Hentig sees as "the victim's contribution to the genesis of the crime," is "that the victim not infrequently requests that the perpetrator be pardoned—even in cases of rape." The idea of victim-precipitated crime represents a bias toward the accused law violator. This idea becomes even more explicit in Howard Becker's presidential address to the Society for the Study of Social Problems (1967) where he phrased the question as "Whose Side are We On?" Becker used the illustration of the researcher developing sympathy for juveniles in institutions for delinquents rather than for the professional staff of such institutions.

Later, an apparent transformation in Sutherland's concern for accused criminals took place. In the 1940s Sutherland argued (1945), at least partially on the basis of moral outrage, that white-collar crime provided appropriate data for sociology even if it did not result in prosecutions or convictions because it is harmful behavior that violates existing criminal laws. Sutherland rejected the idea proffered by fellow criminologist Paul Tappan (1947) that only those actually convicted of white-collar crime could be accurately called white-collar criminals. Sutherland insisted on behavioral rather than administrative boundaries in his description and theoretical explanation of white-collar crime. The extent of his outrage is evident in the following passage taken from his book *White Collar Crime*:

> [T]he utility corporations for two generations or more have engaged in organized propaganda to develop favorable sentiments. They devoted much atten-

tion to the public schools in an effort to mold the opinion of children. Perhaps no groups except the Nazis have paid so much attention to indoctrinating the youth of the land with ideas favorable to a special interest, and it is doubtful whether even the Nazis were less bound by considerations of honesty in their propaganda (1949:210).

The depth of Sutherland's antagonism toward white-collar crime is reflected in the original version of his book-length manuscript on white-collar crime, which contained all the names of those corporations convicted of such violations. But fearing lawsuits, the book's publisher demanded their removal (Sutherland, 1983).

While Sutherland was concerned with the human rights of white-collar crime victims, this seemed totally absent in his study of the crimes of the professional thief. The close identification with the professional thief was clearly something he never wanted with the white-collar criminals. He was concerned with both the human nature and the human rights of the professional thief, but in the study of white-collar crime he was interested in the human nature of these actors and in the collective human rights of society for protection from these powerful law violators—just as in earlier generations Bentham and Goddard had been concerned with the human rights of society.

One explanation for Sutherland's inconsistency is that the primary victims of white-collar crime are middle-class consumers and investors much like himself, while he seemed to have less in common with, and less empathy for, the victims of street crime, including the victims of rape and robbery. It has also been noted that Sutherland was outraged by white-collar crime because, as a believer in the free enterprise system, he worried when the system of free and fair trade was corrupted through collusion (1983:xvi). He worried, for example, about the A & P company controlling 25 percent of the grocery market, saying "A & P . . . is driving the United States . . . away from free enterprise into a socialist economy" (1983:xvii).

Over the years, many criminologists have followed Sutherland's lead, as one might expect given his stature in the field as a former American Sociological Association president and recognizing that his criminology textbook remains a leading seller almost 40 years after his death. Routine concern is expressed by criminologists about white-collar crime, but little anger is reflected about property crimes such as burglary and robbery. The fashion seems to be to effect a value-neutrality in these latter cases. There seems to be little place for moral outrage among academic liberals, reflecting one type of posturing scientific objectivism. Recently, Horowitz (1987:49) observed: "Moral relativists have informed their readers that without norms there can be no deviance. . . . All behavior can be interpreted in morally neutral terms, without consideration of legal or moral institutions. . . . Homicide alone remains a category worthy of the label 'crime.'" For example, it was left to nonsociologists to initially express rage about rape and to specifically analyze the *collective human rights of society* regarding rape (Brownmiller, 1975).

Recognizing that the poor are the primary victims of street crime, surely there is nothing morally wrong with the goal of getting the crime rate down. But few criminologists who have championed the same liberal concerns Sutherland did have been attracted to research with this promise of less crime, except, of course, in the case of white-collar crime. This analysis of the contributions of Sutherland demonstrates the strengths but also the limitations of liberal ideology. While Sutherland recognized the human rights and human nature of most types of accused criminals, he had great difficulty in recognizing the collective human rights of society when confronted with the spector of street crime.

The New Right on Crime and Human Nature

The failure of what has been called liberal criminology set the stage for the development of what by contrast seems to be a neoconservative criminology in the late 1960s. For example, the moral and ethical stance of most of those doing research on crime deterrence in the 1960s and 1970s is reflected in the views of Gibbs (1968), who claimed to be personally opposed to the death penalty but still determined to demonstrate the degree to which it served as a deterrent. Phillips (1980a:139) raised and quickly rejected the issue of the morality of deterrence in a cryptic disclaimer: "In this paper I will be concerned only with the deterrent effect of capital punishment. I will not consider the other important dimensions of this topic, for example, the morality or immorality of capital punishment." Later he explained this decision (1980b): "I have no moral expertise and consequently my opinion on the morality of capital punishment is worth no more and no less than anyone else's." Just as has been true of many liberal criminologists, among these neoconservative researchers we see the claimed value-neutrality. But unlike liberal criminology, nothing is found here about accused criminals' human rights, but there are firm implications about accused criminals' human nature in that humans are sometimes found to be deterred in specific ways by state-imposed terror, which these authors implicitly justify as a rational means of enhancing the collective human rights of society. David Greenberg represents something of an exception in that he became interested in such deterrence research to discredit deterrence researchers' findings that typically supported the efficacy of increased criminal penalties. "As a socialist, it seemed politically important for me to do that" (Greenberg, 1981). Here we see a primary concern with the human rights of accused criminals.

A culmination and combination of earlier ideas has recently emerged with considerable fanfare in a new and widely discussed book, *Crime and Human Nature*, by Wilson and Herrnstein (1985). The authors observed that serious street crime is concentrated in the lower class (1985:28), among those with low IQs (1985:148–172), and that blacks are overrepresented four to one among those arrested for violent crime in the United States (1985:461). Based on such differences, they jumped on this possibility (1985:457): "We think it is important to take note of the principle that cultural differences may grow out of biological differences." And (1985:468): "Even to allude to the possibility that races may differ in the distribution of those constitutional factors that are associated with criminality will strike some persons as factually, ethically, or prudentially wrong. We disagree." They speculate, in an outstanding example of victim blaming (1985:258), that constitutional characteristics of children may produce abusive families and that this may be the reason a correlation is found between delinquency and broken or abusive families. From the evidence they marshal, including black crime rates, these authors conclude that it seems to follow that criminal behavior has genetic as well as the widely recognized environmental causes. But a critic of this work asked, "If blonds were subject to pervasive discrimination and committed crimes, would it make sense to talk of their genes as causing both blondness and crime?" (Kamin, 1986:27).

Wilson and Herrnstein correctly concluded that theories of crime carry an enormous political message. They (1985:79) noted the "lethal perversion" of biological theories of behavior by fascism, but do not suggest why this peversion took place, leaving the impression that it was a chance occurrence. Since Wilson and Herrnstein (1985:42) recognized that people pick theories of crime because they *want* to believe in them, they might well have asked why it is that fascists always seem to want to believe in biological causes of behavior. Perhaps they did not ask this question because they might have been forced to conclude that fascists want to believe in biological theories of behavior because of the type of social policy such theories commend. As an example of the theoretical bias they discussed, the authors noted that when criminology became a sociological speciality in the 1940s this discouraged biological explanations of crime because sociologists were unfamiliar and uneasy with biological concepts (1985:80). Indeed, Wilson and Herrnstein demonstrated their own theoretical preferences (1985:200) in their analysis of the shoddy research on psychopathy: "If we set our expectations for these data at a realistically low level, we should not be disappointed with the findings." Unlike their generosity with psychopath research, they (1985:64, 215) were critical of strain theory, such as developed by Robert Merton, for assuming that people are naturally good and reject the notion of "man as the naturally good" (1985:518) as a part of naive liberal ideology because such reasoning does not "fully consider the extent to which constitutional differences in intelligence and temperment shape the ease with which people can be socialized" (1985:521).

Wilson and Herrnstein (1985:480) cited research showing that welfare destroys families because those families receiving financial subsidies in one study were found to be more likely than others to break up. But still they claim (1985:514) that their ideas must be accepted as scientific fact and are not ideological, neither liberal nor conservative. And Wilson warned in *Time* (1985:94) that "this [book] has nothing to do with conservative times. Do not put this book in that framework." These warnings notwithstanding, several reviewers have seen this book as a product of the current conservative political era (Time, 1985; Kamin, 1986). Predictably, liberal criminology especially worries Wilson and Herrnstein because of its rejection of retribution and its belief in rehabilitation of offenders who liberals view as compelled to commit crimes. And these authors are also concerned about the capacity of liberal criminology to subvert justice.

Conviction of a crime usually requires mens rea or criminal intent, which in turn requires that criminal behavior be freely and intentionally engaged in, but "every advance in knowledge about why people behave as they do may shrink the scope of criminal law" (Wilson and Herrnstein, 1985:504).

Because of what is known about the causes of crime, Wilson and Herrnstein made certain conclusions about its control. They wrote (1985:486): "To the extent there are important constitutional factors at work, then programs would have to be tailored to individuals rather than groups, a difficult and painstaking task." Yet later they suggest that such individualized programs are unjust for they violate the principle of equity (1985:492). Contrary to the rejection of retribution by the noted psychiatrist Karl Menninger, Wilson and Herrnstein claimed that retribution is required for people to see the legal system as just and fair (1985:496). And it follows that legislatures are excellent custodians of this retribution (1985:501): "Society has attempted to deal with the issue of subjectivity (the gravity of offenses) by dispersing the judgment broadly, by having, for example, a representative legislature establishing a range of punishments." This description of "representative" legislatures will come as some surprise not only to the black voters of Mississippi but to most lower-class Americans.

Wilson and Herrnstein concluded thàt if crime is to be controlled, more criminal punishment, more policing, and more control by families is needed—none of which bears any relationship to biological causes of crime. Another need is a general acceptance of the justice of a status hierarchy, which they felt has been eroded and must be restored (1985:414): "As a society becomes more egalitarian in its outlook, it becomes skeptical of claims that the inputs of some persons are intrinsically superior to those of others." This skepticism leads some people to commit crimes against those at the top whose resources are considered by some to be unjustly gained. Wilson and Herrnstein made such assumptions even though they admitted they knew of no research that directly relates to this issue. Even so, these Harvard professors warned that for a crime-free democracy we must guard against the dangerous idea of equality. Their protestations notwithstanding, this emphasis on constitutional crime causes, condemnation of egalitarian ideals, naive support of the American legislative system as a representative democracy, and calls for retribution are every bit as ideological as the liberal criminology which they criticize. Even while claiming to be value-free, they emphasized only the alleged human nature of criminals and the collective human rights of society. But the most damning criticism of such ideas is that "'the definition of crime is variable,' according to [criminologist Frank] Scarpitti. 'It changes from time to time, and place to place. How can we say people are born with predispositions to violate laws which are manmade?'" (Winkler, 1986). Scarpitti implied, as will be argued below, that for a complete understanding of collective human nature we must study the law rather than specific criminal behavior.

More explicit moral outrage about crime than Wilson and Herrnstein's is found in the case of Hirschi (1973), who sarcastically spoke for liberal criminologists: "The oldtimers may have wanted to reduce the rate of deviance, but

not me. I want to increase it. I want to make one big cat house of the world."
Here we find no discussion of human rights of deviant actors but only of the
collective rights of society to have the lowest possible crime rates. But lowering
the crime rate is not as simple as it may seem. Vaughan (1981) noted, for
example, "The very concept of deterrence has immediate ethical implications. A
conventional utilitarian would say that since the reduction of murder rates is
taken as an ultimate ethical good, anything that is required to lower the murder
rate is also ethical, including capital punishment." Vaughan draws our attention
to the ultimate result of a concern with the rights of society, ignoring the rights
of deviant actors.

Within the limits imposed by the range between conservative and liberal
criminology, it seems to be possible to answer some questions about human
nature and human rights, but necessary to ignore others. Conservative criminologists typically tell us about the human nature of accused criminals and the
human rights of society. Liberal criminologists usually offer competing descriptions of the human nature of criminal actors, and usually stress the human rights
of these actors rather than the human rights of society. Liberal and conservative
conclusions about human nature and human rights are quite diverse and, contrary to the conclusions of Wilson and Herrnstein, no immediate means of
arbitrating between their claims is apparent. The fundamental weakness of both
liberal and conservative criminology is their reliance on the human nature of
accused criminal actors, which forces both liberals and conservatives to place
considerable conceptual faith in what is essentially nothing more than an administrative category—the criminal actor—in their search for human rights. But in
neither model is there ever any thorough discussion of the collective human
nature of society. This omission becomes significant, assuming, of course, that
the human rights of both society and accused criminals must be grounded in
knowledge of collective human nature. A thorough understanding of the issue
of collective human nature requires leaving the review of criminological literature to consider the law.

Law and Collective Human Nature

It is incorrect to assume the character of societies' collective human
rights or accused criminals' human rights from individual actors' human nature
as has been done by Goddard, Sutherland, Wilson and Herrnstein, and others. It
has been argued that some verification of collective human rights is required that
is based on information about collective human nature or collective human
needs (Hart, 1961). Once such information is secured, we may then be in a
position to determine collective human rights and then to determine accused
criminals' human rights. The reasoning is that to recognize any individual's
human rights we must first know the collective human nature or needs through
the study of the social and legal structures, moving outside a parochial study of
criminal behavior and criminal actors. Hart (1961) found that given the human
nature of people generally, legal systems must provide certain human rights that

include protecting people from physical injury and breach of promise. Unlike lions, tigers, and the great sharks, humans are not the most vicious of animals and need some protection, as well as some predictability in their lives.

Questions of morality become involved when studying criminal law because historically American criminal law has been based on moral values and the Bible (Rothman, 1971; Haskins, 1960), even though it is now rationalized as necessary for order. Yet even the maintenance of order in any given political and economic system involves questions of morality. Fuller (1966) found that the law always contains the "is" and the "ought." Criminal law contains a specific prohibition and a prescribed penalty, the "is," as well as a clearly implied desired state of affairs discouraging specific behavior, the "ought." Laws prohibiting burglary, for example, often provide a description of the act, which involves breaking and entering with the intent to steal, the prescribed prison sentence or fine, as well as the clear implication that one's place of residence or work should be free from such intrusions. The "ought" is essential in legal systems, for as Wilson and Herrnstein observed, a legal system will control human behavior to the degree that it is considered just and fair, that is, to the degree to which the law is what people feel that it "ought" to be.

In a well-known study in the development of law, Schwartz (1954) compared two Israeli communes that were similar in every way except that in one all property was shared on an egalitarian basis. In the other there was private property and thus some variation in wealth among families. Only in the latter commune was it ever necessary to develop anything like a legal system to coerce noncriminal behavior. One interpretation of these findings is that in egalitarian social systems the distribution of resources is most likely to be generally considered fair, and thus the norms win the voluntary compliance of the people. Moreover, crime, such as theft, generally becomes meaningless when all citizens have exactly the same type and amount of property.

Similar conclusions regarding how well a legal or social system accomplishes the goal of providing a fit environment for human residence is found in Rawls' (1971) twin concepts, the original position and the veil of ignorance. Being in the original position behind the veil of ignorance means that individuals must imagine that they are not a part of any society and have no information on what society they will become a member of, nor what their position will be in any society. In this original position, Rawls argued, we will all select a society, like the first Israeli commune discussed above, with the greatest degree of equality for all citizens. Such decisions will be based on nothing more than the human nature of acting in one's self interest. Dworkin (1977) argued that of the two fundamental human rights mentioned by Rawls—equality and freedom—equality is the most essential, for once equality is achieved, freedom will usually also be maintained as a necesary byproduct of equality. But neither Dworkin nor Rawls assumed that we must first understand human nature to establish human rights. Unlike Wilson and Herrnstein on the one hand, and Hart on the other, Dworkin and Rawls made no assumptions that individual or collective biological characteristics should be consulted in determining human rights. The Rev. Martin Luther King (1963), in fact, claimed that people of all classes, countries, and colors have the same *moral worth* simply because they are human beings, and therefore laws that do not treat them equally are unjust and should be ignored.

To his credit, Sutherland (1924:11) also urged sociological students of crime to study the origins of criminal law because he argued that this would provide the empirical boundaries for criminology and the study of criminal behavior: "An understanding of the nature of law is necessary in order to secure an understanding of the nature of crime. A complete explanation of the origin and enforcement of laws would be, also, an explanation of the violation of laws." These sweeping claims notwithstanding, Sutherland put much less effort into the study of law than into the origins of criminal behavior, and he is much more remembered for his famous differential association theory of criminal behavior than for the two small studies he conducted on the origins of law (1950a; 1950b). A similar relatively heavy emphasis on the origins of criminal behavior is found in contemporary criminology, compared to scant literature on the origins of law. This represents not only an empirical choice but also a choice of methods and morality. If one studies the origins of law rather than the IQs or motives of those who violate the laws, then different actors and different data become the object of focus. Legislators and property owners are studied, for example, rather than prison inmates or juvenile delinquents. Thus in studies of the origins and administration of law rather than the characteristics of accused criminals, one's answers to the questions of the origins of, and solutions to, such problems as embezzlement or drug offenses, for example, will be totally different.

Recalling the deterrence research discussed in chapter 1, as useful as attempts to challenge the empirical findings of deterrence researchers may seem, such challenges only attack empirical findings, or what Hughes (1971) referred to as the *minor premise* of research. For example, some have criticized Wilson and Herrnstein for selectively picking over existing research, often using dated studies, to support their positions (Rose, 1986; Kamin, 1986). The *major premise*, or underlying reason, for conducting any specific type of research is quite different than mere research findings. Hughes (1971) explained the distinction as follows:

> The inequality of the position of the races in this country was once defended by scriptural quotation; now it is defended by what are called "facts" of biology and psychology. And those of us who are interested in getting new light on and more just action in the relations between peoples, take up the chase. If someone says Negros have such poor jobs because they are biologically incapable of learning complicated skills, we set about to prove that Negros can learn to do anything anyone else can learn to do. . . . Then someone comes along with the defense that although they can learn as well, or almost as well, as other people, Negros lack sexual and other controls necessary to the nicer positions in our society; we chase that one. . . . Now I have no basic objection to the making of such tests. . . . What I do object to is giving the terms of the game into the hands of the enemy, who, by inventing a new rationalization every day, leads us a merry and endless

chase. . . . [On the other hand] the major premise is ordinarily not stated in either case by the persons who use the statement; nor is it often stated or answered by those who oppose racial and ethnic discrimination (page 214). . . . in this kind of argument, incidentally, we again play into the hands of the enemy, for in arguing so hard that groups of people whose rights we have limited are without fault we encourage the idea—implicit in the "fault" justification of prejudice and limited rights—that justice and equality are something to be earned (page 218).*

Hughes demonstrated here how political liberals' reliance on the minor premise, that is, on the apolitical pursuit of scientific facts, offers an insufficient reaction to racist research projects. He also notes that this reliance on the facts often causes liberal scholars to overreact in the opposite direction from their adversaries and make empirical errors that are nearly as profound as those they criticize, such as feeling forced to claim that there are no real differences between majority-group members and ethnic and racial minorities. This overreaction surely applies to Sutherland who felt called upon to condemn rape victims in the process of defending those accused of sex crimes.

In any case, only in studying the law as opposed to criminal behavior, does the major premise imply that one can learn about crime by determining how power is exercised in a society. Through the analysis of the origins and administration of the legal institutions of human societies, we come to the conclusion that equality is to be sought rather than avoided, as a means of crime control. But what we choose to study is not inherent in the "facts" themselves, rather our choice represents a moral and political decision. The convention of scientific neutrality must be unmasked, for its use always seems to be directed at the same types of lower-class and minority victims. And contrary to the implications of much of the research reported above, it is not obvious that the scientific facts speak for themselves in molding social policy. It does not really matter if there are profound genetic causes of criminal behavior. In any nation social policy cannot take into the account such supposedly apolitical "facts" without fatal damage to democratic institutions. Surely the world's recent experience with fascism would teach us that.

*Published by permission of Transaction Publishers, from "Principle and Rationalization in Race Relations," in *The Sociological Eye: Selected Papers*. By Everett C. Hughes. Copyright © 1971 by Transaction Publishers.

REFERENCES

Becker, H. S.
  1967 "Whose side are we on?" Social Problems 14(Winter):239–247.
Bentham, J.
  1923 An introduction to the Principles of Morals and Legislation. Reprinted 1948. New York: Hafner.

Brownmiller, S.
  1975 Against Our Will: Men, Women, and Rape. New York: Simon & Schuster.
Dworkin, R.
  1977 Taking Rights Seriously. Cambridge, Mass.: Harvard University Press.

Fuller, L.
1966   The Law in Quest of Itself. Boston: Beacon Press.

Gibbs, J. P.
1968   "Crime, punishment, and deterrence." Southwestern Social Science Quarterly 48(March):515–530.

Goddard, H.
1917a   "Mental tests and the immigrant." The Journal of Delinquency 2(September): 243–277.
1917b   "The criminal instincts of the feeble-minded." The Journal of Delinquency 2 (November):352–355.

Greenberg, D.
1981   Personal communication (June 21).

Hart, H. L. A.
1961   The Concept of Law. London: Oxford University Press.

Haskins, G. L.
1960   Law and Authority in Early Massachusetts. New York: Macmillan.

Hirschi, T.
1973   "Procedural rules and the study of deviant behavior." Social Problems 21(Fall): 159:173.

Horowitz, I. L.
1987   "Disenthralling sociology." Society 24(January): 48–55.

Hughes, E. C.
1971   "Principle and rationalization in race relations." Pp. 212–219 in The Sociological Eye: Selected Papers. Chicago: Aldine-Atherton.

Kamin, L. J.
1986   [Book Review] "Is crime in the genes? The answer may depend on who chooses what evidence." Scientific American 254(February): 22–27.

King, M. L., Jr.
1963   "Letter from Birmingham jail." The Christian Century 80(June 12):767–773.

Phillips, D. P.
1980a   "The deterrent effect of capital punishment: new evidence on an old controversy." American Journal of Sociology 86(July):139–148.
1980b   Personal communication (October 23).

Platt, A. M.
1977   The Child Savers: The Invention of Delinquency. 2d ed. Chicago: University of Chicago Press.

Rose, S.
1986   [Book Review] "Stalking the criminal mind," The Nation 242(May 24):732–736.

Rawls, J.
1971   A Theory of Justice. Cambridge, Mass.: Belknap Press of Harvard University Press.

Rothman, D. J.
1971   The Discovery of the Asylum: Social Order and Disorder in the New Republic. Boston: Little, Brown.

Schwartz, R. D.
1954   "Social factors in the development of legal control: a case study of two Israeli settlements." The Yale Law Journal 63(February): 471–491.

Sutherland, E. H.
1924   Criminology. Philadelphia: J. B. Lippincott.
1937   The Professional Thief. Chicago: University of Chicago Press.
1945   "Is 'white-collar crime' crime?" American Sociological Review 10(April):132–139.
1949   White Collar Crime. New York: Dryden Press.
1950a   "The sexual psychopath laws." Journal of Criminal Law and Criminology 40(January–February):543–554.
1950b   "The diffusion of sexual psychopath laws." American Journal of Sociology 56(September):142–148.
1983   White Collar Crime: The Uncut Version. Introduction by G. Geis and C. Goff. New Haven: Yale University Press.

Tappan, P. W.
1947   "Who is the criminal?" American Sociological Review 12(February):96–102.

Time
1985   [Book Review] "Are criminals born, not made?" (October 21):94.

Vaughan, T. R.
1981   Comments made in session on "Ethics and Social Science: Research on Capital Punishment." Midwest Sociological Society Annual Meeting. Minneapolis, April.

von Hentig, H.
1948   The Criminal and His Victim: Studies in the Sociobiology of Crime. New York: Schocken Books.

Wilson, J. Q.
1975   Thinking About Crime. New York: Basic Books.

Wilson, J. Q. and R. J. Herrnstein
1985   Crime and Human Nature. New York: Simon & Schuster.

Winkler, K. J.
1986   "Criminals are born as well as made, authors of controversial book assert." The Chronicle of Higher Education 31(January 15):5, 8.

NAME INDEX

Whyte, W. F., 185
Wice, P. B., 208
Wilkins, L. T., 244
Williams, K. R., 195
Wilson, J. Q., 33, 187, 190, 191, 193, 194, 199, 266, 348-350, 351
Winkler, K. J., 350
Wirt, F. M., 138
Woetzel, R. K., 103, 104
Wolfgang, M., 55, 114, 115, 118, 123, 128, 133, 223
Wood, A. L., 213, 214
Wood, P. L., 59

Woodward, K. L., 17
Wright, K. N., 110, 294
Wyle, C. J., 127

Y
Yablonsky, L., 248
Young, J., 14, 137

Z
Zimbardo, Philip, 302, 303
Zimring, F. E., 254, 255, 256, 257, 258
Zingraff, M. T., 310

SUBJECT INDEX